TRAVEL WITH CHILDREN
5th edition – July 2009
First published – May 1985

PUBLISHED BY
Lonely Planet Publications Pty Ltd
ABN 36 005 607 983
90 Maribyrnong St, Footscray,
Victoria 3011, Australia

LONELY PLANET OFFICES
AUSTRALIA Locked Bag 1, Footscray,
Victoria 3011
USA 150 Linden Street, Oakland, CA 94607
UK 2nd Floor, 186 City Rd, London, EC1V 2NT

Printed through Hang Tai Printing Company
Printed in China

PHOTOGRAPHS
Cover image: Jonathan Lee Wright/
Photolibrary

Many of the images in this guide are available
for licensing from Lonely Planet Images.
Website: www.lonelyplanetimages.com

ISBN 9781740595025

PUBLISHER Chris Rennie
ASSOCIATE PUBLISHER Ben Handicott
COMMISSIONING EDITORS Bridget Blair,
Janine Eberle
COORDINATING EDITORS Laura Gibb, Alison
Ridgway, Kate Whitfield
COORDINATING LAYOUT DESIGNER Jessica Rose
DESIGNER Mark Adams
PROJECT MANAGER Jane Atkin
IMAGE RESEARCHER Craig Newell
THANKS TO Nigel Chin, Daniel Corbett, Brigitte
Ellemor, Marika McAdam, Jacqui Saunders and
Maureen Wheeler.

CONTENTS

FOREWORD

When I wrote the first edition of *Travel With Children*, Tashi and Kieran (our children) were four and two years old and we had just moved to California to set up the Lonely Planet office.

Although they were very young, they were already veteran travellers. At eight months Tashi had her first taste of life as a Lonely Planet baby, updating our Southeast Asia book. When Kieran was three months we all went to Indonesia, and later that same year to India, Nepal (including a trek) and Sri Lanka.

Travelling was what Tony and I did, and it seemed completely natural to us that when the babies came they would travel with us. Of course, other people thought we were mad, and there were times when I would have agreed. It wasn't always easy; we travelled by public transport or drove ourselves. We stayed in pleasant, family-run places which had local facilities, but not much in the way of the normal amenities families in Australia or other Western developed countries took for granted. When we finally took the children to Europe, Tashi found it hard to believe that she could drink water from the tap in every country we visited.

The children learned a lot – Kieran, aged five, when asked to do a show and tell of his trip to Egypt, insisted that the Sphinx had a moustache. When his teacher gently suggested it was a beard, Kieran asked him had he been there? The result was that an entire class went through primary school convinced that the Sphinx had a moustache, because, after all, Kieran had been there and seen it with his own eyes.

When Tashi was three we were updating the Sri Lanka book and Tony took her with him when he went to check out some hotels. In one of them, the owner, recognising Tony from an earlier trip, offered them some tea. They chatted for a while and then Tony got up to leave. Tashi tugged on his arm and said, 'Daddy, aren't we going to check the toilets?'

Years later, when Tashi was 13, we decided to spend a week at a beach resort with family friends. After a few days, Tashi came to me and asked, 'So, we stay here, we don't go from place to place, we go to the same beach every day – we just hang out?' I replied, 'Yes, that's it'. 'So is this what you call a holiday?' she asked and I realised that although we had travelled all her life, this was indeed her first holiday.

People always assume that it must have been a wonderful childhood, constantly travelling, seeing new places and encountering so many different people and cultures, and it was, but of course it wasn't always easy. Our children were often a curiosity to local people, and they would find a place they loved, but we never stayed

> *'Travelling was what Tony and I did, and it seemed completely natural to us that when the babies came they would travel with us. Of course, other people thought we were mad, and there were times when I would have agreed. It wasn't always easy; we travelled by public transport or drove ourselves.'*

ABOVE. MAUREEN AND TONY WHEELER WITH THEIR CHILDREN, TASHI AND KIERAN

more than a few days. Kieran, even at three months, knew he would rather be home; Tashi loved being on the road. However, travel is woven into the fabric of their lives and both of them can't imagine a future without plans to travel. Kieran spent eight months travelling in Southeast Asia and has since visited India and Europe, and Tashi lived in London for three years and travels whenever she can get the time and money together.

As parents we want to give our children so much, not just material things, but memories and experiences that will help them navigate the rest of their lives. Travelling with your children opens up the world to them and gives you the chance to see it again through fresh eyes, and despite the inevitable anxious moments and the sheer hard work involved, I would do it all again.

Maureen Wheeler

INTRODUCTION

Family holidays, the poor cousin of all other travel genres, tend to get a lot of bad press. You could be forgiven for thinking they're all about package resorts with beaches that look like the human version of a penguin colony. Or group confinement with reviled relatives. Or sulking teens glued to their phones, bemoaning their boredom. Or maybe you've been led to believe that the trip starts with your baby keeping all other plane passengers awake and just goes downhill from there. Mention the idea of travelling with children to some people and they just say, 'Don't!'

But these gloomy images are getting a makeover, as more and more families take to the road with gusto and return with positive tales to tell. Seasoned independent travellers aren't stopping just because they've had children, and some families who've never travelled before are taking the plunge. No-frill airlines, increasing affluence and a recognition of the value of travelling together as a family are all playing a part.

If you want to spend quality time with your children, help them learn, grow and gain a better understanding of the world and humanity, then travelling is a great way to do it. As a travelling family you'll talk and share experiences, which these days we often struggle to find time for in our busy lives. If you've been stuck in a pattern of 'telling off' and whining, travel can get things off to a fresh start. Your children may surprise you with their adaptability and affability when the hold of regular routines loosens. Watching your children engage with different surroundings can change your perspective and invigorate you with a renewed sense of wonder. As your children blossom before your eyes in response to new encounters and experiences, it's hard not to share their excitement. Their questions will reveal the depths of their intelligence and the scope of their understanding, which in turn will enrich your appreciation of your children. Their horizons quite literally expand as they realise that the world is bigger than your home town or city, and with it comes an appreciation of cultural diversity, the seeds of tolerance and empathy, which will stay with them for the rest of their lives. For young children this may come with the simple realisation that people speak different languages – and as their ears become attuned to new sounds they'll probably even pick up a few words in the local tongue.

'Travel with children provides insights into local cultures that you often just don't get travelling childless. In most cultures children are welcomed, if not revered, and become the centre of attention. As a parent, you'll be caught up in the interest generated by your child and will have closer encounters with the locals as a result.'

Travel with children provides insights into local cultures that you often just don't get travelling childless. In most cultures children are welcomed, if not revered, and become the centre of attention. As a parent, you'll be caught up in the interest generated by your child and will have closer encounters with the locals as a result. And although your life may be very different from that of others you'll meet on your travels, parenting provides a strong common bond with people all over the world.

Of course, it isn't always easy travelling with children. Schlepping the luggage while trying to hurry along someone who wants to dawdle every step of the way can be stressful to say the least. But there's a lot you can do up front to minimise aggravation and difficulties. Getting the pace right is vital, and planning and taking the right bits and pieces with you, including the right mental attitude, are key. Starting out in a positive frame of mind and aiming to stay that way will help to deflect tensions. Remaining flexible will save you when your carefully laid plans go off the rails. If you approach the journey with a spirit of adventure, and involve your children in the planning and problem solving, you'll have a better chance of converting setbacks into opportunities.

A big part of getting the planning right comes with choosing a suitable destination and type of holiday for your family. In this edition we've put a lot of thought into providing really useful information on all your options, from camping to activity holidays to resorts and cruises to settling in another country long-term. We've also expanded coverage of our favourite destinations for family travel, by adding new detail on the most interesting places to visit and hotels that welcome children. In order to provide in-depth information, we've chosen to use our limited space to focus on the very best places to go. Each country we cover has been carefully chosen because it is safe and well-suited to family travel.

One of the nice things about this book is that it's not just one person telling you about travel with children – it's a global team of authors with children, offering their best tips and passing on practical information. This book has grown over 23 years and enshrines the knowledge Lonely Planet cofounder Maureen Wheeler gained travelling with her children in their first 15 years, as well as the experiences of Lonely Planet authors, staff and readers.

Travelling with children might not be glamorous, relaxing or extremely thrill-seeking, but families who travel are having their own sort of adventure and deserve to be applauded, encouraged and respected. With a positive attitude and a bit of forethought, travelling happily with your offspring is easily achieved. Things won't always go as planned, of course, but then they never do with travel or with kids.

ABOVE. DIVING WITH A GREEN SEA TURTLE, HAWAII

ABOVE. A SURF LIFE-SAVING CARNIVAL AT NOOSA, AUSTRALIA

TOP 10

BEACH HOLIDAYS

COSTA DEL SUD (SARDINIA P142)
Although you have to drive to the beaches, the water is clean, the sand is white and there aren't too many people: Sardinian beaches are far better than many on the Italian mainland.
www.sardegnaturismo.it

COTTESLOE (AUSTRALIA P181)
Just north of Fremantle and west of Perth in Western Australia, Cottesloe has a beautifully safe beach for kids to swim or snorkel at, and the weather always seems to be perfect.
www.cottesloe.wa.gov.au

DURBAN (SOUTH AFRICA P254)
Washed by the warm Indian Ocean, Durban's city beaches have plenty of free children's swimming pools and lots of family entertainment such as Sea World and Ushaka Marine World.
www.durban.gov.za

KARON BEACH (THAILAND P207)
Family-friendly Karon, with its Flintstone-themed fun park, is a great base for exploring Phuket's beaches and reserves, including Phuket Gibbon Rehabilitation Centre.
www.phuket.com/island/beaches_karon.htm

KAUA'I (HAWAII, USA P160)
Home to plenty of beaches where children can snorkel in very shallow waters and an excellent Children's Discovery Museum.
www.kauai-hawaii.com

AITUTAKI (COOK ISLANDS P193)
Soft sand beaches edge a turquoise lagoon filled with tropical fish. Kayaking, snorkelling and boat cruises are also part of the picture.
http://cookislands.travel/index

NOOSA (AUSTRALIA P181)
Recommended by lots of parents at Lonely Planet's head office as a wonderful place to take the kids. Great beaches, beautiful natural environment (Noosa National Park) and very child-friendly.
www.noosa.qld.gov.au/aboutnoosa

TAVIRA (PORTUGAL P136)
At the eastern end of the Portuguese south coast, this quiet town has a magnificent untamed beach that goes on for miles. And, best of all, you take a boat to get to the beach.
www.visitportugal.com

SAYULITA (MEXICO P227)
A safe, laid-back beach town full of hip North American and European families where you and the kids get 'back to basics'. Every evening both local and gringo kids congregate in the town square to eat ice cream and play games.
www.sayulitalife.com

SANUR (BALI P224)
A quiet little town close to the 'happening' area of Bali with a great little collection of *warungs* (outdoor restaurants) lining the beach at both ends; full of friendly local people.
www.balitourismboard.org

■ **TOP 10** ■

CITY BREAKS

OAXACA (MEXICO P227)

This colourful Mexican city is pint-sized, charming and fun to explore on foot. A central plaza provides plenty of run-around space for kids and there's a vibrant market.
www.visitmexico.com

ISTANBUL (TURKEY P154)

With its mosques, palaces, museums, bazaars, multicoloured carpets, food markets, Bosphorus cruises and sweet apple tea, the children will be fascinated and enchanted at every turn.
www.tourismturkey.org

LONDON (ENGLAND P119)

You could stay in London for a whole year and find interesting things to do with the children every day. In summer don't miss out on playing in the fountains at Somerset House where there's an outdoor ice-skating rink in the winter.
www.visitlondon.com

LOS ANGELES (USA P160)

A good destination for teenagers – choose between the original Disneyland, Universal Studios and Santa Monica. There's heaps to see and do in this sprawling city that encapsulates the American Dream.
www.discoverlosangeles.com

VANCOUVER (CANADA P171)

Vancouver is frequently named the most liveable city in the world. There's lots of water as well as beaches, a huge urban park (Stanley Park) and numerous hiking and biking trails. In addition, all the attractions of the Rocky Mountains are just over 100km away.
http://vancouver.ca/visitors.htm

LISBON (PORTUGAL P136)

With trams trundling up to a castle, a state-of-the-art aquarium and a fascinating museum that explores Portugal's great seafaring past, this city captivates kids. The fairy-tale town of Sintra, too, is a just a short train ride away.
www.lisbon-guide.info

COPENHAGEN (DENMARK P127)

Oozes old-world charm, with a compact city centre, a lively waterfront and pedestrian-only zones. Thrilling rides at Tivoli Gardens and Bakken, a royal palace and museums designed especially for children will keep you busy.
www.visitcopenhagen.com

SINGAPORE (P215)

Safe, clean and accessible, Singapore is a gentle introduction to the cities of Southeast Asia – and an excellent jetlag-busting pit stop on the long haul between Europe and Australasia. Also, Sentosa Island with its beaches, butterfly park, dolphin lagoon and underwater world has to be seen to be believed.
www.visitsingapore.com

SYDNEY (AUSTRALIA P181)

If beaches, swimming pools and numerous ferries aren't enough, there's Sydney Aquarium, Taronga Zoo and the Koala Park Sanctuary, which are all huge hits with the young ones.
www.sydney.com.au

ROME (ITALY P142)

With some of Italy's best gelato, the impressive Colosseum and Castel Sant'Angelo, spooky catacombs under Via Appia Antica and the green spaces of Villa Borghese, the challenge in Rome is not to do too much.
www.romaturismo.it

ABOVE. THE GARDEN AT VILLA LANTE, ROME

ABOVE. SENTOSA ISLAND, SINGAPORE

ABOVE. BANFF NATIONAL PARK, CANADA

ABOVE. RED-EYED TREE FROG, COSTA RICA

OUTDOOR ADVENTURES

ARUSHA & THE NORTHERN SAFARI CIRCUIT (TANZANIA P251)

Feed Lion King fantasies at Tarangire and the bird paradise of Lake Manyara (home to the rare mountain-climbing lion), visit the Ngorongoro volcano, stop by the Serengeti desert and climb Mt Kilimanjaro.
http://tanzaniatouristboard.com/

NAXOS (GREECE P150)

Inland from the beaches and bustling main town lie beautiful untouched villages, rolling hills and low-key archaeological sites.
www.gnto.gr

BELIZE (P236)

Aside from laid-back beaches, there's wildlife galore in the inland jungles, with a jaguar reserve at Cockscomb Basin Wildlife Sanctuary, birdlife at the Mayflower Bocawina National Park; majestic Mayan ruins dot the country too.
www.travelbelize.org

GRAND TETON NATIONAL PARK (USA P160)

Get ready to encounter buffalo, moose, bear, eagles, coyote, deer, foxes, rabbits and more. There's canoeing, horseback riding, hiking, swimming and rafting for older children.
www.nps.gov/grte

KANGAROO ISLAND (AUSTRALIA P181)

A hidden gem off the coast of South Australia, this is a national park with lots of Australian wildlife, caving adventures at Kelly Hill Conservation Park, sleeping seals on the beach and the 'Remarkable Rocks'.
www.tourkangarooisland.com.au

WADI RUM (JORDAN P264)

Hike or camel ride into the dazzling Wadi Rum canyon, then camp in a Bedouin tent.
www.visitjordan.com

MONTEVERDE CLOUD FOREST RESERVE (COSTA RICA P238)

This is where you teach the kids about physical geography – there are lots of trails, a few huts where you can stay the night and an amazing sky-walk above the forest canopy.
www.monteverdeinfo.com

OUTER HEBRIDES (SCOTLAND P124)

Some of the oldest rock in the world is in these islands off the northwest coast, linked by car ferries and bridges. There are plenty of sheep and spectacular scenery, as well as great Scottish breakfasts and ancient sites.
www.visithebrides.com

THE CANADIAN ROCKY MOUNTAINS (CANADA P171)

A great unspoilt wilderness with endless outdoor pursuits – hiking, biking, skiing, fishing, wildlife watching, horseback riding and mountain climbing from the well-known and family-friendly bases of Banff and Jasper.
www.pc.gc.ca/pn-np/ab/banff/
www.pc.gc.ca/pn-np/ab/jasper/

WILSONS PROMONTORY (AUSTRALIA P181)

200km southeast of Melbourne, this national park boasts rainforests, mountains and sandy bays and is a great beach/bush getaway with kids. There are camping facilities and an outdoor cinema as well as great surfing (for the teenagers).
www.promcountrytourism.com.au

■ TOP 10 ■

CAMPING HOLIDAYS

WEST COAST OF THE SOUTH ISLAND (NEW ZEALAND P188)

Lakes and rivers, short walks to magnificent glaciers and a chance to hear the chirps of the elusive kiwi bird. New Zealand has some of the best camping grounds in the world.
www.holidayparks.co.nz

SUNSHINE COAST (AUSTRALIA P181)

Surf or frolic on endless beaches or tramp through the subtropical rainforest of the hinterland.
www.goseeaustralia.com.au

YELLOWSTONE NATIONAL PARK (USA P160)

Geysers, hot springs, wildflowers, bears and bison are only a fraction of the attractions at this over-the-top beautiful park.
www.nps.gov/yell

VANCOUVER ISLAND (CANADA P171)

Spot orcas, fish for salmon and watch eagles soar overhead. Camping options range from RV parks near urban areas to complete back country.
www.vancouverislandabound.com/camping.htm

HVAR & KORČULA ISLANDS (CROATIA P146)

Shady beaches, clear and calm waters that aren't too crowded – yet. There are so many great places to camp in this country it's hard to choose!
www.findcroatia.com/accommodation_croatia/campings_croatia.htm

CORSICA (FRANCE P129) & SARDINIA (ITALY P142)

Get two cultures for the price of one when you board the ferry to island hop from France (Corsica) to Italy (Sardinia). In these spots you'll find white Mediterranean beaches, mountains, amazing food and beautiful campsites.
www.campingcorse.com/indexang.html
www.byguide.com/eng-camping.asp

BORNHOLM (DENMARK P127)

The soft-sand beaches and dunes of this island are perfect for children, and there's a camping ground in a wooded area right next to the beach.
www.visitdenmark.com

SEA OF CORTEZ COAST (MEXICO P227)

The place to go in a camper van. Calm swimming beaches, lazy fishing villages and whale watching are on the menu.
www.ontheroadin.com

KRUGER NATIONAL PARK (SOUTH AFRICA P254)

Excellent kid-friendly facilities in one of Africa's greatest wildlife parks.
www.sanparks.org

CYCLADES (GREECE P150)

The islands of Naxos and Amorgos, among others, have lovely laid-back seaside camp spots.
www.gnto.gr

ABOVE. FOX GLACIER, SOUTH ISLAND, NEW ZEALAND

ABOVE. SANTA TERESA DI GALLURA, SARDINIA, ITALY

Part 1.
BEFORE YOU GO

BEING PREPARED

Good preparation and planning is the key to travelling with children. This doesn't mean mapping out your entire route or booking every night's accommodation but with children in tow you constantly need to think ahead and anticipate everyone's needs. If your child is old enough, they will enjoy being involved in your pre-departure planning: children like to contribute, to 'help' and, more than anything, they love looking forward to something special (as long as it isn't too far ahead).

Travelling with children is hard work: in fact, you'll probably come back from your trip more in need of holiday than ever before. But, if you've researched your destination, packed the right equipment and prepared the children, you're well on your way to a successful and workable time away.

CHILDREN'S AGES

There's no right or wrong age to start travelling with children: your trip can be just as enjoyable with a baby or a teenager. Each age group or stage in your child's development comes with its own rewards and challenges, and your travels need to be mapped out with your child's abilities and requirements in mind. However, a good holiday or trip is one that works for everyone – both children and adults – so remember to take your own travel plans or wishes into consideration too.

Babies

There are lots of advantages to travelling with babies. They have no views on where you go, what you do and how you get there (make the most of it!). In many ways, your first baby need not make a huge difference to the way you travelled pre-children.

Babies are extremely portable, they sleep a lot and they are easily entertained either in the stroller or in a baby carrier/sling strapped to your front. If you want to spend your days out and about, visiting museums, seeing the sights and ending up in a nice restaurant at night then, for most of the time, your baby

will be happy either snuggled up to your front in the baby carrier or being pushed (asleep or awake) in a stroller. For the first eight to ten weeks your baby will probably face towards you when in the baby carrier but after that they can face outwards and start to take an interest in their surroundings. When you're on the move, even though you'll need to stop regularly for feeds and nappy changes, you will have a lot of freedom when travelling with a baby. One of the real perks of this age is that you're still able to go out at night. As long as you're not somewhere smoky or too noisy, babies do not have to go back to their accommodation for bedtime but will often sleep anywhere. In addition, having a baby actively improves your social life when travelling: there's nothing like a baby to stimulate interest and interaction from local people or other travellers.

However, there are some downsides. As the health and safety of your baby is paramount, you'll need to choose your destinations carefully. For more information, see the Staying Healthy & Keeping Safe chapter (p34) as well as the country profiles in Part 4 of this book. This is crucial when travelling with babies (or any child too young to communicate properly) because they can't tell you if they are too hot or too cold or have a stomach ache or a symptom of a serious illness. In addition, you'll have to decide how much travelling you want to do before your baby has had their full course of childhood immunisations (usually given at two, three and four months old). See p34 for more details about immunisations.

Being a newish mum or dad, you'll probably be more anxious about travelling than you will be when your child is older (especially as it is harder to maintain your normal routine for naps, feeding and changing). Some of your anxieties may stem from a lack of sleep – travelling with young children can be tiring but even more so if your sleep is still being disrupted. And, if you're up at night because your baby is crying, chances are that the people in the bedroom next door to yours are awake too. Of course, this knowledge then adds to your night-time stress levels – see p64 for a discussion of what accommodation is best for which age groups.

How you intend to feed your baby is also a key issue. On the road, the easiest and best option is to breastfeed – see p79 for a discussion of the pros and cons. However, if you are uncomfortable with this option (for any number of reasons), you'll need to engage with the slightly more complicated process of bottlefeeding your baby while abroad (see p80 for more details). In addition, if your baby is around six months, you'll be introducing solids and will need to think about regular meal times and preparing foods like baby rice.

But the main disadvantage of travelling with a baby is how much equipment they need – nappies, changes of clothes, bottles, formula, feeding utensils, stroller, baby-carriers, etc. If you're used to travelling with hand-luggage only, it's a big wake-up call; plus babies often have no baggage allowance on planes (see p51 for more details).

Crawlers

From a travelling or holiday point of view, the most wonderful thing about a baby is that when you put them down they stay there. Once your baby can move properly (not just roll over), they need to be watched 24 hours a day. Turn your back for a second and they're off to investigate the hotel balcony or the duck pond or to find out what the toilet brush tastes like. Yes, not only are crawlers a worry because they can crawl off but everything they find en route will go straight into their mouths. In addition, their hands and clothes will be filthy all the time which means that you're constantly washing them (wet-wipes are a godsend) and washing their clothes. And crawlers that are also thumb-suckers need even more hygiene attention.

Apart from this, the bad news is that all the downsides of travelling with a baby still apply to your crawler. Plus, they need more entertaining and are slightly less happy to be in the stroller or carried in a baby carrier when they are not tired.

The good news is that a crawling baby knows that the world is interesting and has decided to investigate it. This means that from now on your baby will become more and more fascinated by what you show him or her while you're away. Usually, crawlers are still good nappers so you can still do what you want to do for much of the time. In addition, from around six months, you don't need to sterilise feeding or eating equipment, which is one less chore to think about.

Toddlers

The most difficult time to travel with children is when they are aged between one and three. They've got bags of energy, they can move like the wind, everything still goes in their mouth, they can have terrible tantrums (in the most public of spaces) because they get frustrated by the things they can't do or aren't allowed to do and you can't reason with them (yet). In addition, they are often fussy eaters, obstinate in their likes and dislikes, their favourite word is 'no', and you can't take your eyes off them for a second. On top of this, toddlers are pretty much at the age where they need a proper bedtime in a proper bed in your hotel, apartment or wherever you are staying. This means that from now on you'll probably spend most of your evenings at your accommodation, having had an early supper with the children who are now in bed (or not, as the case may be). It is at this juncture that babysitters or travelling with other families becomes more attractive (see p28 and p83).

On the plus side, toddlers are probably sleeping better at night and many will still have a long afternoon sleep in the stroller (which can coincide with a museum visit or two). Although they may baulk at some of the food on offer (see p79 for how to cope with this issue), from the age of a year they can drink cows' milk, as long as it is pasteurised, which makes life on the road easier. In addition, toddlers are just starting to communicate. They are full of *joie de vivre*, bringing a fresh interest to everything and giving you the chance to see the world from a different perspective. They love running around in safe environments like parks and playgrounds, they get excited by water fountains and being at the beach, going on public transport (especially trains) is an entertainment in itself, and they adore picnics. Want to remember how wonderful the world is? Then travel with your toddler.

Preschool & Older Children

From about the age of four, travel with children becomes a real pleasure. They are mostly over the tantrum stage, you can have proper conversations with them about where you are and what they are looking at, they will listen to reason and they understand the need for some holiday rules and regulations (see p79 for more details). If your child can communicate properly and act more responsibly, the first thing this means is that travelling to some more adventurous destinations becomes safer. By the age of about eight, many activity and adventure tour operators will accept them on family programs to countries in the developing world. In fact, travelling with kids aged four and older just gets better and better each year. Although the afternoon sleep has disappeared forever, you can make practically anything you want to do interesting for a child aged four to 10. You can keep the younger ones amused by telling them stories, participating in their make-believe, playing games, making up silly rhymes and singing, and the older ones can enjoy acting like grown-ups, keeping a travel diary, creating a holiday website, and telling you what they'd like to do and what they'd find interesting. It is either a pro or a con but from the age of about four, planning how you'll spend your day will be a much more collaborative affair with the children's likes and dislikes taken into consideration. See the Making It Work chapter for more details (p72).

Having said all of this, it can still be hard work as children in this age group can get bored easily. So you'll have to be constantly inventive, active and strict about some quiet time when the children amuse themselves (otherwise you'll run yourself ragged).

Teenagers

Travelling or holidaying with pre-teens and teenagers is a whole different ball game which is why this book has a whole chapter dedicated to this age group (see p88). The world is your oyster (as long as they are not too 'cool' to follow instructions in malarious areas or ones where dengue fever is on the increase). They are much more able to entertain themselves, which is good, but this can throw up issues about keeping them safe if they want to go off on their own (see p89). They may enjoy some of the same things that you do and they'll also remember most of what they experience and get some educational value from it. Your evenings will also be less restricted.

They'll need to be heavily involved in the planning of a trip or holiday – if they are unhappy you will be too. They need to be consulted day-to-day and will probably be clear about what they want to do, where they want to go, and how many 'temple' days and 'ruins' days are a reasonable exchange for beach days or shopping days! Travelling with teenagers can also be more expensive because they may want the privacy of their own room. If it's not the 'done thing' to holiday with the oldies anymore, then suggest they take along a friend.

PASSPORTS, VISAS & TRAVEL INSURANCE

Passports

Identity fraud is one of the planet's fastest-growing crimes. To help combat this, many countries now issue biometric passports and most have caught up with the UK, US and Australia and insist that all children have their own passports. These usually cost less than an adult one because they are often valid for a shorter period of time. In the UK, US and Australia, for instance, they last for five years. This means that it's easy to forget when your child's passport expires, so do check the date regularly.

The introduction of biometric passports is coupled with stricter rules on passport photos (eyes open, mouth closed, no smiling, etc). In some cases, it can be quite difficult to take an acceptable passport photo of a baby or toddler. It is important to read and comply fully with all passport photo instructions and to accept that it may take an afternoon's photography to get the right one.

In addition, in the US both parents need to accompany a child under 14 when applying for or renewing their passport. You also need to bring proof of the child's US citizenship, evidence of the child's relationship to yourselves, and parental identification. These rules are in place to protect against international abduction.

Visas

This is fairly straightforward. If you need a visa then your child will too. As they'll be travelling on their own passport, they'll need their own visas and there are no discounts. Visas mean more form-filling and more photo-taking.

Travel Insurance

Children can usually be included on your travel insurance. Your insurer will need their names and ages and you'll have to declare any pre-existing medical conditions like asthma, ear infections (eg glue ear) and eczema. It usually costs nothing to include an infant (under two years of age) but children from two upwards are often charged at a discounted rate.

Good travel insurance with medical cover of up to at least £5 million and repatriation to

Cost Cutters

Although travelling with children will cost more than travelling on your own or with a partner, significant savings can be made in nearly all of the following areas:

- **Scheduled airlines** With increased competition and airline alliances, flying has rarely been cheaper. Most bargain fares go on sale between six to eight months before departure (you rarely get a good deal last minute). The cost of your ticket depends on your departure date so try to fly out of season. Travel as much as you can with any family members under two because they only pay between 10% and 15% of a full adult fare. In addition, children up to the age of 12 usually pay 67% to 75% of the normal adult fare, plus get baggage allowance. For more information on flying see p51.
- **School holidays** The most expensive time to travel anywhere is during the school holidays so, if you can, avoid this time like the plague.
- **No-frills airlines** Flying no frills started in the US and has now been adopted worldwide. If you book at the right time (usually six to eight weeks before departure) and get the cheap fares, these airlines have opened up the possibility of frequent travel for parents and children.
- **Package holidays** This is often one of the cheapest ways to holiday. You don't have to stay at your resort if you don't want to – why not spend a couple of nights away? The cost will often be cheaper than if you book everything separately. For more information see the Package Holidays & Resorts chapter.
- **Trains and buses** It can be cheaper to travel this way with children than on your own. Do your homework and see what 'family' cards or special fares are on offer at your destination. Also, sleeper trains are a great way to save money on accommodation and give the kids a thrill (wow, bunk beds on a train?!) For more details on train and bus travel see p57.
- **Accommodation** Cleanliness and comfort is more important when travelling with children so accommodation can cost more. Look out for hotels that charge by the room, rather than per person. Don't discount the lowly youth hostel – many now have family rooms and are relaxed, fun places to stay with kids and once they are old enough, camping is a very cheap option. For more information on accommodation see p64.
- **Food** Self-catering will be your cheapest option. But even if you don't want to go down that route, children love picnics and they cost significantly less than meals in a restaurant. See p79 for more information on eating with children abroad.
- **Seasons** If you travel out of season you can get good deals on practically anything. Have a beach holiday in Europe in May or October or go to Australia in July. For a discussion on climate and when to travel see p63.
- **Free stuff** Particularly in cities, there's tons to do that doesn't cost anything. Parks, playgrounds, paddling pools, festivals, beaches, some museums, etc, are all free. Read Part 4: Destinations for more details of particular countries and cities.

For more information on holiday options and their costs see Part 3: Types of Holidays. For more country-specific information, including living costs, see Part 4: Destinations or log onto Lonely Planet at www.lonelyplanet.com/destinations.

your home country is crucial when travelling with kids. According to Direct Line's (www .directline.com) claims data, the top three medical claims made on behalf of children are for:

- Ear infections
- Gastrointestinal problems
- Trips, slips and falls

Also, check that if you need to curtail or cancel your trip due to one member of the family becoming ill, everyone is covered.

If you live in the Economic European Area (EEA) and intend to travel in this region or Switzerland, it is wise for you and your children to apply for a European Health Insurance Card (EHIC) as well as travel insurance. This will entitle most nationalities in this area to reduced-cost or free medical treatment when abroad.

TRAVEL INSURANCE WHEN PREGNANT
It happens. You plan to go travelling or book to go on holiday months in advance and by the time you depart you're pregnant. A handful of travel insurance companies will insure you up to the 32nd week including any complications of pregnancy and care of a premature baby, and give medical cover of up to £10 million. However, most companies won't insure you after the 28th week of pregnancy.

After 32 weeks you won't be able to get travel insurance for love nor money. However, the date beyond which airlines will not allow pregnant travellers to fly differs from company to company. With many, it is 36 weeks, but for others it's 34 weeks or less. This means that any travel after 32 weeks is not insured.

If travelling when pregnant, you must inform your airline or ferry company. In addition, if you are more than 28 weeks at the time of your return trip, most airlines ask for a medical certificate from a GP stating that you are fit to travel.

For information on travelling when pregnant see p44.

Other Documents
If you don't have the same surname as your child and you are travelling alone with them, things could get complicated. Wherever you are headed, it is wise to obtain a letter from the father or mother whose surname your child possesses, giving you permission to travel with them. This letter, accompanied by a copy of their birth certificate showing you as father or mother, should ensure you have few problems when crossing borders.

If you are travelling with a child under 16 who doesn't belong to your family (ie a holiday companion for your teenage daughter or son), you will need a letter from his or her parents saying the same thing.

However, sometimes you may need this letter to be 'notarised'. Basically, this means that the signatures are witnessed by a person who has the professional authority to do this (eg your solicitor). For more information, the website http://travelwithkids.about.com/cs/ carplanetips/a/crossborders.htm gives a good overview of this issue.

Country entry and exit requirements change continually so, whenever you travel with children, you must check up-to-date border requirements with your travel agent or the appropriate consulate. In addition, the US Department of State's Bureau of Consular Affairs website (http://travel.state .gov/travel/cis_pa_tw/cis/cis_1765.html) gives all the current details of entry and exit requirements for all countries in the world.

MONEY & COSTS

There's no doubt that travelling is more expensive than staying at home. However, the costs of long-term travel with your family can sometimes be offset by letting your family home and selling the family car. See p22 for other tips.

Some of the main factors that impact on how much you'll spend include: how many family members are travelling and their ages; what type of holiday or trip you want (eg independent travel or a package holiday); where you go (eg will the cost of living be cheap or expensive); what you do when you get there; and how you want to travel (eg on a shoestring or five star all the way). Within this, the two most expensive elements of any trip will be accommodation and transport.

PACKING

When you are a new parent, you could fill the entire hold of an A380 (one of those superjumbo planes) with equipment for your one baby. When your child is slightly older, it is still tempting to pack everything but the bunk beds as you plan for every eventuality.

OK, time for a reality check. When travelling with children you need to keep it simple. Take as little as possible and remember that, unless you're going bush, you can buy much of what you need at your destination or you'll be able to improvise or 'make do'. If it helps, start packing a couple of weeks before departure and each day take something out of the suitcase. If you travel a lot, consider keeping a bag ready packed with everything but the children's clothes in it so you're not continually referring to your checklist when you go away.

How many pieces of luggage you take is also crucial. If you've got too many you won't be able to look after the children and keep an eye on all your gear. If you are travelling on public transport, try to fit all but the bulky items in one bag and allow each adult one day-pack only. If you are taking a stroller, a baby carrier/backpack and/or a baby car seat, then that's five or six pieces of individual luggage already and that's quite enough to remember.

Some parents like to give older toddlers or preschool children their own day-packs to carry. This can make them feel involved and help them take early responsibility for some of their own possessions. Other parents, however, find this over-complicated and find these daypacks usually get left behind somewhere (often in the airport toilets – landside when you're now airside!), causing anguish or delay.

What to Bring

This depends on the age of your children, where you are going, what you are doing and how you're getting there. Following are some guidelines for your checklist:

BABIES & CRAWLERS

This group will need the most equipment and there'll be very little room left in the luggage for your clothes.

Feeding Equipment

If you're bottlefeeding or supplementing breast milk with formula you'll need:

- **Baby food** It's wise to pack a few jars of your baby's favourite food, just in case it takes a while to find something similar when you're away
- **Bottle brush** Otherwise you'll never get them clean
- **Bottles and teats** Enough for one day's feeds

- **Disposable presterilised bottles** Although wasteful and environmentally unfriendly, one of two of these might be useful as a back-up; large chemists often stock them
- **Formula milk** If you can, take enough for your whole trip, as different brands of formula taste different and your baby might not be so keen
- **Cloth squares** Take as many as you can and use as bibs, adult shoulder protectors etc
- **Plastic formula containers** These are segmented and hold enough premeasured formula for three feeds allowing you more freedom to make up feeds when you're out and about
- **Sterilising equipment** Tablets or microwavable sterilising bags that you put all your equipment in (then hope to find a microwave) are common ways to deal with this
- **Travel kettle** To boil the water for feeds. On top of this, remember your baby food container, spoons and plastic or disposable bibs and, most importantly, wet wipes. If you're breastfeeding, bring along a nice big shawl to use in public places or countries where breastfeeding is more of a private affair.

Nappies (Diapers)

If you're travelling in a warm climate there'll be times when your baby can go without nappies but, for the majority of the time, you'll need either disposable nappies or cloth ones. See Part 4: Destinations for information on nappy availability at your destination.

Disposable nappies are easy to use and light to carry, although they are bulky to pack and relatively expensive. Of course, environmentally friendly nappies are the way to go, especially when you're travelling, as you don't want to leave anything in a country that will be there in a couple of hundred years' time.

Cloth nappies are easy to pack, reusable, relatively inexpensive and environmentally friendly. However, you'll need to carry the soiled ones around with you until you can wash and dry them. If you use cloth you'll need to carry a minimum of a dozen nappies.

As well as nappy cream and biodegradable nappy sacks, other bottom-related items are:

- **Portable changing mat** Invaluable for when you need to change your baby on an airline seat or on the floor of the toilets
- **Gaffer tape** For when the tabs on your environmentally friendly nappies fail
- **Baby wipes** Invaluable for wiping up everything from top to bottom

Baby Carriers, Strollers & Car Seats

For babies up to eight months or so, a baby carrier or sling (you can use a sarong or shawl or buy one custom-made) that you strap to your front is a travel must. Babies love being carried in front and will often be lulled to sleep by your heartbeat and movement (when they're not carried face-out so they can admire their surroundings).

Just as important is a folding, light-weight stroller with a well-fitting rain cover. Buy one for newborns that lies flat so your growing baby will always sleep comfortably and you won't have to rush back to your accommodation for naps. One with larger wheels is better for travelling because it can negotiate more terrains than the strollers with smaller ones can. For many parents, a baby carrier and stroller is not an either/or choice: they always take both. Babies and young children love having the option: the baby carrier is good for when your child is alert and

BEFORE YOU GO

interested in the surroundings and the stroller is better when he or she is sleepy, taking less interest and wants to see the world from a different perspective. In addition, a stroller is useful in restaurants where the child can be strapped in an upright position to eat without having to keep them on your knee.

A lightweight stroller is no good if you plan to go trekking on mountain paths, isolated tracks or beaches. But it's really useful for day-to-day excursions to restaurants, shops, hotels and around towns. All-terrain, three-wheeler strollers will get you to more places but they tend to be heavier and bulkier so fitting through the doors of shops or getting onto public transport is more difficult.

Unless you plan to do any travel by car, it is debatable whether you need a baby carrier, a stroller and a car seat. For many parents it is one carrying system too far but it's a personal choice. However, it can be good if you are flying long-haul; see p53 for more information.

Travel Cots

Considering their size when erected, collapsible travel cots fold down quite small. However, if you're carting them from place to place you might find them too heavy (plus it's one more piece of equipment to think about). Many places you stay in will be able to provide a cot (for a small extra charge) and if they can't, it's easy to improvise with sleeping arrangements. However, take a look at the many lightweight, pop-up travel cots that are on the market; most can be used until babies are eight or nine months.

Bedding

What you take depends on your destination and accommodation choices. However, unless you are camping, you rarely need to pack much bedding at all.

Having said that, some parents like to travel with their baby's lambskin or similar. Lambskins are good if your baby is sweaty because the wool never feels damp. It is always soft and cuddly, and keeps a child warm when they are cold and cool when they are hot. Lambskins are washable but need a full, hot day to dry them. However, they are extremely bulky to pack, which is a major disadvantage.

In hot climes, cotton sleeping bags (the type that goes on like a nightgown over the head and arms, but fastens down the middle and are sewn along the bottom like a bag) are cooler for babies than sleep-suits. And, of course, if your child sleeps with a favoured blankie for comfort, don't forget to pack this too.

Clothes

Again, what your baby or crawler wears will depend on where you're going. This age group will need more clothes because everything gets dirty the moment it's put on. As such, a range of tops and bottoms is good because you can simply change whichever part has the most food/sick/dirt down it. Also, pack a travel clothes line to give you as many drying options as possible.

If you're travelling in a hot climate you'll need to pack lightweight, loose-fitting clothes. Cotton clothing absorbs sweat and will help keep your young ones cool. Synthetic clothing doesn't get so creased and dries out easily but can make your baby feel clammy. Long-sleeved tops and trousers are good because they give vital protection against the sun and biting insects. Most important of all is the sun hat, but make sure it protects the back of your baby's neck.

In a colder climate you'll need plenty of layers and perhaps some thermal underwear. Woollen tights under trousers are also good for keeping babies warm. Don't forget mittens and a warm hat.

Toys & Cuddlies
Unless there's anything your baby or crawler is particularly attached to (like a blankie), revel in the fact that at this stage you'll probably need only take a rattle or two and one of those clip-on stroller books.

TODDLERS & PRESCHOOLERS
As your child gets older, the amount of special equipment you need to pack reduces and changes as follows:

- **Clothing** Older children might need junior walking boots or waterproof sandals. Comfortable tracksuits for flying, fleeces for cold weather, trousers that convert into shorts for warmer climes and some wet weather gear are all recommended.

- **Emergency nibbles** A jar of Marmite/ Vegemite or peanut butter, crackers, a container of cornflakes and packs of sultanas ensure your fussy three- year-old always has something they'll eat, even when noses are turned up at everything else on offer.

- **Feeding equipment** Your toddler may still want their bedtime milk in a bottle. Otherwise, all you'll really need are spill-proof drink cups, a handful of baby spoons, a strainer if your child doesn't like the 'bits' in juice and possibly a bowl.

- **Strollers & backpacks** Even for children up to the age of five, a stroller can be useful, especially if you like active holidays where you're walking a lot. For toddlers and children up to the age

of four years, you'll swap your baby carrier for a backpack. They are rarely comfortable for sleeping (the head lolls) but children love to see the world from up high on your back.

- **Toilet equipment** Until your child is dry at night you'll still have to pack the nappies (diapers). If you're toilet training you may want to take a potty (although it's one extra thing to carry). For preschool children, a waterproof mat is sometimes useful: even older children can have the occasional accident when they're very tired or in new surroundings.

- **Toys** Writing pads, activity books, coloured pencils, magnetic drawing boards (where you erase what you draw), a favourite book or two, some DVDs (depending on the nature of your travels and whether you're taking a laptop) plus one cuddly toy is plenty to keep this age group entertained.

OLDER CHILDREN & TEENAGERS
The main thing to think about is what will keep them amused. Drawing, writing, taking photos and keeping a travel diary (see p32) works for children from five upwards. If you're travelling in countries where English-language children's books are scarce, think about swapping with other travellers or if you're travelling long- term get new ones sent from home. Older children will want to take their MP3 players, portable electronic games and, if they're into them, puzzle books.

For more information on entertainment in the car see p60.

Medical Kits
These are very important to pack. See p35 for details of items to include.

BEFORE YOU GO

HOLIDAYING WITH OTHERS

One of the lovely things about travelling as a family is that you usually spend more time together when away than you do at home. Particularly with older children, it can be a really good time to catch up with everyone and to bond again. However, travelling with youngsters is often hard work and, depending on their age, it can be difficult to grab any 'you' time (or 'us' time if you're with a partner).

This is where a holiday with the grandparents can be very attractive. Many families try to fit in at least one holiday like this a year. Hopefully, grandparents will appreciate spending some quality time with your children and from time to time you might get to read a book or go out to dinner while they babysit. There are pros and cons to this set-up but if everyone tends to get on well, and everyone is fit enough, this holiday option is a good one all round.

A subset of this type of holiday is going away with another family. This always sounds great when you're discussing it at a dinner party – your children can play together and you can take it in turns to babysit. However, in nine out of 10 cases, this option is only 100% successful if both families know each other extremely well. Will the children actually play together or will there be constant tears and fights? Do the parents have a similar parenting style (what about manners, discipline, sweets, bedtimes etc)? Will both families be travelling on a similar budget? If this option works, it works really well. If it doesn't, it could be one of the most annoying and frustrating holidays you've ever taken.

For a discussion of taking your teenager's best friend with you on holiday, see p90.

WHAT TO DO ABOUT SCHOOL

When your child hits school age, it gets a little more complicated to travel with them for an extended period of time. Having said that, there are increasing numbers of parents being posted overseas or taking career breaks with their children.

As a parent, you have a legal obligation to ensure that any child of school age is receiving suitable full-time education. However, you have a lot of flexibility about how you discharge this responsibility.

If you are travelling abroad but staying in one place for a reasonable length of time, you might want your child to attend school. If this is the case you have a number of options, depending on what country you are in, what visa you have and what languages you speak.

In most cases, if you have the right of residence in, or permission to enter, a developed country, you can apply for your child to attend a local non-fee-paying school. In addition, under European Community law, visiting nationals of the European Economic Area (EEA), which includes all member states plus Iceland, Norway and Liechtenstein, have the same rights to education as citizens of any of these countries.

Any offer of a school place would be subject to availability and, for the most part, it is unlikely that firm offers would be made until you are resident within that country. At this point, a school or local authority will probably want to inspect a copy of your child's birth certificate (so remember to bring it) and your family's passports.

As every country is different, you will want to research the education system and admissions policies for overseas children before you leave home. A good place to start is a country's Department of Education. In the UK this is the Department for Children, Schools and Families (www .dcsf.gov.uk), in Australia the Department of Education, Employment and Workplace Relations (www.deewr.gov.au) and in the US, the US Department of Education (www .ed.gov). Another resource is Expat Focus (www.expatfocus.com) which discusses schools and schooling in each country's section.

A few issues to consider when choosing to send your child to a local non-fee-paying school are the national curriculum, the national qualifications, class sizes, school facilities and the national language. In general, if your children are of primary school age, you may think that attending a local school in the local language will be a great experience for them and that there'll be plenty of time for them to catch up when you get home, if necessary.

However, if your child is of secondary school age you may want them to follow an international curriculum, to take internationally recognised exams and, if your first language is English, to be taught in this language. If this is the case, then you will need to consider sending your child to a private school.

Of course, if you are intending to send your child to school in a less-developed country then, whatever their age, you'll probably be thinking of this option too (class sizes, school facilities, etc, being a consideration).

In terms of a private education abroad, many parents choose to send their children to an international school. At these schools the teaching is in English, the curricula are internationally recognised and the education is of a high standard. Of course, all of this comes at a cost and this will mean paying fairly steeply for your child's education.

There is a range of organisations that give information about international schools around the world but two particularly useful ones include the Council of International Schools (www.cois.org) and the European Council of International Schools (www.ecis .org). Otherwise, the consulate of the country you are travelling to will have information on international schools. Places in international schools tend to fill up quickly so apply well in advance and be prepared for some sort of interview or selection process, which may take place over the phone.

Another option is to go the 'total immersion' route and send your child to a private school that teaches in the local language. Again, the consulate will have details on how to find information about private schools within their country and so will websites like About.Com (http://privateschool .about.com/od/schoolsonlineworldwide).

Of course, attending some sort of bricks and mortar school only works if you're planning to be in one place (or a series of places) for more than a term. However, what do you do if you want to be on the move with the children?

One option is for your child to attend some sort of cyber- or correspondence school. These work in a variety of ways but you pretty much have a curriculum that you follow and your child sends in their course work to be marked by post, fax or email. There are

School & Teenagers

Younger school age children often return from a spell abroad with a reading level well above that of their peers. If they have fallen behind in other areas, it's likely they will catch up quickly. Teenagers, however, are different. When they come home they may face important exams that can impact on their choices for higher education. It may not be practical or affordable to find a school to educate them in these subjects. Your ability to teach them yourself may be hindered by your ignorance of the material. So, here are a few tips on how to cope with this dilemma:

- Consider travelling with a laptop. Before leaving, download exam-prep material, lessons, articles and anything else you can think of.
- Ask your child's teachers for a teaching plan. They may have digitalised copies of textbooks and other instructional materials that you can also download
- Find a local tutor. This more flexible and cheaper than finding a school. It's also a good way for your teenager to meet other young people. If there is a university at your destination, ask around the appropriate department or ask someone at the local high school to recommend a bright, upper-level student.
- Allocate a significant proportion of the family's baggage to your scholar's books. Since you left your own reading material behind, read these books along with your child and muddle through together.
- Make sure your teenager keeps a travel journal. In addition to helping with their writing skills, it will likely come in handy for reports and projects after your return.

Fritz Burke

then options to have tutorials online and support phone calls. There are a number of international organisations that offer this service but two worth checking out include the World-wide Education Service (www .weshome.co.uk) and Clonlara School (www .clonlara.org).

However, a good many travelling families choose to educate their children themselves. In many countries there is a long history of home-schooling or home education and doing it on the road is very similar. You can usually choose whether you want to follow your own national curriculum or develop your own curriculum based on your travels. And, of course, the educational benefits of seeing the world can be huge: there's nothing like going to a rainforest instead of learning about it in a geography lesson at school or visiting the Tower of London and learning about the Tudor period of English history rather than looking at the pictures in a textbook. Reading and writing can be made fun as your child writes letters home or reads emails from friends and the value of maths suddenly becomes apparent as your child uses the local currency in shops or works out how many miles to the next destination.

Your child's current school might be willing to guide you but it is a good idea to contact organisations in your home country which help those who want to educate their children themselves. In the UK, contact Education Otherwise (www.education -otherwise.org) or the Home Education Advisory Service (HEAS) (www.heas.org .uk), in Australia there's the Home Education Association (http://hea.asn.au) and in the US log onto A to Z Home's Cool Home-schooling (http://homeschooling.gomilpitas.com).

If you are away, educating your children yourself and want them to take examinations abroad, this can usually be arranged through an organisation like Edexcel International (www.edexcel-international.org).

CHILDREN WITH SPECIAL NEEDS

If you are a parent or carer travelling with a child who has special needs, you are the best person to know what destinations, accommodation options and transport choices are suitable for your child. Depending on the individual, having special requirements might not limit your travels but it does mean more planning. Consult your medical specialist before you go and contact support organisations where people may have already had the same kind of experiences. And a good generic website to look at is http://www .worldtravelguide.net/appendices/4/appen dix/Facilities-for-Disabled-Travellers.html.

Before You Go

If your child has a health issue that may require urgent medical attention, make sure you discuss a standard medical plan with your doctor as well as an emergency plan and be sure to have lots of extra medication with you. Check out in advance where the nearest doctor and hospital emergency departments are in the places you will be staying. Make sure you have adequate travel insurance and that your insurer is fully aware of your child's pre-existing medical condition. Also, ensure that your policy will cover replacement or theft of any medical supplies. If you need any electrical equipment make sure you know the voltage in your destination and take an adaptor.

If you're taking a wheelchair, explain the facilities that will be required when you book your accommodation – easy wheelchair access to the hotel, a ground-floor room or lift access, a room with access to the bathroom and reasonably level surroundings. Also book ahead for hired cars or taxis that can accommodate not only wheelchairs but special equipment and everyone's general luggage. Check with the local tourist office or a special needs organisation in the country you're visiting for details of wheelchair access in the general area. And remember to pack your wheelchair repair kit.

Planes

When travelling by plane keep your child's medication in the hand luggage in case your luggage in the hold is delayed or lost. Using cramped toilets is an issue for many kids with special needs: ask the airline what they can do to assist. For instance, some have a couple of designated accessible toilets and others will provide a screen so the door can be left open to allow more space to move.

When booking a flight, provide all relevant information such as any help your child might need during the flight and special dietary requirements. Reconfirm these details 48 hours before and check in early so that you can get a seat that will suit you. Some airlines require a medical clearance form, so check if your child will need one of these. If your child needs a special restraint in the car take it with you. Depending on the type of restraint and the age of your children you may also be able to use it on the plane.

If your child is in a wheelchair, give the airline as much notice as possible so they can provide assistance. They should be able to organise a wheelchair once your child has been checked in and have yours waiting for you at the end of your flight. However (as with strollers) ask exactly where the wheelchair will be at your destination, otherwise you'll have a time-consuming run-

around trying to discover its whereabouts. Provide instructions on how it should be reassembled and take detachable pieces such as the wheelchair cushion on the plane with you. The wheelchair is usually not included in your baggage allowance. If you have a folding wheelchair it may be possible to take that on board.

Trains

Wheelchair access to platforms is often via a lift and these can be slow and at the wrong end of the platform. You need to allow much more time than you think for boarding and transfers, especially to make connections that require a change of platform. As with flying, when booking rail tickets make sure the company knows you're travelling with a wheelchair as they have to book a space for it.

DOCUMENTING THE JOURNEY

There are lots of fun and enjoyable ways that children can record their trip, depending on their interests and inclination. Below are a few ideas that might appeal:

- **Keeping a travel journal** For younger children this may be more of a scrap book of tickets, postcards, stamps, etc. For older ones it can be a proper diary with alternating lined and blank pages.
- **Taking photos** Children of all ages love to take photos. Hard-wearing digital cameras designed especially for children are available, and disposable cameras also have their advantages.
- **Online Travel Diaries** Older children and teenagers can subscribe to an online travel diary site and write journal entries, plot their route on a map, upload their photos and email friends and relatives.

Preparing Your Child to Travel

It is said that travel broadens the mind. With a little help from you, it might eventually lead your child to a better understanding of the world they'll one day inherit.

At a more practical level, giving them some information about their destination can go a long way towards helping them cope when they get there and it might also get them excited about the prospect in advance. Here are some ideas that can easily be incorporated into your everyday life:

- **Map** Pin up a map of the region or country you are visiting. Older children could mark on it where they'd like to go (and keep your fingers crossed that it resembles parental plans).

- **Books** Get some guidebooks and picture books from the library about where you're going and look at them together (perhaps before bed). Try to find books of legends or children's stories from the region. You may be surprised at how much sticks. See the country profiles in Part 4 of this book for kid-friendly suggestions.

- **Films** There's nothing like a good movie to get kids excited about a place and give them a visual image of what it will be like, so hire some DVDs before you go. For instance, what child that's watched and loved The Sound of Music does not want to go straight from the sofa to Salzburg?

- **Restaurants and home-cooking** Even if you're only going away for a couple of weeks, it's fun to take your children to a restaurant that serves the same cuisine as the country you're going to. Although most young children will recoil on principle when anything new is offered, they will sometimes try new food in a new country when it is served up in a restaurant. If you're planning a longer trip, try introducing a few different foods or flavours into your home cooking so the food on your travels won't be completely new.

- **Learning the language** If your children can say 'Please' and 'Thank you' in the local language, this will endear them to every shopkeeper, hotelier and restaurateur in the country. If they can say more than this then well done for being a great home-educator. We all know that learning some of the local language can be useful as well as enjoyable and it will help your children's confidence if they can converse with a few key words. Children usually pick up languages quickly, particularly the younger ones.

- **Internet** Older children can be encouraged to go online and do some research on your holiday destination or route planning if you're travelling for longer. Depending on their age (and on how brave you feel), you might even give them the responsibility of booking some tickets.

STAYING HEALTHY & KEEPING SAFE

Ask any parent what they worry about most when travelling with children and they'll list health and safety as their main concern. The health and safety of your child will impact on almost every decision you take – from where to go, to what you do and what precautions you take when you get there.

HEALTH

Any pretrip planning should take into consideration not only the potential health risks of your destination, but also the age and temperament of your children.

Before You Go

DOCTOR & DENTIST

It's a good idea to make sure your child is as healthy as possible before you go. Talk to your doctor about illness prevention and work out a plan of action for common problems. If your child has an ongoing condition like eczema, diabetes or asthma, be clear about what to do if the condition worsens while you're away.

It's worth making sure your children have a thorough dental checkup before going away and remember to leave enough time for any treatment to be carried out if necessary.

IMMUNISATIONS

Children should be up to date with all routine childhood immunisations and they'll need the same travel-related vaccines as you. Most fully immunised school-age children won't need further doses of routine immunisations, but babies and younger children who haven't completed their normal childhood immunisations may need to complete the schedules earlier than normal. Ask your doctor about immunisations when you start planning your trip. Travel-related vaccines your child may need are listed below, including some vaccines with age restrictions – your doctor should be able to help you with these.

- **Diphtheria, tetanus, polio, pertussis and Hib** The new five-in-one vaccine can only be given after six weeks of age
- **Hepatitis A** This vaccine can be given from the age of one year (two years in the US)
- **Hepatitis B and tuberculosis** Though not used in the US and some European countries, these have no lower age limit but are important for long-term travel
- **Measles** This can be given at six months of age if necessary (but not recommended for use under 12 months unless there are very special circumstances and revaccination should then be considered at 12 months)
- **Rabies** You can vaccinate from birth. Rabies can be caught from a lick, scratch or bite. Rabid animals can sometimes appear docile and could either be a domestic pet or a wild animal.
- **Typhoid** This vaccination isn't normally given under two years of age but can be given from 12 or 18 months, although this may lead to a poor immune response
- **Yellow fever** This disease is potentially life-threatening and this is sometimes one of the vaccinations you need to cross borders. You can vaccinate from the age of nine months upwards.

If kids are going to react to an immunisation, it will usually happen about 48 hours after the injection and can generally be settled with paracetamol (acetaminophen). Children can go on to have further reactions and sometimes develop rashes 10 days after the immunisation, so the earlier you get kids immunised, the better.

If you're coming from a region where yellow fever is an issue – such as South America or Africa – you may need certificates of vaccination to enter some countries. It's a good idea to keep records of vaccinations, and ask your doctor for up-to-date information about vaccination requirements. Also ask about malaria prevention, particularly if you're visiting Africa, Asia or South America.

A good website for travel health advice is Fit for Travel (www.fitfortravel.scot.nhs.uk).

MEDICAL KIT & MEDICATIONS

It's essential to take a child-specific medical kit as well as your own basic medical kit. If your child takes any medications regularly (for asthma, eczema or diabetes, for example) you'll obviously need to take a good supply of these medications with you. However, remember to keep some of this medication close to hand, especially when you're in transit and your main bag is inaccessible. Also, drugs have different names in different countries so check what yours are called in the countries you're visiting before you depart. It's also wise to get a letter from your GP explaining any pre-existing medical conditions and medications, which can help you at border crossings. You'll also have to bear in mind how you're going to store these drugs as some need to be kept in controlled temperatures.

A basic medical kit for children should include most of the following:

- Anti-acid tablets – useful to comfort mild stomach irritations
- Antibiotics – if you are planning on going to extremely remote areas for extended periods of time, then you could consider packing broad-spectrum antibiotics. You must discuss what these might be with your travel health professional.
- Antihistamine tablets, creams or liquids for bites and stings
- Antiseptic wipes and antiseptic liquid or spray
- Barrier cream or Vaseline for nappy rash
- Calamine cream or aloe vera gel for heat rash and sunburn
- Measuring implements for liquid medicines like plastic spoons (5mL and 2.5mL) or syringes
- Motion sickness remedies (see p37)
- No-water washes – good for keeping children's hands clean when you're out and about
- Nonadherent dressing and nonallergic strapping tape
- Oral rehydration salt sachets (flavoured)
- Plentiful supply of Band-Aids (waterproof for swimming but fabric to help the wound heal)
- Remedies for pain and fever like paracetamol (acetaminophen) and ibuprofen child syrups. These often come in premeasured sachets and work well in combination, as you can reduce the intervals between doses if used together. Also pack cold and flu remedy drinks and decongestants (Karvol).
- Sunscreen
- Thermometer (digital or forehead if very small child)
- Tiger balm and arnica cream
- Tweezers and nail clippers
- Wet wipes

If you do need to give your child medication when you are away, remember children need a child-sized dose and not all medications are suitable for children. Follow the dosing instructions given by your doctor or on the packet. Doses are generally based on your child's age and weight. You should also check that your child's medication is legal at your destination.

Before you go, it makes sense to do a general first-aid course so you'd know what to do in most medical emergencies, especially those relevant to children like choking.

While You're Away

Being informed, taking precautions and knowing what to look for if your child becomes unwell is important when you are abroad. Children are at risk of the same diseases as you are when you are away. Because children can't always tell you what's wrong and in many cases don't show typical symptoms of diseases, it's even more important to seek medical help at the earliest opportunity. Always get medical help if you have any concerns about their condition.

CLIMATE

Children can be adaptable to climate change. However, they need time to adjust to extremes. Ideally, this means spending a minimum of three days in your new destination upping your fluid intake and allowing time to relax.

Heat

If your child is not used to a hot climate, they will need time to acclimatise. Children tend to acclimatise easily, but young children (with their greater surface area relative to their body mass) can lose fluid very rapidly through sweating, and become dehydrated and vulnerable to heatstroke. Babies and young children may not be able to tell you how hot they're feeling, although obvious symptoms like lethargy, flushing and clamminess are the danger signals. Otherwise, if you're getting hot, check to see how your child is coping, and whether they are dressed appropriately. Try to discourage mobile youngsters from rushing around in the heat of the day. Baby backpacks or slings are a handy way to carry children, but it can be easy to forget how exposed they are to the elements.

Because babies and children can become dehydrated relatively easily, they require a significant increase in their fluid intake. As a general rule this should be doubled and they should be encouraged to drink water containing rehydration salts, which increase the amount of fluid retained by the body. In these conditions, you can take pleasure in allowing your child to eat salty crisps and to indulge in sweet/fizzy drinks. This is because salt, which helps retain water in the body, is lost through sweating and sugar helps the body to absorb salt. You can also encourage them to eat lots of juicy fruit and vegetables. Keep an eye on how much urine they are passing – small amounts of dark urine or dark urine-stained nappies in babies mean you need to increase their fluid intake.

Cold

Children feel the cold, as they lose heat very rapidly, especially if they are immobile in a carrier, so wrap them up well and check them regularly for signs of cold. Appropriate layers of clothes are vital for keeping kids warm, including mittens and warm hats. Give children plenty to eat and drink, as they can use up their energy reserves quickly and this makes them more vulnerable to the cold.

Altitude

Altitude sickness can be fatal if not recognised and treated properly.

If you're planning on going to high-altitude destinations, remember that littlies are just as vulnerable to the effects of altitude as adults and they may not be able to tell you about their symptoms. Altitude sickness may have nonspecific symptoms, such as nausea, headache or vomiting, which can be easily confused with other kids' illnesses. Keep a close eye on your children and familiarise yourself with symptoms by discussing altitude sickness with your doctor, especially if you're trekking or going to be higher than 2000m above sea level.

The longer you take ascending to altitude, the better; flying into somewhere high like Quito (Ecuador) should be treated with extra care. You should descend promptly if your children show any signs of altitude sickness.

Treatment drugs such as Diamox are best avoided with young travellers.

TRAVEL-RELATED HEALTH ISSUES

Motion Sickness

This is extremely common in children and can turn even a short journey into a trauma. If you know that your children are particularly susceptible to this, it is only fair to take a good supply of your normal motion sickness remedy with you on holiday.

Otherwise, ginger is a good remedy. You can buy ginger capsules from many health-food stores; check that the capsule dosage will be suitable for your children's weight and age (and that they can swallow capsules).

The use of sedatives like promethazine (Phenergan) which have traditionally been used to sedate children on long journeys (particularly when flying) is now frowned upon by the medical establishment. If you

BEFORE YOU GO

ARPAD BENEDEK | ISTOCKPHOTO

think this is an alternative you may want to seek medical advice before you depart. A natural soothing alternative is camomile.

Flying

On flights, air-pressure changes can cause ear pain in babies and young children. Give babies a drink as this happens, as the swallowing reflex will clear their ears, and older children can be given chewy sweets or drinks, or encouraged to blow their noses, which should help their ears to pop. Younger children and babies can be given decongestant nose drops if necessary (get these from your doctor or pharmacist before you go) as well as paracetamol (acetaminophen) syrup to ease the pain. If your child has an ear infection or a bad cold, this will exacerbate your problems.

Infections

Your children can catch an infection three main ways: from insects, from food and water; and through contact with humans and animals. A lot of these can be immunised against but some can't.

You don't want to avoid contact with humans, but be aware of the importance of good hygiene procedures and know the symptoms of diseases caught from other people, such as meningitis and diphtheria.

Diarrhoea

Children – especially young children and babies – are more likely than adults to get diarrhoea when they are away. They also tend to get more severe symptoms and for longer. It's partly because children are less discriminating about what they put in their mouths and it's hard to keep little hands clean, but it may also be because they have less immunity to disease-causing bugs.

Babies and children can become rapidly dehydrated through diarrhoea and vomiting, and it can be difficult to make sure they drink enough. The best fluids to give children are oral rehydration salts (ORS). You need to start giving them ORS as soon as diarrhoea or vomiting appears – you can make ORS more palatable by adding flavours or look for ready-flavoured sachets of ORS. Avoid food if kids are vomiting.

You don't need to give your child ORS if you're breastfeeding, but make sure you're taking in enough fluid yourself. If your child is being fed a milk-based formula, you need to replace this with ORS until the diarrhoea is better. As the diarrhoea improves introduce diluted milk feeds then, and if your baby is over six months and on solids, reintroduce these too. For older children follow the same dietary guidelines as for adults, avoiding milk and milk-based products until your child is on the mend.

The World Health Organisation gives the following guidelines for the quantity of fluid replacement:

- Under two years: one quarter to one half-cup per loose stool
- Two to 10 years: one half to one cup per loose stool
- Over 10 years: as for adults (two cups per loose stool)

If children are vomiting, allow the stomach to rest for about an hour before trying to give them fluids. Then reintroduce fluids very slowly – 5mL every 15 minutes for the first hour and build up from there. If your child is refusing to drink, try giving them small amounts by teaspoon or syringe every few minutes. Seek medical help earlier rather than later, especially if you notice any of the following symptoms developing:

- Prolonged vomiting and diarrhoea
- Refusal to take fluids
- Listlessness
- Fever
- Blood or mucus in the diarrhoea

In children, faeces may take 10 to 14 days to return to normal (though sometimes longer). As long as the faeces are not too frequent, you shouldn't worry about slightly loose faeces in an otherwise fit and recovered child.

Note that symptomatic antidiarrhoeal medications ('stoppers') are not recommended for children and should be avoided. If your child is ill enough to need antibiotics, you should seek medical advice. If you are in a remote area away from medical assistance, trimethoprim, amoxycillin or the new azithromycin are suitable antibiotic options.

Insect-Borne Diseases
Biting insects carry a number of serious diseases. The most common of these are malaria and dengue fever.

It is extremely important to protect your child from bites. Make sure your child is covered up with clothes, socks and shoes, and use insect repellents on exposed areas of skin. In hot, humid conditions, DEET-based products should be applied once an hour and the more natural repellents containing lemon eucalyptus etc, once every half hour, as all insect repellents will sweat off quickly. Also, children have very sensitive skin and whichever repellent you choose for your child should be trialled on them well before you leave. The best way to do this is to do a 'patch test'. This involves putting a small amount of the repellent on the inside of your child's arm, and covering it with a plaster for half an hour to see if they react. Permethrin-soaked

mosquito nets or coils will keep the nasties away at night and during daytime naps. Make sure the net has plenty of room in it, as children can thrash about at night and poke an arm or a leg outside the protected area.

However, coils can be smoky, so it's best not to use them indoors with young babies. Don't put repellent on babies' hands and feet, either – they'll end up eating it.

Malaria
Malaria is a problem in much of the tropical world. It is a fatal illness and children are more susceptible because of their smaller body mass. This means the parasite gains control more rapidly and in some cases can cause coma within 24 hours.

Malaria can be avoided with a few sensible preventative measures. Firstly, malaria is more prevalent at certain times of the year so try to travel in the height of the dry season and avoid the middle to late rainy seasons. Secondly, mosquitoes go into a feeding frenzy at dawn and dusk so always be protected at these times. However, they are generally night-time biters. As such, bite avoidance is your first line of defence (see above).

In addition to these precautions, your children must take preventative drugs. All antimalarials must be taken regularly so if you are in any doubt that your child will find this difficult then don't enter a malarial area. Most antimalarials are in tablet form and will need to be disguised before your children will take them (eg you can crush tablets and hide them in jam on toast). The dosage of tablets for children is done on weight and some of these tablets can be taken from birth. Not all antimalarials are suitable for all areas so seeing a travel-health specialist is imperative, so you can discuss any possible side effects your child might experience. Nothing will give you 100% protection, so always look out for severe fevers and flu-like symptoms.

Also, bear in mind that antimalarials do not prevent your child from catching malaria, they just kill the parasite once it enters the body to stop the disease spreading. This is why you must practise bite-avoidance at the same time as taking the drugs.

Dengue Fever

This disease is on the increase in much of the tropical world. In fact, it is often found in most places of the world where malaria is a problem. It differs from malaria in that the disease is carried by a daytime-biting mosquito. There are no preventative drugs and there is no drug treatment once caught. So, if you're going to a dengue fever–infested area, bite avoidance is crucial all day. This disease is not commonly fatal in adults or children but the vast majority of serious cases do occur in

kids. Dengue fever is known as break-bone disease and will make your child feel truly dreadful for two to three weeks.

ANIMAL BITES, STINGS & LICKS

It's hard to stop children from stroking animals and bites are not the only danger – it only needs a lick from a rabid animal on an open wound for the infection to be passed to your child. A rabies vaccination is important for your peace of mind and will allow you the time to get medical help should your child come into contact with a rabid beast. See p34 for rabies vaccination information.

Snakes can also be an issue for inquisitive children who are constantly picking up stones and raking around in undergrowth. It is worth noting that if your child gets bitten, there's only a 50% chance that the snake will pass venom. Remaining calm and slowing down blood flow is the key to survival. It is shocking to be bitten by

PHILIP & KAREN SMITH | LONELY PLANET IMAGES

a snake, which is why you'll need to calm your child. You can slow down the spread of the venom by applying gentle pressure around the bite area (ie a crepe bandage below and above) and elevate the area. Do not try to apply tourniquets or suck out venom, as seen in the movies; this will cause more harm than good.

Insect repellent has limited effectiveness against bee and wasp stings so if your child is stung, apply sting relief sprays and creams, pain killers and lots of sympathy. Antihistamines are good for bad reactions to lots of bites and stings, so pack some of these.

Often the shock of being stung is worse than the actual effect. If you know your child is allergic to bee stings, discuss this with your doctor before you leave and pack adrenaline (epinephrine) in your emergency kit.

Also see Insect-Borne Diseases (p39) for more information.

FOOD, DRINK & HYGIENE
Wherever you are in the world, cleanliness is important when eating and drinking. However, different destinations require different approaches. In particular, if you plan to take the children to areas in the developing world, you will need to take extra precautions.

Food
The following advice will help your little ones avoid stomach problems when travelling in less-developed countries:

- Always eat hot, freshly prepared food
- Only eat fruit and vegetables that you can peel
- Approach salads and buffets with caution (food that has been left to stand)
- Avoid reheated rice and chicken
- Avoid seafood (eg prawns, crabs); fish is OK

- Avoid dairy products, unless they have been boiled
- Try not to eat sauces that have been left to stand on tables
- Avoid dirty plates and/or cups (take your own or clean them yourself before use)

If your child is really craving familiar foods, this is the one time when heading for a Western fast-food outlet shouldn't fill you with guilt; these places have strict guidelines on food preparation.

If you can, try to prepare any food for babies yourself, making sure that the utensils you use are sterile (take along some sterilising tablets). Also, you might want to consider taking your own cooker so that home-cooked meals are an option. For details on making up feeds for baby, see p24.

Loss of Appetite
Some children eat very little when they first start travelling or go on holiday (sometimes they appear to have given up completely). If this happens, try not to worry – they probably do this at home as well but you're more relaxed there and it isn't so obvious.

Children eat when they are hungry, so don't start worrying that this trip will end with starved, malnourished children. However, carry some children's vitamin supplements with you and, more importantly, ensure that they continue to drink lots of fluid.

Water
Unless you are travelling in a first world country, it is safer to assume that all water is unfit to drink. This is the case even if it is being consumed by local people who may have built up a tolerance to the bacteria in it.

However, all water will be safe to drink as long as it has been boiled thoroughly (approximately five minutes). If your children are very young, you cannot use chemicals for water purification, so boiling or using a nonchemical filter (ceramic filters) are good alternatives. Otherwise, stick to bottled water. However, mineral water that is high in magnesium can cause diarrhoea and mineral water that is high in carbonates can cause constipation. As such, it is best to stick to 'drinking' water, as opposed to 'mineral' water.

Always avoid ice in drinks, as you don't know where the water came from. Also, be ready to refuse your children ice lollies and ice creams, unless you are 100% sure they will be safe.

Hygiene
Good hygiene will avoid many stomach problems caused by hand-to-mouth contamination either through food and water or from person to person. Children who are crawling or just walking are particularly at risk of diseases spread in this way.

Wash children's hands and faces frequently throughout the day, especially if you're travelling on public transport and particularly before they eat. Another good preventative measure is to discourage hands wandering into the mouth, eyes and nose as much as possible. A supply of wet wipes can be invaluable, especially on long journeys. It is a good idea to give your children a supply of their own wet wipes so that good hygiene becomes a bit of a game. Of course, keep their fingernails short to avoid trapping dirt and germs. Carrying a supply of no-water washes based on alcohol is also a good idea because the gel remains on the skin and will kill bacteria.

If you get sick with diarrhoea yourself, be extremely careful to wash your hands after using the toilet to avoid passing diarrhoea to your child. Be careful with nappies if your child has diarrhoea to prevent it passing to you.

SKIN PROBLEMS
Cuts & Scratches
In hot, humid climates cuts and scratches can easily become infected and it is difficult to keep children clean. You'll need to take a bit more care of abrasions than you would normally. Wash any break in the skin carefully with soap and water or antiseptic solution (or an antiseptic wipe if you haven't got access to water) and keep it covered with a sterile, nonstick, nonfluffy dressing (a sticking plaster is fine if the wound is small). Always check for infections – if the wound is weeping, there is redness and it's hot around the wound site, this will probably mean the wound is infected and you should seek medical advice because you'll need antibiotics.

It's probably worth checking your child carefully at the end of each day for cuts, scratches and potentially problematic bites. Always treat wounds with liquid or powder antiseptics, as creams will keep the wound moist and inhibit healing.

Sun
Anyone can get sunburnt but little ones are especially vulnerable. Keep children and babies covered up. A note about hats – these are hard to keep on children's heads unless they like them, so let them pick the hat themselves. Also, check for clothes with a high ultraviolet protection factor (UPF) rating. Apply liberal amounts of the highest factor sunscreen you can find and reapply it frequently.

Prickly Heat & Nappy Rash

Prickly heat is caused by an allergy to sweat. It tends to be more of a problem in children than in adults.

Calamine cream can soothe the irritation and, if needed, antihistamines can also help. You can help prevent the rash by dressing children in loose cotton clothing, bathing them often and drying them carefully, especially any skin folds and under their arms.

Nappy rash can be a lot worse in the heat. Take a good supply of barrier creams (such as petroleum jelly, zinc and castor oil cream, or Sudocrem). Wash the affected area with water after your child has a bowel movement, dry it well and apply barrier cream before the new nappy goes on; also, try to keep the nappy off as much as possible.

If the affected area is red and painful, and the rash doesn't clear up with simple treatment, it may be due to a fungal infection. Try applying an antifungal cream twice a day (options include clotrimazole, or Canesten; or an antifungal with hydrocortisone if it is very red and painful). Check your child's mouth, as they may have a fungal infection (thrush) there as well, indicated by white patches on the tongue that are difficult to remove. Treatment is with antifungal drops (such as nystatin). Remember to change rubber teats and feeding utensils as soon as treatment is started and halfway through. Continue antifungal treatments for a couple of weeks after all symptoms have disappeared.

IS MY CHILD UNWELL?

Children can quickly change from being well and active to being ill, sometimes seriously ill. In young children especially, the signs can be quite subtle and difficult to interpret, which can be a worry.

As the parent, you will know your child best of all and any change in their behaviour should be taken seriously – listen to your sixth sense. Babies up to six months may become quieter than usual, miserable and start crying without apparent cause. They may not want to eat or drink, or they may develop more specific signs, such as diarrhoea, coughing, vomiting or rashes.

Older babies and toddlers may stop walking, stop sitting up, stop feeding themselves or being as developed as you are used to. Children of this age are unable to tell you what's wrong and this may be the only sign before a rash or a cough appears.

Don't rely on a child's skin temperature as an indication of whether they have a raised temperature or not. Instead you should always carry and use a thermometer (preferably a digital one or a fever strip – less accurate but easier to use). It is important to have an actual reading of the child's temperature. A child who is cold to touch may have a raging temperature, and the reverse is also true. If you have any cause for concern, check the temperature and make sure your child is taking at least enough fluids to pass urine twice a day, even if they have gone off their food.

Fever

This is very common in children wherever they are and is always a cause for concern. In addition, a high temperature can sometimes cause a convulsion in babies and young children. Skin temperature is a confusing and unreliable sign – see the section above. If you think your child has a fever, for example, if the child is flushed and irritable and obviously unwell:

- Take your child's temperature and then take it again 30 minutes later as a check

- Put your child to bed, removing most clothing (perhaps covering the child up with a cotton sheet) and making them comfortable (protecting them with a mosquito net if necessary)
- Wipe your child's face and body with a sponge or cloth soaked in tepid (not cold) water or place in a tepid bath to help lower the temperature
- Give paracetamol (acetaminophen) syrup or tablets every four to six hours to help lower the temperature
- Use a fan or open window to get a breeze but be aware of mosquitoes coming in
- Prevent dehydration by giving small amounts of fluid often – make up oral rehydration salts with bottled or boiled water, or fruit juice diluted half and half with safe water; give 5mL every 15 minutes for the first hour
- Conditions like viral infections, colds, ear infections, urinary tract infections and diarrhoea are common causes of fever. If you've been travelling in malarial risk areas, you must always consider the possibility that a fever could be malaria.

Take steps to lower the child's temperature and also seek medical help urgently in the following situations:

- If the temperature is over 37.7°C (100°F) in a baby of less than six months
- If the temperature is over 39°C (104°F) in any infant or child
- If your child has had fits in the past
- If it could be malaria. Malaria should be suspected with any high fever if you are in a malarial area or have been within the last three months.

- If the fever shows no sign of improving after 24 hours (take your child's temperature regularly to show you if it's going up or down)

Colds, Coughs & Earaches

Children are particularly likely to succumb to new germs in new places, so be prepared. Asthma (cough, wheezing) may occur for the first time while you are away and can be frightening especially if your child has never experienced it before. You should seek medical advice if your child is having difficulty breathing, especially if you notice that their ribs are being drawn in with each breath.

If you suspect an ear infection consult a doctor, as antibiotics will be required for a middle ear infection. If your child does get an infection try to avoid water getting in their ear for two weeks. If they do have grommets in their ears, your doctor will generally advise that they shouldn't swim.

After You Get Back

Consider getting a checkup for yourself and your children if you've been on a long trip or have been travelling rough. Make sure your doctor is aware you've been travelling and where. Of course, if you've been taking antimalarial tablets, don't forget to finish the course.

PREGNANT TRAVEL

Being pregnant doesn't have to put an end to your travels. Plenty of women either choose or end up travelling while they are pregnant, without any adverse effects on mother or fetus. However, there are some important considerations if you are planning to travel while pregnant. The information included in this section gives you an idea of the issues that are involved – you should get medical advice well before you plan to go on any trip. You should also think about your travel insurance (see p21 for more details).

If you have had complicated pregnancies before or you're expecting twins, it would be best to postpone your trip until after the birth. You also need to ensure you understand the risks of travelling to any parts of the developing world while pregnant. If things go wrong, the standards of medical care may be poor and the environment dirty.

When

Most doctors suggest that the best time to travel in pregnancy is during the middle 12 weeks, when the risk of complications lessens, the pregnancy is relatively well established and your energy levels should be getting back to normal.

Before the 12th week, there is a relatively high risk of miscarriage (which could require surgical treatment like a scrape of the womb lining or even a blood transfusion) or tubal pregnancy, which occurs in about one in 200 pregnancies. Tubal pregnancy nearly always requires surgical treatment and is an emergency situation. In addition, many women experience morning sickness in the first three months (sometimes for longer), which could make travelling less than enjoyable. Occasionally, it can be severe enough to require treatment in hospital. More mundane, but just as incapacitating for travelling, is needing to empty your bladder more frequently as the enlarging womb takes up more room in the pelvis and presses on the bladder.

Note that most airlines prohibit flying after the 36th week of pregnancy (sometimes this

can be waived if you have a doctor's certificate to say that there are no complications) – this is because airlines don't want to risk a woman going into premature labour during a flight, not because there's thought to be any intrinsic danger to the pregnancy.

In the last three months, major complications – such as premature labour, blood pressure problems and problems with the placenta – can all occur, so you would probably not want to risk a trip of any length during this time.

Immunisations

Generally, it's best to avoid all vaccinations in the first 12 weeks of pregnancy. However, if they cannot be avoided you need to weigh up the benefits and the risks. In addition, 'live' vaccines ideally should be avoided at any time during pregnancy; 'live' vaccines include oral typhoid. Hepatitis A is a much more serious illness in pregnancy, so it's important to have the immunoglobulin injection or the hepatitis A vaccine as well as taking food and water precautions. A tetanus booster can be given safely in pregnancy and tetanus protection is conferred to the newborn. Make sure you are clear on what your travel health insurance covers during pregnancy.

Special Considerations

If this is your first pregnancy, it's a good idea to read up on it before you go so you have an idea of what to expect (such as tiredness, heartburn etc) and are familiar with any minor problems that may arise. Discuss these with your doctor or midwife, and work out strategies for coping in advance.

In the first three months, you'll be surprised how hungry you get. If you miss a meal due to travelling by train or bus or arriving late you may feel sick or even faint, so always carry something to eat with you, and snack on fruit, biscuits, or anything you can find to keep you going.

Don't try to do all the things you did before you got pregnant. Take frequent rests, particularly in the first three months when you're still adjusting to pregnancy. If you have one day of hard travel, have a day or two of rest and just plan to travel at a slower pace. Finally, don't be alarmed by how often you'll need to find a toilet. You'll need to go to the toilet more often than you thought physically possible. It's wise to dress for quick and convenient toilet visits.

SAFETY

When travelling with children it is easy to become fixated about their health. However, statistics show that by far the largest risk to you and your child's well-being abroad is being involved in a traffic or drowning accident. Safety is obviously important whatever the age of your children, however, the younger they are the more vigilant you need to be.

On the Roads

Depending on your destination, driving is often more dangerous overseas, particularly in the developing world. Some countries or regions have a reputation for difficult road conditions, badly maintained vehicles or dangerous driving (eg drinking while driving or driving in the shade). As such, in some countries you may want to give your children a safety talk before walking around big towns or cities. Difficult road conditions may also make you think twice about where you hire a car and how you choose to get from A to B.

Water

What parent does not know the risk of hotel, villa or resort swimming pools to children? Yet, every year, there are terrible accidents involving young children and water. They mostly come about where a pool is not adequately fenced off; even an alarm on a pool is only useful if it's turned on, working and someone nearby hears.

If you are renting a villa or an apartment with a pool that a nonswimming or weak-swimming child can easily access, make sure you know where your child is, especially when you are engaged in a busy activity.

Beach safety is also key. It goes without saying that children should be allowed on safe beaches only and that constant supervision is a must. When your children are old enough, make sure they know what to do in a rip current as these can occur anywhere in the world and even in river mouths and estuaries.

Risk Assessments

Parents usually find it becomes second nature to look for and anticipate any potential risks to their child. However, the nature of travelling – wherein you are in an unfamiliar place and rarely in control of your surroundings – requires you to double these efforts.

Every time you arrive in a new place, do a quick risk assessment. In a new hotel room check the floor for anything unsafe that's lurking under the bed or in plain view that housekeeping has not cleaned up. Check if the room has a balcony, how safe it is and whether it can be easily accessed. Make sure you know what you need to do in the event of a fire and go and inspect the fire escape.

If you're visiting friends or relations, you may think you're relatively safe. However, you still need to do a risk assessment of the house and garden.

Getting Lost

It is every parent's nightmare: you take your eye off your child for one second and they're gone. Young children can move frighteningly quickly and by the time you've looked in the wrong direction for a couple more seconds, they've made their getaway.

Here are some precautions to practise daily:

- If you're travelling with another adult, always know whose responsibility it is to look after the children. If you don't, you both might take your eyes off them at the same time to deal with some travel issue (eg asking directions, buying tickets etc)
- Always carry an up-to-date printed photograph of your child and know your child's height
- Dress your children in bright clothes that stand out so you can spot them from a short distance
- Note each day what they are wearing (in case you need to describe it to anyone)
- Be very careful in crowds or places where there are lots of children like playgrounds and theme parks
- Keep children under three safely strapped in the stroller or firmly holding your hand if they are walking
- Establish clear ground rules, explaining to your child that they are expected to hold your hand (or the hand of whomever they're with), and praise them as they do the right thing. See p79 for more information about road safety.
- Ensure your children always wear some form of identity bracelet or band. If you find they fiddle with these and take them off, resort to writing your mobile telephone number in ink on their tummies.
- As a parent always carry a mobile phone and, if you're travelling with older children, allow them to have one too
- Drill your children about what to do if they become separated from you and encourage them to ask permission before going somewhere. If your children are old enough, you can arrange always to have a meeting point. If they are young, ensure they know their personal contact details and tell them to go into a shop, find someone in a uniform that's serving and explain what's happened.

It will be second nature but the moment you realise you don't know where your child is, call out their name and shout to everyone who can hear that you've lost a child. If you can't find them immediately, head to the most dangerous place first (the duck pond, the open gate, the road etc) to ensure they're not there. If the worst comes to the worst, you must seek official help and see the consular section of your embassy.

World Events

Particularly if you're travelling long-term, make sure that you keep up to date with world news. If you're from the UK, log on regularly to the Foreign and Commonwealth Office website (www.fco.gov.uk); if you're American, to the Bureau of Consular Affairs at the US Department of State (www.travel.state.gov); and for Australians the Australian Department of Foreign Affairs and Trade site (www.dfat.gov.au/travel). Logging on or tuning into the BBC Service News (www.bbc.co.uk/worldservice) is also worthwhile.

TRANSPORT

Children are fascinated by means of transport, which is why there are so many books, films and TV programs about planes, trains, cars and buses aimed at youngsters. They can find travelling on public transport an adventure, something that fires their imaginations, and, with your help, journeys can usually be turned into fun, interesting and educational activities.

AIR

Flying with children of any age has its own particular challenges. One issue to bear in mind when flying is the general health of youngsters, regardless of their age. Children with colds or flu (or any condition that may affect their ears) can suffer badly from the change in cabin pressure at take-off and landing. If your child is unwell the day before you are due to fly, take them to your GP for advice and help.

Children's Ages

BABIES & CRAWLERS

Babies need to be at least a week old before they fly at all. Some medical professionals advise against flying long-haul with your newborn until they are three months old. This is because the air in an aeroplane is so dry that it is difficult to keep very young babies properly hydrated. Another concern is the recycled air inside the cabin, creating a less-than-clean environment that's not ideal for very young babies, who have low immunity. Having said this, you often see babies much younger than three months flying long distances to see friends and relations, so you need to do what you think is best.

However, as long as they are taking sufficient fluids, flying with a baby is easy; all they want is you and flying is a lovely opportunity to give them exactly that. Whether you manage to get a sky-cot or not (see p55), the motion of the plane often just soothes them to sleep. Of course, there are certain challenges like changing nappies in cramped toilets, eating your meal with a baby in your arms and perhaps warming bottles but other than this, make the most of travelling with your easy bundle.

Once your baby becomes more mobile, you will have to work a little harder to keep them happy for the duration, although older babies still usually sleep for a good part of any flight. Nappy changing and meal times become somewhat more complicated: the larger and wrigglier your baby the more difficult it becomes to fit them on those tiny aeroplane changing tables and you'll have to plan what your weaning child will eat on the plane (see p55).

TODDLERS

Any child under three can be hard going as a travel companion and long flights can be pure torture for them and for you. Herculean efforts are required to amuse and distract them with books, toys and snacks and it seems that however many times you ask them not to, all they want to do is kick the seat of the person in front of them. Of course, toddlers still need a lot of sleep, so try to time your flights to coincide with their naps. Try not to worry too much about any negative reactions from other passengers. You'll probably never see them again! See the Travel Games Appendix for ideas on keeping the young ones amused on long-haul flights.

PRESCHOOLERS

At the age of three or four years, the wonder of flight kicks in and time can be spent talking about how planes fly, looking out of the window, seeing the buildings getting smaller and chatting about the clouds and why the plane bumps a little as you pass through them. Flying with preschool children is not too difficult. Almost all airlines have children's activity packs on board medium- to long-haul flights which will complement the toys and activities you've brought. Plus, many airlines now have good audio and visual entertainment for children so they can plug into the children's audio channel and also watch the kids' movies or shows. Although spilling food and drink is still part and parcel of this age group, they can feed themselves from their tray and a meal is one more interesting distraction.

OLDER CHILDREN & TEENAGERS

Oh, what a pleasure. For the first time in years you'll get to read a book or a newspaper on a flight while your older child listens to their MP3 player and gets on with any number activities that do not demand your constant attention.

Which Airline

As cost will be an important issue when flying as a family (see p51 for information on fares), you might decide to fly with the airline that offers the best discounted tickets. However, with children there are other factors that you may want to consider.

SAFETY

When you have children, airline safety becomes even more important. A good website to check for information on airline safety is AirSafe.com (www.airsafe.com).

SCHEDULED OR CHARTER

This can be a hard decision. Charter airlines are usually cheaper but this is because they make savings in other areas. For instance, charter airlines tend to pack in the passengers which means you have less leg room and less possibility of the seat next to you being free. They are also delayed more often because scheduled airlines will always take priority. All of which is not great when travelling with children.

More importantly, charter planes often fly at inconvenient times: very late at night or very early in the morning. With children, being able to choose when you fly can be important. For instance, you may want to fly when you know your child is due for a nap or, if you're travelling long-haul, it can be good to fly overnight.

NO FRILLS (LOW-COST CARRIERS)

No-frills airlines – also called LCCs (low-cost carriers) and VBAs (value-based airlines) are most active in North America, Europe, Southeast Asia and Australasia. Almost all fly short-haul – up to four hours or so – though easyJet now has flights that are over five hours, and V Australia links Sydney with Los Angeles. Child fares are almost unknown, but fares can be so low relative to the competition this doesn't matter. Infants up to two years old who do not occupy a seat travel only for an administration charge.

To get the best fares, you will need to book early and fly off-peak – on a less-popular date and/or an inconvenient time. Seats are usually unassigned, but families with children under 12 usually get priority boarding. Note that many no-frills airlines now charge extra for luggage and, with children (especially young ones), this can increase the overall cost of your flight significantly.

NONSTOP OR STOP-OVER

If flying long-haul, to stop or not to stop is the question. With children who are of preschool age and younger, many parents feel that a nonstop flight is best because it involves less getting to and from airports, carrying of luggage and general disruption. With older children and teenagers, it can be nice to show them a different country and a new culture.

What you will want to avoid if possible is a stop where you change planes only; with children this is an added complication that you really don't need. And children dislike being woken up in the middle of the night in order to stand around an airport terminal even more than adults do.

SERVICE

Most of the big international airlines are relatively child-friendly these days. Some have the following services: preboarding for families, a policy to seat families together if seats are not already preassigned, children's meals, activity packs, in-flight entertainment with dedicated children's channels, nappies and baby food for infants, and special children's meals.

Some airlines, however, stand out for a particular service or facility on their long-haul flights, as follows:

- **American Airlines** Infants under two years of age who travel within the United States, Canada, Puerto Rico and the US Virgin Islands may be held in an adult's lap at no charge.
- **Air France** At peak times, 'Family Assistants' help cabin crew on flights where a high proportion of children are expected. They can be found on particular flights operating over the West Indies, Indian Ocean, Africa and Middle East network.
- **British Airways (BA)** If you are seated in a bulkhead position, BA can provide an infant seat for those aged between six months and two years (maximum weight 13kg). These sit on top of the sky cots.
- **Cathay Pacific** Cathay has two different activity packs for children: one for those aged three to six and one for those between the ages of seven and 12. Baby packs and infant packs are also supplied (these contain items such as nappies and nappy sacks).
- **Emirates** Infants not occupying a seat are permitted 10kg of free baggage allowance. The airline operates a stroller delivery service at Dubai airport enabling parents to have access to strollers as soon as they leave the aircraft (great if you're transiting but also useful if Dubai is your final destination because you can use it to reach your carousel in baggage reclaim). Their in-flight entertainment system called Ice features lots of audiovisual entertainment and games for children.
- **Gulf Air** There are now over 150 sky nannies, all trained at the renowned Norland College in Bath, operating on Gulf's international flights.
- **Singapore Airlines** Three types of kids' meals are provided in three age-group categories – the under ones; those between one and two; and for youngsters aged between two and seven. There are over 90 computer games to choose from, which will keep teenagers occupied and there's also on-demand TV channels for children, as well as channels with children's music and audio stories.

○ **Virgin Atlantic** For newborn babies, infants and children up to a maximum weight of 20kg (44lb) or a maximum height of 100cm (40in), Virgin provides an infant/child seat that attaches to normal passenger seats.

Before you decide to book on one of these carriers, however, remember that the practice of code sharing means that you may buy a ticket with one airline but fly with a different one (its partner). This is annoying if you've made your choice based on a certain service but there's nothing you can do about it.

Fares & Baggage Allowance

In the world of international flights, passengers under the age of two are called 'infants'; those between the ages of two and 11 are called a 'child'; and those from the age of 12 onwards are called an 'adult'. These definitions sometimes apply for domestic flights but you'll need to check when you book your tickets. The age of your child at the time of departure is the key factor in determining whether he or she is an infant or a child; so if they have a birthday while away you probably won't be asked to pay more for the fare. Check this directly with the airline when making your booking.

On international flights, infants pay 10% to 15% of the full adult fare, provided they are accompanied by a fare-paying adult. Only one 10% to 15% fare is allowed per adult and any other under-twos have to pay a children's fare. This is because infants on 10% to 15% fares do not get a seat – they're expected to sit on your lap, and you can't have more than one child on your lap at the same time. Some airlines provide infant meals but most don't; you're supposed to bring food for them or let them pick off your tray. On a related note, many airlines have certain regulations about the ratio of

infants or children to adults so do check this with your travel agent.

On international flights, children usually pay 67% to 75% of the adult fare and get a full baggage allowance. Once your child has turned 12 all discounts end; they're full-fare.

Infants often get no baggage allowance (which is ironic considering how much stuff they need). However, necessary items (like food, nappies and clothing) for your baby can usually be brought on as cabin luggage. Your stroller, which you can use right up until the plane door, is not counted towards anyone's baggage allowance and neither is your car seat (if you are allowed to fly with one; see opposite for more details).

If you're travelling long-haul with an infant and feel that an extra seat is imperative, think about purchasing one at a child's fare. Yes, this will be more costly but you may think the extra room is worth it.

Equipment for the Flight

The rules concerning cabin luggage can change at a moment's notice and may be very strict so always check with your airline in advance of flying and stay up to date. On some flights you may be allowed very little; on others, a lot. In all events, try to take as little as possible, but here are some suggestions for what you may find useful.

BABIES, CRAWLERS & TODDLERS

On most long-haul flights, airlines will carry emergency supplies of nappies and, upon request, can provide jars of baby food. However, it's best not to rely on this service and be as self-sufficient as possible. In your baby bag, try to take:

- Nappies and baby wipes
- Nappy sacks
- Portable changing mat

- Food and drink (especially water, as cabin staff never seem to bring enough)
- Changes of clothes
- Muslin wraps and a favourite blankie
- A few toys

The crew will usually take away used disposable nappies but they must be in a plastic bag to meet health regulations. And, although there are changing tables in the toilets, it can be easier to change your baby on a changing mat at your seat, unless it's going to make you too unpopular with other passengers.

With toddlers, in particular, it can be a good idea to bring your own rubbish bag because you will probably create rubbish at a faster rate than the cabin crew can clear it away. For those out of nappies, take a few pairs of pants because accidents can happen even to toilet-trained children when they are excited or have to wait too long for a toilet.

PRESCHOOLERS, OLDER CHILDREN & TEENAGERS

Your three- or four-year-old may need a change of clothes but, apart from that, all kids of this age need are some snacks and drinks (in a spill-proof drink cup for your three- or four-year old) and some toys. For preschoolers and older children, story CDs, drawing material and diaries are good; they'll also be given an activity pack. For your teenager it will be their MP3 player, perhaps loaded with some interesting podcasts, plus a good book.

COMFORT

Planes are very dry, which can make everyone feel uncomfortable. If you are allowed to bring it on board, moisturising cream is good to ease tight, dry skin. A chapstick is also useful for dry lips and toothbrushes and toothpaste are important when you want to freshen up.

If you find the dry air causes sore noses or sinus discomfort, try putting a scarf or handkerchief around a child's face, like a bandit. Something made of light material placed across their noses may cause some localised humidity and ease the discomfort.

STROLLERS & CAR SEATS

When you check-in at the airport, you can keep your stroller with you. This is a godsend if you have to spend any quantity of time at the airport, if your departure gate is miles away from anywhere or if you have a tired or sleepy child. When boarding planes from an airbridge, you can push your child straight to the entrance of the plane and then fold-up your stroller for it to be stowed in the hold. If you're boarding from the tarmac you can push it to the boarding stairs. As you don't check in strollers, they are not counted as part of your baggage allowance. At the other end, your stroller will either be waiting for you as you alight the plane or it will appear somewhere in the airport – possibly on the carousel or where the oversized items appear.

When restricted cabin-baggage allowances are not in place, many airlines will allow you to take your car seat on board the plane. If you plan to do this, you will need to purchase a passenger seat (at a child's fare) in order to use it. You are allowed to strap your child into the car seat during the flight, but you will not be allowed to use it during take-off and landing. Your car seat must fulfil certain criteria and these will differ from airline to airline. In addition, some aviation authorities have different regulations in regards to front-facing or rear-facing car seats. Check with your airline for up-to-date information.

In most cases, car seats do not count towards your cabin baggage allowance.

WHAT TO WEAR

Comfort is the main consideration when deciding what to wear. Regardless of your destination or the weather, dress for the conditions in the plane and in airports (particularly if you're changing planes). Planes can either be too hot or too cold (and airports are often very cold due to energetic air-conditioning). This means layers of clothing, which can be removed or added as required, are a good idea.

Airports

Most airports are like crowded, busy villages and because you might be distracted by passports, tickets or check-in they are an easy place to lose your child. A good idea is to attach a small, loud whistle to your child's jacket. If they get lost or even momentarily separated from you, they can give a good piercing blast.

At some airports children can happily spend ages watching planes take off and land, and some have play areas or family areas. However, many are just like retail parks and you'll have to be resourceful to keep the children entertained before boarding.

Checking-in

When you book your tickets you can request certain seats through the travel agent or the airline. Some airlines charge for this service and others don't. Some allow you to check in online 24 hours before your flight and this is a good way of securing the seats you want, although there are no guarantees and seats can still change when you get to the airport.

If you want to be sure of getting those seats or to have any choice at all in their allocation, you will need to arrive at the airport early. Nevertheless, check-in staff do try to give families more choice than other passengers and to seat them together.

Boarding

Almost all airlines will board passengers with children first. This is great if the seating isn't preassigned (as on no-frills flights) but on scheduled flights think carefully about whether you want to do this. Boarding first means that you're stuck inside the plane for about 20 minutes longer than other passengers and you might prefer to spend this time playing boisterously at the gate area. If you're last on the plane, you also have a good idea of where any empty seats are and you can make a dash for them when the seat-belt sign has been switched off.

Seating

Planes with lots of empty seats are the best ones as far as flying with children is concerned. With a couple of seats to stretch over, small children can sleep just as comfortably as they do at home.

Where you sit doesn't really matter on a quick flight from London to Paris but on longer journeys it is important. Parents with small children are generally placed in the first row of seats facing the bulkhead (the front wall of the cabin); this includes window-to-aisle seats, which can be a cosy option if you're travelling with an infant. This is wonderful news if you have requested a sky-cot because it means you've been allocated one: all the sky-cots are fixed onto the bulkhead (see the next section for more information on these). This position also has the advantage of having more leg room so your child can play, and seating you with other sympathetic parents.

The main, big disadvantage with these seats is that generally the bulkhead seat row has fixed armrests that the tables fold down into. This means that even if you are lucky enough to score a vacant seat beside you, your child can't lie flat because the armrest won't budge. Finally, being seated with other parents and children could work against you. If your child doesn't usually cry, sitting beside children who do might just set them off!

Working out where to sit on the plane is a black art with websites (eg www.seatguru .com) devoted to the subject. However, for children who no longer need sky-cots there are several alternatives:

- Request seats in the middle rows because there are generally more seats in this section than between the aisle and the window, so there's more chance of being able to stretch out if there are vacant seats.

- If you and your family have three seats in a row of four and an individual stranger sits down in the remaining seat, one look at your contingent is usually enough to send them off seeking alternative seating, so you may still wind up with an extra seat.

- If you have two adults and two or more children you can always go on a scouting trip through the plane. You may find that by splitting up you can get very comfortably organised for sleeping.

- If there are only two of you, window and aisle seats fill up first so if you request these seats, you may find that people won't choose to sit between you.

- If you're travelling with an infant too old for a sky-cot but you want extra room, you could always consider paying for an extra seat (which would cost the same as a children's fare).

Bear in mind, however, that if you're travelling with an infant you will be restricted to rows of seats that have an extra oxygen mask, in case of emergencies. And you'll have to forget all about the emergency exit rows, as children are not allowed to sit in them at all.

Sleeping

All airlines carry a number of bassinets or sky-cots on long-distance flights, but the number of babies on board often outnumbers the bassinets. In many cases, sky-cots cannot be prebooked or, if they are, it is not guaranteed you'll get one. More often than not, these are allocated on a first come first served basis upon arrival at check-in. In addition, these cannot usually be prebooked if you're checking in online 24 hours before your flight. Check with the airline at the time of booking and if you can reserve one it is definitely worth going for it.

Sky-cots usually clip onto the bulkhead. Their dimensions are between 58cm and 76cm long, between 30cm and 36cm wide, and around 16cm to 20cm deep. The maximum weight they can take varies from 10kg to 16kg which, in most cases, means babies up about two years of age. They come fully equipped with bedding.

If young children can stretch out on vacant seats they'll sleep like babies. Otherwise, regardless of how uncomfortable they look, youngsters have an uncanny knack of finding a fairly comfortable position in an adult seat and sleeping fairly well on a longish flight. The flight attendant will bring blankets and pillows to make them comfortable.

Safety Inflight

If you are travelling with an infant, some airlines will insist you wear an infant restraint belt that goes around the child's waist and is attached to your seat belt. You have to wear these for take off and landing. It is advised, however, that children wear seatbelts at all times when they are seated. This is just in case the plane hits unexpected turbulence – in the most extreme cases a child can easily shoot out of your arms.

If your older children are sleeping, make sure they have their seat belts around them over the blanket so the cabin crew don't need to wake them to check seatbelts are fastened during turbulence.

Food & Drink

If you are travelling with a baby that takes a bottle or a child that's weaning, bring all the food and drink you'll need for the flight. Try to bring enough bottles containing sterilised water for the whole flight and then make them up when you need them. Most airlines will heat up bottles and also provide baby food upon request. However, it's better not to count on the airline providing everything because supplies will become depleted if there are more babies on the flight than expected and they can dry up completely if there are unexpected delays. Many airlines also have specific meals for children, although you might not approve of the burger and turkey twizzler options.

In many cases, airlines do their best to cater for children but there'll still be times when they can't eat when they want to. For instance, they might get hungry between meals or they may want something when the cabin crew is busy. To help you through these moments, bring along a few favourite snacks.

Everyone gets dehydrated on planes, so nursing mothers have to be especially careful to increase their fluid intake. Juice, soft drinks and water are available at almost any time, so make a habit of ordering drinks for the children before they tell you they are thirsty.

Finally, if there are two adults travelling with a baby or young child, ask the cabin crew to delay one of your meals so that one of you can look after the baby while the other eats.

Health Issues

If your child is prone to motion sickness, they might feel unwell on the plane, especially when the plane starts its descent for landing. Another common ailment is ear pain during take off and landing, due to the changes in cabin pressure. For more information on both of these see p37.

If you are particularly worried about how your active youngster might cope on a long-haul flight, talk to your GP. Sometimes the drug Phenergan (in the UK) or Benadryl (in the US and Australia) is used by parents who travel frequently to make their children drowsy on flights. However, with some children these drugs can have the exact opposite effect. This practice is usually frowned upon by the medical community.

Time Zones

Even though children are highly adaptable, some can be particularly susceptible to changes in time zones. There are a few things you can do to minimise the disruption to their internal body clocks. For instance, night flights are often considered better: if you have a long flight ahead, keep your children awake during the day and evening so that when you board the plane they'll fall asleep immediately. With luck that's between seven to nine hours of the flight already gone by the time they wake up. When you reach your destination, the faster you can get on to the new time, the faster you and the children will adjust.

Although you may feel like falling into bed as soon as you arrive, if it is early- or mid-morning, try to keep going for the rest of the day. Of course, everyone will want to relax and wind down, but try to make your bed time an appropriate one. This doesn't mean you have to keep the children awake come what may, but try to make sure that any naps are short-lived. When bedtime (at last) arrives, your normal bedtime routine (eg bath, bottle/breast, stories and bed in whatever combination) will be all-important.

FERRIES & BOATS

In some parts of the world, there's a good chance that one of the first forms of transport you'll take with your child is a ferry. This will certainly be the case if you are travelling around Europe, visiting the UK and Ireland or spending time in the Greek Islands.

It is hard to generalise about travelling with children on ferries and boats because safety standards and amenities vary wildly, depending on where you are and which shipping line you use. However, travelling by sea can be a good option for children because you and they are not confined in the same way as you are to varying extents on planes, trains, buses or cars. Having said that, if your child wanders off on a ferry or a boat you're in much deeper trouble than you would be on other forms of transport. But, as long as your child does not suffer from sea sickness, children love the idea of life on the high seas – going out on deck to spot wildlife, sleeping on a bunk bed in a cabin or watching the sea spray from the comfort of a window seat.

If you're travelling to or from the UK, these ferries carry large numbers of children all year round and are set up to cater to youngsters.

They often have soft-play areas, video rooms, children's entertainers, and staff that organise painting or drawing sessions, and some of the ships that do the longer crossings (eg between the UK and northern Spain) have swimming pools. As these ferries are often like floating villages, there is always plenty to see, do and buy as well as a good choice of eating options.

Of course, one of the main reasons why ferries continue to be so popular in Europe is because it's an easy way of transporting your car overseas. But, boarding a ferry in your car can be a long process with lots of waiting around in the holding area wondering why every car lane but yours is being invited on board. For children, this can be a frustrating part of the journey and for this reason it's good to get to the port early so you're one of the first on board the ship.

In parts of the developing world, taking ferries and boats may be slightly riskier as boats can be older and safety standards lower. Even in the Greek Islands, you'll have to take extreme care on some of the smaller, more crowded ferries with skimpy barriers between the deck and the sea.

Two things to consider on ferries or boats the world over are smoking restrictions and appropriate clothing. If you're on a boat or ferry that has no smoking restrictions or where smoking is restricted to certain areas only, with children you can sometimes still feel like you're travelling in a buoyant ashtray. Ferries and boats are always colder than you think, especially if you want to go out on deck, so fleeces, blankets and jumpers are often the order of the day (or night).

Children's Fares

The surest thing you can say about the cost of travelling with children on ferries and boats is that infant and children's fares do exist. However, the definition of infants and children vary according to which shipping line you use. For instance, many that cross the English Channel or operate between the UK and the Continent will consider anyone up the age of three to be an infant, from four to 15 to be a child and from 16 onwards an adult fare is charged. However, in Greece the under-fours travel for free and children between the ages of four and 10 pay half the adult fare.

TRAINS

There are lots of advantages to travelling by train with children. Although there's less space than on a ferry, there's still room to move around a carriage, walk up and down the aisles, visit the buffet car and even do some keep-fit exercises in the boarding areas. Unlike when you're in the car, you can concentrate 100% on the children, you don't have to worry how to get from A to B and trains are often faster with fewer hold-ups. If you've got a child that suffers from motion sickness, a train is often one of the only forms of transport that doesn't make them feel queasy. All in all, travelling by train is a stress-free way to see a region or country and a good opportunity for a family to have quality time together.

A table between two seats of two works especially well as there's room for the youngsters to do their art work and to eat a picnic. Many countries (eg Croatia) still operate the old-fashioned types of trains where you get your own compartment. These are great with children of any age because you don't have to worry about how much noise they make and, if they are younger, they'll happily play 'house' and when they are tired you can pull the seats together for naps. And, if you're travelling overnight, children love the novelty of sleeper trains and sleeper compartments.

Some countries (eg Germany) are completely set up for travel by train with family carriages and plenty of space to put a stroller. Others will be an interesting challenge. Nonetheless, as long as the windows are not so dirty you can't see out, train travel is an education for your children because it's a good way for them to see a lot of the country you're travelling in.

Of course, it has its disadvantages too. Train stations tend to have more staircases than escalators which means that competency in weightlifting can be an advantage, especially if you're changing trains and platforms on a tight schedule. Boarding and disembarking can also be an interesting process with lots of luggage and children in tow. As with ferries, smoking can also be an issue.

But, if you live in northern Europe, one of the fastest and most hassle-free ways of getting to and from the UK with children is by train. Eurostar (www.eurostar.com) travels to three Continental hubs that can all take you deeper into Europe: from Brussels there are frequent trains to Amsterdam or Vienna; from Lille the warm climate of the south of France beckons; and from Paris you can pick up trains to Italy or Spain.

Children's Fares

While airlines worldwide generally define children as being under 12 years of age, there is simply no standardisation among the planet's railways. Under-twos travel free everywhere, but the railways of the USA, Canada, Colombia and Namibia charge half the adult fare from the second birthday onwards. Taiwan does the same from age three, but in other countries what you pay depends on how tall your children are. Those taller than 90cm pay half fare on trains in the Philippines; in Thailand it is 100cm; in

Chile and China, 110cm. In nonmetric New York, the height is 3ft 8in (112cm): until this height, you travel free on New York's subway and buses. Four is also the age when you have to pay on the trains of Australia, New Zealand, and on Eurostar trains through the Channel Tunnel. In Tunisia, you start paying 75% of the adult rate. Most British and European rail operators charge half-fare from the age of five onwards, while Japan charges half-fare from six years. The most generous train operators are in southern Africa – Zambia, South Africa and Botswana – where charging half price starts on a child's seventh birthday. But at the same age, adult fares start applying in Madagascar, and by eight years you're an adult on Indonesian Railways. On the railways of the nations of the former Soviet Union, adulthood begins at age 10.

BUSES

Long-distance bus journeys are probably the most crowded and uncomfortable form of transport with any child past the baby phase. For crawlers, toddlers and preschoolers, they can be torturous, especially as you often have to hold young children on your lap. Even if you decide to purchase an extra seat for your infant, chances are your space will be eroded by other passengers.

One of the worst things about travelling on buses with children is what to do when they want to go to the toilet. Bus drivers all over the world know what is coming when they see you lurching up the aisle with a youngster in tow, although do this too frequently and you'll quickly make a lot of enemies.

Unless you're in a country where the buses are pretty comfortable and even have on-board toilets, it is wise to avoid long-distance bus journeys with children under the age of

10 or 11 years. If you can't, try to break the trip into smaller sections and if you can't do this, grin and bear it. Take all the food and drink you could possibly need and if you are travelling overnight make sure you take a blanket or warm clothes.

After a long trip, try to make sure that the next few days are spent somewhere nice and relaxing so your child can get the journey totally out of their system. If you don't space your trips out sufficiently, you may have a mini riot on your hands the next time you approach anything that looks like a long-distance bus station.

In the developing world, another important consideration about bus travel is safety. Check what the road conditions are like and the reputation of the bus company you're planning to travel with.

CAR

When travelling *en famille,* there are advantages to renting a car or taking your own. You can travel when you want and drive for as long as you want, you can stop for the toilet upon request and have breaks along the way at playgrounds and parks. But probably the most attractive reason to travel by car is that you don't have to carry your own luggage and, if you're in your own car, you've got few luggage restrictions.

However, there are disadvantages to car travel with children. Youngsters don't like to be contained and restrained, they will often put up with the car but don't actually look forward to journeying in it. You can't pay them much attention because you're either driving or navigating. Plus, many children suffer from car sickness and this makes every journey, even the smallest, a test of endurance for both you and your child.

HIRING A CAR

If you intend to hire a car overseas it is best to bring your own car seat. You will also need to check that the car you intend to hire has safety belts in the back. Many car companies will allow you to hire car seats but nine times out of 10 you'll find they are not as good as yours or that the message has not got through to the pick-up point. The destination profiles in Part 4 of this book have country-specific information about child safety seats. Also see p101 for information on travelling in motor homes, camper vans or recreational vehicles.

DRIVE TIME

The age of your children will influence the length of your day's drive. It can be easy to travel for hours with babies and young children if you leave when they're almost due for a sleep during the day or drive at night when they are sleeping; though the latter option can make for tired parents. With older children you can either pace yourself and not travel more than two to four hours a day, or do a long stint of six to eight hours and then stop for a few days when you get to your destination. You could also start very early in the morning, let the kids fall back to sleep in the car and drive for a few hours until breakfast time to give you a good start for the day. This is particularly useful to avoid the morning peak hour traffic if you're driving out of cities.

If travelling with older children and teenagers you can plan the driving with them. If you're really brave (and they are old enough to sit in the front seat) you can even allow them to help navigate.

CAR ENTERTAINMENT

Lots of families travelling in their own car have invested in portable DVD players which are wonderful on long journeys. Otherwise, invest in MP3 players and plenty of variety in children's or adult CDs or cassettes, plus an infinite variety of verbal and visual car games (see the Travel Games Appendix on p272 for lots of ideas).

Local Transport

You'll find yourself taking local transport with your children not only because you want to get somewhere but because they'll find it interesting and fun.

Children love water taxis, river cruises and gondolas. Some of the best ways to see a new town are on open-topped tourist buses, on a rickshaw or *tuk-tuk* (although you need to make sure no one falls out of these three options). If your children are old enough, hiring a bicycle is a good way of getting around, as long as the roads are safe and you can find children's safety helmets to rent.

All local public transport, however, will be a challenge with a stroller. Trams, for instance, are sometimes so high off the ground that lifting strollers on and off them is strenuous work. City underground systems are often riddled with stairs and on buses there may not be room for strollers meaning you'll first have to unload the contents of storage baskets then fold them up.

As with long-distance transport, each new destination will have child or family discounts. As soon as you arrive somewhere, make sure you know who you need to pay for and who travels free.

DECIDING WHERE TO GO

When planning a holiday or longer trip with children, health and safety will be one of the most important factors to consider in choosing your destination. Your children's ages and holiday costs will determine the kind of trip you'll be able to have. Today, travel is cheaper than it has ever been so you may decide to take more than one holiday, trip or short break a year. This means you'll be able to choose from a wide variety of travel experiences. For instance, you may opt for one beach holiday a year (for the children) but temper that with a more adventurous trip (for you) later on. In between times, both you and the children might decide on a few short, cultural city breaks.

BEFORE YOU GO

INFLUENCING FACTORS

If you're visiting friends and family or are trying to weave a holiday into a work trip, you may have little choice about where you end up. However, if you are starting with a blank slate, there are lots of practical and inspirational things to consider. Following are a few ideas to think about:

CHILDREN'S AGES

There's no getting away from it, the younger your children the more restricted your holiday options might be. For instance, with children under three (or older) you may decide to travel to destinations where they don't need any jabs or antimalarial medicines, and where there is a low risk of dengue fever.

With older children, you can get more adventurous in your destination and also your activities. Developing countries become a much safer option and it's fun to think about trekking, cycling or horseback riding. For more information see the Activity & Adventure Holidays chapter (p94).

WHAT DO THE CHILDREN WANT TO DO?

There are no prizes for knowing what young children want to do on holiday. Given the choice, it's often to go to a beach. As predictable as this is, it is important to listen to

such a request and to somehow build it into your holiday plans. When they start school and find that friends have been to Disneyland, gone to Lapland to see Santa, or fed the spring lambs on a farmstay, then you can expect a little more variety in their choices.

Older children or teenagers may have quite sophisticated tastes. For instance, the perfect holiday for your teenage daughter could be a four-day shopping trip to New York.

WHAT DO YOU WANT TO DO?

Travel with children must work for everyone, including you. Remember to take your own wishes into consideration. After all, you're the one paying for it and holiday time is precious.

TRAVEL EXPERIENCES

Sometimes it is nice to make your decision based on a 'wow' factor: what would really impress your children? Would it be the Northern (Aurora Borealis) or Southern (Aurora Australis) Lights? Swimming with dolphins? Visiting the JFK Space Centre in Cape Canaveral? You might also like to try camping, cruising or volunteering with your children (for more ideas see Part 3 of this book).

EDUCATIONAL VALUE

In school your children learn about the world's natural features (mountains, volcanoes, deserts, rainforests, canyons) as well as the world's wildlife. A holiday can be an opportunity to bring their learning alive and to show them these natural wonders in real life. Travel with your children can also make history come alive through visiting ancient civilisations or exploring impressive museum collections together.

EVENTS & FESTIVALS

Look at the interesting events or festivals that occur around the world and time your trip to coincide with one or two of them. For younger travellers, many beach resorts hold sandcastle festivals, for older children there are ice-sculpture festivals, Mardi Gras and an exhilarating range of celebrations in places like India. For more information see the information about different destinations in Part 4 of this book and log onto What's On When (www.whatsonwhen.com).

DISTANCE

You might not want to stray too far from your backyard, particularly with young children. As such, when you first start travelling with your youngster, you might only consider destinations within a certain flight or drive time. And, if you've always overlooked what is right under your nose, having young children can be a wonderful excuse to explore those countries or areas closest to you.

TRANSPORT OPTIONS

How will you get there? To a certain extent, this will impact on your choice of destination. If your children don't like travelling by car then a driving holiday is out. If you can't face a string of long-distance bus journeys, then you won't be travelling through Central America. Whichever mode of transport you choose, make the journey

fun – see the Transport chapter (p48) for more information.

COMFORT ZONES & CULTURE SHOCK

When travelling with children, it is wise not to choose a destination that is out of your comfort zone, let alone the children's. If you're worried about infrastructure, how basic the standard of living is, how strange the food might taste and how totally different everything might be, go there another time.

If 'another time' is 'this time', think about how your children will react to what they see and experience. Children experience culture shock just as adults do and they face it head on, always wanting to know 'Why?'. If you are not ready to explain about the world's inequalities, if your children are not old enough to understand them, or if life on the street will be too upsetting, think again about a particularly challenging region of the world.

ATTITUDES TOWARDS CHILDREN

Many cultures will openly show affection for your children, who will get a lot of fuss made over them. Others will be less understanding when your children are being boisterous and overenergetic.

However, in some cultures, local people may react to your children in more surprising ways. For instance, here is an excerpt from a reader's letter we received from parents who took their son to Vietnam:

Our son has extremely blonde (white) hair which caught the attention of locals, as we anticipated it would and prepared him for. What we weren't expecting was the large number of people that groped his genitals. This happened numerous (dozens) times

throughout the country and included people pulling his pants down and inserting hands inside his underpants on occasion. The perpetrators included both men and women of various ages, up to 70 years old. Older women tended to be the biggest culprits. We were told that it was to bring good luck. It was very hard to guard against, as it could literally happen anywhere, by anyone and was generally over in a flash.

CLIMATE & SEASONS

The climate and the seasons will affect not only where you choose to go but also at what time of the year.

One of your biggest decisions will be what you want to do about holidays in sunny climes. Exposure to the sun is one of the main factors responsible for the rise of melanoma, the most dangerous form of skin cancer. As such, you may want to steer away from taking beach holidays at the hottest time of the year, when the sun is at its most dangerous for your child. (Avoiding the peak season will also be kinder on your pocket.) For information on protecting your child from the sun's rays see p42.

Avoiding extreme cold is good too. Visiting Antarctica is the trip of a lifetime but most tour operators won't take children under 12 due to extreme temperatures.

Try to travel outside the season for monsoons, hurricanes or other extreme weather conditions. It is easy to forget that if you're travelling to a malarious area, the best time to go is in the height of the dry season because the risk of being bitten, and therefore catching malaria, is far less.

GOING BACK

Children love what they know (which is why they ask you to read the same story night after night). While you may want to experience something new, your children might just want to go back to where you went on holiday last year. And this is fine. A place that you and they get to know well, that they grow up visiting, that they feel an attachment to, possibly getting to know the local children, makes for some very happy childhood memories.

ACCOMMODATION

Where you stay is a key component of your holiday or trip. If you're travelling long-term, you can mix and match your accommodation options to find the ones that suit your family best. If you're planning just a few weeks away, you'll want to do more research and get this right first time around.

With children, where you choose to stay becomes more important because you usually spend more of your time there. Having children also makes you more fussy: what was acceptable to you on your own is no longer so with little ones in tow.

Wherever you stay, remember to do a quick risk assessment (see p46 for details).

Youth Hostels

Do not discount the humble youth hostel. Over the years, these have changed and many are now set up beautifully for children with family rooms, en-suite facilities, gardens, play areas and lots of comfortable communal space. In a youth hostel there's usually lots of noise and lots of energy so your children will blend in perfectly. These days they usually have pretty good in-house bars, cafes or restaurants but you've still got the option to self-cater (the best of both worlds when you've got children). Of course, they are also relatively inexpensive and help defray the additional costs of travelling with kids. For

more information or to book see Hostelling International (HI; www.hihostels.com).

Hotels & Pensions

Sometimes a hotel or pension can make you feel right at home and sometimes they make you feel like your children should be on their best behaviour all the time.

Although it is hard to generalise, two-star or three-star places can be better with younger children, especially if they're family-run. Any more stars and the other guests might not be so pleased to share a lounge or dining area with you. However, there is one huge benefit to staying in a slightly more expensive establishment and that's the minibar (these are also starting to appear in more budget accommodation options, especially in hot countries). Rearrange its contents and use it as your fridge. This is an invaluable piece of equipment if you're bottle-feeding and useful for storing snacks and self-catering supplies such as cheese.

If you're travelling with a baby or crawler who wakes in the night and cries, your main concern will be how thick the walls are. Only one thing is worse than you being up yourself with a crying baby and that's the knowledge that everyone else on your floor is awake too. To this end, renting a villa or a house might make you feel more comfortable at night. Strollers are also a hindrance in many smaller hotels or pensions. If there is a lift it will probably be too small for you, the stroller, your child and all your luggage and if there isn't then you're back to lifting everything up and down stairs again. One way around this is to ask for rooms on the ground floor when booking your accommodation.

Many hotels have family rooms or charge by the room as opposed to per person. This option is good with younger children because they enjoy the novelty (or not) of sleeping in the same room as the adults and your hotel bill is cheaper. But there are downsides to this arrangement too. The main one is that when it is time for your young ones to sleep, there's no separate space for you either to read, chat or watch TV without disturbing everyone. One solution to this dilemma is to stay in a place that has rooms near a dining area or bar. That way you can go and eat (or drink) when the children have fallen asleep but check on them every 10 minutes to see that they are still OK. With older children or teenagers, the 'all-in-one-room' arrangement might not give them the privacy they now require. At this point, you'll have to bite the bullet and watch your accommodation bills soar.

If you're travelling in parts of the world where heavy smoking is part of the culture, remember to ask for nonsmoking rooms. The pungent smell of air freshener in a smoking room is almost as bad as the smell of smoke.

Hotels with baths rather than showers are best for a young family as a bath is often part of the bedtime routine, plus many young children don't like the sensation of a pounding (or dribbling) shower on their bodies.

Best of all, however, are hotels with swimming pools. Children will forgive you almost anything during the day if they're allowed to go swimming when they get back to their hotel. In plenty of destinations, hotels with swimming pools are not considerably more expensive that hotels without.

Bed & Breakfast

If the owners are child-friendly, and the B&B is not positioning itself as a romantic getaway, then B&Bs can be a good option with kids. They're more intimate than a hotel or pension, and you can usually make yourselves at home and use the fridge (to

store milk), the microwave (to heat baby feeds) and make specific dietary requests for the children. Often, the B&B's pet cat or dog is a big hit, as is the stack of children's toys in the corner waiting for someone to play with them.

Some of the best B&Bs to visit with children in tow are those that are also working farms. The owners of B&Bs are sometimes up for a spot of babysitting if you want to escape for a rare evening of adult entertainment.

Self Catering
APARTMENTS, VILLAS OR HOUSES

Most families choose self-catering accommodation when they go on holiday, especially with young children or babies. It can certainly be a good option if you're staying in an area for a while. As well as being more affordable than a hotel, it provides space for you and the children to spread out, more privacy and you may also have more connection with the local community. The big plus, however, is that you can cook what you like when you like for your children and you don't have to fit in with hotel mealtimes or strange food on foreign menus. In addition, when the children are tucked up in bed at night, there's a much greater choice of where you might spend the rest of the evening – relaxing in the living-room, eating in the kitchen or sampling local wines on the verandah. Another bonus of the self-catering villa or house is that they are easily shared with friends and other families so can be a very sociable option.

However, self-catering accommodation can sometimes be a little too much like being at home. You do all the cooking, you do all the washing-up, you do all the cleaning; plus, your kids can eat baked beans on toast every evening if they want.

If you are travelling long-term, it can make a nice change, and if you're going on holiday with the under-fives, it can be an easy option. Otherwise, you may want your children to experience more of the local customs and cultures (including food) than can sometimes be possible in your own little self-catering cocoon.

Home Exchanges

At first, the thought of having a family you don't know stay in your home while you stay in theirs may have little appeal. However, there can be a number of advantages. Obviously, there's the cost – exchanging homes is less expensive than staying in hotels or self-catering accommodation. Usually an exchange is arranged with families that have similarly aged children so much of the equipment you might need, especially for youngsters or babies, will already be there (plus a ready supply of babysitters). In addition, you might be able to exchange cars (as long as insurance isn't a problem) and if both families have pets you can organise to look after each other's goldfish.

Home exchanges can also work with older children because the kids can get to know each other by email or instant messaging beforehand and possibly slip into a ready-made network of friends upon arrival. Plus, from a cultural point of view, homestays are always a fascinating insight into the lives of other people.

There are many home exchange organisations as well as some hospitality exchange organisations on the internet. However, two that are up-to-speed on the issues of exchanging homes when children are involved are: HomeExchange.com (www.homeexchange.com) and Home Base Holidays (www.homebase-hols.com).

MEPPU | ISTOCKPHOTO

Holiday Homes

A second home either in your own country or abroad is now a feature of an increasing number of family holidays and weekend breaks. One step up from self-catering accommodation and home exchanges, your own place in a location that the family loves can work well for many a family holiday.

There are downsides, of course; the initial upfront cost or second mortgage; maintenance and utility bills; and the feelings of guilt if you don't visit regularly enough. However, regardless of your child's age, the advantages tend to outweigh the disadvantages, as kids love the familiarity of a place they know well, enjoy inviting friends and family to stay and benefit from an ongoing connection with local ways and local people.

Staying with Friends & Relatives

In a category of its own, taking your children to stay with friends or family can either be a great success or a dismal failure. Much of it depends on whether their house is set up for children. Are the mantelpieces full of dainty china figurines? Is there a brilliant white thick-pile carpet under the dining-room table or a medicine cabinet within easy reach? The most common place for youngsters to swallow household cleaning fluids or other people's tablets is in the house of someone you know (see p46).

INDEPENDENT TRAVEL VS ORGANISED TOURS

Independent travel may be what you are used to but jetting off into the great unknown on your own is different from taking off with a baby in your backpack. However, with or without a youngster in your arms, there are pros and cons to each style of travel.

Independent

With 'no-frills' airlines on the increase and more career-breakers with kids opting to travel, you may consider going it alone. After all it is probably one or all of the following:

- **What you know** If you are used to travelling in this way you know what to expect and it can be difficult to change the habit of a lifetime, even when you've got little ones
- **The cheap option** Travelling independently will usually be cheaper than going on an organised tour and, depending on how many children you have, this is a key issue
- **Your choice** If you're used to choosing where you stay, how you travel, where you eat and what time then you may find it hard to fit with plans that others have made, particularly when you have children
- **Highly flexible** Independent travel means you are free to go at your own pace – to stay longer in one place because the kids adore it or to move on quickly because they don't
- **Adventurous** Regardless of your destination, independent travel is always adventurous because you never know what will happen next. This can either be good or bad with children in tow but there's certainly never a dull moment.

Organised

The cons of independent travel are basically the pros of an organised tour. There's no doubt that independent travel, particularly with young children, can be hard work. An organised tour has the following advantages:

- **A choice of family-friendly tour operators** Within the travel industry, travel with children is a growth area and there are now a good range of tour operators catering for families.

- **Help with the luggage** This is a big advantage of travelling with a tour operator that caters for families – there's very little lugging of luggage that you have to do yourself.
- **It's the easy option** One of the problems of travelling with children (particularly young ones) is that parents can come back from a holiday needing another one. With an organised tour there's less to think about, and very little to organise which leaves you freer to enjoy being with the children.
- **Time to relax** If you're lucky, you may get to read a book while you're away rather than be on constant toddler watch. In addition, if you are surrounded by other families, your children will have a range of instant playmates.
- **Certainty** When travelling with children, 'adventure' is not always at the top of your holiday wish list. Sometimes it is nice to know where you are staying, how you're going to get there and what you're doing for the rest of the week.
- **If there's a problem…** you're usually in safe hands. It is always a comfort to be escorted by a travel guide who knows the country, speaks the language, understands the systems and is trained to deal with emergencies.

As always, balance is good. Many parents choose to travel independently some of the time but choose a package holiday or an organised tour at other times. For more information on tours see p94 and for package-holiday advice, see p106.

HOLIDAY IDEAS

Beach Holidays

Ask almost any child where they want to go on holiday and, unhesitatingly, they'll say, 'to the beach'. They want to feel the sand between their toes, build sandcastles, collect shells, paddle or swim in the sea, write their names in the sand with pieces of driftwood and play with bats and balls.

However, a beach holiday with children doesn't necessarily fill every parent's heart with glee, particularly if you've got youngsters. For you, it means constant vigilance, to check for sun protection and water safety.

In addition, unless you want to read and relax and have older children who can occupy themselves, going to the seaside isn't necessarily very interesting. Choose a beach destination within reach of some great walks or near a city; it can make a big difference to the success of your holiday or travels. See p9 for the Top 10 beach holiday ideas.

City Breaks

With the increase in 'no-frills' flying, the world's cities are full of children on weekend city breaks and, in general, they're having a wonderful time. Cities are very easy with kids because there's always so much to see and do, whether it be aquariums, museums, parks, galleries, open-top bus tours or something familiar like swimming in the local (or hotel) pool.

With children in tow there are two main issues to consider. The first is how long it will actually take you to arrive at your destination. Although flight or train times might be only a few hours, door-to-door journey times when going abroad can often be between seven to 11 hours (depending

Top Five Christmas Markets

Predominantly a European tradition, Christmas markets first started in Germany but they have now sprung up in lots of central and northern European cities. There's nothing like a good Christmas market to get you and the children in the seasonal mood with lots of mulled wine (for you, not the kids), festive music, lights, decorations, Christmas trees and sometimes an appearance by Santa Claus.

Start looking out for them from late November onwards. You can visit them independently, or go as part of an organised tour. These are six of the best:

- **Dresden (Germany)** Look out for Dresden's Christstollen cake made from nuts, dried fruit and cinnamon with icing sugar.
- **Nuremberg (Germany)** Held in the main square, this market always offers lots of entertainment for children.
- **Strasbourg (France)** There has been a market in La Place de la Cathedral since 1570 and it's one of the largest in France.
- **Prague (Czech Republic)** There are often several markets in Prague but the most spectacular are those in Old Town Square and Wenceslas Square. They both remain open until the 12th day of Christmas (6 January).
- **Lille (France)** Sometimes small is beautiful and this is the case with Lille's Christmas market which always features a big-wheel and a lovely old-fashioned merry-go-round.
- **Bath (England)** Set in the World Heritage site of Georgian Bath, this addition to the Christmas market scene is going from strength to strength. The chalets huddle around Bath's celebrated Abbey and Roman Baths.

BEFORE YOU GO

on your destination). For younger children, this is certainly a lot of travelling for what may be a shortish stay in a city. The other city issue is one of pollution: particularly in the developing world, some of the most intriguing cities (eg Delhi, Mexico City etc) are now choked with car fumes and it is hard to spend time there when you know how unhealthy it is for your children.

See p10 for the Top 10 cities for travel with children.

Christmas Holidays

Children who live in the southern hemisphere get their long summer break during Christmas holidays, but in the northern hemisphere it's a different story. Regardless, in books and films, Christmas is always portrayed as a time of winter and when you've got children it is sometimes nice to indulge that view and take them skiing, Christmas shopping in New York (a particular treat for the teenagers) or across to Lapland to see Santa Claus.

However, if you live in the northern hemisphere you might be just as keen on finding a little winter sun so the youngsters can go outside without their scarves and gloves on. Otherwise, if you live in or are travelling in Europe, a resort like Center Parcs (www.centerparcs.com) rings the changes because the kids can swim all day long in their huge indoor aquatic bubbles and it feels like you've taken them to the Caribbean at a fraction of the cost.

Part 2.
ON THE ROAD

MAKING IT WORK

If you travel on your own, you can please yourself. When you travel with other people you need to be more considerate, take into account what your travel companions would like to do or are feeling, make group decisions and be ready to compromise. Exactly the same process applies to when you travel with your children but it can sometimes be more challenging to reconcile the needs and wants of a child with those of an adult. However, it is important that travel with children works for everyone and that a healthy balance is maintained between what you might like to do and what is attractive to your young charges.

Spending time with your children on holiday should be fun but, like anything, you've got to work at it because it doesn't happen automatically. However, if you give some forethought to how your trip might pan out and you've got a few coping strategies up your sleeve, it will make a big difference to everyone's enjoyment level during the trip.

PACE

If you did a lot of travelling pre-kids, you might be used to arriving in a new place, hitting all the main sights and activities in a couple of days and then moving on. When you're travelling with youngsters it doesn't work that way. The first lesson to learn is that your pace and your schedule will be much slower.

Children are difficult to hurry along: they don't see the need for it and they don't enjoy the process. For starters, just getting them out the door every morning with everything you and they need for the day, plus having everyone do their wees, takes time. Then, when you want to catch the 10.30am City Walking Tour which leaves from the square in the Old Town (not advised for anyone under six) they'll find a hundred interesting things to do on the way, from playing on the old street railings to watching the fish in the aquarium of a restaurant you pass.

With children, everything takes longer and you will need to change your expectations of how much you do or achieve in one day. You'll need to build in time for them to dawdle and get distracted. And, you'll probably need to leave your plans a little looser because sometimes it's really nice, for example, when the children suddenly spot a playground in a nearby park, if you can let them go and play immediately. Or, on the other hand, what you'd planned to do today might simply not fit in with your child's mood and so perhaps you can all decide to do something different today.

Of course, when you've got a train or plane to catch, then there's much less time to be flexible, but this is when you'll really appreciate the value of giving yourself lots of time. There's nothing worse than running for a train or plane, particularly when you've got youngsters trying their best to keep up or strollers to lift up and down steps, along with your normal luggage.

Tiredness

Travelling or being on holiday somewhere new can be quite tiring for young children. There are three main reasons for this: the actual journey (getting from A to B) always takes more out of children than you'd expect; when you're away from home you usually spend more time than usual out in the fresh air which is fantastic for kids but does wear them out more quickly; and normal sleep routines (bedtimes, afternoon naps,

ON THE ROAD

etc) can be disrupted. Plus, you tend to do more walking on holiday which is good for everyone's health but, again, possibly more tiring than normal for young ones.

Like everyone else, however, young children cope badly with life when they are in need of rest. Trying to avoid getting them overtired is easier said than done, but try to structure your day around your kids' needs. Think about what you want to do and then how best to do it. If you have a long train journey to your next destination, think about doing it later in the day to coincide with an afternoon nap and spend the morning outside giving them some fresh air.

It is also nice if you can fit in some unstructured playtime each day where they can catch up with themselves and quietly process some of their experiences. Perhaps they'll want to do this watching TV in your hotel bedroom or playing with their toys. Sometimes, waiting at airports or waiting around for other forms of transport can be a time when children can tune out or relax.

Routines

Depending on the age of your child and your parenting style, routines will either be important to keep up or you'll just do your best and not worry too much.

However, in a world that has suddenly changed for a young child, nice, safe, familiar routines can reassure your youngster that not everything is suddenly different and hard to understand in his or her new (albeit temporary) life. One of the most crucial routines to try to continue is the one at bedtime: if your child is used to the three 'Bs' – bath, bottle/breast and bed – then do this when you are abroad. A story or a bedtime read is usually important (or appreciated) for children up to the age of 10 or more and

it can be nice to make something up about the experiences you've had that day (or older children might like to make one up and tell it to you). Having said all of this, bedtimes are usually later when you're on holiday or travelling so watch for the tell-tale signs of children who've not had enough sleep.

Afternoon naps are an easy routine to keep going for anyone who still fits in the stroller (sometimes up to the age of five or six). They are also a great opportunity for you to have some time to yourself (you could have some adult time in a museum, read a book, relax at a cafe).

Eating at your children's usual times might not happen when you're travelling, especially if you've got several journeys to make in a day. However, this is when your supply of sneaky snacks comes into its own (see p79 for more information).

The older your children are, the less you need to worry about everything in this section. However, see the Travelling with Teenagers chapter to see what it is you do need to think about.

WHAT TO SEE

The world is full of sights, sounds and smells that your children will find fascinating, particularly if they are allowed to touch as well. This means that the things you want to see and do can be just as interesting for your children, as long as you make it so. For instance, many museums these days are geared towards younger visitors and either have free art and craft activities or special children's trails to follow (which will often open up the collection to you too). If they don't, museums almost always display something that will pique the interest of your child, such as Egyptian mummies, the remains of a dinosaur, a whale's bone and historical costumes.

Ruins, statues and historic buildings can also be made fun. Some statues can make great climbing frames, but be aware of cultural sensitivities – for example, children should not climb on Buddha statues. Many churches or temples have roofs or spires you can climb for great views from the top, scary crypts you can visit at the bottom or activities like brass-rubbing in between. If you fear a particular sight might hold little appeal to your child then be ready to retell some stories and legends associated with what you're visiting. See the country profiles in Part 4 for ideas on child-friendly sites.

Of course, it is important to pick and choose what you want to see. Children will quickly become immune to too much of anything, whether it's Roman ruins or Norman castles (the first was probably really exciting). Guided tours are too long and difficult to understand for most young children (unless you've timed them to coincide with a sleep in the stroller). Instead, go at your own pace, explain things along the way, let them follow their own interests and if they are not interested in anything, play some of your normal family games ('I spy' is good because they don't realise you're getting them to do exactly what they found boring a moment ago).

If you are travelling with teenagers then you have more flexibility. For instance, they might be happier to explore places themselves and meet you at a designated spot outside (see the Travelling with Teenagers chapter for more ideas and information).

Creating a Child-friendly Itinerary

Just about everywhere in the world, you can find things that seem to be tailor-made for children. Kids will be intrigued by the obvious differences from life at home – the houses, the different forms of transport, the way people dress and the local customs. Equally, there'll pick up on funny little differences (often at their own height) that you've totally overlooked. For instance, the flashing green and red men that indicate what to do at pedestrian crossings in France are incredibly thin, and young children can talk to you for hours about how many croissants they need to eat to grow bigger.

There are some activities that children the world over love to do and it is nice if one or two of these can be incorporated into your plans for each day. Parks and playgrounds are always a big draw, regardless of whether the facilities are good or not. Also, most children love anything to do with water so if you're not within reach of a beach or don't have a swimming pool at your accommodation, a trip to the local baths is a lovely treat. Otherwise, what about visiting waterfalls, paddling pools, wishing-wells and boat museums and going on river cruises? Kids will also look forward to activities involving animals – the local zoo, farm, or animal sanctuary, riding in a horse and cart (or on an elephant), or visiting a butterfly house. Natural features such as caves with stalactites and stalagmites, volcanoes (safe ones) or geysers all set their imaginations on fire. The list of possible attractions just goes on and on…for more ideas see Part 3 of this book.

Something for older children or teenagers might be a visit to the cinema, especially if it is possible to see a film abroad which has not yet come out in your own country. And shopping is always a good one, especially in colourful, local markets. Give your older children some local money and encourage them to make transactions – they'll be amazingly adept at working out how much their money is worth in a number of currencies and it's great for their maths skills.

A Child's Perspective

Allow your children to experience things in their own way. The Taj Mahal may be impressive to you, but if your son is more interested in the vendor of sticky drinks, don't think that the trip is a failure and that he would have been better at home. You might be surprised at the memories children take away, and the insights they will have of the culture and people they met. As long as your children find something that excites or interests them every day, no matter what it is, your trip will be a success.

Talking & Listening to Your Children

From the age of about four, your child will have a view on what they want to do today and in what order. Unfortunately, this probably won't coincide with your ideas. However, involving your youngsters in day-to-day plans will make them feel more involved and will help them take more ownership of the holiday. With older children and teenagers you can obviously consult with them a lot more.

Also, if you've missed a train or some form of transport, discuss what's happening with the children so they're not just picking up that something's wrong but aren't sure what it is.

Taking Turns

With very young children you may enjoy a gallery visit more if you go solo, so if there are two adults you can split up. One can stay with the children and one can visit the museum, and the next day vice-versa. Some travelling parents take it in turns to have one day to themselves each week.

Once your children are a bit older you can take turns at each doing an activity. You choose to visit a museum in the morning, but in the afternoon they get to choose what they want to do, whether it is playing in their room, present shopping for friends, going to a playground or swimming pool, or doing some sightseeing. If you have a full day on a bus or in the car, make the next day a rest day, when you all relax and the children get to choose the activities.

You can extend this further and adopt a system where each family member has a turn at being the leader for the day, deciding what you'll do that day, where you'll eat and what you'll see. It spreads the responsibility, helps build a child's confidence and makes them feel like it's their trip as well. And you may end up doing some things that you wouldn't have done otherwise!

Making Time for Treats

Children young and old respond well to having something to look forward to. You know best what treats your child likes but if it's a chocolate ice cream, a mug of hot chocolate in a cafe, a picnic, or to return to a place that's become a favourite (for example, a playground or a special shop) then, as long as you've told them that this is on the agenda, it can help keep little people happy for longer. A phrase that parents can be heard muttering all over the world is, 'After we've done xx, I promise we'll go and have a xx'.

Finding Friends

Children enjoy being with other children. On your holiday or travels, chances are your child will find a playmate or two. Initially they may need some encouragement but youngsters bond very quickly, regardless of whether they have a language in common. If your child develops a good friendship while travelling, it may be worthwhile adjusting your plans to spend a bit longer with their friend in that place. Obviously, you can't do this every time but sometimes it can work out well.

There are some types of holidays which positively promote 'friend-finding', such as skiing (where all the children go to ski school), camping (particularly if there is a games room on site) and any holiday experience that involves a kids' club (regardless of how frequently you use it). However, if you plan to be on the move, good places for your children to meet other little ones include: the children's section of a local library; local or hotel swimming pools; playgrounds; and even the hotel lobby.

Rainy Day Activities

Sometimes a wet weather day makes a nice change and your children are ready for some indoor activities (drawing, writing, watching DVDs/TV, playing hide and seek in the hotel room). But, at some point they'll need a change of scene and you'll have to brave the weather and make a dash for a place where they can let off steam – a swimming pool, sports centre or indoor play centre is ideal. Otherwise, it'll have to be something like a museum, the theatre or the cinema.

If your plans are fairly loose, a wet weather day can be a good opportunity to move on. Children prefer being in the car or on public transport if it's not sunny outside.

PEOPLE & CULTURE

The people you meet will probably be the most important memories your children take home, especially if you are travelling in a culture quite different from your own. You will be surprised at how many people they remember. In many countries tourism is a two-way process and often you and your child are the centre of attention.

Being the Centre of Attention

Travelling with children opens doors and it is quite likely your children will regularly be the centre of attention in another culture. They may be talked to by adoring adults, given sweets (without anyone asking your permission first) and generally admired. You're likely to receive lots of praise and maybe some advice. In a number of cultures it's common for children to be passed around or to get admiring pinches on the cheek. Some children will love the attention, but others won't be used to strangers acting like relatives. If your child has difficulty coping with tactile affection from people they don't know, you can often protect them from most of it by having them ride on your shoulders or in a backpack. Although you'll talk to your children about how things are different in different societies and how no one ever wants to offend, your offspring need to set their own limits and know you'll support them.

Local Children

One of the nicest aspects of travelling with young children is that no matter where you are or what language is spoken, your children will make friends and communicate beautifully with the local children.

As they get older, children tend to need a common language before they can play together for any length of time. Even a few words can go a long way. Despite communication difficulties, children do notice and study each others' behaviour. It is interesting to discover what your children are noticing and what they think of it. The beach is a good place to observe cultural differences and also a place where your children can engage in noisy, boisterous games with the local children without relying on spoken communication.

However, one thing to be aware of on the beach is that not every culture places an importance on teaching children to swim. So, even if your children are good swimmers, keep an eye on the children they are playing with in case they are led out of their depth and experience difficulties.

Culture

If you are travelling in parts of the world that have very different cultures and customs from your home country, you may find that your children become very clingy. This is normal. When everything familiar has disappeared they will hang on to what remains. Don't try to make them 'snap out of it' but try to be extra comforting and keep them informed about where you are going and what you hope to see there. Let them know that everything is perfectly normal and fine, and just give them a bit of extra coddling to reassure them. Generally it doesn't take too long for children to regain their sense of security.

Of course, you may also be feeling disoriented and a bit uncertain yourself, especially if it is your first trip in a more unfamiliar environment. If you are, try not to let your children sense this. During the first few days, stay close to your accommodation, make short walking trips in 'your neighbourhood', eat at your accommodation if you feel more comfortable there and set off on excursions only when you feel ready.

Experiencing other cultures and societies with your children is a great way to teach them respect for people who are different from them. And, as always, the best way to teach is by example and your children

ON THE ROAD

ANANTHA VARDHAN | ISTOCKPHOTO

will copy how you speak about the people you meet and how you talk to them. As such, try not to give way to expressions of disdain when you are talking about the local people. This is something we may do more often than we realise. Remember that your children use you as their role model and will rely on you even more now that their world is totally different and their usual guidelines are gone.

The fact that some grown-ups don't understand English may cause your children some hilarity; they may feel superior when someone uses the wrong word, for example. It's a good opportunity to introduce your kids to the language of the country by teaching them a few basic words. You can make them aware of their relative position by asking them how much of the local language they can speak. See the country profiles later in this book for country-specific cultural issues.

If you are travelling in the developing world then at some stage, depending on your children's ages, they may become upset by the poverty and suffering they see. When this happens it needs to be dealt with sensitively. Talking to your children before you travel about what they may see or experience is obviously important. In addition, kids of all ages like to think that they can 'help'. One way to facilitate this is to involve your children back home in a charity that you know works in the areas you intend to travel in. Or, if your children are in their teens, you could think about doing some volunteering while you are travelling (for example, doing some shifts at a soup kitchen in Nepal) – for more information on international volunteering read Lonely Planet's *Volunteer: A Traveller's Guide to Making a Difference Around the World.*

SMOKING

When you travel with your children in certain cultures, you become very sensitive towards their attitude to smoking. In some countries, the level of smoke in restaurants or on public transport can become an issue and you'll need to take it into consideration when choosing where to eat or stay (in a hotel, for instance, ask for a nonsmoking room).

ENCOURAGING GOOD BEHAVIOUR

Travelling with your children will create many happy memories for your kids to look back on fondly. But the intensity of travelling together can also create conflict and put parenting skills to the test.

While parenting on the road creates different situations from those you may be used to at home, the issues are basically the same, and consistency of approach is key. By sticking to your usual rules about behaviour, you'll be maintaining some comforting predictability in your child's life while travelling – it will be one less thing that's different.

You will need to make allowances, though, because there will be times when your children are out of routine and when they need more attention to make them feel secure in a strange environment. Answering all their questions and giving lots of reassurance about what's going on will be especially important.

If there are two of you, try to be united in your approach. Working together means there's someone else you can rely on and get support from when you're tired, and it lessens overall conflict.

Staying positive, listening to your children and remembering to praise and thank them for the things they're doing right will get things off to a good start.

Rules for the Road

Clear ground rules, especially for things that could affect the safety of you and your children, are crucial. Make it plain at the start of the trip what the rules are; work them out as a family and discuss why they are needed and what they mean. For example, if you decide it's a rule that you must ask permission before going somewhere, be clear what that means.

There are several rules about rules that can make them much more effective. Firstly, for rules to work they should be positively stated so that the child knows what to do – if kids hear 'don't' over and over they are likely to tune out and also get frustrated because they're not clear on how you *do* want them to behave. Secondly, there should only be a few rules, so that the child can remember them easily and isn't overwhelmed. Thirdly, the rules should be enforceable (you'll need to be able to do something if they are broken). The rules should also be fair and applicable to everyone. Finally, the rules should be easy to follow. As your children learn to follow the rules, praise them for doing the right thing – often. When you've really got the hang of this it can be surprising how rarely your children have tantrums or test the limits of your patience.

If your children do the wrong thing or behave inappropriately, tell them to stop, and tell them what they are doing wrong and why it is a problem. Then tell them what to do instead and give them a chance to practise.

If your children continue to behave in a difficult way despite your best efforts, it can be helpful to reflect on what they might be trying to achieve with their behaviour (though obviously this can be tricky in the heat of the moment!). Perhaps it is more personal space, or maybe more of your attention? If you can pin down the reason for the behaviour, you'll be able to respond to the cause, not the symptoms. In some situations it may be appropriate for the family to solve the problem together so everyone feels part of the solution; for example, seating arrangements in the car can be decided with everyone's input.

Even though you may sometimes feel stressed yourself while travelling, it's important to remember that discipline is about *teaching* your child about acceptable and unacceptable behaviour. Try to remain realistic with your expectations, and keep an eye on your own behaviour as well as your child's!

FOOD & DRINK

As a parent, you're always concerned about whether your children are eating and drinking properly. The only way to have any real control over this is to choose self-catering accommodation whenever you travel. However, this is not always possible or desirable which means it is sometimes easy to worry. Are the children eating enough fresh fruit and veg? Are they becoming dehydrated? The answers are usually 'yes' and 'no', respectively, but it's wise to keep a close eye on both issues.

Breastfeeding

If you're happy breastfeeding, your milk will provide a safe supply of nourishment that is also a comfort to your child. On the road, it is also much easier and more convenient than bottlefeeding. All the usual advice to nursing mothers applies when you are travelling. However, if you've got any specific concerns about breastfeeding while travelling, ask your

ON THE ROAD

GP or local travel clinic. Two common queries include: can you breastfeed and still have your travel jabs? The answer is yes, but always confirm this with the travel health clinic pharmacist. What about breastfeeding if you get a bout of diarrhoea and vomiting while on your travels? Again, this is fine, although you'll have to work doubly hard to replace lost fluids.

Different cultures react differently to a mother breastfeeding her baby, so sensitivity or good camouflage (a big shawl, for instance) will be the order of the day.

Also, remember to take care of yourself as well as the baby. You will need to drink enough fluid to make sure you don't become dehydrated because this will have an effect on your milk supply. Also, it's wise to take things more slowly so you're less tired and more relaxed. Breastfeeding on demand can also help make sure you always have sufficient milk for your baby.

Bottlefeeding

If you plan to bottlefeed you have three main issues: sufficient supplies of formula; clean water; and sterile equipment. Because different brands of formula vary in taste (and your baby has probably got used to one type) try to bring all the formula you need for your trip. The water you use to make up your feeds should always be boiled (bring it to a 'roaring' boil for a couple of minutes) which is why a travel kettle is invaluable. If you're using bottled water you should still boil it because bottled water is not sterile. Sterilising bottles and teats can be a long-winded process when you're not in your kitchen at home. The best methods are either to boil them in a pan (you may become rather familiar with the kitchen staff at your accommodation), use sterilising

tablets or pop them in a sealed sterlising bag that you then pop in a microwave (if you can find one). Strictly speaking, you don't need to sterilise everything after your child has reached six months but you may choose to continue to do so.

Making up feeds is also a bit of a challenge. If you don't have a fridge (or a minibar) or if you do but don't want to be tied to it each time you need a ready-made up bottle, make up the feeds as you go along. Have your bottles of cooled boiled water and your premeasured formula in containers and then make up the bottles as you need them.

Snacks

Once your children are weaned, it is a good idea to always carry some snacks with you, particularly if you are out and about or travelling by bus, train or car. You could take your child to local markets and ask them to choose some fresh fruit, which you can then supplement with foods that you know your child definitely likes. Sultanas, raisins, biscuits and cornflakes are always good bets, as is a small jar of Marmite, Vegemite or peanut butter to spread on crackers or bread. Also, invest in a water bottle for your child and always have this on you (filled up). A knife for peeling or cutting fruit is also a good idea.

Places to Eat

Even if you have your own kitchen facilities, you'll probably eat out quite a lot. Depending on where you travel, you will find a range of the usual options: family-run eateries or restaurant chains, street stalls, fast-food outlets or hotels with dining for nonguests.

Although you'll probably want to sample a variety of local dishes, chances are that a child under the age of eight might not be so keen. Hence, when you come across a menu that also serves something familiar like spaghetti bolognese, chips or pizza it makes life very easy. At home you might avoid feeding your child from worldwide fast food chains, but allowing your child a meal they recognise can help them feel a little more secure and also reassure them that they won't have to eat 'strange' food forever. As a last resort, most big hotels can provide a suitable copy of food your child might like to indulge in and sometimes it is worthwhile to see the pleasure it can bring.

Unfamiliar food or not, there are some great dining possibilities that children will love. Food that is colourful or arrives sizzling or with flames on it will usually appeal. While it certainly makes ordering easy you may have to dissuade your child from ordering the most luridly coloured dishes. Remind them they have to eat the meal as well as look at it.

One thing you'll have to get used to with young children is eating your evening meal fairly early. A child between the ages of three and nine often needs to eat before 6pm or 7pm. This can mean you get your meal over before the main rush of the evening or it can mean that restaurants open that early are hard to find. In Spain, for instance, it's hard to find places that will serve you before 8.30pm. Otherwise, what about having your main meal in the middle of the day? This option can be a pleasant and restful way of passing time during the hottest part of the day and a good way of avoiding the problem of evening restaurants opening later than children's bedtimes.

When choosing a restaurant for children, one of your first considerations is always how safe the food will be. Although not a foolproof method, look out for busy restaurants because there's less likelihood you'll be served something that's been hanging around for days. Also, a restaurant with locals in it is a sign of repeat business and therefore a reputable establishment. Of course, in some cultures, an inspection of the restaurant kitchen is actively encouraged and this can be reassuring (or not).

Of second or equal concern is whether you and your children will be made to feel welcome. Expensive restaurants, those with starched white tablecloths or places where lots of couples are dining romantically maybe not be the best place to take the kids, of course. What you want with children is something more casual, where the table cloths are paper (fantastic for drawing on) or where there are no table coverings at all. Outdoor restaurants are worth looking out for; as are restaurants where there is plenty of space inside or something about them that might appeal to kids (for example, an aquarium or fountain). Small or family-run restaurants are often a good bet because they might remember the thrills and spills of eating with youngsters. Depending on your destination, another good indication of whether a restaurant likes children or not is whether it has highchairs or not. And then there's the menu. If there's nothing on it that your children will like, it's not an option but if there's a children's menu, then it's probably a good bet.

If you are dining with children under 10, it's good to have a few notebooks and pens up your sleeve to produce while you're waiting for the food to come (this is when those paper tablecloths come into their own). If you're accompanied by very young children, you may have to take them for a little walk or explore during the delay.

ON THE ROAD

Alternatives

Children of almost any age adore picnics. Not only are they a relaxed alternative to a sit-down lunch or dinner, but it gives children more control over what they eat if they've also helped you with the food shopping.

Another option is the humble street stall. If it's a popular joint where fresh food is cooked in front of you and served piping hot then it's probably a safe and fun mealtime alternative.

At the end of a busy day, sometimes the last thing you want to do is drag your youngster out to find a suitable restaurant. At times like this, a quiet meal where you're staying or room service can be a terrific alternative. Children usually love room service and if it is kept for those special occasions, it can be another one of those treats you dish out from time to time to keep everyone happy. In the privacy of your room they can eat how they like, in their pyjamas perhaps, ready to go to bed as soon as they've finished eating.

Alternatively, if you can't bear to pay the inflated prices that most hotels charge for room service, one of you can go on a food-finding mission to a local fast-food place, a restaurant with takeaway, or even a night market or food stall and then bring it back to the room. Obviously, this idea only works if you've got two or more adults travelling with children.

TOILETS

In this world, only three things are certain: death, taxes, and that your children will want to go to the toilet five minutes after you've left a convenient place for them to do so.

When it comes to wees and poos, travelling with a baby or young child in nappies is so easy; your only concern is finding nappy-changing facilities. In the majority of countries these are scarce but as long as you have your changing mat, you can improvise. Park or street benches, bus seats or car bonnets (as long as you take sensible precautions) – in fact, any flat surface will do if you're desperate. And it is amazing how quick you become at the whole procedure, especially if it's a bit nippy and your baby's bottom is exposed to the elements.

Travelling with children who are toilet-training or just trained is the most difficult stage because if you don't find a toilet quickly enough there'll be an accident in the back of your car or on the bus floor. For times when you know finding a toilet will be difficult take some large nappies with you to hold out for your child to use and then dispose of them afterwards.

With older children, hygiene can be more of an issue because they can do everything themselves, including touching filthy toilet rims, germ-ridden flushing handles and dirty door catches (and this can often be after they've washed their hands). See p42 for more information about hygiene. An issue with preschool children who want to be independent is when they don't want to come into the same toilet cubicle as you. If you're in a situation where you go into different cubicles, get your child to sing so you know that they are still there and safe, although you're not in with you.

In some places toilets are of the squat-down, 'hole in the ground' variety. In many ways, these are quite hygienic because your child ends up touching very little, as long as you're aware that the soles of their shoes will be rather revolting. However, to begin with they can be a bit scary because some young children are afraid they are about to disappear down the hole. If this is the case, you'll either have to go first to reassure them and/or hold their hand and keep talking to them while they have this new experience.

LAUNDRY

Unfortunately, this will need to be done frequently which is why some parents return from a villa holiday saying that the best thing about their trip was the washing machine in the utility room. And they're not joking.

Hotel laundry services are usually quite expensive so if you don't have a washing machine you'll probably either be hand-washing or using the local laundries. If the former, this is where your travel clothesline comes in handy. If you are hand-washing, do it every second day so it doesn't build up and mornings are best because you've got more drying time.

BABYSITTERS

If you're not travelling with grandparents, friends or an au pair, it is sometimes nice to employ babysitters from time to time. However, you obviously need to trust them 100% with your children.

Many large hotels in tourist areas can often make babysitting arrangements, but it's much nicer when the hotel you are staying in is run by a family and the daughters would just love to look after your children (you'll obviously need to pay). Otherwise, some child-friendly hotels are set up with 'baby-listening' where your room is monitored at reception for noise and you can spend time in the hotel bar or restaurant, only being called if your child starts to cry. Some parents also travel with their own baby monitors to achieve the same

effect. In both cases, however, it's a good idea to go and check on your children at small regular intervals, regardless of whether you can hear any noise or not.

See the country profiles in Part 4 for more information on babysitter availability at different destinations.

COMING HOME

Part of making travel work is making your home-coming work too. Just as you did when you went away, give your youngsters enough time to adapt to being home again. Travelling can be tiring so when they arrive back, children often just want to be quiet for a few days and relax around their immediate neighbourhood.

Resuming the routines of home, going back to school and catching up with old friends can all be unsettling experiences for youngsters. And don't underestimate how much they might miss your company and all the attention you gave them while you were away, being there almost 24 hours a day for them.

To help them readjust, talk to them about the forthcoming changes and get them excited about the things they love at home (for example, play dates with friends, seeing their pets or visiting their favourite park). But take things slowly and try your best to be around as much as possible to ease them back into life at home.

Remember that children are highly adaptable and usually go with the flow. They'll soon settle down again, get back into the old swing of things and in a couple of weeks they'll be too busy living their immediate life to get the post-holiday blues. Those are just for you.

TRAVELLING AS A ONE-PARENT FAMILY

Whether you're a parent with sole custody of your child, have access on weekends or during holidays, or are temporarily alone with your offspring on a flight from A to B, taking kids travelling on your own can bring logistical challenges, physical and mental exhaustion, and feelings of isolation. Not to mention economic downturns. But, like all travel with children, it presents a unique opportunity to bond with your kids and can be a kind of hothouse for enriching your relationship. And if anybody needs a break from the grinding daily routines of home, it's the parent who does it alone.

Most of the general pointers in this book apply to sole parent families, but some tips are especially worth heeding. For instance, booking accommodation with some space where you can relax outside the children's room – be it a balcony, lounge or separate bedroom – is vital so that you can get some 'me' time. And involving your children in the planning of your trip will cement you together as a real team. Most importantly (and apologies if this sounds trite), stay positive. By keeping things in perspective and engaging in events with a spirit of adventure, you'll be playing a part, along with your offspring, in creating very fond lifelong memories.

FINDING COMPANY

When your family unit doesn't fit the typical mould, it can be tough watching all the happy-looking nuclear families doing their holiday business. And it's not just isolation that the holidaying solo parent has to contend with; tiredness and a lack of respite are also big issues. Being on vacation may turn out to be more exhausting than staying at home!

While the main focus of your trip is likely to be spending time with your children, you should also factor in some time for adult activities (say, going to a movie, bar or art gallery) without the family. For a lot of people it's important for their own sense of self to have an identity outside nappy changing and cooking alphabet noodles. Clearly this involves locating someone to babysit, be it hotel staff or a travel companion.

Going on holiday with another single-parent family can work well, especially if the other parent is a sibling or close friend. You can take turns babysitting and share cooking and other jobs. You'll also have some adult companionship, which is especially necessary after the children have gone to bed. The kids can play together, and you'll save money by sharing accommodation costs, especially if you rent a house or apartment.

As a single parent it's likely you've already had to rely on help from your extended family, so also consider taking grandparents on holiday with you, especially if they're seasoned travellers (adding an anxiety-ridden granny or grandpa to the mix might not work so well). If your kids feel comfortable with them, they won't mind if you leave sometimes to do your own thing. Remember, though, that grandparents might not have your stamina and need some time out too. And, if travelling with Nan and Pop, tailor your trip accordingly – somewhere with comfy beds is likely to go down better than a campsite with smelly drop toilets.

The usual cautions apply to travelling with others (even the closest friendships can unravel under the strain of 24/7 on-the-road contact), but you should also give some thought to the parenting styles of any potential travel partners. If you're planning to play fast and loose with routines but your companion is already working out what time her four-year-old needs to sleep on the plane, you may need to find a meeting of the minds. It's also worth discussing how you will share responsibilities and help each other. If either of you has a young baby, for instance, you can probably reach an understanding whereby that parent is let off the hook a bit when it comes to cooking, shopping and other chores.

STAYING SANE

Because it can be very hard work to be both mum and dad, especially when you're lugging all the baggage, it really pays to put a lot of forethought into your trip – possibly even typing up a detailed (but flexible) itinerary if you are so inclined. Most importantly, you need to keep your holiday stress-free and relaxing for all involved, so go for something simple. Darting all over the globe at a mile a minute will most likely fry your nerves and turn your children into unhinged lunatics. Renting a beach house for a couple of weeks will let you all chill out and keep the rhythm of your days nicely intact.

Although it can be tempting to load up each day with preplanned activities and excursions, you'll all have a more relaxing holiday if each day contains lots of unstructured time to just hang out. You may want to plan half-day activities so that there's always an afternoon or morning playing on the beach or at home base. The more kids get hooked on constant activities, the more

they're likely to demand nonstop diversions ('I'm bored!'), which is very wearing for the sole parent. Just spending quality time together is a valiant aim.

Remaining calm is very important when there's only one of you to deal with tantrums and other imperfect behaviour, but it's most vital to avoid stress-inducing situations altogether. Stress is contagious and can escalate quickly. Make sure you're really early for flights – the airport is not the ideal place for meltdowns, especially when you're running to catch your plane. In this era of lengthy security checks, you can't expect to show up at the last minute and board your flight. If you're driving, have plenty of rest and food stops. Once the kids get cranky, there's only one of you to encourage peace and harmony – a big ask when you're tired from driving.

When there's no other adult to discuss worries with (and even when there is!), parents sometimes share stress and fears with their children – which can in turn make kids feel insecure and anxious. There's no need to hide all your worries – open communication with your children is essential – but if you can put a positive or humorous spin on the trip's trials and tribulations, it's more likely you'll coast through delays and other hindrances. Approaching dramas with patience and a light heart will make for a much happier family unit.

PACKING & LOGISTICS

If anyone needs to heed those ludicrous rules about travelling light ('once you've packed your bags, take out half the clothes and put them back in the wardrobe') it's the sole parent taking to the road with the kids. You really need to travel super light, since you're the only one carrying it all (unless your kids are old enough to shoulder some

ON THE ROAD

of the load) – and that means being able to carry all your gear for at least 300m, not just lift it. And remember, you'll probably have to lug your bags with you if someone needs to go to the toilet at the train station or airport. Think about whether you really need to bring all those 'essentials'; you can probably buy them once you arrive. Don't skimp on nutritious snacks and water, though, whether you're flying or driving; you'll save money and avoid stress if you have sustenance on hand to quell hungry beasts.

Cabin baggage should be cut to a minimum, too, and leave your hands free so that you can fish around for crucial documents, tickets and money easily. Investing in mini-luggage on rollers (and preferably with cartoon characters) for your child is well worth it – as long as you don't get lumbered with it. Give thought to whether your child is old enough to take charge of it.

Sole parents aren't known for having much cash to splash, but you might want to consider treating yourselves to a few luxuries en route. Even if you intend to rough it by camping or hostelling, it's worth booking your first night's accommodation in a nice hotel so that you are collected from the airport. And if you're travelling alone with a baby, and can afford it or have frequent-flyer miles to burn, why not upgrade to business class?

TYPES OF HOLIDAY

Independent Travel

Travelling independently can save you money (when compared to package tours) and works very well if you pick the right destination. Somewhere with other kids about and where you can find a reasonably priced self-catering apartment is ideal, especially if it's in close proximity to a beach. If you stay in hotels and your kids are still

PHILIP & KAREN SMITH | LONELY PLANET IMAGES

quite small, you can save some pennies by all squeezing into a double bed – many places don't charge for children sleeping in the parental room or bed. And always ask if there are discounted rates for children staying with a single adult (as opposed to a couple).

The cheapest possible holiday (aside from gatecrashing your relatives) is a camping trip somewhere within driving distance of home. This can be fabulous if you pick a spot with other children and somewhere to explore (such as the forest or beach). The most basic version is to take a tent but many camping grounds also have cabins and on-site caravans (trailers) that can be very cosy. See p101 for more information.

You can also save money by taking a break overnight or over a long weekend rather than for a week or more. You'll still feel like you've been away but won't have to shell out so much for accommodation. Taking a vacation outside high season will also cut costs, both at hotels and camping grounds. And with fewer crowds you'll have a bit more room to move.

Package & Resort Holidays

Most package holidays are geared towards the 'average' family of two adults and two children and offer no discount if there's only one adult. You might think that twin-share accommodation would work well for a parent and child, but there's usually no child discount.

Some tour companies and resorts are cottoning on to the sole-parent market, however, and there are now quite a few offering to not only put you up in a room but to matchmake as well! Some are also adding activities to the mix. Going on holiday with a gang of other single-parent families has all sorts of advantages. One of the biggest pros is that a sort of instant megafamily is created. The kids all play together and the parents have adult company. The parenting workload tends to diminish, too, as all adults pitch in with supervision, cooking and chores. See Listings, below, for details of tour companies specialising in travel for sole-parent families.

Paperwork

There can be extra red tape to negotiate when travelling as a sole parent. Depending on where you plan to travel (and your circumstances) you may need a notarised letter from the nontravelling parent giving permission for your child to travel outside the country. See p23 for details.

Listings

The following companies specialise in holidays for sole-parent families:

UK

HELP (Holiday Endeavour for Lone Parents; +44 (0)1427 668717 ; www.helphols.co.uk) Organises inexpensive holidays for sole parents at more than 80 sites, mostly in the UK.

Mango (+44 (0)902 373410; www.mangokids.co.uk) Runs trips in the UK and to the Continent for single parent families; daily group activities and communal evening meals are included.

USA

Single Parent Tours (www.singleparenttravel.net) Based in the US; offers trips and advice for sole parent families, along with personal ads!

AUSTRALIA

Holidays with Kids (www.holidayswithkids.com.au) Hosts an annual getaway for single-parent families in Australia.

INTERNATIONAL

Small Families (www.smallfamilies.co.uk) Escorts single-parent families to resorts in Portugal, Lapland, Croatia, Tunisia, Morocco and elsewhere.

ON THE ROAD

TRAVELLING WITH TEENAGERS

Most teenagers do not look kindly on family vacations. It is their job as adolescents to grow more independent from their parents. Understandably, the idea of being stuck with them on the tourist trail strikes many teenagers as the ultimate regression. Besides, they couldn't possibly be separated from all their friends – certainly not from their latest romantic entanglement. If you force your teenagers to march through cathedrals with their parents and embarrassing younger siblings, they will hate you, or tell you they do – neither of which fosters a positive outlook toward the proposed journey.

So why do it? Well, for one thing because travel does indeed lead to personal growth. Exposing your teenagers to the beauty and complexity of the earth and its peoples will give them a useful perspective as they go about the task of defining themselves as adults. In most cases this education occurs in ways that you don't anticipate. For this reason it is usually not wise to force-feed culture. This is not to say that you shouldn't expose your child to the rich architecture of Mexico City as long as you're in the neighbourhood. (You never know what may slip by an unguarded brain receptor.) But don't be surprised if instead of an understanding of Mexican history, they end up, as a result of keen observations of the fashion, style and buzz of the street scene (which you as unhip old person were unaware of), with an understanding of the modern teen culture. Teenagers are full of surprises. You may have thought your child spent their entire holiday lying on the beach in Phuket listening only to music, but months later you'll hear them speaking enthusiastically and with remarkable insight about life in Thailand.

But the most compelling reason to travel with your children has little to do with the destination. It has to do with family. A family that breaks the separate routines of their usual life and is thrown together physically will almost certainly become closer emotionally. This is particularly gratifying for adolescents and their parents who have grown more emotionally distant. Our most cherished photographs are not of the Grand Canyon but of the family standing in front of it. The shared experiences will endure long after your teenager has left home. The disgusting hotel room in Chihuahua, the 10-day rain in Marrakech, the evening-long card games in hotel lobbies – these are the stories that bind a family together.

PLANNING

Teenagers can voice their opinions with the determination of a three-year-old. It is sometimes unfortunate that they have a more sophisticated ability to express them. True, the opinion to skip the Wat Phra Kaew and Grand Palace to catch up on TV in the hotel room may seem self-centred, lazy and stupid to you; but it's also true that teenagers cannot assert the independence their growing maturity requires without distancing themselves from their parents. Without negotiating a rigid itinerary, decide how you will spend your vacation in a way that respects your teenagers' more mature influence on family decisions. Anticipate potential problems (such as the whiny attitude, curfews, the extra bedroom, icky food and spending money) and discuss them before leaving. If your teenager is studying a foreign language at school, consider travelling somewhere it is spoken. Give them responsibilities (such as banking, shopping and arranging transport) that require its use.

Some other tips to consider:

- Leave books about your destination lying about conspicuously
- Have short language, historical and cultural lessons each night at dinner
- Pore over a map together
- Budget for accommodation that will allow your teenager some privacy

FREEDOM & SAFETY

Every parent and teenager struggles with this issue and the conflict is essentially the same wherever the combatants find themselves. What's different on the road is that your teen's need for privacy is more acute at the same time that your ability to make judgements about safety is compromised. There's no easy way to resolve this, but if teenager and parent are stuck together 24/7, the whole family is likely to be miserable. So you'll probably have to take off the training wheels. Unless your teen is an experienced traveller, allow them to find their balance someplace with a safe and hassle-free reputation. Ask other parents – locals, expatriates and tourists – for advice.

Experienced independent travellers form conclusions about the safety of a neighbourhood through a complex matrix of data they are only vaguely aware of. Ask yourself how you come to your own prudent conclusions and teach these methods to your child. They will learn better on their own, but try to give them a baseline of travel skills. Encourage your teenager to read the Staying Healthy & Keeping Safe chapter in this book (p34) and, since hormonal impulses are not suspended while on vacation, consider augmenting this information with a discussion of sexual safety and romantic customs appropriate

ON THE ROAD

OREN HARVEY | LONELY PLANET IMAGES

ON THE ROAD

to your destination. Your daughter may discover that her usual ways of dealing with unwanted sexual advances are ineffective – even dangerous – in a different culture. Single women who have travelled your path can let you know what to expect and how to deal with it. Travel blogs and venues such as Lonely Planet's Thorn Tree contain these discussions.

BRINGING A FRIEND

It's likely that your teenager will be more enthusiastic about the family vacation if you let them bring a friend along. Indeed, this may be the only way you'll get them to agree to the idea at all. Despite the problems of being responsible for someone else's child and other logistical issues (see p23), it's worth considering. Peers are important to teenagers in part because close friends help them to define themselves and the adult they are becoming. By the end of the trip your teen's friend will have become your friend also. You will probably discover that this bond brings you closer to your own child as well. Besides, teenagers together project confidence toward unfamiliar settings, and confidence is critical to getting the most out of a travel experience.

But, since a friend will have a strong influence on the family dynamic, he or she should be a good match for everyone, not just your teenager. If you or your spouse don't care for your child's 'best friend' or don't think they would travel well, insist on another choice. Make it clear to your teenager and their friend what their responsibilities as family members involve. If there are younger siblings, it is important the friend is willing to spend time with and help care for them. Younger siblings also raise issues of fairness, since presumably you can't take along a playmate for every

member of the family. These decisions are never easy, but extra teenagers, in addition to being able (mostly) to take care of themselves, can also help babysit, cook, pack, carry and navigate. Also, your younger children still need you, while your teen needs to get away from you. You will probably be more comfortable with this if he or she has a companion.

PARENT AS SOCIAL COORDINATOR

Teenagers are at a self-conscious age. If they spot another teenager, the potential companions can take days to hook up. There's no time for this on the road. As parent you need to facilitate and expedite these social encounters. This may embarrass your teenager at the time, but they'll probably be grateful later. The following strategies will help you make contact with other teenagers:

- Mark the location of internet cafes, video game parlours, schoolyards and other teen hangouts
- Scout for other travelling families at hotels, restaurants, bus stations, on trains and at other tourist hotspots. Don't be shy. Find an excuse to chat up the kids and their parents. Chances are they're in the same situation.
- Lurk around the edges of football, basketball and volleyball games. Sooner or later someone will ask you to join in. With luck these will be daily events your teen will look forward to.
- If no such game presents itself, find a beach, park or playground and pull out your Frisbee.
- Look for places and activities popular with young adults, college students and travellers in their 20s. They will give your teenager a peek at what it would be like to travel independently.

Holiday Ideas for Teens

With younger children you have to accept that you will take in fewer sights; with teenagers you have to start taking in some different ones. If you want to spend time together, both parent and teen will need to work out the family itinerary. You may both be surprised to discover things you didn't know you'd like. The following suggestions may help:

- **High Adventure** For many teenagers fun is an active concept. So activities that are dramatic, exotic, exhilarating and x-treme are likely to be a hit. Look around for white-water rafting, quadbiking, volcano climbing, diving and snorkelling, rock concerts, rock climbing, windsurfing and anything else that pushes the envelope. See the Activity and Adventure Holidays chapter (p94) for more information.

- **Voluntourism** Family volunteer experiences such as building schools, digging wells, planting trees and rebuilding after a natural or political disaster can be very rewarding. This is a way for the family to have shared experiences, common goals and meaningful connections with a different culture (see p115). It is also an opportunity for both you and your teenager to make contacts and friends, which may well endure long after your journey ends. There are thousands of organisations that offer these experiences. The Idealist website (www.idealist.org) is a good place to start.

- **Ecotourism** Teenagers are often interested in environmental and ecological issues – perhaps because they are beginning to have a political consciousness and understand that these issues will affect their generation. For these emerging adults a guided trip into the rainforest, African game park or alpine zone may give them an idea of what's at stake.

- **Package Holidays & Resorts**If you can only get away for a week or a weekend, or if you need a relaxing break on a longer trip, there's always the all-inclusive resort. Many of these places cater to teenagers. Here you can kick back on the beach or in the ski lodge with a good book while your teen hangs out with other teenagers who have also managed to ditch their parents. But choose carefully if you want to see your child for more than the occasional meal. Many packages are designed to schedule as little parent/child contact as possible. See the Package Holidays & Resorts chapter (p106) for more information.

ON THE ROAD

ACTIVITY & ADVENTURE HOLIDAYS

Roping a single activity into your holiday can be exhilarating. Lassoing a few and pursuing them as the main focus of your trip can lead you and your family on the adventure of a lifetime. Participating in an activity is also a great way to do something together as a family and to cross boundaries of age and interest. Increasingly, tour operators are specialising in family adventures, or alternatively, you can easily sprinkle activities into independent travel.

Adventure holidays and activities are ideal for children with lots of energy, and kids' attention spans can grow exponentially when given the opportunity to try something thrilling and new or that caters to a particular interest. Sailing in a hot-air balloon over Austria's mountaintops, tumbling on a white-water raft down a raging Canadian river, snorkelling with parrotfish in Hawaii or spotting lions on an African safari – these are experiences your children won't forget in a hurry. Travel is always an adventure, but throw in a pair of snowshoes or a saddle and the excitement can expand tenfold.

ACTIVITIES

With so many options, it can seem difficult to pinpoint the ideal activity. Try to choose something that will interest the entire family. If Jake loves animals but Katie is terrified or if you're itching to go sailing but your kids yawn at the thought, reconsider. Activities generally require proactive energy and family members who are less than interested will make the trip a chore for everyone. A holiday isn't the time to convince your kids that golf is actually fun.

The older your children are, the greater the number of possibilities for activities. Nevertheless, even with toddlers in tow, you can find activities that suit the whole family. More and more operators are offering activities that cater to smaller children's needs. Other activities, like cruising in a glass-bottomed boat or going on forest walks, are ideal for kids of all ages.

Always check the safety record of a tour group or activity operator and whether they have first-aid and necessary equipment (such as life jackets) to hand. If you're planning your trip around one particular activity, check seasonality, availability and eligibility closely.

On the Water

Hop on a paddleboat up the Mississippi River, rent a rowboat in Hyde Park or strap yourself into a speedboat for a 100mph trip down New Zealand's Shotover River – going **boating** can be thrilling for kids (and parents) of all ages. Trips in glass-bottomed boats are perfect for those not keen or able to snorkel, giving smaller children a look at colourful coral life in places like Florida or Hawaii. For short distances or island-hopping, travelling by ferry rather than plane lets kids experience the sea. Joining fishing trips can be exciting for kids, and many operators offer catch-and-release trips. (For smaller kids these can be painfully dull.) Cruise boats are also an option, but be careful to choose one that caters to families and includes lots of stops; otherwise it can feel a bit like being trapped in a hotel room for days on end. Trips on boats are generally suitable for the entire family. Small, uncovered jet boats tend to have an age restriction of six years old and a height restriction of 112cm. Small, covered boats might only allow children over four years (or 102cm).

Canoeing or **kayaking** on still lakes or down slow rivers is possible with kids as young as five (although some operators require children to be eight or 10). With younger children, double kayaks or canoes in water that's shallow enough for you to stand in is ideal and can be a fantastic way to explore in destinations like New Zealand, Hawaii and France. Also consider **rafting**; while you won't like be hitting any rapids with kids under 13, slower rivers can generally be done in family groups with children five and over.

Children who are confident in the water will discover a whole new world with their **snorkel**. This can often be done directly off-shore in many tropical destinations; check first and acquaint your kids with any local sea life to be wary of. Learning to **surf** and **boogie board** is also something most kids can't do at home; places like Hawaii and Fiji offer family lessons and cater to kids.

EQUIPMENT & COSTS

Costs for boat trips vary, depending what's on offer. To rent a boat in New York's Central Park is US$10 while a jet boat trip past Niagara Falls will set you back US$60. Check life-jacket regulations before you go. Many countries require that life jackets be onboard for each passenger but in some countries these will all be adult-sized and it can be worth bringing children's flotation devices from home.

Family canoe and kayak trips are generally half-day excursions and are very affordable; all equipment is provided. Rafting trips are often a little pricier but well worth it. Snorkelling equipment is extremely inexpensive and is sometimes available for use from hotels. You'll have to dig deeper for surf lessons; children eight and younger often require private lessons.

On Land

Walking and **hiking** are fantastic ways to experience the great outdoors. Many national parks maintain well-marked trails with rating levels; start off on the easiest trails to get a feel for how your kids manage. If things get too tough (or steep), turn back. When walking as a family, seeing wildlife, exploring forests and arriving at lakes and seasides are more likely to be highlights than the pedometer reading.

For short distances, **cycling** can be a fun way to explore, particularly in parks. Even if your children are very stable on a bike, stick to areas that have cycling trails, preferably nowhere near the road; different road rules plus a strange bike can be dangerous. In many cities, you'll also find cycling tours geared for families.

TYPES OF HOLIDAY

Pack Your Bags & Head to...

- West Coast Canada for kayaking, whale watching, snowshoeing and cross-country skiing
- New Zealand for swimming with dolphins, walking and rafting
- Southeast Africa for wildlife safaris and snorkelling
- Costa Rica for jungle safaris and boating
- France for canoeing and cycling
- Hawaii for snorkelling, surfing and swimming
- Croatia for boating, walking and sandcastle building
- Thailand for wildlife watching, hiking and swimming

Volunteering Holidays

Giving something back to the community you're visiting is a great way to experience local culture first hand and an excellent way to show your kids the positive impact they can make on the world through travel. This might involve working with endangered animals, lending a hand in a local school or helping rebuild communities after natural disasters. Many tour operators offer volunteering options that you can tack on to a tour; see Intrepid (p100), World Expeditions (p100) and Adventure Company (p99).

If you'd like to make a community project the main focus of your visit, take a look at Wara Yassi Community (www.intiwarayassi.org) in Bolivia that gets you involved in rehabilitating wild animals; Casa Guatemala (www.casa-guatemala.org) where you can help out at a riverside community for poor and impoverished children; or the Millennium Elephant Foundation (www.eureka.lk/elefound) that's dedicated to the welfare of Sri Lanka's sick and retired elephants.

A few hours on **horseback** can be thrilling for everyone and can make a scenic tour the highlight of a youngster's holiday. Kids under six generally ride with an adult. Introduce your kids to the horses first to ensure they're going to be comfortable during the ride; nervous riders can make for nervous horses. In the States, you can bunk down at a dude ranch for a few days; in India, consider a **camel safari** and in Thailand you can hop on an **elephant** for a ride around the jungle.

EQUIPMENT & COSTS

Other than park entrance, walking is free! Bring along sturdy shoes, a carrying pack for baby and a day-pack for a map, supplies and a mini first-aid kit. You can rent bikes pretty much anywhere that cycling is safe and popular and it's also a very economical activity. For children too small to pedal on their own, tandem trailers and carriages are increasingly available in Europe, North America and Australasia. Be sure to take along plenty of water and first aid for any tumbles.

Horseback riding can be pricey so it pays to shop around. An hour or two in the saddle sometimes seems less worthwhile than a half-day excursion where food and sometimes even cultural activities are included.

Winter Activities

Winter can be a magical time to explore as a family – picture snuggling into your cabin with a mug of hot chocolate and the snow falling gently outside as you reminisce about the day's activities. **Skiing** can be exhilarating; consider **cross-country** which is easier to do as a group, regardless of ability. Most resorts offer ski lessons for beginners and for children in particular.

Many parks maintain winter trails for **snowshoeing**, an activity that's generally open to children three and up. Join a tour or set out as a family on marked trails. **Dog-sledding** or **mushing** is also possible in many northern regions, particularly Alaska, Canada and across northern Europe.

In many city centres, you can strap on a pair of **skates**; slide across the pond in New York's Central Park or London's Hyde Park.

EQUIPMENT & COSTS

Skiing is not a cheap holiday, particularly when you add on the costs for renting equipment and lessons. Nevertheless, if you're staying in self-contained accommodation on the mountain, there's often not much else to spend your money on – no museum entrances or endless restaurant bills. Cross-country skiing eliminates the lift fees.

Where snowshoeing and skating is possible, rental equipment is generally also available. These are very economical winter activities. Dog-sledding is pricey but the experience of a lifetime. For all winter activities, ensure you have proper thermal clothing and sunscreen.

Wildlife Watching

It's not just kids who will thrill at the sight of a whale or giraffe. Wildlife watching can be exceptionally memorable. Some activities, such as walking or kayaking, offer the possibility of seeing wildlife en route. If spotting animals is your main goal, boost your chances by joining a tour that specialises in it. **Safaris** in southeastern Africa give you the chance to spot leopards and wildebeest and to experience mass animal migrations. Central and South America also offer fantastic opportunities for tropical safaris. Many operators will tailor safaris to suit all ages.

New Zealand, both coasts of North America, Scotland, Italy and many other destinations offer **whale watching**; depending on where you are, you may also spot porpoises, puffins, sea lions, penguins and dolphins. For open, Zodiac tours, children generally need to be around eight years old; for larger boats, children of all ages are welcome. **Swimming with dolphins** is an unforgettable experience; the minimum age is usually eight years and all participants must be confident swimmers. Most operators follow strict ecofriendly regulations, but check before signing up.

ELEMENTAL IMAGING | ISTOCKPHOTO

TYPES OF HOLIDAY

EQUIPMENT & COSTS

Other than binoculars and a camera (and perhaps a dose of bravery) you won't need much. Tour operators supply all equipment. Costs are invariably high; if there's a particular animal you really want to see or a type of tour you're keen on (such as a safari), it pays to shop around. Many adventure tours include wildlife watching as part of the tour.

ADVENTURE TOURS

There are many reasons why you might choose a tour over independent travel. If you're keen to do an activity you've never tried before, if you're concerned about the safety of an activity and want knowledgeable guides on hand, or if it's something like dog-sledding or a camel safari that are nearly impossible to plan on your own – paying for someone else to take care of the nitty-gritty can make your trip less stressful and more of a holiday.

When choosing a tour operator, look for one that specialises in family travel, rather than one that's simply willing to allow kids to tag along. You want activities and days planned with children and their abilities and limitations in mind. Other points to consider when choosing an operator:

- Safety record, first-aid qualifications and plan should an emergency arise
- Age of other participants – whether there will be a number of families or if your kids will be the only nonadults
- Group size – big groups often mean less interaction with the local culture and less opportunities to tailor the tour to your families interests; smaller groups mean less impact on the environment and make it easier to meet people
- Suitability of accommodation and whether family rooms are available
- Meals – whether the food will be acceptable to your child's palate
- Tour length – overly long tours can be exhausting for adults and children alike
- Ethics – whether the operator works with local communities and abides by animal welfare standards
- Whether the fitness levels required match those of your family and if there's

Full of Hot Air

There's little that ignites the imagination like the thought of sailing over trees and fields in a hot-air balloon. Drift at dawn over Australia's outback; sail over the moonscape of Cappadocia in Turkey; get a bird's-eye view of Spain's Segovia Old Town; or join a balloon safari in South Africa.

Opt for a trip in a larger basket; smaller ones can make for extremely rough landings. With larger baskets, the ascent and descent is as soft as feathers; and happening upon a deer, seeing the sun sink below the horizon or peering down on the narrow lanes of a village can be truly magical. Trips are usually open to children from the age of four or eight. Balloons move with the wind and so are extremely gentle with virtually no chance of motion sickness. Small children may be frightened by the noisy firing of the burner which happens regularly; consider kitting them out with ear muffs.

For a directory of ballooning companies around the globe, check out eballoon.org. If you're booking a tour with a travel company, ask for ballooning opportunities.

A good balance of free time versus organised activities
○ Whether activities appeal to everyone in the family, including mum and dad
○ Whether the climate will be suitable for everybody, if there's extreme heat or cold
○ Whether you will get any adult time through kids-only activities or accommodation that allows you privacy
○ Whether equipment is provided, including baby-carriers, children's life jackets

Operators

All of the operators below employ a responsible tourism policy and run family tours with a maximum group size of 16 to 20 people. Unless otherwise noted, all prices listed do not include airfare. See individual websites for more details.

UK

Activities Abroad (+44-(0)1670 789991; www .activitiesabroad.com) Visit Tuscany or join a husky safari in Canada. Covering many destinations, family tours include lots of activities along with a pulse rating to let you know just how much adrenaline is in store. Where possible, it aims to match families with children of similar ages and have specific trips for families with teenagers. Children need to be at least eight. A week canyoning, biking and kayaking in France costs £495/395 per adult/child, while a week in Jordan is £1030/980 per adult/child. Reasonably priced flights can be booked for you too.

Adventure Company (+44-(0)845 4505316; www .adventurecompany.co.uk) With trips catering to families with children aged five and up, the Adventure Company travels the globe. It also has a handful of Infant Adventures that welcome toddlers from two years, Teenager

Adventures and specific departure dates for single parents. You can opt for trips with a single base to avoid moving around or have a tour created just for you. Ride elephants through a Thai jungle, join a cowboy camp in the wild West of the USA or sail down the Nile. For 11 days in India you'll pay £1250 per person, for eight day in the Pyrenees it'll cost £700 and 17 days in the USA will set you back £2570. Prices include airfare.

Bushbaby Travel (+44-(0)1252 792984; www .bushbabytravel.com) Offering huge flexibility, from accommodation only to international flights, activities and car rentals, Bushbaby is adept at tailoring your trip to your family. You can expect malaria-free destinations, transfer cars equipped with booster seats, and family-friendly accommodation that offers babysitting. Destinations cover South Africa and the Indian Ocean and activities include safaris, ballooning, snorkelling and horseback riding. Prices vary; seven nights in Omar and Dubai is £1280/380 per adult/child while a week on a South African safari goes for around £1800/1150 per adult/child.

USA

Aardvark Safaris (+1-858-794-1480; www .aardvarksafaris.com) Run by parents who have travelled through Africa with their children, Aardvark offers tailor-made-tours to off-the-beaten-track parts of southeast Africa and Madagascar. Based on your children's ages and interests, it will recommend activities like canoe safaris or a day at a local school. It can also keep your tour within malaria-free zones. Accommodation options range from bush camps to family cottages, all of which have been personally vetted. Prices start from US$6000 per person.

Backroads (+1-510-521-1444; www.backroads .com) Very active family holidays get you out on bikes, camels and walking trails. With lots of trips in the US and across the world, Backroads will match you with a tour based on ability, age and attention span. Choose from small inns or campgrounds. Kids can try local cuisine or stick to what they know. Tours are available for children as young as one and include child-only activities to give parents time alone. Six days cycling in Tuscany costs US$3300 and six days walking and camel riding in Morocco is US$4700; kids receive a 10% to 75% discount, depending on their age.

Kumuka Worldwide (+1-718-923-0351; www.kumuka.com) Offering tours to almost everywhere imaginable, Kumuka runs trips tailored to families with children aged five and older. Cruise on a traditional *gület* in Turkey, spot orang-utans in Borneo, fly kites in China or horseback ride in Brazil. You'll experience family-friendly accommodation, lots of free time and interaction with local kids. Tours include everything except international flights. For 12 days in Brazil you'll pay US$4990/3960 per adult/child. A week in Borneo will be around US$1460/1150 per adult/child.

AUSTRALIA

Intrepid (+61-(0)2-8354-3200; www.intrepidtravel.com) Synonymous with interactive holidays, Intrepid ensures you try out the local transport, meet the local people and experience the local culture. Family trips are very much about you spending time as a family, with a balance of activities and free time. With offices and trips around the globe, you should find something to suit your interests. Spend two weeks in Turkey, visiting a Cappadocia cave house and jumping into the hot springs of Pamukkale for A$1425, or dash over to New Zealand for 12 days, paddling down the River Avon and hiking on Franz Josef Glacier for A$1635.

Peregrine Adventures (+61-(0)3-8601-4444; wwwperegrineadventures.com) With 30 years' experience under its belt, Peregrine can take your family to just about anywhere you want to go. Join two or three other families and head to the Middle East for 12 days of sailing a felucca, crawling through the pyramids and snorkelling on the coast for A$1700. Travel through Botswana, Zimbabwe and South Africa for 12 days, taking in wildlife reserves, river cruises and Victoria Falls for A$3600. Tiring travel is kept to a minimum for kids; children must be at least six years old.

World Expeditions (+61-(0)2-8270-8400; www.worldexpeditions.com.au) Specialising in trekking and activity holidays across seven continents, World Expeditions now has trips specifically designed for families. Running at a slower pace but taking in culturally diverse destinations like Borneo or India, most family tours include children from four years old, with trips to Europe suitable for two-year-olds. Thirteen days in Vietnam costs A$2290/1550 per adult/child while exploring the Amazon is A$3500/2800 per adult/child.

Information & Inspiration

Visit familyonabike.org for extraordinary stories of families on adventurous journeys. Responsibletravel.com links travellers with responsible operators and accommodation; visit the Families page for hand-picked adventure holidays that positively affect the community and environment. For parent forums on family travel, head to takethefamily.com.

TYPES OF HOLIDAY

CAMPING & CAMPER VANS

Camping, whether in a tent or a camper van, is the classic family holiday and an ideal way to travel on a budget. The magic of the outdoors can bring new angles of discovery to any destination, from nearby wilderness parks to foreign lands. While these trips take more time in the planning stages, the independence of having a portable home and the thrill that kids get from being outdoors make this one of the most child-compatible forms of travel. Of course if something goes wrong – torrential rains, swarms of biting insects or having all your food eaten by forest critters – parental responsibility increases tenfold.

If you haven't camped as a family before, consider trying a weekend practice run before embarking on longer trips to make sure you've mastered the basics. Getting everyone involved as much as possible in setting up and packing up camp can be a blast when you're camping. You could plan your meals before you go, with the kids helping to choose ingredients so you're sure they'll eat what you bring.

The internet has made planning a camping trip a walk in the woods. Unless you're going to camp in developing nations or obscure regions, you'll find that nearly all parks, government-run campsites and endependently owned establishments have websites where you can book or make enquiries. With prior research into available camping areas, travel distances and seasonal availability, you could move around on a whim, leaving that mosquito-ridden lakeside for that place you saw earlier with a pool, whenever the fancy strikes.

WHERE TO GO

When most people visualise a family camping trip, they think of packing up a vehicle and leaving directly from home. While this is great fun, you shouldn't forget that camping is a safe, family oriented way to travel throughout most of the world's developed nations as well as some less developed regions. In most of Europe for example, camp areas are very popular with families and are a great way to meet locals with kids. New Zealand has some good deals on camper van rentals (try www .nzroadtrip.com) and has everything from modern holiday parks to quiet campsites. The USA is rich with famous national parks but you could also camp five minutes from Disneyland. Latin American nations such as Chile have some fabulous campgrounds to drive or hike into where it's easy to make friends and experience the culture. Adventurous camping in Asia and Africa is possible independently but many families choose to play it safe by organising through a specialised tour company (see p94).

Wherever you choose to go, the places that children enjoy most are the ones with the most action. While sleeping in bear country might not be every family's choice, do try to find areas with some wildlife. Deer, squirrels, birds, frogs and bugs will keep young minds entertained for hours. Fishing, even if the adults don't know what they are doing, is almost always fun. Turning over rocks and finding bugs and tadpoles can even be more exciting that the actual fishing if nothing's biting.

As with any form of travel with children, your best bet is to have a central base and do short hikes in different directions, rather than pack up camp regularly.

See p14 for great camping holiday ideas.

TYPES OF HOLIDAY

WHAT TO EXPECT

Your camping experience depends greatly on the age of your children. Babies are easy to keep an eye on but need oodles of equipment; toddlers will adore being in nature but require a keen eye to keep them safe and sound. The magic years for camping with children begins at around age four. At this age, tykes are old enough to take some care of themselves, and are fascinated with the outdoors.

Most kids will associate camping with campfires so if possible, find a site where you can build a fire (making sure you have all the necessary permits) and have all the accoutrements, such as marshmallows and a snappy song. Get everyone involved in gathering firewood and building a fire, then clean up any sign of your revelries when you leave. Making sure a campsite is 'cleaner than when you found it' helps develop a sense of pride.

Try to let kids be as free as possible while they are outdoors. Collecting bugs, chasing birds or playing hide and seek with a field mouse is what will make the trip fun, so keep the schedule and attitudes loose. Your main job is to make sure there are plenty of snacks and clean water (by boiling or filtering) available to keep young energy from plummeting.

CAMPING WITH INFANTS & TODDLERS

What happens if your toddler ingests a stink beetle? Will an eight-month-old crawl out of the tent in the middle of the night and get lost to be raised by bears? Camper van camping is, without a doubt, the best solution to camping with the tiniest tots but car tenting and back country camping can be a rewarding adventure with enough preparation and patience. While you might not be able to

stop children from eating Mother Nature's creations, reading up on local plants and fauna can help you be on your guard and prepare for the worst; in general the woods are cleaner and much safer than city streets.

If you're car camping and fretting about the little guy going on a midnight wander, you might consider upsizing your tent to accommodate a portable crib or play pen. In the back country, you'll have to get creative about blocking and securing tent entryways and it's not a bad idea to nest newly mobile children between parents during night-time sleep hours.

Back country camping with kids in nappies presents challenges. In the case of cloth nappies the problem is washing; for the disposable variety you'll need to think about disposal. For cloth nappies consider bringing a portable pressure cooker for washing, but this means you'll have to tote weighty fuel as well as the contraption (available online and at specialty camping stores). Disposable nappies are often burned in campfires but this is not an ecologically responsible practice. Although a chore, the best thing to do is to remove and bury any recently produced biological matter, dry the nappy in the sun (so it's not so heavy) then pack it in a sealed plastic bag. If your child is recently potty trained, bring a few pull-up nappies for nights and emergencies – a wet sleeping bag will ruin any camping trip and can even be dangerous in cold conditions.

Babies and children are more sensitive to altitude than adults and some doctors recommend not taking unacclimatised children under three on camping trips above 2000m. Take the ascent slowly no matter how old your child is and be ready to backtrack if anyone gets unusually irritable, becomes short of breath or vomits. In cold weather be very cautious if you are carrying your child in a backpack – immobile children get cold very fast.

EQUIPMENT & COSTS

Camping requires more equipment than your average family holiday – what you bring will depend on how luxuriously you want to travel and how far you have to walk. The basics include tent, sleeping bags, sleeping pads, first-aid kit, torch, matches, cooking equipment and a water filter. For babies and young children take some kind of mat or tarp you can use as a clean space for them to play on and a child carrier if you plan on taking moderate to long walks. If you are starting from zero, your investment could easily come to UK£150/US$250/A$325 per person.

Leave special or complicated toys at home. Sticks, rocks, dirt and flowers will keep kids very occupied. For rainy days, bring paper, pens, board games and books.

Camping Gear

Tents and sleeping bags offer hours of fun for toddlers to preteens and they'll often end up playing with the stuff back home long after the adventure is over. How much you need to spend on this sort of equipment depends on the weather you expect to encounter, whether you are hiking or driving and how often you think you'll use it in future. A cold kid will make camping a miserable experience so if you are going anywhere where temperatures are low at night, you'll need a good bag. Half-length sleeping bags used by climbers (try the Taiga half-bag for around UK£100/US$150/A$200) are ideal for children and are much better quality than the average child-sized sleeping bag. If your children are tall or over age eight or nine, it makes sense to get an adult bag (sometimes available in short sizes) since a

Keeping the Outdoors Safe

Living in the woods creates freedom and danger that you'll need to manage in order to keep children safe and enthusiastic about camping a second time.

- Plan trips carefully, check weather reports and be flexible enough to turn back
- Stay in a group: adults must always be able to see small children and kids should be told to keep an adult in sight
- Make sure kids know what to do if they get lost: tell them to stop, stay where they are and make lots of noise. Hanging a whistle around their necks isn't a bad idea.
- Keep a complete first-aid kit handy
- Make sure everyone has comfortable, worn in, appropriate footwear, and carry blister-protection tape
- Give kids small pictorial field guides on flora and fauna so they can learn fun, handy facts and know what to be careful of
- Keep everyone hydrated
- Sunscreen, sunscreen, sunscreen

good sleeping bag will last into adulthood. In tropical climates, the sleeping bag won't matter as much but you will want a tent that provides plenty of ventilation along with rain and bug protection. For comfort camping, aim for a tent that is at least 3m by 4m for two adults and two kids. Prices increase for gear that is constructed to be lightweight and/or compressible (indispensable for trekking or long journeys).

Self-inflating thermal sleep pads are the Mercedes of camping mats while less-expensive flat roll-up mats are less comfy and warm. Car campers can get massive inflatable mattresses with an air pump.

Clothing

Make sure kids wear bright clothing so they are easier to see. Wool, polypropylene or polar fleece are the best fabrics for cooler areas since cotton offers little warmth, especially when wet. In hot weather, nothing beats lightweight cotton. To avoid blisters, invest in polypropylene socks because cotton absorbs moisture which provokes blisters; blisters are among the most frequent hikers' ailments. If you are going to be hiking you'll have to carefully balance how much clothing to bring versus how much you are willing to carry. If the weather is warm and dry, you can wash clothes as you go and get away with bringing less.

Food

You can buy preprepared, lightweight food from outdoor stores but this can be expensive and surprisingly spicy. It's better to pack your own meals. Anything that comes powdered or freeze-dried is great and don't forget trail mix, muesli bars and fruit for snacks. Cooking on a campfire (you might need to pack a grill) is the most fun way to cook but a portable gas stove is a boon when fires are illegal, the firewood gets wet or you just want to heat something quickly without bothering to build a fire. Make sure if you are travelling internationally that you'll be able to find the specific gas bottle and type for your stove.

Listings

Cool Camping: England This book by Jonathan Knight features English campsites chosen for their beautiful locations.

Little Trekkers (www.littletrekkers.co.uk) This children's outdoor gear company is based in the UK and has everything from child carriers to cooking equipment.

First Treks (www.firsttreks.com) This USA-based outdoor gear company specialises in high quality children's products.

Outdoor Kids (www.outdoorkids.com) This company was started by a US mom and has a huge range of quality outdoor gear for kids.

Camperman Australia (www.campermanaustralia .com) This company offers camper van rentals and sales plus buy-back options, good rates and one-way rentals.

Minti (www.minti.com/parenting-advice/2263/camping -with-kids) You can ask questions and chat with other camping families in Australia at this online forum for parents.

Backpacking with Babies and Small Children This book by Goldie Silverman focuses on camping-based holidays with preschool-aged children and is not destination specific.

Camping France (www.campingfrance.com) This website allows you to order the *The Guide to All the Camp Sites in France* (€12 plus postage), published in February each year.

Idea Merge (www.ideamerge.com) This site has good information about renting camper vans by country throughout Europe, North America, Australia and New Zealand plus links to rental companies.

www.motorhomesworldwide.com Rent a motor home nearly anywhere in the world.

PACKAGE HOLIDAYS & RESORTS

The resort world is one where you don't need a map to locate your hotel because your package includes transfers; where you leave your wallet in the safe because food, drinks, snacks and activities are included; and where your children would prefer to learn tightrope-walking at a kids' club than hang out with you. It's a world independent travellers may not be familiar with but, take hear; a resort holiday may actually be fun and relaxing.

When is a resort holiday a good travel option? Probably when you really need a good, solid chunk of time out. Perhaps it's time when the thought of traipsing around a country with a mad-as-a-hatter toddler and an 'are-we-there-yet?' tween makes you not want to go away at all.

Another reason to pick a package is that sometimes a flight and a hotel package costs only a little more than air only, providing you with a base from where you can set off to explore the country – maybe only spending two nights at the hotel at the start and end of your trip. Your children might find it comforting to have a familiar base, too.

WHAT TO EXPECT

You may think of package holidays as insular experiences. They can be. Culturally, it's possible that the only locals you meet are the ones turning down your beds. Resorts in exotic locales might hold a few local dancing and singing performances, but don't expect to be blown away by culture shock. If you sit around on a deck chair all day and limit yourself to the provided entertainment it'll be more like a culture murmur – and that's just from exposure to your fellow holidaymakers. Your children might have more opportunities to get some cultural immersion thanks to a kids' club. Some kids'

clubs put on local language and grass-skirt making or tie-dyeing lessons, and your children will probably enjoy making friends with others from around the world.

One sure-fire way to add a cultural element to your resort experience is to drag your family out of the resort for a wander.

Most parents go on holiday to spend time with their children, but if the draw of a kids' club proves too strong, check it out yourself first because the standard of childcare may be lower than in your home country. There have been personal-safety issues involving children in resort-based childcare in the past, so quiz your resort on the qualifications their childcare staff holds and the child-protection regulations they have in place.

If you've been dreaming about sending the young ones skipping off to a kids' club, check it's on when you're there. Some resorts only run a kids' club during peak periods, and some then only have a few places. They are usually open for business from 9am until 10pm; some resorts require you to collect your charges for lunch and dinner. Center Parcs only offers an evening kids' club (during the day you're encouraged to take part in the activities as a family).

From cheap and nasty to full-on luxury, in the resort world your accommodation can be a lucky dip. Even expensive resorts can let you down, so read current reviews and ask questions. It's rarely going to be inexpensive, so make it worth it.

Cruises operate in a similar way to land resorts (except there's little chance of escape). If it's a dedicated family cruise then your children may have entire floors dedicated to their entertainment. Thankfully there are adults-only sections on board so you don't have to live and breathe your – and everyone else's – children. Carnival Cruise Lines is a Disney competitor that entices kids (and adults) on board with the temptation of a 24-hour pizzeria and an educational focus to some of its kids' club programs including lessons in art, reading, geography, science and physical fitness. Some Disney cruises include a combination of a few days at sea and then time at Disney World; this land and sea option is a good choice if you and your children love variety.

WHERE TO GO

Where you want to go depends on what your family wants to do. If you and your charges are happier straddling a bicycle than holding back the queasy feeling of one-too-many rollercoaster rides, then maybe Center Parcs suits you better than Universal Studios. Ski bunnies can hit the slopes thanks to ski nannies, and – oh my goodness – Disney even operates cruises.

Europe's 20 Center Parcs are a cycle-around-the-forest, swim, but pay-for-everything-else experience. There are two distinct opinions on Center Parcs: some people book for next year before they leave; others vow never to return. Their domed 'Subtropical Swimming Paradise' is popular for year-round swimming. Children might feel inspired by the location of one of the

UK's Center Parcs: it's in Robin Hood's Sherwood Forest.

Beach-seekers could head for Europe's well-trodden family resort towns in the Balearics, Greek Islands and Canaries. Europe also houses Paris's EuroDisney – where dreams come true in French.

Queensland's Gold Coast is Australia's resort playground, and has the bonus of being reasonably close to the Great Barrier Reef. Like America's Florida, the Gold Coast celebrates its cartoon-character-infested theme parks, the beach and the sun. It's here that you'll find Sea World, Warner Bros Movie World, Wet 'n' Wild Water World, Dreamworld and Australia Zoo.

The friendly Pacific and Caribbean islands are popular for cruising (P&O Cruises covers the Pacific from Australia) and are dotted with sprawling resorts.

The Caribbean and Mexican Riviera are popular family cruise destinations because you cover different places in just a few days of cruising. Carnival and Disney's family cruises depart for these areas from Port Canaveral in Florida, which is conveniently close to Universal Studios, Disney World, Sea World and the Kennedy Space Centre. Three of America's top family resorts also reside in the region, and one of them, Disney's Animal Kingdom Lodge, is where you may struggle to get your children to go to sleep. How will they when they know there are giraffes, wildebeests and zebras roaming the surrounding savannah?

Skiing is a popular family resort holiday choice and www.ifyouski.com links you with child-friendly European ski resorts. While far from cheap, the family-friendly Ritz–Carlton at Beaver Creek, Colorado, USA, has a ski nanny that delivers your children to and from ski school. Cool.

WHAT TO BRING

For cruises and resort stays you won't need to pack much more than clothes (and perhaps something formal for the cruise dinner), toiletries, medication and a few 'getting there' toys.

Confirm when you book, but many resorts and cruise liners will make your room resemble a baby goods shop by supplying a baby bath, stroller, cot and highchair. If requested, some of the better ones will even childproof your room (including installing child safety gates) before you arrive.

To save paying rental, some people take bikes to the England-, France-, Germany-, Belgium- and Netherlands-based Center Parcs villages (riding your bike and swimming are two of the few free activities), and some self-catering families bring their own food instead of shopping at the more-expensive on-site shopping centres.

COSTS

Brochure prices are a reflection of the highest amount you'll pay and because they are printed months in advance use them as a guide only. Political upheaval, inclement weather and sudden declines in tourist numbers can yield great bargains. Brochures help to give you some idea of cost and facilities, but internet sites, including www.airtours.co.uk, are worth searching for discounts and last-minute deals. In the UK, online packages can be up to UK£400 cheaper than brochure and travel agent prices.

Costs vary dramatically for resort stays but expect to fork out an absolute minimum of UK£1600/US$3000/A$4000 for seven days all-inclusive for two adults and two children on a cruise or at a resort. Club Med in Australia with its all-inclusive way will set you back double that. Two nights in low season at Disneyland Resort Paris for four is around UK£550/US$1000/A$1300 and a bargain week for four at Disneyland, Florida will cost around UK£800/US$1600/A$2000. Cruise prices for children vary from one third of the adult's fare to just a few dollars cheaper. All US citizens now require passports for travel to Mexico, the Caribbean and Canada, so keep that extra cost in mind when you're budgeting.

The following questions are important to consider when booking cruises and resorts:

- Are taxes included in the price you've been quoted?
- Do you have to tip?
- Is there a surcharge for the cot?
- Are transfers included?
- How much is babysitting? (Minimum is around UK£3/US$6/A$8 per hour)
- What's included in the all-inclusive offer?

All-inclusive can work well if the variety and quality of food is good. Some resorts include alcohol and snacks, but there's no industry

Cruise Tips

- Write your ship's name, room number and level on a piece of paper and keep it in your child's pocket
- Check minimum ages of children – for US-based cruises it's usually four months and Australia-based P&O cruises won't take children under the age of 12 months

standard. If you're not going the all-inclusive route then you'll probably have more choice about what and where you eat, but resort food is generally expensive. The cost and quality is definitely the source of most resort guests' complaints. It's not unusual to hear comments like 'we needed the free wine to help swallow the food'. If your wine's not free, then budget for double what you would normally pay to eat out and you're almost there. On the bright side: a budget will help you avoid buffet fever and you might go home thinner.

'Bring the kids for free', or 'kids eat and drink for free' offers pop up frequently. Conditions usually include paying full price for two adults, so only work for single parents who take a friend. When kids eat for free you usually need to purchase a (possibly overpriced) meal yourself.

Most places offer babysitting at an extra cost; check how much it is when you're booking, as prices can be as much UK£20/US$40/A$50 per hour.

Single parents generally pay a single supplement, but a few companies offer resort specials for single parents. Beaches Resorts in Jamaica and Turks and Caicos waive the single supplement twice a year during their 'Single Parents Program', for example. For more information on packages for single-parent families, see the Travelling as a One-Parent Family chapter.

Listings

UK

Center Parcs (www.centerparcs.co.uk) A forest-based family package holiday where you'll have little option but to get active; it's likely everyone else will be!

Mark Warner (www.markwarner.co.uk) Mark Warner looks after ski and sun packages with multitudes of active possibilities and different types of kids' clubs.

USA

Beaches (1888 BEACHES; www.beaches.com) From special 'vacations with Elmo and friends' and annual single-parent holidays, Beaches resorts are proudly all-inclusive.

Best Family Beach Vacations (www.best-family-beach-vacations.com) A family-holiday-oriented information and booking website.

Carnival Cruise Lines (1888 CARNIVAL; www.carnival.com) This cruise line has Camp Carnival for children and cruises from three to 16 days' duration, including transatlantic crossings.

Disney (+1 407 939 7675; www.disney.com) From cruise liners to theme parks and a whole series of hotels and campsites, this children's icon has got the family travel sector covered.

AUSTRALIA

P&O Cruises (+61 13 24 69; www.pocruises.com.au) P&O Cruises (Australia) mostly goes around Australia, New Zealand and the South Pacific.

Sea World Resort (+61 (0)7 5591 6200; www.seaworldresort.myfun.com.au) Next door to Sea World itself is one of the Gold Coast's best-known child-friendly resorts.

Travel With Kidz (+61 1300 729 541; www.travelwithkidz.com.au) A website with links to travel agents who specialise in family travel.

INTERNATIONAL

Club Med (www.clubmed.com) With 80 'dream locations' around the world, Club Med is a major resort player, but not all of those have children's activities, and only some offer a 'baby welcome', so select carefully.

TYPES OF HOLIDAY

LONG-TERM TRAVEL & LIVING ABROAD

It's a quiet revolution but it's happening: career breakers and travel addicts are packing up the kids and going – long-term. And it's not as hard as it sounds! While some people choose to be nomads on round-the-world trips or continent exploration, other families decide to keep the adventure focused on a single destination where they can live, learn the language, find local employment or work as a volunteer (see the boxed text on p115). The choice really depends on the disposition of your family but, in general, kids get tired of moving around sooner than adults do – vast exploratory trips might need to be slowed down to keep kids happy. A good way to cover more ground is to intersperse wandering with settling in one place every few weeks (see p72).

Most parents who choose to live abroad with their families are missionaries, academics, students, teachers, military personnel or international business people. If you're one of these, there are books, websites and even psychological studies on the subject (see p114); there is little support, however, for long-term wanderers or folks who want to live abroad independently on a budget.

Going to one place for an extended time with children has plenty of benefits. During short trips you might end up missing lots of 'boring' museums, sights and nightlife; however, when you stick around one place, chances are you'll find a good babysitter or activities for your kids, giving you the time to enjoy the nuances of a place. If kids are in school or have the chance to meet other children, their immersion into a culture can often exceed that of their parents; the doors to integration can often be opened through your children. From a child's perspective, going on a long trip means living out of the box – when they get home they might find themselves less wrapped up in the school rat-race and more free to be unique. Kids who don't like school will appreciate the change and maybe appreciate school more when

they return. Whatever the case, most families find that they spend more time together when they are travelling long-term or living abroad. This is a time to bond, work through problems and really get to know each other on terms different from the everyday routine.

WHAT TO EXPECT

Culture shock (see p63) and schedule upheaval is hard for some kids but exhilarating to others. For babies and very young children, keeping to a schedule and easing slowly into any necessary dietary changes will help them adjust. Unfortunately some kids have a hard time with sleep especially if you are moving around a lot, and the only thing that helps (and even this isn't a sure bet) is to stay put awhile somewhere.

PREPARATION

It's good to keep kids over the age of eight informed of your travel plans as early on as possible. Younger children can be told three months prior or slightly later – if told too early they could become overanxious. If you're moving, get as much information as you can about your new home and share it with your kids. When there will be a different language it can be fun to listen to some language CDs or switch DVDs to that language so the sounds will be more familiar.

Some toddlers and young children will feel like the people they are leaving will never be seen again. Older children and teens, especially those who are very social, might find that being away from friends is the hardest issue. If kids are anxious about leaving friends and family, consider throwing a predeparture party. Take lots of pictures and have everyone personally contribute to a small going-away gift (such as a book with drawings from all the guests) that can be packed as a memento. On the road give kids plenty of opportunity to email, call or write to their friends and family.

A limited number of countries allow you to pack the pets and bring them along without having to quarantine them (see www.defra .gov.uk/animalh/quarantine/pets for a list of approved countries). Otherwise you'll have to find a willing friend, relative or pet-sitter (call your local SPCA or see Listings on p114) to take care of Fido and Fluffy while you're gone.

One of the biggest questions folks have is what to do with all their stuff and how to tie up loose ends. A particularly family friendly option if you own your own home is a home swap (see Listings on p114). Besides saving money on lodging, and having someone take care of your home, trading with a family with children in the same age group gets you a house that will probably have everything you need including a whole new set of toys. Otherwise, you'll have to arrange selling or letting out your home, find a housesitter or even leave it empty. Renters have the option of just packing everything into storage or finding out if it's possible to sublet for the time you are expecting to be away.

For information about how to manage school issues, see p28.

DARIO BAJURIN | DREAMSTIME

TYPES OF HOLIDAY

ESSENTIALS FOR THE LONG HAUL

Finding other kids to play with on the road can ease the pain of separation and helps to liven things up. Go to places where kids can meet other kids. Language schools, homestays, volunteer organisations such as WWOOF (World Wide Opportunities on Organic Farms; www.wwoof.org), and even family-oriented resorts are great places for children to socialise with their peers (for more on teen travellers, see the Travelling with Teenagers chapter). Sometimes it's possible to arrange for friends or family to meet you somewhere on the road – for kids this is the ideal situation. If everyone misses the pet, you might be able to find an SPCA (or similar) that takes volunteers to walk dogs – in this way you could have a 'dog for a day'.

Make sure that if you are working, volunteering or partaking in another activity, that you have plenty of time set aside for the children. Kids need all the support and companionship they can get when adjusting to new circumstances. If you are staying put, try to encourage interests like sports or the arts that will allow them to explore the culture and meet people – it might take a few weeks or even months before shy children feel comfortable branching out. In some cases, parents might have to take on several additional roles such as teacher, best friend and coach.

A few favourite food items are a good idea to have along when kids are easing into a new culture. You'll run out eventually but these things can help get past initial discomforts. You'll have to get used to local brands of nappies, lotions, formula and baby food unless someone can regularly ship you care packages from home. Find out before you leave about the availability of special medicines and talk to your doctor about how to manage this.

IF SOMETHING GOES WRONG

Accidents do happen and it's always possible that you, your partner or your children will want to go home early. Prepare yourself with good travel insurance and a plan B before you leave. In the heat of the moment you will not want to be making big decisions so talk about this as a family prior to your departure. Other morbid details to consider are writing up a will and completing legal papers to ensure that your children will be cared for by the people you choose (and that they agree) if anything should happen to you. Giving a trusted friend or family member power of attorney at home can help resolve countless legal problems that might arise.

Remember that most accidents happen in the home. Being well prepared will put your mind more at ease.

EQUIPMENT & COSTS

Calculated on a per-day basis, long-term travel or overseas living gives you the most bang for your tourist buck. Costs and what you decide to bring depend entirely on whether you're planning to be on the move or to stay put. Once you fork out the airfare, daily costs may be on par with or considerably less than what you would spend at home, or they may be more – depending on your home country and where you're travelling to.

Find out what your health insurance will cover. If you will staying in one country, it might be cheaper to insure yourselves there. See p21 for information on travel insurance.

Coming home is another expense you'll need to consider. If you are coming home to a home and a job, you'll have no worries; otherwise you'll need several months of living costs saved to get you through to your next job and maybe your new life.

LONG-TERM TRAVEL

The more you're planning on moving around, the less you should bring unless you're travelling in your own vehicle. Toys get lost easily on the road so it's best to try to leave special items at home unless that will create separation anxiety. In the case of indispensable security toys like a special stuffed animal, you'll have to keep an eye on it almost as if it were another child. For other toys, pack lightly since people love to give children gifts and you'll find that as some get lost, others appear. Pens, paper, a deck of age-appropriate cards and a disposable camera (you can buy more later) or inexpensive digital camera are the only basics you might want to bring from home. Keep clothing to a minimum but make sure you're covered for a variety of situations.

Strollers, baby carriers and car seats will be useful depending on the country. In cities and well-paved nations, an umbrella stroller will be worth the extra weight; for countries with poor roads, rural conditions or lots of mountains or jungle, a baby carrier might make a better choice. Packing both will weigh you down but this is a personal, country-specific choice. If you are planning on buying a car definitely bring a car seat. Otherwise find out about the availability of seats at car-rental companies. If you bring your own car seat, stroller or baby carrier, consider donating it to a local family when you leave if these items are a luxury or hard to come by in that country.

Older kids will be able to carry their own packs but make sure the pack is made with a child's fit and isn't too heavy. A good intermediate option is a backpack with wheels that can either roll or be carried. Younger kids can carry small packs with a few toys and snacks.

LIVING ABROAD

Moving is another story entirely. If you're going for a few years and have the means to move your belongings to your new country, do it. All that familiar stuff will help kids adjust much faster. International moving agencies (see Listings, p114) do everything from finding specialised sturdy packing materials to dealing with shipping schedules and customs fees. Taking this a step further (in service and in fees) a relocation company will take care of the movers as well as help arrange schooling and housing, provide

(see Listings, p114)

TYPES OF HOLIDAY

Third Culture Kids

A mix of two or more cultures but not fully a part of any, 'third culture kids' (a term coined by Dr Ruth Hill Useem) are children who spend a significant part of their developmental years in cultures other than that of their parents. In general, these children make roots more in people than in place and characteristically become highly independent adults. For more information check out www.tckworld.com (a US– based support site for third culture kids) or *The Third Culture Kid Experience* by David C Pollack and Ruth Van Reken.

you with an in-country 'sponsor' to help you settle in and much more.

If you're moving for a year or less and are on a budget, think about shipping out a few boxes of belongings and not much more. Discuss your family's needs with them when you decide what to bring. In some cases you might all decide to only bring what you can pack onto the plane.

Listings

INTERNATIONAL

BritishExpats.com (www.britishexpats.com) You will find articles, a forum and classified ads on this useful website.

Expats Australia (www.expatsaustralia.com) This company has tools for job seekers abroad plus a great links page about everything on the subject of living overseas.

Home Base Holidays (www.homebase-hols.com) Based in the UK but with several international offices, this company has been helping people swap homes since 1985.

HomeExchange.com (www.homeexchange.com) This is the site used in the Hollywood movie, *The Holiday*. It is internationally represented and huge.

International Movers (www.intlmovers.com) Interactive tools to find international movers and relocation companies worldwide.

Moving Your Family Overseas This American perspective by Rosalind Kalb and Penelope Welch explores the issues of raising children internationally with a mobile lifestyle.

National Association of Professional Pet Sitters (www.petsitters.org) This valuable association is a US-based company.

Raising Global Nomads: Parenting Abroad in an On-Demand World This book by Robin Pascoe is a handy guide that helps parents understand the expat experience for kids and how to help them through it.

Tales From a Small Planet (www.talesmag.com) This American-run online magazine has lots of informative articles and links.

SAMUEL, MIKEL, BOWLES | ISTOCKPHOTO

Volunteer?

Clare Wearden and her husband worked as volunteers with Volunteer Bolivia (www .volunteerbolivia.org) and brought along their children aged 16 months, five and eight. In total, the family was overseas for over 18 months. Here she gives pointers for families wishing to volunteer.

- Make sure that the organisation is positive about children – we had definite negative vibes from two other organisations before we found Volunteer Bolivia. They put us in contact with people they knew with kids around the same age as ours so that we could ask about schooling, the main concern for us before we set off. Also, [check] that they are willing to help with visa requirements for children if you are staying beyond the time of a tourist visa – you can't find this out easily from the UK and [their help] was invaluable to us.

- Make sure you decide how the voluntary work will fit in – I think it is very easy to get carried away and end up working full time and leaving your kids to someone else. We decided to put our kids into the Bolivian system where schooling is only on offer for one four-hour session (either morning or afternoon) and then we worked it out between us to be with them in the afternoons. We also decided to live in a very residential area with a garden, outside the town centre so that the kids had neighbours to play with, as lots of poorer countries don't have play parks.

- Make sure the kids know where and why they are going and what the place is like, what the people look like, how it will be different etc. We got maps, videos and books of Bolivia for them. We even managed to get some children's films in Spanish – *Buzz Lightyear* and *Toy Story* – and we did a little bit of Spanish before we left – name, age, colours, numbers etc. Taking them out of the UK system for five terms has had absolutely no ill effects. We did no home tutoring at all and they went to a Spanish-speaking school within two weeks of arrival. They settled incredibly quickly. They are doing really well at school now and are eager to repeat the experience – with or without us.

- We settled so quickly into life in Bolivia that the challenges were no more than if we were living in the UK – probably less daunting as we had so much more time together as a family. It is the best thing we ever did and a totally different experience of a country from going as a single person.

Clare Wearden

Part 4.

DESTINATIONS

180 AUSTRALASIA

TOP THINGS TO DO

- Snorkel on the Great Barrier Reef
- Tour the wetlands of Australia's Kakadu
- Watch mud boil in New Zealand's Rotorua
- Step into Middle Earth, via New Zealand
- Claim a perfect beach in Fiji

198 ASIA

TOP THINGS TO DO

- Spot tigers from an elephant's back, India
- Unearth treasures at a Thai night market
- Go toy shopping in Tokyo
- Meet baby turtles in Sri Lanka
- Face off ancient warriors in Xī'ān, China

258 THE MIDDLE EAST

TOP THINGS TO DO

- Sail on a dhow boat in the Gulf
- Make sulphuric mud-pies at the Dead Sea
- Explore the wonders of Petra, Jordan
- Stay with the Bedouin in Wadi Rum
- Marvel at the Jeita Grotto caves, Lebanon

EUROPE

GREAT BRITAIN

Scotland's lochs and highlands, Cornwall's sandy beaches, Wales' pointy Snowdonia, England's storybook farmlets, quaint villages and big old trees – Britain really can seem like it has emerged from the pages of an Enid Blyton novel. Thirty centuries of history, brought to life by battlefields, castles, palaces and mystical standing stones, make it a richly fascinating destination for anyone over the age of about three. Cathedrals might not be every child's cup of tea, but the awesome scale and gravitas of York Minster, Durham, Canterbury or Westminster are bound to impress even confirmed heathens. And then there's London, one of the world's top cities, with superb museums, royal sights, verdant parks and a tangible buzz.

Britain is expensive compared with many other countries, but you can control costs by planning ahead and shopping around. You can also save money by self-catering, camping and choosing activities that are free. Visiting the sights needn't cost a bomb – entry to the Natural History Museum, for example, is gratis. Accommodation and meals cost substantially less outside London, and there are usually hefty child discounts at camping grounds, hostels, hotels, museums and historic sites.

WHAT'S TOPS

- Scanning the depths for the monster at Loch Ness
- A walk and steam-train ride through dramatic Snowdonia, in Wales
- A whirl on the London Eye, a modern-day Ferris wheel
- The Tower of London's sparkly Crown Jewels, dim dungeons and pike-bearing beefeaters
- Bath's watery Roman ruins
- Sideshows on Brighton's Palace Pier
- The mysterious pillars of Stonehenge and Avebury
- Wild and wonderful exhibits at London's Natural History Museum
- York's Jorvik Viking Festival, in February, with horned helmets and longboats galore
- Guy Fawkes Day, held on 5 November, with fireworks and towering bonfires

WHERE

England

Some of England's attractions have been designed specifically with children in mind. **Eureka! The Museum for Children** (+44 (0)1422 330069; www.eureka.org.uk; Discovery Rd, Halifax), in West Yorkshire, is big on play-based learning and is the designed with everything – from push buttons to toilets – at child height. Bristol's **Explore** (+44 0845 345 1235; www.at-bristol.org.uk /Explore; Anchor Rd, Harbourside, Bristol) is an engaging science museum. Budding rocket scientists will love the **National Space Centre** (+44 (0)116 261 0261; www.spacecentre.co.uk; Exploration Dr, Leicester), with zero-gravity toilets and other cosmic wonders. **Alton Towers** (www.altontowers.com), near Stoke-on-Trent, is England's most infamous theme park, with roller coasters for the very brave. Blackpool's **Pleasure Beach** (www.blackpool pleasurebeach.com) is another favourite fun park, with some old-school rides in the mix. **Tales of Robin Hood** (www.robinhood.uk.com), in Nottingham, is a somewhat silly romp through models of Sherwood Forest, with occasional falconry and jester workshops.

LONDON

Where to start? London has a daunting range of activities, museums and historical sites that go down very well with children. Long-standing top attractions include the British Museum, with Egyptian, Greek and Roman booty; the Tower of London, with sparkling Crown Jewels and creepy dungeons; and

DESTINATIONS

the changing of the guard at Buckingham Palace. But lesser-known activities and sights, such as brass-rubbing in the Crypt at St Martin-in-the-Fields Church, splashing in the fountains at Somerset House, watching Tower Bridge open and close, and visiting London Aquarium and the Science Museum, are also great kid-pleasers. And don't forget to book ahead for city's hottest attraction, the London Eye, with its glass-bubble gondolas that look out over the city.

London's green spaces are a delight. Primrose Hill Park, Hyde Park, Regent's Park and Hampstead Heath are all fine places to unwind and run about, while Kew Gardens, with its magnificent conservatories and Climbers Creepers (an interactive botanical play area), is the place for a big day out.

Villagelike Greenwich is worthy of its own maritime-themed day trip, with highlights such as the *Cutty Sark* (the fastest ship in the world when it was launched in 1869) and the National Maritime Museum. The *Cutty Sark* was ravaged by a fire in May 2007 and will be reopen to the public in spring 2010. Older children will enjoy climbing the hill to the Royal Observatory, where a brass strip in the courtyard marks the Prime Meridian,

dividing the world into eastern and western hemispheres. Greenwich Park, with a boating pond and excellent playground, is a fine place for a picnic.

SEE

Natural History Museum (+44 (0)20 7942 5000; www.nhm.ac.uk; Cromwell Rd; 10am-5.50pm Mon-Sat, 11am-5.50pm Sun) There's a lot more going on here than dusty stuffed animals. Interactive displays on human biology, animatronic dinosaurs and a dramatic earthquake simulator are just some of the mind-blowing offerings.

V&A Museum of Childhood (+44 (0)20 8980 5200; www.museumofchildhood.org.uk; Cambridge Heath Rd, Bethnal Green; 10am-5.45pm daily) Family-centric performances, movies, activities, tours and creative workshops make this an ideal place to while away a few hours. There's also a never-ending collection of dolls, teddy bears, children's clothing, dolls' houses, nursery equipment and toys dating from the 16th century. And there's a great onsite cafe with half-portions for kids.

STAY

Arran House Hotel (+44 (0)20 7636 2186, www .arranhotel-london.com; 77-79 Gower St, Bloomsbury; $) This cosy child-friendly hotel a short walk from the British Museum has kitchen facilities, a patio garden and a lounge where parents can unwind. It also provides cots, highchairs, paints and babysitters.

Mayflower Hotel & Apartments (+44 (0)20 7370 0991; mayflowerhotel.co.uk; 26-28 Trebovir Rd, Earl's Court; $$) The Mayflower's rooms and self-catering apartments (which cost only a fraction more than rooms) have an up-to-date feel, with lovely teak furnishings and colourful fabric flourishes. There's a lounge and juice bar, and a little tropical garden outside the breakfast room.

Harry Who?

Locations used in the *Harry Potter* films are dotted across England. Hogwarts School is a composite of interiors and exteriors from Gloucester Cathedral, Wiltshire's Lacock Abbey, Northumberland's Alnwick Castle and Oxford's Christ Church College. The most popular site for visitors, though, is Hogsmead Station, which in real life is the charming Goathland Station on the North York Moors.

THE SOUTH

From London, head southwest to seaside **Brighton** for a look at the onion-domed Royal Pavilion and a walk out on Palace Pier, then on to **New Forest** for some walking or horseback riding. Wiltshire's prehistoric **Stonehenge** is nearby, along with quaint villages such as **Lacock** (a *Harry Potter* site), **Devises** (with canals, lochs and horse-drawn carts from the local brewery) and **Avebury**, site of a massive stone circle where kids can run around. The **Isle of Wight** is also nearby, and makes an interesting detour. Devon and Cornwall, with sandy beaches (such as those near **St Ives** and **St Agnes** and along the **Roseland Peninsula**), wild moors where you can go pony trekking, and historic towns like maritime **Plymouth** and **Fowey**, and fishing villages such as **Polperro** and **Looe**, are also options from here. Near **St Austell**, the Eden Project holds flora and fauna from around the globe in three gigantic greenhouse biomes (tropical, temperate and desert). Also in Cornwall, **Tintagel Castle**, the legendary birthplace of King Arthur, will appeal to fans of Merlinesque fantasy. The Roman baths, excellent museums and elegant honey-coloured Georgian terraces of **Bath**, once home to Jane Austen, are a delight for history buffs, and you can cross shop-lined Pulteney Bridge to take a punt on the Avon here as well.

STAY

Brighton's **Seaspray** (+44 (0)1273 680332; www.seaspraybrighton.co.uk; 25 New Steine; $$) is one of the few hotels in this groovy city that cater to families. In Avebury, **Manor Farm** (+ 44 (0)1672 539294; www.manorfm.com; $) has flowery rooms in a farmhouse surrounded by a walled garden. On a grassy cliff top on the Isle of Wight, the **Brighstone Holiday Centre** (+44 (0)1983 740244; www.brighstone-holidays.co.uk; $) has

Price Guide

$ budget $$ midrange $$$ top end

tent and caravan sites and very cute cabins. In the delightful old port of Fowey, the **King of Prussia** (+44 (0)1726 833694; 3 Town Quay; $$) and the **Ship Inn** (+44 (0)1726 832 230; Trafalgar Square; $) are atmospheric old pubs with family rooms. In Bath, the minimalist and friendly **Koryu** (+44 (0)1225 337642; japanesekoryu@aol.com; 7 Pulteney Gardens; $$) has family rooms with en suite.

YORKSHIRE

Yorkshire's dales, moors and wolds and thriving cities like **Leeds** make it a gritty, rousing antidote to the rose gardens of the south. In historic **York**, the rich stained glass of the massive 1000-year-old York Minster is worth a look, as are the Jorvik Viking Centre and the National Railway Museum. Within the town walls the city is pedestrian-only during the day. **Skipton** has one of the country's best-preserved medieval castles and a lively street market. A ride on the well-preserved **North Yorkshire Moors Railway** (www.nymr.co.uk) is a must, especially for *Harry Potter* fans. Avid readers can also explore the countryside that inspired the Brontës and James Herriot, around **Haworth** and **Richmond**, respectively. **Whitby**, with narrow streets winding down to harbour quays with colourful fishing boats and stacks of lobster pots, is Yorkshire's most rewarding coastal town. It's also where explorer James Cook was apprenticed to a shipowner and HMS *Endeavour* was built.

STAY

York International Youth Hostel (+44 (0)845 371 9051; york@yha.org.uk; 42 Water End, Clifton; $), in

HUNTING DINOSAURS

~ ENGLAND ~

BY ROSIE WHITEHOUSE

There's driving rain and a force-nine gale as we drive into Lyme Regis but nothing is going to deter my daughters. They've got an appointment with local dinosaur-hunter Steve Davies and they aren't going to miss it whatever the weather.

Pulling on his waterproof jacket, Davies laughs at me when I ask him if we are still going fossil hunting. 'Of course, this is marvellous weather for fossils. Anyway, the sun will be shining by the time we get on the beach!'

As chief palaeontologist for the multinational company BP, Davies spent months excavating the frozen oilfields of Alaska. 'Kids make great fossil hunters,' says Davies, as he guides us towards the beach. 'You've got to get as close to the ground as possible and they've got a natural advantage!' Pushing the baby twins in the double pram, I have to run to keep up. Davies found his first fossil here on a school outing and now runs *Dinosaurland,* the local museum.

By the time we reach the seafront the sun is shining and the waves are lapping quietly on the rocks. Davies is bubbling over with enthusiasm. Esti and Rachel are entranced. With eyes wide they listen to Davies as he tells them that we're standing at the bottom of what was once the

Tethys Sea. 'Two hundred million years ago this place was paradise on earth. It was bursting with marine life. There were ichthyosaurs, plesiosaurs and heaps of ammonites and belemnites. When they died they sank to the bottom and were covered in mud.'

The girls immediately identify with the 12-year-old, Mary Anning, who found the first complete ichthyosaur, a kind of Jurassic dolphin, here in 1811. Mary used to gather shells and fossils to sell to visitors. The tongue twister 'She sells sea shells by the sea shore' is all about her. Davies' 13-year-old son, Christopher, is helping out on this walk along the beach. He's a natural-born fossil hunter too. When he was just 11, he found the head of a baby ichthyosaur lying at his feet.

The girls follow Davies like the Pied Piper. Their bucket is soon bursting with flint and pebbles. Shells prove a major distraction but one boy who's with us finds an ammonite the size of a small coin!

'Esti and Rachel are entranced. With eyes wide they listen to Davies as he tells them that we're standing at the bottom of what was once the Tethys Sea.'

I'm left dragging the double buggy back over the rocks. You can only get to the fossils at low tide and it's very easy to get cut off, I can't see us getting out of here in a hurry. I've never been here before or seen the film *The French Lieutenant's Woman*, that made Lyme Regis really famous, but the tiny painted cottages look familiar. Esti is certain she's seen them in a storybook at home. She's right. Beatrix Potter immortalised Lyme in *The Tale of Little Pig Robinson*. So did Whistler and Jane Austen but they're not in the same league.

Coming back empty handed is a bonus as now we can spend an hour or two cruising the souvenir shops. There's an ichthyosaur for a small fortune but thankfully Esti and Rachel settle on a tiny box of fossilised shark teeth, a couple of pencils and a purple teddy bear key ring.

Behind Lyme Regis is some of the most beautiful countryside in England. Steep green valleys, thatched cottages and ancient woodlands. The girls love it when we find the road blocked by cows on the way home for milking. The twins sleep off the excitement as we drive along the coast to Abbotsbury. The view from the cliff edge is spectacular. There's a double rainbow. The girls have their cameras out and are snapping.

Abbotsbury is a real Miss Marple village but it's deserted. It's famous for its swans and there are hundreds gliding in and out of the reeds in the estuary. We feel like bit players in *The Ugly Duckling*. Eve baulks as she comes eye to eye with a three-foot hissing swan.

It's time to head for civilisation and I've booked the cottage in a hurry forgetting

'The view from the cliff edge is spectacular. There's a double rainbow. The girls have their cameras out and are snapping.'

to read the small print. As we arrive back in Stoke Abbot the mobile phone cuts out. It's a real chocolate-box village, just like it said in the brochure, but like Abbotsbury it's deserted. Our cottage is literally dug into the edge of the graveyard that looks as if it's stepped right out of a horror movie! The graves rise up from the kitchen window and when you turn on the tumble dryer the whole kitchen smells earthy and damp.

Alone with four children, I almost turn tail and run but you can't tell them you're scared of ghosts can you? The next day, as we drive back to London across the moors, Dorset looks sinister in the grey light. Thomas Hardy wouldn't recognise it. I ask Esti if she'd noticed anything about the house. She did but had decided it was wiser to keep quiet.

an old mansion near the river, is surrounded by lawn and has family rooms. In Haworth, a lovely village of cobblestone streets that was home to the Brontës, the rambling stone **Aitches Guest House** (+44 (0)1535 642501; 11 West Lane; www.aitches.co.uk; $) welcomes children. Whitby's **White Horse & Griffin** (+44 (0)1947 604857; 87 Church St; www.whitehorseandgriffin.co.uk; $) has stylish rooms and self-catering cottages.

Wales

Bucolic Wales has gorgeous countryside, but children are likely to get more excited about the unpronounceable town names and the local castles, of which there are over 600. **Caernarfon Castle** is perhaps the most famous, but **Cardiff** also has a great fairy-tale castle with peacocks and a Norman tower. It also has Techniquest, a hands-on science and discovery centre. In **Brecon Beacons National Park** you can go pony-trekking or take a canal cruise along the valley of the River Usk; this area is also famous for its local produce, so it's worth having a proper sit-down nosh-up in one of the villages. **Snowdonia**, in the north, is an area of impressive jagged mountains that loom over the coast. You can drive up high and then walk to the summits, or take the Snowdon Mountain Railway to the very top. There are numerous other narrow-gauge railways in the region; see www.walesrails.co.uk for details.

STAY

In Cardiff, the high-rise **Big Sleep Hotel** (+44 (0)2920 636 363; www.thebigsleephotel.com; Bute Tce; $) has interior cool and views that are an absolute bargain. In Brecon, the hub of the Beacons, the quaint family-friendly **Grange Guest House** (+44 (0)1874 624038; www.thegrange -brecon.co.uk; $) has a courtyard garden and children's video library. In pretty Beddgelert in the heart of Snowdonia, **Plas Colwyn**

Guest House (+44 (0)1925 765 702; www.plascolwyn .co.uk; $) has a comfy family room and offers hearty breakfasts. Near Barmouth, a placid beach resort on the edge of Snowdonia, **Llwyndu Farmhouse** (+44 (0)1341 280 144; www .llwyndu-farmhouse.co.uk; $) has superb lofty family rooms in a converted granary and serves up exotic breakfasts.

Scotland

Bagpipes, kilts and tartans do a lot to cement Scotland as a tangible national concept in the minds of children. While the highlands, islands and lochs steal the show up here, the city of **Edinburgh** is not to be missed, with winding cobblestone streets, stately Georgian houses and a hilltop castle. Glasgow's Science Centre and Dundee's Sensation are interactive science museums designed for kids. **Oban** makes a pleasant, bustling bayside base for exploring the western highlands and has ferries to the Inner and Outer Hebrides, most notably **Mull**, with spectacular beaches and scenery, a miniature steam train, castles, brightly painted cottages and a marine discovery centre. Scotland's **northern highlands** are great for a bit of walking or driving, and children will get a buzz out of spotting yak-like highland cattle. A visit to **Loch Ness**, the largest body of freshwater in Britain, is obligatory.

STAY

In Edinburgh, **Mingalar** (+44 (0)131 556 7000; www.mingalar.eu; 2 East Claremont St; $) is a charming B&B with large family rooms in a Georgian house; guests are free to use the kitchen, and a highchair and cot are available. For something a little fancier, there's the elegant **Dukes of Windsor Street** (+44 (0)131 556 6046; 17 Windsor St, www.dukesofwindsor.com; $) with a columned portico, luxurious rooms with crisp bed linen and fluffy towels and a chic breakfast menu that includes vegan and wheat-free options. In Oban, the sky-blue **Maridon Guest House** (+44 (0)1631 562670; www.west-scotland-tourism.com/maridon-house; $) is renowned for its friendly owners and comfy rooms with views over the water. In the picture-postcard village of Tobermory on Mull, the exquisite **Failte Guest House** (+44 (0)1688 302495; $) has beautiful rooms overlooking the bay. For cottages near Loch Ness, visit www.wildernesscottages.co.uk.

WHEN

The British obsession with the weather is well founded, as changeable conditions keep everyone guessing. Summer (June to August) has the greatest number of sunny days but can also bring cloud and rain, and winter can deliver surprising spells of crisp clear days between snow falls. Spring brings blossom, wildflowers and daffodils, while in autumn red apples hang from huge old trees, and leaves turn various shades of russet. May to September is probably the best time to visit, though tourist sites can be busy in July and August, and London can get stinking hot at the height of summer. Travel in winter outside the cities is to be avoided, as it's chilly just about everywhere and gets dark very early.

HOW

Transport
Britain is a hectic airline hub, with London, Manchester and Glasgow in particular receiving frequent flights from around the world, and a boom in no-frills airlines is resulting in very cheap flights from the Continent to regional British airports. There are car ferries from the Continent and Ireland, and the Channel Tunnel funnels cars and Eurostar trains from France.

MARK DAFFEY | LONELY PLANET IMAGES

ABOVE. **FUN ON A HOT DAY IN THE PICCADILLY GARDENS WATERJETS, MANCHESTER**

DESTINATIONS

Compact England, Scotland and Wales are all wonderful to explore by car, but the fun stops in city centres, where parking can be hard and expensive. Car hire is often exorbitant, so look for fly-drive deals in your home country when booking flights. Petrol is also pricey in Britain. An overseas driving licence is valid in Britain for 12 months. Although a car restraint is compulsory for children under 12, this rule is waived when taxis and hire cars don't have restraints. If you're planning a lot of driving in a hire car, choose a company that provides a restraint.

Trains are fast and efficient but expensive, with fares roughly double that of long-distance buses (coaches). To save on fares, keep your dates flexible so that you can snap up special deals, and book early, or consider buying either a discount or unlimited-travel train pass.

Catching a ride with a postbus (mail-delivery van) is a novel way to see remote rural areas without a car. For information and timetables, contact Royal Mail Postbus (www.postbus.royalmail.com).

London's now-decommissioned old double-decker buses have begun a new lease of life travelling on two heritage routes: Bus 9 trundles from the Royal Albert Hall to Aldwych via Piccadilly Circus, while bus 15 runs from Trafalgar Square to Tower Hill via Fleet St; they run every 15 minutes. Driving in London is a nightmare: traffic jams are common, parking space is at a premium and there are annoyingly dutiful traffic wardens. Plus, if you bring your car into central London from 7am to 6.30pm on a weekday, you'll need to pay an £8 per day congestion charge.

Shopping & Essentials

You can get just about anything you might need in Britain (yes, even Vegemite), so just bring essentials. Rain jackets, warm clothes and comfy shoes are all vital, even if you're visiting in summer, but even these can be bought once you arrive.

Most shops are open Monday to Saturday from 9am till 5pm (or later), and sometimes on Sunday from 10am to 4pm. In country areas shops usually close on weekends and for lunch, and occasionally on Wednesday or Thursday afternoon too.

Most museums and historical attractions have nappy-changing facilities, as do department stores.

Health

Britain presents no real health risks to the travelling family. Regardless of nationality, anyone needing help will receive free emergency treatment at the emergency department of an NHS hospital. Reciprocal arrangements allow citizens of some countries (including Australia) to receive subsidised care from GPs and dentists.

Breastfeeding in public can still raise the occasional eyebrow but is certainly OK.

Food

The fact that sliced white bread, sausages, fish 'n' chips and mashed spuds still loom large on the British culinary map probably gets a big thumbs up from many children. Of course, it's no secret that the food scene in Britain is actually much more sophisticated and worldly than its traditional reputation these days, with curries the most popular takeaway food and a bevy of inventive celebrity chefs making their mark with organic produce. But that doesn't mean you won't be able to find a Spam sandwich if you want one.

Children are not especially catered for in the form of kids' menus but you may be able to ask for a small portion. Breakfasts in B&Bs are often of the huge half-a-farmyard variety, with bacon, eggs, sausages, tomatoes, mushrooms and baked beans, but cereal, toast and a single boiled egg are usually on offer too. The standard pub ploughman's lunch of bread, cheese and pickles can be fun, while pies and pasties (best in Cornwall) are good for eating on the run. The humble and ubiquitous British caff is just made for kids, with meals like omelette and chips and toasted cheese sandwiches – and everything is usually inexpensive (rightly so).

DENMARK

Home to Hans Christian Andersen, Lego and a real-life fairy-tale princess, Denmark is the stuff children's dreams are made of. It's a very family-oriented place, where kids (børne) are revered. There are plenty of playgrounds, and restaurants, hotels and hostels all welcome little ones. Travel in the Danish archipelago is likely to involve ferries, no matter whether you travel by bus, train or car – and that's always fun. And while the weather isn't exactly tropical, somewhere offering the uniquely Danish concept of 'cosiness' is always nearby.

Denmark ain't cheap, but it's not as expensive as its Scandinavian neighbours. Hotels, car rental, meals and supplies will all take a toll on your wallet.

There are a couple of engaging websites where children can do their own pretrip research: the kids' section of www.denmark.dk, and www.ambwashington.um.dk/en/menu/ForKids.

WHAT'S TOPS

- Copenhagen's Zoologisk Have, a huge zoo with thematic adventure trails
- The 45 million bricks that make up Legoland
- The 2000-year-old bodies of the bog people in Silkeborg
- The reconstructed Viking ships at Roskilde
- Ribe VikingeCenter, a hands-on Viking village in Jutland
- Rolling down the white sand dunes at Dueodde
- The excavated Viking ring fortress at Trelleborg
- Low-tech fun at Joboland, on Bornholm
- A canal-boat tour of Copenhagen
- Borrowing a bike in Copenhagen, as part of the free Bycyklen bicycle scheme

WHERE

While Copenhagen and its island of Zealand are eminently explorable, visitors with a bit of time should also check out other islands in the archipelago. **Jutland** has the unmissable Legoland and Denmark's oldest and best-preserved town, Ribe, while **Bornholm** is a delightful slow-paced island. In **Funen**, you'll find bucolic countryside dotted with thatched-roof farmhouses, as well as Egeskov Castle, surrounded by moats and formal gardens.

To rent seaside cottages anywhere in Denmark, contact DanCenter (www.dancenter.co.uk).

ZEALAND

The island of Zealand has castles, beaches, fjords, Viking ships at **Roskilde**, the

Viking ring fortress at **Trelleborg** and the delightful towns of **Sorø** and **Vallø** – and the national capital.

Copenhagen is devoid of the skyscrapers that dominate most other cities, and its old buildings and compact city centre keep things to a charming human scale. Parks, fountains, squares, gardens and pedestrian-only zones lace the city, and there are fun waterfront areas. There's a lot going on for kids, including two fun parks (Tivoli Gardens and Bakken), a zoo and the Experimentium science centre, and the Children's Museum (in the National Museum). Royalists might want to explore Rosenborg Castle, where the crown jewels are on display and there are puppet shows. A climb up the spiral stairs to the top of Rundetårn, a round tower dating from 1642, provides bird's-eye views over the old city's red-tiled rooftops.

STAY

In Copenhagen, the **Avenue Hotel** (+45 35 37 31 11; Åboulevard 29 DK-1960; www.avenuehotel.dk; $$) has newly decorated family rooms with beds as comfortable as clouds, as well as flat-screen TV, fridge and en suite. There's a tranquil patio and inviting lounge too. **Danhostel Lyngby Vandrerhjem** (+45 45 80 30 74; Rådvad 1 DK-2800; www.lyngbyhostel.dk; $) is nestled in the peaceful old village of Råvad, which is buried within the gorgeous wilds of Dyrehaven. This friendly hostel is a destination in itself, and it's well worth mellowing out here for a couple of days to commune with the Danish countryside. Rooms have a homely feel and sleep two to six people, and there are shelters in the forest that sleep up to seven. The hostel provides baby tub, change table, outdoor toys and highchair, and there's a great kitchen.

BORNHOLM

This pleasantly varied island is a gem. It has white-sand beaches and dunes, cycling trails, forests, round churches, windmills and unspoiled fishing villages such as **Gudhjem** and **Svaneke**, with mustard-yellow half-timbered houses and the quaint Joboland amusement park. Offshore is the tiny well-preserved fortress island of **Christiansø**.

STAY

Dueodde Vandrerhjem & Camping (+45 56 48 81 19; www.dueodde.dk; $) is in a wooded area next to the gorgeous soft-sand beach at Dueodde that is perfect for children; if you haven't brought a tent you can stay in an on-site van or in the hostel, which has family rooms with en suite. Facilities include a playground, sauna, indoor pool and jumping castle. **Therns Hotel** (www.therns -hotel.dk; $), a simple inn on Gudhjem's main street, has family rooms and there are ample areas to run amok, such as the lounge, garden and restaurant with outdoor terrace.

WHEN

Denmark's winter months (cold and short on daylight) are not very hospitable. The weather warms up in late April, and stays pretty nice until October. May and June can be lovely months to visit, with fresh green leaves on the trees and fields covered in flowers, and the days are long (peaking at over 17 daylight hours in late June). During July and August there are open-air concerts and longer opening hours at museums and other attractions. Autumn tends to be hazy and dull, as many farmers burn crop waste in the fields. Expect to see a fair bit of rain, no matter when you visit.

HOW

Transport

Flights from all over the world fly into Copenhagen, but overseas visitors may find it cheaper to fly to another city in Europe first and then travel onward to Denmark by boat, bus, train or car. Ferries travel from Sweden, Norway, Germany, Poland, England, Iceland and the Faroe Islands, and also operate within Denmark.

Danish roads are well maintained and signposted, and traffic is manageable. The parking system in cities involves a clock-like parking disk, available from petrol stations and elsewhere. Scenic routes are collectively known as the Marguerite Route and designated by signs with a white daisy. Children under 135cm need to use a child seat or restraint appropriate to their size. Car rental is expensive, costing as much for a day as for a week in Germany. Booking from abroad is usually cheapest. Either a national licence or International Driving Permit is accepted.

Denmark has an efficient and reliable train system and the intercity (IC) trains come with play areas for children and baby-change facilities. Trains between Zealand and Funen roll right onto the ferries.

Shopping & Essentials

All supplies are easy to come by, but because of value-added tax and high prices most people won't want to be stocking up excessively in Denmark. Keep in mind that even in the warmest months, cool weather and rain are not uncommon – so bring jumpers, warm socks and light jackets.

Health

Denmark poses no health risks for travellers and has modern, well-run health care. Emergency treatment at hospitals is free to all travellers. Many medicines that can be bought over the counter at pharmacies elsewhere in Europe are available on prescription only.

The tourist office in Copenhagen gives out a guide to public toilets in the city.

Food

Danish food tends to be hearty, with meat, fish and butter playing prominent roles. Many restaurants have a separate children's menu, called a *børnemenu*. Open sandwiches made from rye bread and topped with roast beef or pork, shrimps or fish fillet and finished with garnishes are the staple, along with buffet-style spreads of foods such as pickled or smoked fish, salads, cheese and meatballs. Bornholm is renowned for its smokehouses, producing treats such as smoked herring, while the nearby island of Christiansø makes the best spiced herring in the country.

FRANCE

Travelling *en famille* in France means you'll probably have to abandon dreams of eating five-course meals and savouring the Louvre. But it hardly matters when there's so much you can all enjoy together, whether it's running through fields of lavender, picnicking on baguettes and brie, or paddling on the Atlantic coast.

Accommodation and restaurant meals are usually expensive, even from a European perspective. But self-catering and camper-vanning are enjoyable ways to rough it and save money, and long-term rentals can also work out quite cheaply.

WHAT'S TOPS

- Taking the lift or climbing to the top of the Eiffel Tower
- Disneyland Resort, just outside Paris, where cast members speak French
- The Jardin du Luxembourg in Paris, with crêpes, playgrounds and ponds
- The Cité des Sciences et de L'Industrie, in Paris, with an aquarium, experiential installations and adjacent Parc de la Villette
- Pottering on the lovely beaches of Île de Ré, on the Atlantic coast
- Learning to ski at a *jardin de neige* in the Alps
- La Rochelle's state-of-the-art aquarium
- Going canoeing in the Dordogne
- The green parks and puppet theatres of Lyon
- The enchanting Christmas markets, decorations and celebrations of Alsace

WHERE

France is a diverse land, and every region has its own very unique topography, history, traditions and sights. Normandy is a land of apples, seafood, dairy cows, half-timbered farmhouses and **Mont St-Michel**, the magical abbey encircled by tidal waters. Celtic Brittany is known for its old-world fishing villages, seaside resorts such as **Carnac**, **Camaret** and **Morgat** and islands like the aptly named **Belle Île**. The Loire is peppered with chateaux, most notably **Chambord** and islandlike **Azay-le-Rideau**, as is Burgundy. In **Lyon** you can visit the world of 19th-century silk weavers, along with verdant parks, puppet theatres and casual eateries. The Atlantic coast is a rewarding region for families, with long stretches of wild beach and the lively ports of **La Rochelle** and **St-Jean de Luz**. The Alps and Jura are another paradise for families, with soaring cable-car rides, ski slopes, forest walks and interesting towns like **Annecy**. The prehistoric cave paintings (and accompanying theme parks and museums) in the **Vézère Valley** and at **Lascaux**, both in the Dordogne, are real eye-openers for kids and there are also delightful flower-filled villages and great canoe trips in this river-rich region. At the **Gouffre de Padirac**, southeast of Carennac, it's possible to take a boat along an underground river. Nearby, in **Quercy**, you can rent house boats and travel along the River Lot. The conical-topped buildings of the medieval walled town of **Carcassonne**, in Languedoc, send children's imaginations into overdrive, but beware of stifling crowds in high summer. Provence, land of lavender and sunshine, has some wonderful markets – in towns like **Aix**, **Apt** and **Arles** – and Roman ruins. The Côte d'Azur, a mix of chic seaside towns and traffic gridlock, has some relatively uncrammed sandy beaches west of St-Tropez.

PARIS

For most kids, Paris means one thing: the Eiffel Tower. Oh, and Disneyland. But they'll are a few other treats in store, such as the illuminated fountains at the Trocadero Gardens, the Palais de la Découverte (a science museum), the modern Parc de la Villette and Cité des Sciences et de L'Industrie, the peaceful and kaleidoscopic Ste-Chapelle and the climb up the gargoyle-encrusted towers of Notre Dame. For a look at the city's dirty underwear, visit the below-ground Musée des Égouts (Sewers Museum). Queues in Paris can be very long, so it's worth getting an early start, especially for popular sights such as the Eiffel Tower. Beyond the Ring Road, the Bois de Boulogne has boat rides, farm animals and playgrounds galore, while, further afield, Chartres and Versailles both make enchanting day trips.

Paris is one of the best places in France to sample North African, Middle Eastern and Vietnamese food, in eateries that are often less expensive and more family friendly than traditional French restaurants.

SEE
Batobus (08 25 05 01 01; www.batobus.com) Getting around Paris on the metro is fun (unless you're wrangling a stroller up and down its stairs) but this hop on/off boat along the Seine is more fun. It stops at the Champs-Élysées, Eiffel Tower, Hôtel de Ville, Jardin des Plantes, Musée d'Orsay, Louvre, Notre Dame and St-Germain des Prés.

Jardin du Luxembourg (Luxembourg Garden; 7am-9.30pm Apr-Oct, 8am-sunset Nov-Mar) When the weather is fine, everyone flocks to the formal terraces and chestnut groves of this quintessentially Parisian park to relax. Children are very much part of the picture, with the sand pit, pony rides, miniature boats and carousel all part of an enduring tradition. Punch and Judy puppet shows take place at the park's Les Guignols in Théâtre des Marionnettes on Wednesdays and weekends.

STAY
Apart'hotels Citadines Paris St-Germain des Prés (+33 01 41 05 79 05; www.citadines.com; 53 ter, quai des Grands Augustins 75006; $$$) Overlooking the Seine and Île de la Cité, apartments here have sleek furnishings, fully equipped kitchen and a babysitter option. There are also properties in Les Halles, Montmartre, Opéra Grands Boulevards and elsewhere, some more expensive than others.

DAVID H. LEWIS · ISTOCKPHOTOS

ABOVE: **HIT THE SLOPES FOR A DAY OF ALPINE FUN**

DESTINATIONS

EIFFEL OR MOUTHFUL

~ FRANCE ~

STEPHANIE LEVIN-GERVASI

Last summer, I cobbled together enough money for two plane tickets to Paris – one for me, the other for my daughter. I had lived in Paris during the 1980s, so I emailed my French friends and said to be on the lookout for us. We boarded the plane without plan or itinerary.

This isn't to say I didn't have a maternal portrait percolating in my brain. I fancied a kind of storybook vacation with my eight-year-old. Camille and I were excited to be in Paris, but we had entirely different agendas. A Francophile and a French 'foodie', I longed to sashay arm-in-arm with my daughter through one of the city's oldest markets, Rue Mouffetard. The open-air food market – stuffed with culinary counsellors hawking cheeses, oysters and sumptuous produce – is the most colourful market in Paris. Camille's raison d'etre: the Eiffel Tower and a ride on the Ferris wheel, the one she had seen on television during the millennium celebrations.

Food was our biggest challenge. In a city where food is an art, Camille lived on sliced ham and baguettes. She had a litany of complaints about French food: the dollop of crème fraiche crowning the ice cream didn't taste like American whipped cream, the cheeses smelled like stinky feet and the mustard was the wrong colour yellow. We frequented *boulangeries*, corner stores,

'A Francophile and a French 'foodie', I longed to sashay, arm-in-arm with my daughter through one of the city's oldest markets, Rue Mouffetard.'

pizza places and discovered a plethora of Chinese restaurants in the 13th arrondissement (Place d'Italie). Each morning we ferreted out croissants, hot chocolate and cafe au lait at corner cafes. We didn't starve.

Once we solved the food conundrum, we tackled the nasty lines snaking around every monument or museum. I hate standing in line, ditto for my daughter. Thankfully, I had the foresight before leaving the States to contact Rail Europe in New York for French Rail Passes. The pass allowed us to bypass long lines at the train stations. That was our only reprieve from lines. The queue curling around the Louvre looked like a line for a sold-out Stones concert.

'Forget the Louvre,' I said. We took the metro to the Eiffel Tower. 'I knew we should have come early in the day,' I groaned, checking out the four-hour line for the two elevators. 'That's OK, mom, we can wait in the short line and walk up,' suggested Camille good naturedly. An hour later we shelled out our entry fee and started up the mighty monument. Actually, Camille bolted up the steps while

I huffed and puffed. Thankfully, we could only go to the third tier by foot. Because I avoid lines, this was my first trip to the Eiffel Tower. And, like every other tourist, I oohed and aahed at the high-rise views of Paris. We bought postcards, posted them from the Eiffel Tower post office and headed down.

Get an early start, and you're less likely to stand in lines in Paris during the summer. We never got started before 10am and our days sorely lacked structure. We needed to mend our ways. Our casual approach to Paris was whittling away precious days. We hatched a plan. Since the French do not eat on the run, we decided not to either. We packed picnic lunches – baguettes, cheese, ham and fruit, then ate in a different park every day. Camille got to ride the Ferris wheel after our picnic in the Jardin des Tuileries. In the park behind Cathédrale de Notre Dame, we munched our sandwiches under watchful gargoyles, then strolled across the Seine and boarded the *Bateau Mouche*. The *bateau* glides down the Seine, past the Palais de Justice, l'Île Saint Louis and the Statue of Liberty in less than an hour.

Paris is stunning after dark and it stays light until around 10.30pm in the summer. The Left Bank is the hot spot at night and the square in front of Notre Dame always has something going on. Forget Quasimodo's bell tower, Camille was dazzled by the daredevil skateboard competition in the square. A tin-can toss from Notre Dame sits Shakespeare & Company – the English-language bookstore crammed with literary treasures and reading alcoves. We purchased *Harry Potter*.

We put a lot of mileage on our feet peeking into store windows, soaking in

'We put a lot of mileage on our feet peeking into store windows, soaking in the street theatre and stopping for sugar crêpes on the street.'

the street theatre and stopping for sugar crêpes on the street. Sometimes our feet got sore and our tempers frazzled, but we remedied this by riding the metro.

Every metro station has a gigantic map with colourful buttons that lead to different metro lines. I let Camille pick a point, within reason, and we would ride to that destination. In Bois de Vincennes we discovered a little zoo, and in Place Des Vosges, Camille found kids to play with.

We spent a brilliant day at La Vilette – the city of science that proved to be an ingenious marvel. Every hands-on scientific secret is here to explore. The cavernous halls are designed for various ages and tickets are sold in hourly chunks so that the exhibit halls and geodesic dome IMAX theatre don't overcrowd.

Our week in Paris was coming to an end. It was time for our next adventure, a train ride to see our friends in a tiny village near La Rochelle. But that's another story.

Hôtel des Grandes Écoles (+30 01 43 26 79 23; www.hotel-grandes-ecoles.com; 75 rue du Cardinal Lemoine, 5e; $$) This wonderful, welcoming hotel with its own garden has one of the loveliest situations in the Latin Quarter, tucked away in a courtyard off a medieval street. There are quad rooms and extra beds can be added to smaller rooms. Rooms 29 to 33 have direct access to the garden.

ATLANTIC COAST & BASQUE COUNTRY

The charming port of **La Rochelle**, a lively place full of holidaying families, is in one of the sunniest regions of France and has child-friendly museums and an aquarium. Close by, **Île de Ré**, featuring whitewashed fishing villages and a long sandy beach with safe shallow water, is similarly popular with families, and its scenic, hollyhock-lined lanes make it perfect for bicycling. Futuroscope, inland near **Poitiers**, is a cinematic theme park, with 3-D IMAX films, cybergames and water-spouting play areas. With miles of sandy beach and relaxed resorts such as **Arcachon** (linked by bike path to Europe's highest sand dune) and **Soulac-sur-Mer** (with a surfing school) the Côte d'Argent is another top spot for a seaside holiday. And **Bordeaux**, the regional capital, is a gleaming gem, especially now that its centre has been pedestrianised.

Further south, in the French Basque Country, don't miss the glitz and surf scene of **Biarritz**, the lively seaside **St-Jean de Luz** and the very pretty pilgrim stop of **St-Jean Pied de Port**, a great launching place for walks into the surrounding hills.

STAY
Hôtel la Jétee (+30 05 46 09 36 36; www.hotel-lajetee .com; 23 quai Georges Clemenceau; $), on Île de Ré, has mezzanine family rooms arranged around a leafy central courtyard. In Arcachon, **La Forêt** (+30 05 56 22 73 28; route de Biscarosse; $) is a well-run camping ground with cute family cabins shaded by pine trees. For a touch of Biarritz glam, opt for a family room at **Hôtel Plaza** (+30 05 59 24 74 00; www.groupe-segeric.com; 20 av Édouard VII; $$), a refurbished art deco dazzler overlooking Grande Plage. Other sparkling family-oriented hotels in Biarritz include the colourful **Hôtel Palym** (+30 05 59 24 25 83; www.le-palmarium.com; 7 rue du Port Vieux; $); the bright **Hôtel St-Julien** (+30 05 59 24 20 39; www.saint-julien-biarritz.com; 20 av Carnot; $); and **Hôtel Maïtagaria** (+30 05 59 24 26 65; www .hotel-maitagaria.com; $), with a two-room family suite, lounge area and garden. In St Jean de Luz, the chalet-like **Hotel-Villas Les Goëlands** (+30 05 59 26 10 05; www.hotel-lesgoelands.com; $$) welcomes children with open arms, supplying highchairs, changing mats, bottle warmers and babysitters.

FRENCH ALPS & THE JURA

The snowy peaks of the Alps are most famous for their ski slopes, and all the major resorts have ski schools and 'snow gardens' (for toddlers). **Chamonix** (with extremely gorgeous scenery, accessible by train) and **La Clusaz** (near Annecy, with plenty of village charm) are just two of your many options. There are also some fascinating towns to explore. Surrounded by jagged mountains and sitting on a large lake, chic **Annecy** is laced with Venetian-style canals bordered by overhanging medieval buildings. In summer it's possible to swim in the lake, or you can take to it in a pedal boat, canoe or cruise boat. Sophisticated **Grenoble**, the capital of the Alps, features an imposing 16th-century fort reached by cable car.

The forested hills and granite plateaus of the **Jura Mountains** are an invigorating place to escape the alpine hordes and get a taste of traditional mountain life. The area is popular for its hiking and cross-country skiing and is especially beautiful in summer, when lush meadows are carpeted with wildflowers. The **Parc Naturel Régional du Haut-Jura** is filled with glacial lakes, mountains and low-lying valleys and its town of **Moirans-en-Montaigne** is known for its wooden toys.

STAY

In Annecy, **Le Pré Carré** (+30 04 50 52 14 14; www .hotel-annecy.net; 27 rue Sommellier; $$) is a swish contemporary hotel with impeccable service; children under 12 stay free, and facilities include a communal family room and play area. **La Mainaz** (+30 04 50 41 31 10; www.la-mainaz .com; 5 route du Col de la Faucille; $$), a traditional chalet at the edge of Haut-Jura National Park, has spacious, comfy rooms and a huge terrace with panoramic views of the Alps.

WHEN

Spring has some of the best weather and it's usually warm enough for the beach in May. Autumn isn't necessarily cold but short days mean limited sunlight, even along the Côte d'Azur. Winter is snow season in France's Alps and Pyrenees, reaching a crowdy peak over the Christmas school holidays. Most city dwellers take their annual vacation to the coasts and mountains from mid-July to the end of August, and the emptied-out cities tend to shut down at the same time.

HOW

Transport

Numerous budget airlines serve France, especially from the UK. High-speed Eurotunnel trains shuttle cars, motorcycles and buses through the Channel Tunnel from England to northwestern France. Rail services link France with every country in Europe, and the Eurostar

travels between London and Paris in just two and a half hours. Car ferries travel to France from Italy, the UK, the Channel Islands and Ireland, with additional services and routes operating in summer. There are also ferries between Corsica and Sardinia.

France has an efficient and far-reaching rail network with superfast TGVs travelling in all directions. Reduced fares are available for adults travelling with a child aged four to 11, in addition to child discounts.

Most foreign licences can be used in France for up to a year. Arranging car rental from abroad can be less expensive than doing it once you arrive. Rental companies can provide child car seats (necessary for children less than 18kg) but these must be arranged when making the reservation. If you're going to be in France for between two weeks and six months and you're *not* an EU resident, purchase-repurchase plans from Peugeot and Renault are much cheaper than renting.

Shopping & Essentials

Bring rain gear for Brittany, Paris and the mountains, and sunhats and insect repellent for elsewhere. A pocket knife is handy for picnics, but you can always buy an interesting local one once you arrive. Supermarkets open Monday to Saturday from about 9am or 9.30am to 7pm or 8pm; some open on Sunday morning. Many food shops take a midday break from noon or 1pm to 2pm or 3pm (except in Paris) and are closed on Sunday afternoon and all day Monday. Most towns have a vibrant market selling fresh fruit and vegetables. Disposable nappies, formula and fresh milk are widely available, but limited and unfamiliar opening hours can leave you stranded without supplies for days.

DESTINATIONS

Health

Excellent health care is easily accessible and pharmacists can give advice and medications for minor ailments. Altitude sickness can affect children at 2000m, and babies at lower altitudes, so keep an eye on your troops. Hypothermia, too, can be an issue in the mountains, so carry warm clothes even in summer. All tap water in France is safe to drink; when it is not (eg at public fountains or on trains), a sign will usually say *'eau non potable'*.

No one is likely to blink if you breastfeed in public, but you may not see many other women doing it.

Food

French regional dishes that really appeal to children include Brittany's crêpes and galettes, Provençal pizza and cheesy fondue and raclette from the Alps. But eating out can pose a few challenges. Highchairs, children's menus and half-portions are thin on the ground, and French children do not usually frequent anywhere more sophisticated than a corner cafe. When they do go to a proper restaurant, their manners and behaviour are expected to be impeccable. *Cafétérias* usually have simple dishes like *croque monsieur* (toasted cheese and ham sandwich) and ready-made food you can see before ordering, something that works for many kids. Picnicking and self-catering are probably the best ways to keep the family fed, however. Grab a *baguette*, some cheese, a bunch of grapes *et voilà!* Markets sometimes sell takeaway pizza and roast chicken – perfect picnic food – and takeaway baguettes filled with cheese or ham are a great way to eat cheaply in Paris.

If you are eating out, having the main meal at lunchtime can work well for families. Dinner can often take hours, and many restaurants, especially in the south, don't open for dinner until 8pm.

PORTUGAL

Portugal is a supremely child-friendly place. It has a gentleness lacking in its brash neighbour, Spain, which can be felt in all sorts of ways. The often slow pace of life, endearingly old-fashioned shops, villages and restaurants and doting locals all contribute to an impression that you've stepped into a loving national embrace.

Lisbon is a star city, with dramatic hilly topography that slopes down to the vast mouth of the Rio Tejo, and its faded grandeur is captivating. Outside the city, there are beautiful landscapes aplenty, from cork oak plantations to lush river valleys lined with vineyards to dramatic coastlines. All over the country there are unspoilt and charming towns and villages.

Simple *pensãos* (pensions) are often the most family-friendly places to stay. They're almost always spotlessly clean and can usually rustle up a cot, especially if you request it when you book your room. Camping grounds, which are widespread and cheap, can be great places to meet other kids. At the other end of the spectrum, Portugal has an amazing array of *pousadas* (www.turihab.pt, www.pousadasportugal.com and www.manor-houses-portugal.com), mansions and palaces that have been converted into upmarket places to stay, many of which cater to families.

Portugal remains one of the most affordable destinations in Europe, and meals especially are often great value.

WHAT'S TOPS

- Catching a cable car, tram or funicular *elevador* in Lisbon
- Sintra, the spectacular mountain retreat brimming with palaces and castles, which you can explore by horse and carriage
- The quaint seaside town of Tavira, with a sandy island beach, expansive salt flats, lovely cobbled streets and a fishing fleet
- Hilltop castles at Óbidos, Marvão, Castelo de Vide, Valença and Elves
- Coimbra's Portugal dos Pequenitos theme park, featuring architectural miniatures from all over the old empire
- Catching dolphin and seal shows at Zoomarine theme park near Albufeira
- Having a laugh at Casa dos Bonecos, Évora's puppet theatre
- Barcelos market, held every Thursday, with loads of handmade wares as well as fresh bread and piled-high fruit and veg
- St Martin's Day, celebrated on 9 November, when chestnuts are roasted and kids paint their faces with charcoal from the fire

WHERE

Portugal is a compact, compelling country to explore, especially if you've got your own wheels. Thanks to its rectangular shape, it's not too difficult to cover all corners – and the middle – either.

The rugged Atlantic coast has a succession of fishing villages and faded beach resorts, usually with cute whitewashed houses edged in blue. There is sometimes great surfing and swimming to be had (but keep an eye out for undertows and rips). Special spots along here include the fishing village **Ericeira**, which also has good surf; low-key **São Martinho**

do Porto, with a calm swimming beach; **Figueira da Foz**, with surfing and the Serra da Boa Viagem forest (which has a fantastic wooden playground at one of the picnic sites); **Aveiro**, with pastel-coloured houses built along canals; and the lace-making town of **Vila do Conde**, with a laid-back feel and beaches that are great for kids. Further north, in the Minho valley, delightful villages and vineyards dot the hilly landscape.

The Algarve begins at Portugal's southwest corner (and it really is a corner), at the dramatic clifftop town of **Sagres**, and stretches along the southern coast to Spain. Much of the Algarve is an overdeveloped package-tour precinct, but kids love its sandy beaches and enthralling water parks, zoos and castles.

With so much to do along Portugal's coast it's easy to neglect the hinterland. But inland there are stunning traditional villages, sometimes with castles and nearly always with eye-catching Manueline buildings. **Monsanto**, **Sortelha** and **Manteigas** are some of the nicest towns and are all in the mountainous Serra da Estrela, where there's fine walking, skiing, canoeing and horseback riding to be had.

Porto, the second-largest city after Lisbon, can seem a bit rough around the edges, so is not for everybody. But it is certainly worth passing through for the views alone. Five dramatic bridges span the rocky gorge carved by the Rio Douro, linking the higgledy piggledy neighbourhoods that tumble down the city's hillsides. Its tram museum is great fun for kids, as are the day-long river cruises that go up and down the Douro valley.

LISBON

Draped over steep hillsides that spill down to the wide mouth of the Rio Tejo, Lisbon is a fascinating city to simply wander around.

DESTINATIONS

Bright yellow trams wind through curvy tree-lined streets, and everywhere Lisboêtas are out strolling and chatting at tiny patio restaurants and cafes. Aside from soaking up the atmosphere, children will love the mosaic-paved footpaths, the huge aquarium and the hilltop Castelo de São Jorge, which has a fabulous playground. A roller-coaster ride on tram 28 through the ancient Alfama district to the Castelo is great fun and good for saving small legs. There are also three *elevadores* and *ascensores* (funiculars) that travel up the city's steepest hills; the Elevador de Santa Justa – a frilly, wrought-iron lift that goes up to a cafe with a superb view – is the most fun.

Just outside Lisbon, the magical setting of Sintra, with its fairy-tale palaces, castles, forests, toy museum and horse-drawn carriages, will please budding princesses and knights alike.

SEE

Oceanário de Lisbon (+351 218 917 002; www .oceanario.pt; 10am-7pm Apr-Oct, to 6pm Nov-Mar) In the riverfont Parque das Nações, this aquatic wonderland is home to 450 different species of sea creature – everything from giant mantas to sea otters and penguins. Children can even stay overnight and sleep with the sharks! Kids will also dig the hands-on Pavilhão do Conhecimento, minitrain and cable car, all in the park surrounding the aquarium.

Museu de Marinha (Naval Museum; +351 213 620 019; 10am-5pm Tue-Sun Oct-Mar, to 6pm Apr-Sep) Among the armadas of model boats, this museum has gems such as Vasco da Gama's portable wooden altar and the polished private quarters of the royal yacht *Amélia*. There are also ornate royal barges, the biggest of which is a 1780 neo-Viking number. A children's museum offers creative activities on weekends.

STAY

Residencial Horizonte (+351 21 353 95 26; www .hotelhorizonte.com; Avenida António Augusto de Aguiar 42; $$) This refurbished hotel is right across from the Parque Eduardo VII, which has a lake and playground. The neighbourhood, while pleasantly leafy, is a bit of a hoof from central Lisbon, but a metro stop in front of the hotel means you can be in Baixa or Bairro Alto in minutes. Rooms have TV and en suite. The hotel also has a lounge and bar, good for post-bedtime relaxing.

Cinco (www.stayatcinco.com; $$) This pretty stone house is in the centre of beautiful Sintra, a 40-minute train ride out of Lisbon. The ground floor of the house has been converted into an apartment that can be rented nightly or weekly. It's bright and cheerful, with an immaculate bathroom complete with big tub. Gardens surround the house, and there's a pool.

MINHO

The northwest corner of Portugal is traditional and very beautiful. Blessed with rich soil and a lush climate, this is wine-growing territory – so don't miss the local *vinho verde*. In late summer the landscape is ablaze as the vines change from lime green to fiery red.

Braga has a fine cathedral (the oldest in Portugal) and other fine churches, but these are likely to bore the pants of the kids – unless they're architecture buffs or particularly devout. Near Braga, however, is the **Citânia de Briteiros**, the remains of an ancient Celtic hill settlement and quite possibly the last stronghold of the Celto-Iberians against the Romans. **Guimarães**, nearby, is the World Heritage–listed cradle of the Portuguese nation and packed with history. Again, it has lots of churches, monuments and museums, which may not be of interest to all kids, but the picture-book castle and balconied houses of the medieval quarter are bound to impress. **Barcelos**, a bit further west, is worth popping into on a Thursday for its famous market; it's also the home of the painted cockerel figurine that's akin to a national symbol.

Viana do Castelo, at the mouth of the Rio Lima, has an excellent sandy beach (reached by a short ferry trip), rococo palaces, Manueline mansions (built with fortunes accrued during the cod boom), a castle and loads of quality places to stay and eat. There's a market on Fridays, breathtaking views from the top of Monte de Santa Luzia, and the town has a fine museum with antique treasure chests. Boat trips run up the river, and there's even an adventure playground on the riverfront. Further upriver is the delightful town of

Ponte de Lima, in the verdant Lima valley. It has an old Roman bridge, a marble-sand beach, cute guesthouses and restaurants and a lively market every second Monday. Things are still done the old-fashioned way here – it's not unusual to see women toting loaves of bread, bundles of shopping and even gigantic bouquets of flowers on their heads. There are also idyllic walking paths in the area – beside the river and along cobbled lanes trellised with vines – and rowboats and canoes can be hired 400m downstream from the main bridge.

STAY

Viana do Castelo, which makes a great base for exploring the Minho region, has plenty of straightforward, friendly *pensãos* including the **Pensão Dolce Vita** (+351 258 824 860; pizzaria.dolcevita@iol.pt; $$). For novelty value, it's hard to beat the hostel on board the **Navio Gil Eannes** (+351 258 821 582;

ABOVE **PORTUGAL'S COAST OFFERS FAMILIES MANY ACTIVITIES, INCLUDING SWIMMING, WINDSURFING AND BOAT RIDES**

www.pousadasjuventude.pt; $), a former hospital ship built for Portuguese fishermen travelling as far afield as Greenland, now docked in Viana. There are dorms and double rooms, all with porthole views. The ship is a museum during the day, which means that guests are locked out – so it's probably best for an overnight adventure rather than a drawn-out stay.

Beautiful Ponte de Lima is awash with posh *pousadas*. The quaint **Cottages at Torre de Refoios** (www.manorhouses.com/mh cottages/refoios.html; $$$) are among the more affordable. They're spectacularly sited beside an ancient fortified tower, close to the river, and have fireplace, kitchenette, television, private garden and pool, and there's even a play area with toys.

ALGARVE

With breathtaking cliffs, scalloped beaches and long sandy islands, the Algarve is a stunner. It may be alarming for adults, what with its hordes of holidaying Brits and towering blocks of timeshare apartments, but it's one of the best places in Portugal for kids. The **Zoomarine** aquatic park at Guia near Albufeira has a captivating dolphin show and swimming pools, while there are **water-slide parks** near Albufeira, Carvoeiro, Lagoa, Guia and Quateira. There are **zoos** at Omega Parque, near Monchique, and Lagos. And at Silves there is an imagination-stirring castle and the wonderful **Fábrica do Inglês**, which has kinetic fountains and a children's playground. Near Alcoutim, the **Parque Mineiro Cova dos Mouros** is an ancient mine where, if kids aren't digging the history, they can ride a donkey. Most resorts run boat trips, and many have little trains. Lagos and Albufeira offer **dolphin-spotting** boat trips.

On either side of the tourism developments that stretch from Lagos to Faro, there are plenty of unspoilt towns and beaches (including those on the sandy offshore islands known as the *ilhas*) and there's some pretty countryside in the Algarve's Serras de Monchique and Caldeirão. Picturesque **Tavira**, at the eastern end of the south coast, is remarkably unspoilt and has elegant old mansions, a river with colourful fishing boats, a garden-edged castle, evocative salt pans (which sometimes attract pink flamingos), a market (held Monday to Saturday), and a gorgeous beach along the Ilha de Tavira.

STAY

Skyscraper apartment buildings line the coast but you should check the location carefully before signing up – often the apartments are too far from the beach for children to walk, and parking near a beach can be a real problem in high season. An alternative to the high-rises is **A Maré** (+351 282 695 165; pt.algarve.co.uk; $$), 15km east of Faro in Salema, with great self-catering apartments overlooking the beach.

Tavira makes the nicest base along the coast, and there are plenty of simple places such as **Pensão Residencial Castelo** (+351 281 320 790; $), which has rooms with balconies and castle views. For something really special check out **Quinta do Caracol** (+351 281 322 475; www.quintadocaracol.com; $$$), a 17th-century farmhouse overlooking a large garden. There are nine separate apartments with kitchenettes, each handsomely designed with traditional Algarve furnishings.

WHEN

Portugal's high season runs from mid-June to mid-September, when temperatures average around 25°C to 30°C and the crowds descend on the Algarve. In July and August, it can get very hot, with the mercury sometimes climbing to over 45°C. Spring and autumn are lovely alternatives, though the water can be a bit nippy. During the winter, the rains arrive, falling most heavily in the north.

HOW

Transport

Most travellers fly into Lisbon or Faro, often by charter flight. It's also possible to arrive by bus or train from Spain or farther afield.

Nationals of EU countries, Brazil and the USA need only their home driving licences. Others (including holders of the UK's old, pre-EU green licences) should bring an International Driving Permit and their home licence. Car rental is usually much cheaper if booked from abroad, though small Portuguese firms can offer good rates. Rental cars are especially at risk of break-ins in larger towns, so don't leave anything of value visible in the car. Fines and tow-aways for illegal parking are common: check signs carefully.

Car seats are required for children up to age four, and can usually be provided by rental car companies (check when booking). Some taxi companies (eg www.rentacar-algarve.co.uk) can provide baby and booster seats if the taxi is prebooked.

Train travel is a great way to get around, especially if you've time to take things slowly.

Shopping & Essentials

It's worth bringing sunhats, sunscreen, sunglasses, sturdy sandals and a phrasebook. Good-quality disposable nappies are available in supermarkets, as is formula. Most shops open from 9.30am to noon and 3pm to 7pm. Banks usually close at 3pm.

Health

Good health care is readily available and for minor illnesses pharmacists can give advice and sell over-the-counter medicines. Most pharmacists speak some English.

Food

You can eat well and cheaply all over Portugal, and it's not unusual for a main dish (or *dose,* portion) to be big enough for two (when in doubt, ask the waiter). For kids, you can often order a *meia dose* (or half-portion), usually at half-price. Side dishes follow strict conventions: fish comes with peeled, boiled potatoes; meat dishes come with chips. Both also come with rice and some lettuce and tomato.

All along the coast, you'll find a wide variety of fresh fish (usually grilled over sizzling hot coals) and paella-like seafood stews. Sardines are everywhere, and even fussy kids may well be converted by these tasty freshly grilled little numbers. *Bacalhau* (dried salt-cod) is served many ways and many children like its bland taste. Nearly every town has a restaurant that serves *frango* (grilled chicken). It's cheap, tasty, and there's usually a takeaway counter where you can get your bird to go.

Markets have a delectable range of seasonal fruits, goat and sheep cheeses, fresh breads, plump olives and other self-catering supplies.

Portuguese cakes, pastries and sweets are spectacular and every village seems to have its own local delicacies, often with names like *papos de anjo* (angel's breasts). Mostly these sweet treats are very rich, with eggs, cheese or nuts as well as a strong dose of sugar. *Pasteis de nata* (custard tarts) are a national treasure, available everywhere, while *pudim flan* (crème caramel) is the standard way to conclude a meal.

ITALY

Yes, it's actually true: Italians love *bambinos,* and they will constantly ply your youngsters with smiles, affection and treats. But friendly locals aside, there's plenty of history – Pompeii, Rome's Colosseum and Forum, and Greek temples in Sicily, to name a few – to capture young imaginations, as well as natural wonders including volcanoes and alpine lakes, not to mention the floating city of Venice. Some children even find basilicas, chapels and art galleries interesting, but many won't share their parents' enthusiasm. For a truly child-friendly visit to Italy, it pays to keep the focus on gelato and the pace low key.

Italy is one of the most expensive destinations in Europe, which can make it prohibitive for visitors from Australia, Asia and even the US. If you're coming from northern Europe, prices won't come as such a shock but be prepared to pay top euro – for accommodation in particular – in Venice and Rome. Hotels and pensions fill up fast, so book in advance to avoid having to trawl the streets with the little ones in tow.

WHAT'S TOPS

- A glimpse of ancient life at Pompeii
- Rome's Colosseum and Forum, which seem even bigger when you're small
- Genoa's giant aquarium
- Learning about the tilt of the leaning tower of Pisa
- A gondola ride in Venice
- Rides and dolphin shows at Gardaland amusement park, near Lake Garda
- A delectable, multicoloured gelato from Rome's San Crispino
- Pedal boats and pony rides at Rome's Villa Borghese
- A boat ride to Capri (or Sicily)
- Christmas nativity scenes at Rome's Piazza Navona

WHERE

Families often find it most fulfilling to base themselves in one or two places and to take day trips from there, although a whistle-stop tour is also possible, especially if you have a car and camp along the way.

Though the cities contain a wealth of cultural attractions, many children will find them unspectacular. Venice, in particular, has extortionate prices, and the novelty of canals and gondolas can wear off very quickly.

Italy's countryside, on the other hand, offers a lot to families. The alpine north has lovely lakes, while the area around **Naples** has stunning coastal scenery and offshore islands. Tuscany has pleasant rolling hills and quaint towns such as **San Gimignano** and **Volterra** – and there are farmhouses to rent aplenty. Off the beaten track, Puglia's **Promontorio del Gargano** is blessed with ancient forests, cheerful fishing villages and sandy beaches backed by sheer white cliffs. Puglia is also famous for its *trulli* – circular whitewashed houses with conical roofs. The islands of **Sardinia** and **Sicily** are destinations in their own right, with fascinating history, captivating towns and spectacular beaches such as Sardinia's Costa del Sud.

Aside from those in Sardinia and Sicily, the cleanest beaches are on **Elba** and in the less-populated areas of the south.

ROME

The multitude of Rome's attractions is overwhelming, and traipsing around with children can be exhausting – so, avoid trying to cram too much into any one day. Between gelato stops the kids are bound to get a buzz out of the Colosseum, Castel Sant'Angelo and the spooky catacombs under Via Appia Antica. If they have really ghoulish tendencies, a trip to the bone display at the Chiesa di Santa Maria della Concezione is in order. Green spaces also offer fun, with Sunday puppet shows on Janiculum Hill and the picnic-worthy Villa Borghese. On the museum front, Explora, designed for the under-12 set, is your best bet. And don't forget to throw some coins into the Trevi Fountain!

SEE

Time elevator (+39 06 977 46 243; www.time-elevator .it; Via dei Snatissimi Apostoli 20; 10.30am-7.30pm) At this multisensory crowd-pleaser, kids can take a 45-minute journey through 3000 years of Roman history. Panoramic screens, flight-simulator technology and surround sound make this a moving experience. Not recommended for the under-fives.

Villa Borghese Bring a picnic and take a walk through this lovely, leafy park northeast of Piazza del Popolo. It has a zoo (the Bioparco), a lake full of ducks, swans and turtles, and fountains. Enter at the Viale delle Belle Arti entrance for pony rides, a minitrain and paddleboats. Bicycles and in-line skates (and kneepads and helmets) can be rented near the Porta Pinciana entrance. There's also little cinema that shows kids' flicks in summer.

STAY

Welrome Hotel (+39 06 478 24 343; www.welrome .it; Via Calatafimi 15; $) The chatty, maternal owner of the Welrome takes huge pride in her small spotless hotel and enthusiastically points out where's good to eat, what's good to do and how best to get there. There are large family rooms with TV, refrigerator, en suite and double-glazing, and wooden cots are provided on request.

Hotel Santa Maria (+39 06 589 46 26; www.hotel santamaria.info; Vicolo del Piede 2; $$) Housed in a converted 17th-century cloister in Trastevere, the Santa Maria is a haven of tranquillity. Its attractive rooms with satellite TV and en suite are set hacienda-style around a central courtyard garden. The friendliness of the staff is the icing on the cake. Bicycles can be borrowed free of charge.

NAPLES, POMPEII & THE AMALFI COAST

Campania has a lot going on: the glamour island of **Capri**, brooding **Mt Vesuvius**, revelatory archaeological sites at **Herculaneum**, **Pompeii** and **Paestum**, the seaside resort of **Sorrento**, the cliff-hanging town of **Positano** and neighbouring **Amalfi** and **Ravello**, and the throbbing city of **Naples** itself (which has great museums and the Edenlandia fun park). This part of the country is jam packed in more ways than one, so be prepared for crowds and traffic snarls in high summer.

STAY

The lively town of Sorrento makes a great base. There are trains to Pompeii, boats to Capri and buses to Positano (from where you can catch a boat back to Sorrento).

Hotel Desiree (+39 081 878 15 63; Via Capo 31b; www.desireehotelsorrento.com; $), a 10-minute walk from the centre of town, has fabulous sea views, cute '50s decor, a TV lounge and an elevator down to a private beach. Some rooms have a balcony and there's a huge rooftop terrace. In Praiano, near Positano, the **Hotel Pensione Continental** (+39 089 87 40 84; www.continental.praiano.it; $) has sparkling rooms and apartments, a pretty garden with lemon and olive trees, and steps leading down to a beach.

THE LAKES
Lombardy's enchanting alpine lakes and towns make it a mellow yet invigorating region for families to explore. The mountain setting of blue-green **Lago di Como** lures visitors from far and wide, and its wiggly western shore is especially pretty. **Lago di Garda** is the most popular of the lakes, with busy but elegant towns and two giant amusement parks – **Gardaland**, the largest in Italy, and **CanevaWorld**, with an aqua park and movie studios. The atmospheric old town of **Malcesine**, south of Riva del Garda, is crowned with a castle and there's a cable car with rotating glass cabins that climbs up nearby Monte Baldo. To escape the throngs go to **Lago d'Orta**; it's surrounded by woodlands, its town of **Orta San Giulio** has cobbled lanes and medieval squares, and you can visit its island, once thought to be inhabited by dragons.

STAY
In Orta San Giulio, on Lago d'Orta, **Piccolo Hotel Olina** (+39 0322 90 55 32; Via Olina 40; www .orta.net/olina; $) has comfy family rooms and apartments and a fine restaurant. **Ostello La Primula** (+39 0344 3 23 56; www.menaggiohostel.com; $), a top-notch hostel on the western shore of Lake Como in Menaggio, has family rooms with en suite, and bike and kayak rentals. Between Lake Como and Lake Lugano, 2km east of Porlezza in Riserva Naturale Lago di Piano, **Camping OK La Rivetta** (+39 0344 7 07 15; www.campingoklarivetta.com; $) is a clean, green and peaceful camping ground with bungalows, a swimming beach, canoe hire, two pools, a playground, and a pinball and video arcade.

ABOVE. CHILDREN CAN LET THEIR IMAGINATIONS LOOSE ON THE ATMOSPHERIC BEACH BENEATH CLIFF-CLINGING POSITANO, ITALY

WHEN

The best period to visit is April to June, when the weather is sunny without being stifling, and the countryside is inundated with wildflowers rather than tourists. In July and August, prices soar and the country broils. In the Alps, winters are long and severe, while elsewhere they range from dull and rainy (in Milan) to mild (in Rome and further south). Sicily has very long summers and short winters – it's usually possible to take a dip in the sea between May and October.

HOW

Transport

Car rental is expensive (as are petrol and *autostrada* tolls), and is best arranged before leaving home. Car seats for infants and children are available from most car-rental agencies, but you should book them in advance. If you don't have an EU licence, you'll need to bring an International Driving Permit as well as your local licence. Driving and parking in big cities can be very stressful, so consider using public transport into and within cities.

Large car ferries travel between the mainland and Sicily and Sardinia, while smaller ferries and hydrofoils run to other islands. There are also ferries between Sardinia and Corsica. Many ferries travel overnight, in which case a cabin is worthwhile.

There are taxi ranks outside train and bus stations and elsewhere, or you can telephone for one. It's illegal for them to stop in the street if hailed, so look out for designated taxi stands. Be warned, though, that taxis can be pricey.

Shopping & Essentials

In fashion-conscious Italy, everyone (kids included) will need at least one set of smart clothes; grimy T-shirts and dusty sandals just don't cut the mustard. Also bring sunscreen and sun hats, and a day pack.

Shops are usually open from 9am to 1pm and 3.30pm to 7.30pm, Monday to Saturday. Pharmacies sell infant formula and disposable nappies, as do most supermarkets.

In cities take precautions against pickpockets (keep valuables in a money belt) and watch out for bag snatchers, especially on public transport and at outdoor cafes and markets.

Health

For emergency treatment, head straight to the *pronto soccorso* (casualty) department of a public hospital. Pharmacists can give valuable advice and dispense over-the-counter medicines for many illnesses.

Noise and air pollution are problems in the major cities, and children are sometimes advised to stay indoors if the air is particularly heavy. Smoking is banned in all closed public places, and many hotels have nonsmoking rooms (ask when you book). Traffic is a real hazard, with cars rarely stopping for pedestrians, even at crossings. Public toilets are usually user-pays, sometimes with an attendant who collects your coins.

Food

Italian children start eating out from a young age, and kids are more than welcome at all eateries. Highchairs are often available and it's perfectly acceptable to order a half-portion (*mezzo piatto*). On the flipside, children are expected to be well behaved – if they start crawling under the table, you'll need to bring them into line.

Italian food is all about regional specialities, though there are some staples that bind the nation. Around Naples, simple tomato and mozzarella pizza reigns supreme, while around Bologna it's all about prosciutto, *parmigiano reggiano* cheese and fresh pasta such as *tagliatelle al ragù* (the original spag bol) and lasagne. Sumptuous Ligurian pesto is served with pasta mixed with a few tiny green beans and new potatoes. In the north, butter replaces olive oil, and rice (usually served as *risotto*) and polenta are often eaten instead of pasta. Sweets, too, are sublime, from the ubiquitous gelato to Sicily's sweet ricotta *cassata*.

Pizza al taglio is a great on-the-run snack, as are *panini* from little grocery stores. Markets everywhere, including Rome's Campo de Fiori, are bursting with inspiring picnic supplies like salami, cheese, olives, bread and fruit.

CROATIA

With over 1100 islands, Croatia is a superb destination for families seeking sun and fun. Boat travel, deep blue water, fragrant pine forests, grand castles and terracotta rooftops all conspire to create a particular brand of paradise. Don't come expecting to find sand – most of the 'beaches' along Croatia's jagged coast consist of slabs of rock sprinkled with naturists – but the waters are sparkling clean, even around large towns.

Croatia is still reasonably inexpensive as a Mediterranean destination, but prices soar in July and August, especially for accommodation. Self-catering apartments often cost little more than a hotel room, so can be a great option for families. Privately run rooms are also often a better bet than hotels, which tend to be sterile and unfriendly. If you are not accosted by room owners on arrival, the local tourist office or travel agency will be able to help. There is usually a 30% discount for stays longer than three nights.

WHAT'S TOPS

- The very evocative Trakošćan Castle
- Bocárski Dom, a park with a great playground, in bustling Zagreb
- Skradinski Buk falls in Krka National Park – the rock pools are great for wading
- Walking the wooden walkways over turquoise pools in Plitvice Lakes National Park
- The strange notes of Zadar's sea organ
- The dramatic walled town of Dubrovnik
- Taking a boat to the monastery on the lake on the island of Mljet
- The International Children's Festival, in Šibenik in mid-July, with puppet shows, street performances, films and music
- The gentle beaches at Lopar, on the island of Rab

WHERE

MAINLAND

Zagreb, a relaxed city with a delightful medieval quarter and a couple of sights that children will enjoy (the Technical Museum and Natural History Museum), is a fine starting point for a tour of Croatia. **Plitvice Lakes National Park**, a wonderland of greenery and waterfalls, has wooden boardwalks (without rails – hang on to those toddlers!) that traverse blue lakes. South on the coast, **Zadar** has old city walls, streets of marble and the world's only sea organ – a system of pipes and whistles that descend into the sea, producing strange, mournful tunes. There's also a swimming area with a small park and a cafe on the coastal promenade off Zvonimira. The pleasant town of **Šibenik** near **Krka National Park,** where you can swim under waterfalls and paddle in rockpools is not far away. Nearby villages such as **Tribunj** (fish ragout with polenta is the local speciality) and medieval **Primošten** are worth a visit. Further south, **Trogir,** with a beautiful old town on an island, has a Venetian cathedral and a fortress. Lively seaside **Split** has the remarkable Diocletian's Palace and a spectacular mountain backdrop. The entire western end of town is a vast, wooded park with beaches below. **Brela,** further south along the Makarska coast, with palm-fringed coves, is a lovely area for kids to swim. Last stop on the mainland is the shimmering walled city of **Dubrovnik,** in a lush agricultural region punctuated by rocky coves. A 10-minute ferry ride whisks you to the forested island of **Lokum,** where there's a botanical garden and family-friendly beaches.

STAY

It might not be everyone's cup of tea, but on the outskirts of Zadar at Borik, the all-inclusive **Funimation** (+385 23 20 66 36; www.falkensteiner.com; Majstora Radovana 7; $$) is a family resort with nicely configured rooms, a water park, an adventure playground and childcare. In the centre of Trogir, the wonderful **Hotel Pašike** (+385 21 88 51 85; www .hotelpasike.com; Sinjska bb 21 220; $$$) occupies an original stone house. For apartments in Trogir, including some beauties in the old town, check **TrogirOnLine** (www.trogir-online .com). There are loads of apartments for rent at Brela. Accommodation in the town of Hvar is tight in summer, so book well ahead for the light, bright **Hotel Croatia** (+46 31 742 400, Majerovica bb; www.hotelcroatia.net; $$). Also on Hvar, in Jelsa, **Pansion Murvica** (+85 21 761 405; www.geocities.com/gurdulic2001; Gradine; $) has sweet studios with a children's bunk room,

and there's an excellent restaurant on site. The loveliest place to stay in Dubrovnik is the cosy **Apartments van Bloemen** (+46 31 323 433; www.karmendu.com; Bandureva 1; $$), almost on top of the ramparts; a cot can be supplied free of charge and extra beds squeezed in for kids. **Villa Adriatica** (www.dubrovnik-online.com/ villa_adriatica) is another fine option, with antique furniture and a spacious terrace overlooking the harbour.

ISLANDS

Croatia's islands are exceedingly beautiful. Most are elongated from northwest to southeast, with high mountains that drop right into the sea.

Krk, in the north, is the country's largest island and though quite touristy is worth visiting for its medieval town and Baška, a superb stretch of pebbly beach. From Baška you can catch a boat to **Rab,** where around Lopar there are fabulous gently sloping sandy beaches fringed by pines – perfect for children. **Hvar,** near Split, is the sunniest and greenest of the Croatian islands and has a stunning interior with lavender fields, peaceful villages and pine-covered slopes. From Hvar water taxis run to the Pakleni islands, where there are shallow, clothing-optional swimming spots off rock ledges. **Korčula** is graced with indented coves, secluded beaches, rolling hills and a walled town that resembles a miniature Dubrovnik. In summer, water taxis at the east harbour take passengers to fine sandy beaches at Lumbarda, nearby, and Orebić on the Pelješac Peninsula. Forest-covered **Mljet,** near Dubrovnik, is one of the Adriatic's most breathtaking islands. A national park occupies the western third of the island and surrounds two saltwater lakes – Malo Jezero and Veliko Jezero – where you can take a boat to a small lake islet and have lunch at a 12th-century Benedictine monastery.

STAY

On Krk, private rooms and apartments can be organised through **Autotrans** (+385 51 222 661; www.autotrans.hr) at the bus station; look for rooms at Baška if you like to be close to the beach. Rab's cheery yellow **Hotel Istra** (+385 51 724134; M de Dominisa bb; www.hotel-istra.hr; $$) has pretty rooms, an outdoor restaurant and can supply a cot on request. On Korčula, **Depolo** (+385 20 711 621; tereza.depolo@du.t-com.hr; $) is a pleasant guesthouse with a tiny beach out the front; it's located close to the old town. Also on Korčula, near the laid-back village of Lumbarda, **Pansion Marinka** (+385 20 712 007; marinka.milina-bire@du.t-com.hr; $) is a working farm and winery that offers rooms and apartments within walking distance of the beach; guests are invited to participate in farm activities (though this is not compulsory!).

WHEN

Most people visit between April and September, when there are warm days and clear skies. It's too cold for swimming in April but accommodation is much cheaper than in high summer. July and August are the most expensive months to visit, and popular places can become unbearably crowded. If you can, wait until September, when temperatures have come down a bit and the hordes have thinned out.

HOW

Transport

Croatia has international airports in Pula, Zagreb, Rijeka, Dubrovnik and Split, which all receive flights from Europe. There are no direct flights from the US to Croatia, but services from Canada are pending. Cheap flights from the UK into nearby Trieste can

ABOVE. TAKE YOUR LITTLIES TO JOIN IN THE LAUGHTER AT A LOCAL FESTIVAL

also be an option. There are trains from neighbouring countries as well as from Germany and Austria, and ferry links with Italy and Slovenia.

If you're solely interested in islands and seaside towns, there's no need for a car – you can travel by ferry along the coast from Rijeka to Dubrovnik, stopping at Split and the islands of Hvar, Korčula and Mljet. There are also ferries that connect other offshore islands with each other and the mainland. Ferry schedules change with the seasons (with fewer boats outside high season) and car ferries to and from Italy and between the islands fill up fast in July and August. Train travel is about 15% cheaper than bus travel and more comfortable, but it is slower and there are no trains along the coast.

Any valid driving licence is sufficient (an International Driving Permit is unnecessary). Travelling by camper van can work very well, as there are camping grounds all over the place. Car-rental companies can provide child seats but don't always manage to supply one that's age-appropriate – check carefully or bring your own. Few taxis have working seatbelts of any kind, let alone car seats.

Shopping & Essentials

Bring rubber shoes or neoprene/plastic sandals for wading along Croatia's rocky coast, as well as high-protection sunscreen. A set of utensils for picnics can come in handy. Strollers and prams will encounter some difficult terrain, including cobbled streets, so instead bring a baby backpack or sling. Buses and trams are also usually too crowded to fit strollers.

Disposable nappies, formula and jars of baby food are easy to find in supermarkets and pharmacies.

Health

Good health care is readily available. Pharmacists can help with minor ailments and point you in the right direction if you need more specialised help.

Breastfeeding in public is uncommon but generally accepted if done discreetly.

Croatia presents few health risks. Ticks can transmit Lyme disease and encephalitis, but the latter is only a risk for those hiking or camping in mountainous forest areas. Sea urchins are present around rocky beaches – wear shoes for protection. Some remote areas still contain landmines, including the Danube region in eastern Slavonia and Krajina. Don't stray into fields or abandoned villages.

Food

It's hard to get a truly bad meal anywhere in Croatia, though there are sharp regional differences. Coastal cuisine reflects its Italian heritage, featuring risotto, pasta and fish (usually grilled with a garlic sauce), while up north you'll find hearty meat and bean dishes.

Signing up for half-board in a family-owned pension is usually cost effective and you're likely to sample some very good home cooking; this scenario doesn't hold true for hotels, however, where the food is likely to taste very institutional.

As in Greece, having a late long lunch in a restaurant as the locals do can work well, especially with the complicated sleep schedules of young children. Other meals can be conjured up from market-bought cheese, ham, bread and fruit. Turkish-style bureks make great on-the-run snacks, as do ćevapčići (spicy meatballs) and ražnjići (shish kebab).

GREECE

Plonk a kid on a beach and their happiness is almost guaranteed. Greece has many charming attributes – scrumptious food, faultless summer weather, warm child-doting people – but it's the constant presence of sparkling Aegean waters, bordered by gorgeous beaches, that makes it so perfect a place to travel with kids.

Ancient ruins might not be a hit with every kid, but children with vivid imaginations or who just love running around will have lots of fun exploring archaeological sites.

Most accommodation is simple and family friendly. Even basic *domatia* (rooms) usually have an en-suite bathroom and a fridge and many also have a kitchenette, often making them a better choice than hotel rooms.

Prices in Greece have been creeping up and it's no longer really a budget destination. Food can be cheap – even seafood if you choose carefully – but room rates are now often higher than in Italy or France.

WHAT'S TOPS

- The frescoed Minoan palace at Knossos, on Crete, guaranteed to stimulate young imaginations
- Delos, a whole island of archaeological treasures
- Ancient Delphi, home of the oracle, where kids will enjoy enquiring about their future
- The colossal monastery topped rock towers of Meteora, with great climbing and hiking
- The medieval ghost town of Mystras in the Peloponnese
- Apokreas, the pre-Lenten Greek Carnival season, with its riot of silly costumes and bawdy songs; on Clean Monday, 40 days before Easter, the entire nation heads to the countryside for picnics and kite-flying
- Orthodox Easter, with candlelit processions, feasting and dancing
- Catching a movie at an outdoor cinema; these pop up everywhere in summer, and movies are usually in English with Greek subtitles

WHERE

Most of the islands are ideal family destinations. Some islands are large and have plenty of scope for exploring over a week or more. Others are small, and if you're not content with lying on the beach all day, you'll probably hanker to jump on a ferry and investigate the island next door. If you want to do a lot of travel by ferry, stick to the **Cyclades**. These compact islands are close together (sometimes only half an hour away) and connected by frequent boats. If you'd like to go to a single island, then **Crete** is the obvious choice. It has some lovely towns, a wild mountainous interior and spectacular beaches. **Thasos**, in the north, has beautiful forests and white-sand beaches and is a good option if you can find a charter flight.

The mainland, too, has plenty to offer, especially if you rent a car. The beautiful **Peloponnese** region is laden with olive and citrus groves and carpeted with wildflowers in spring. Its ancient monuments include **Mycenae**, **Epidavros** and ancient **Olympia**, and there are mysterious mesmerising Byzantine towns such as **Mystras**. There's also an enthralling old rack-and-pinion railway between Diakofto and the mountain resort of Kalavryta. **Halkidiki**, the three-pronged peninsula jutting out east of Thessaloniki, has dense forests and 500km of superb coastline, though much of it is gobbled up by package tourism. If you're prepared to camp, the middle finger, Sithonia, is a fine option. **Thessaloniki** and **Kavala** are vibrant, pretty cities with long colourful histories. They're far less hectic than Athens, making them more enjoyable for visiting families.

CRETE

The island of Crete is a great spot for a family holiday, whether you explore its mountainous interior by car or stay put by the beach. The atmospheric town of **Hania**, which has many pedestrian-only streets, intriguing Venetian architecture and a lively waterfront, makes a lovely base for a few days. The bustling city of **Iraklio** is less prepossessing but has a superb archaeological museum and is close to the captivating palace at **Knossos**. The western end of Crete is less touristy than the east and there are beautiful swathes of soft white sand at laidback **Paleohora** and more remote **Elafonisi** and **Falasana**. **Myrtos**, at the east end of the island, is another great beach option, with a welcoming whitewashed village.

STAY

The atmospheric old Venetian quarter is the best area to stay in Hania. **Pension Eva** (+30 (0)2821 076 706; eva-pension.gr; 1 Theofanous & Zambeliou; $) has a roof garden and kids under six stay for free. **Nostos Hotel** (+30 (0)2821 094 743; www .nostos-hotel.com; $$) occupies a 600-year-old building and has stylish split-level rooms with kitchenettes. Right on the beach in Paleohora, the **Poseidon Hotel** (+30 (0)2823 041 374; $) has

apartments and studios with kitchenettes. In Myrtos, the **Myrtos Hotel** (+30 (0)2842 051 227; www.myrtoshotel.com; $) looks like a concrete white elephant but has clean and comfy rooms with the option of half-board.

CYCLADES

A Cycladic itinerary featuring **Naxos**, **Koufonisia**, the archaeological site of **Delos**, and perhaps **Amorgos**, gives you the best of all worlds. Naxos has a buzzing main town topped with a medieval castle, beautiful villages and some exquisite green back country to explore. Tiny Koufonisia's white sandy beaches are possibly the most beautiful in Greece and it remains relatively undeveloped. The entire magical island of Delos (accessible only as a day trip from Naxos or Mykonos) is a fascinating archaeological site. Laid-back and traditional Amorgos, popular with French travellers, is another good beachy family island. It has plenty of dazzling whitewashed Cycladic architecture and the spectacular Moni Hozoviotissis, an 11th-century monastery that clings to rugged cliffs near the unspoilt town known as Hora.

STAY

By the beach at Aegiali on Amorgos there's a shady **camping ground** (+30 (0)2285 073 500; http://camping-aegiali.amorgos.net; $), and some great apartments at **Lakki Village** (+30 (0)2285 073 253; www.aegialis.com/accommodation/lakki-village .html; $$). On Naxos, try **Hotel Anna** (+30 (0)2285 025 213; hotelannanaxos@yahoo.gr; $) and **Hotel Apollon** (+30 (0)2285 022 468; $), which both have kitchenettes in their rooms, or **Athina Studios** (+30 (0)2285 041 153; www.studiosathina.gr; $$) at Plaka Beach. For houses to rent check out www.naxosisland.com/accommodation .html. On Koufonisia, comfy **Villa Ostria** (44 7808 403 069; $$) has a nice courtyard.

WHEN

There's usually great weather from mid-May until October, with the tourist season at its height in July and August. Think twice before going to Santorini or Mykonos in August – there is quite literally no room to move. In spring or late summer you'll beat the crowds and save a packet on accommodation and car rental. Ferry schedules can be a little erratic in shoulder seasons, but this isn't usually a problem if you keep your itinerary flexible. Winter (November to March) can be very cold and wet, especially in the north (where snow is common), and also sees the closure of many restaurants and hotels and the drastic scaling back of bus and ferry services. Unless you're planning to help with the olive harvest, or are drawn to the tranquillity of empty streets, the warmer months are a better time to visit.

HOW

Transport

Most travellers fly into Athens before catching a ferry or flight to an island. If you are heading to an island, give serious thought to taking a connecting flight straight away and bypassing the city of Athens altogether. Athens is an archetypal Mediterranean city: the chaos, traffic and noise can be overwhelming, especially for kids. If you really want to see Athens, it makes more sense to visit on your way home, after you've been to the islands – especially if you're catching ferries. Ferry travellers should plan to arrive back in Athens at least a day before an international flight, as it's not uncommon for ferries to be cancelled due to inclement weather.

Ferries, including fast catamarans and hydrofoils, leave Athens from the port of Piraeus, which is a quick metro or bus ride from downtown. Although the fast boats will

ABOVE. **BETTER THAN BUILDING BLOCKS: A ROCKY BEACH IN SANTORINI**

get you to your destination twice as fast as a regular ferry, their 'stay seated at all times' requirement means they're not great for young children. Big ferries provide plenty of room for running around and exploring (but also pose some dangers for littlies – probably a good idea to keep them inside unless they are held by a very firm grip). Ferry hopping between various islands can be a lot of fun, but remember this sometimes involves catching a boat at 2am – not a time when most children (or adults for that matter) are at their best. For long journeys, a cabin can be well worthwhile, especially during high season when it's hard to find floor space to sleep on. It's a good idea to bring some snacks, fruit and bottled water with you. For something more substantial, the onboard restaurant usually serves decent, reasonably priced meals that are a better alternative than the greasy pies on offer at the snack bars.

Greeks have a fairly lackadaisical attitude to car restraints – often travelling without seatbelts (even though this is illegal) or with kids on their knees. However, international car-rental firms will usually provide a child car seat free of charge – check this when you make enquiries and remind the company a few days before arrival. If you're travelling in a taxi you'll need to hold any young children (unless you bring your own car seat).

Although bumpy cobblestone streets make backpack baby carriers a good option, a lightweight stroller can also come in handy, particularly in cities or if your child can sometimes nap in it.

Shopping & Essentials

It's worth bringing sunhats, sunscreen, sunglasses, sturdy sandals and walking shoes.

Good-quality disposable nappies are available in supermarkets, as is formula.

Most shops close for a siesta from 2pm to 5pm, then open till 8pm. Almost all are closed on Sunday. Banks are open only in the morning, though some in cities and large towns open 3.30pm to 6.30pm. ATMs are widespread on all but the tiniest islands.

Health

If someone gets sick, head straight to the (probably chronically under-funded) local hospital. Usually you'll see a doctor quickly and this service is free. Pharmacies can dispense medicines that are available only by prescription in many other countries, so for minor ailments the pharmacist should be your first port of call.

Breastfeeding is widely accepted as the usual way to feed a baby, so there's no need to go and hide.

Official public toilets, sometimes with an attendant who hands out leaves of toilet paper for a tip, can occasionally be found in parks. But usually you'll need to duck into a cafe. For some bizarre reason thought to date back to ancient times, Greek plumbing doesn't handle toilet paper very well. You'll need to put used paper in the bin provided.

Food

Greeks love to eat out, whether it's an hours-long feast at a taverna or some snacks to go with an ouzo at the local *kafeneio* (traditional cafe). They also tend to eat late, having lunch after 2pm and dinner around 10pm. That said, tavernas usually open for dinner at 7pm, and in tourist areas may not close at all between lunch and dinner. If the kids need to be in bed early, it can work to have the main meal at lunch and a light snack in the evening. Or you can just let the routine go out the window, since it's nice to eat with the locals. There are usually tavernas right on the beach, which is perfect for families with restless youngsters.

There is almost always a tantalising selection of dishes on offer, and the further away from tourist resorts you are, the more interesting the food will be. In Greece, everyone (including the kids) shares whatever is on the table. This isn't limited to *mezedes* (small dishes for sharing), but these do offer a fun way to sample lots of different things. Dips, feta, calamari, salads, meatballs, roast chicken (often one of the cheapest things on the menu) and even grilled sardines will be gobbled up eagerly. If you have a fuss pot on your hands then turn to the chips, which are usually freshly made and fried in olive oil. Pasta, too, is ubiquitous. Shops stock great supplies for self-catering – it's hard to go wrong with tinned dolmades, olives, fresh tomatoes and cucumber, local cheese, creamy yoghurt, fresh bread and juice. Cheese-and-spinach pies are great for eating on the run. The ice cream is pretty good, too – try the sour cherry and mastic version.

TURKEY

Turkey, where the orient rubs shoulders with Europe, is an intriguing country. The landscape and, indeed, culture is varied, spanning a beautiful bucolic interior, familiar-feeling tourist enclaves along the Aegean and Mediterranean coasts, and remote eastern regions well off the beaten track. Ancient sites aplenty, including Troy, Pergamum, Ephesus and Dalyan, and intricate palaces and mosques evoke a rich history. Natural wonders such as Cappadocia's lunar landscape and Pamukkale's terraced travertine pools are stunners. And, wherever you go, the hospitality of the people, and their wonderfully fragrant cuisine, guarantee a heart-warming, gratifying trip.

Travel in Turkey is not the bargain it used to be. Accommodation prices are climbing steadily, especially in Istanbul and coastal resorts, but meals remain good value and you can eat very cheaply if you self-cater.

WHAT'S TOPS

- The strange fairy chimneys and underground cities of Cappadocia
- A night in one of Safranbolu's Ottoman inns
- A scenic ride on Istanbul's antique tram
- Steaming up, down and across the Bosphorus on a ferry
- Souvenir shopping at Istanbul's Grand Bazaar and Spice Bazaar
- Walking north across Istanbul's Galata Bridge at sunset and dining on a fish sandwich from one of the fishing boats in Eminönü

- A cruise on a *gület* (wooden yacht) along the southern Aegean and western Mediterranean coasts
- The ice-cream city of Kahramanmaraş, where local *salep* (wild orchid root) is the key ingredient of deliciously viscous ice cream

WHERE

Cappadocia, with lunar landscapes, ancient churches and cave dwellings, is one of the most rewarding regions to visit, and one where the impact of tourism has been remarkably restrained. Impeccably preserved Ottoman towns such as **Safranbolu** and

Amasya await you in Central Anatolia. In the northeastern corner of the country, close to Georgia, the scenery turns alpine, with lush green pastures, fir trees and chalets. At **Pamukkale**, there are terraced travertine pools (now off limits), as well as the ruins of the ancient city of **Hierapolis**. The Aegean and Mediterranean coasts are beautiful, with evocative ancient ruins and pretty beaches.

For the very best small hotels, check out www.nisanyan.net.

ISTANBUL

Beguiling Istanbul's heady mix of east and west can be quite intense for children unaccustomed to raucous mopeds, traffic squalls and labyrinthine bazaars – but mostly they'll get as much of a buzz out of it as their parents. After all, the background noise includes delights such as muezzins calling from minarets and the distant sounding of ferry horns. While there aren't all that many attractions designed specifically for children, the awe-inspiring Aya Sofya and Blue Mosque, massive Grand Bazaar (hand-holding obligatory) and fragrant Spice Bazaar, opulent Topkapı Palace, darkly fascinating Basilica Cistern and wildly whirling dervishes will captivate the whole family. The kitsch-coated Miniatürk theme park, which has scale models of the country's most famous landmarks, delights some children, mostly because they can ride on a miniature train.

The city's trams are a quick and efficient way of getting around, and the quaint antique tram that runs from Tünel station to Taksim Square, in particular, is great fun for the kids. A ride on one of the ferries scudding along the Bosphorus is even more enthralling. But remember to walk the streets – this is the key to discovering the city.

SEE

Rahmi M Koç Müzesi (+90 (0)212 369 6600; www.rmk-museum.org.tr; Hasköy Caddesi 27; Hasköy; 10am-5pm Tues-Fri, 10am-7pm Sat & Sun) For those who delight in deconstructing gadgets and pushing buttons on machinery, this museum of transport, communications and industrial stuff is a must. Right on the Golden Horn, it even contains a restored shipyard with moored boats. There's also an outdoor playground with a traditional carousel.

Contemporary Lovers of Mevlana at Sikerci (+90 (0)212 458 8834; Platform 1 Exhibition Hall, Sikerci Railway Station) This version of the whirling dervish *sema* dance is more child friendly than the one at Galata's Mevlevihanesi, and older kids will get a buzz out of the dance, especially if they have read up on it. Remember the dance is a religious ceremony, so kids need to keep still and quiet (no clapping).

STAY

Hotel Empress Zoe (+90 (0)212 518 2504; www.emzoe.com; Adliye Sokak 10, Sultanahmet; $$) Arriving at Empress Zoe is like stepping into a dream. The garden is gorgeous, the wisteria-draped terrace has superb views, and the immaculate rooms have lush Byzantine-inspired decor and hammam-style marble bathrooms. There's a multitude of beautiful suites to choose from, some with private terrace or garden.

Istanbul Holiday Apartments (+90 (0)212 251 8530; www.istanbulholidayapartments.com; cnr Camekar Sokak & Galata Kulesi Sokak, Galata; $$) Tucked in behind Galata Tower, halfway between the rush of Taksim and the tourist sights of Sultanahmet, these apartments have every mod-con, including washing machine and dishwasher, and decor is comfy and contemporary. Some apartments have views of Old Istanbul and the Golden Horn, while others have a private courtyard.

WESTERN MEDITERRANEAN

Turkey's southwestern coast, also known as the **Turquoise Coast**, is dazzlingly beautiful. Unfortunately, the challenge is navigating a path that's reasonably clear of crowds, but it is possible to find serene coastal villages, untrampled archaeological sites, and more than a postage stamp of sand on which to perch. This is prime territory for a four-day cruise on a wooden *gület*, and these usually run from **Fethiye** to **Kale**, or else from **Marmaris** to Fethiye.

One of the nicest things about this region is the mix of history and holiday to be found here – a walk to a sandy beach at laid-back **Olympos** or **Patara** will take you past Lycian tombs and Corinthian temples. Sea-kayaking over the sunken city of **Kekova**, near Kaş, is spectacular. And the eternal flames of the **Chimaera**, leaping out of a mountainside near **Çıralı**, really do bring dragons to mind; make you visit after dark (bring a torch) for optimum atmospheric viewing. Çıralı and Patara beaches are also breeding places for the loggerhead turtle. There are Lycian ruins everywhere, including at **Xanthos**, **Dalyan** and Kale/Demre **(Myra)** – from whence St Nicholas (Santa Claus) hailed.

STAY

Çıralı, a superb beach backed by mountains, makes a great base for a few days or weeks. **Azur Hotel** (+90 (0)242 825 7072; $), a five-minute walk from the beach, has rooms nestled in a lush garden with hammocks swaying between the trees; there are also expanses of green lawn, roaming ducks and rabbits and an adventure playground. **Canada Hotel** (+90 (0)242 825 7233 www.canadahotel.net; $) is another option, and it features a kids' pool and pleasant garden.

In Patara, the **Akay Pension** (+90 (0)242 843 5055; www.pataraakaypension.com; $) has bright rooms with balcony, a comfy Ottoman lounge, a leafy garden and good home-cooked food.

Near the ancient ruins of Phaselis, **Sundance Nature Village** (+90 (0)242 831 4165; www.sundancecamp.com; $) is an idyllic eco hideaway at the end of an arc of beach; bungalows and treehouses are nestled under pines and there's an organic restaurant. Trips with local fishermen and horseback-riding lessons are beach alternatives.

CAPPADOCIA

The lunar landscapes and cave dwellings of Cappadocia fascinate children. The secluded **Soglani Valley**, frescos at the **Göreme Open-Air Museum**, ancient churches of the **Ihlara Valley**, and underground cities at **Derinkuyu** and **Kaymaklı** are all must-sees. Boutique accommodation carved out of the tufa in **Üçhisar**, **Ürgüp** and **Avanos** is the icing.

STAY

The stand-out place to stay in Göreme is the **Kelebek Hotel and Pension** (+90 (0)384 271 2280; www.kelebekhotel.com; $), with atmospheric, beautifully decked out cave and fairy-chimney rooms and suites. In the quiet village of Avanos, **Sofa Hotel** (+90 (0)384 511 5186; www.sofa-hotel.com; $) is a collection of 15 lovingly restored stone houses crammed with kilims, cushions and curios; there's a central courtyard and on-site restaurant. Ürgüp has some spectacular lodgings, including **Kemerli Ev** (+90 (0)384 341 5445; www.kemerliev.com; $$), a restored dervish monastery that epitomises elegance. For something more homely, try the flowery **Hotel Elvan** (+90 (0)384 341 41 91; www.hotelelvan.com; $), where rooms surround a courtyard.

WHEN

Spring (April to June) and autumn (September to October), when temperatures are warm but not stifling, are the best times to visit Istanbul, the Aegean and Mediterranean coasts and Cappadocia. April to September is best for the Black Sea, as the rains abate then. The east is snowy before May and after mid-October. Most tourist-related businesses close in the winter, with the exception of those in Istanbul.

HOW

Transport

Istanbul is the main international air hub, and to reach other Turkish airports you usually have to transit Istanbul. Most people need a 'visa' (really just a stamp in your passport, issued at the point of entry) to enter Turkey, so if you arrive by air you should first join the queue to get the stamp and then join the queue for immigration.

It's also possible to arrive in Turkey by bus or train from neighbouring countries and by boat from the Greek islands, Italy and Northern Cyprus. Relations with some neighbours are tense, and borders are not always open – check before setting out. Also, there are no efficient intercity train services from Western Europe to Istanbul, making rail a slower and more uncomfortable option than bus if you're coming from Greece.

Turkey's intercity bus system is a wonder, with big, modern coaches that run frequently and cheaply. You probably won't need to travel any other way, though domestic flights are increasingly competitive. The rail system is slow and trains are run down, with threadbare carriages and dirty toilets – not a very appealing prospect for family travel!

ABOVE. **CHILDREN CAN EXPERIENCE ISTANBUL FROM ALL THE ANGLES: FROM THE STREETS, THE MOSQUES AND EVEN FROM THE WATER**

DESTINATIONS

Driving in Turkey gives you fantastic freedom to explore but also requires extreme caution. You should practise defensive driving, and avoid driving at night. An International Driving Permit is useful but not required. Renting a car can be quite expensive; shopping around in advance of your trip or going with a smaller local agency will yield the best deals. Rental agencies can usually provide a baby seat on request.

Few taxis have seatbelts, so you'll be holding the baby.

Shopping & Essentials

Bring sunscreen, insect repellent, sturdy walking shoes/sandals, sunhats and a universal sink plug. A headscarf and cover-up clothing must be worn by women when visiting mosques. If you're venturing away from touristy places, a Turkish phrasebook is also likely to come in handy.

Ultrapasteurised milk is sold everywhere, as are nappies, while pharmacies and supermarkets sell formula. Jars of baby food can be hard to find, but hotel and restaurant staff will usually prepare something for a baby or young child.

Shop owners often offer tea when you enter their shop, but you should decline if you don't plan on buying anything. Grocery stores generally open 7am till 7pm daily in tourist areas. Outside tourist areas some shops close at lunchtime and on Sunday.

Health

The standard of healthcare in Turkey is varies from world-class private hospitals in Istanbul and Ankara to depressing state-run clinics in the provinces. It's not uncommon for patients to contract hepatitis during their stay in hospital (or from the dentist) and medical supplies often need to be purchased from the local pharmacy. Investing in very good travel insurance is essential. Pharmacies can give good advice and dispense many medicines that would require a prescription elsewhere.

Most Turkish women breastfeed their babies (discreetly) in public and no one is likely to mind you doing the same.

Drink only bottled or boiled water. Dairy products, including milk, cheese and yoghurt, are safe to consume. Rabies is not unheard of, so don't let your kids near dogs and other mammals. Malaria is present in southeastern Turkey, and sandflies can transmit leishmaniasis. Avoid malarial areas and cover up with insect repellent if sandflies are about. Some vaccinations may be needed, so consult a travel health clinic well before departure.

You'll encounter both pedestal and squat toilets (which may take some practice). Paper is usually provided but not always, so it's a good idea to carry some with you.

Food

Turkey is a foodie's paradise, with herb-laden, spice-dusted delicacies at every turn. Though restaurants aren't always used to kids, almost all are pretty welcoming, and some even have highchairs. The usual practice of sharing whatever goes on the table (especially mezes) means that children can pick and choose from a selection of dishes. Favourites are likely to include dips with freshly baked bread, smoky kebabs, meatballs, tasty soups, *manti* (ravioli), pancakes, yoghurt and *kuru fasulye* (baked beans). *Börek* (small pies), *pides* (pizzas topped with cheese, egg or meat) and döner kebabs are great for snacks and meals on the run. Turkish breakfasts are savoury, with bread, eggs, cucumber, tomatoes, olives and cheese, but there's usually honey or jam to spread on the bread as well. Cereal-eaters aren't catered for, so bring a box with you if that's the usual breakfast staple in your family.

USA & CANADA

USA

Hugely diverse and just plain huge, the United States (US) can cater to virtually any holiday dream. Fancy rounding up cattle on horseback? Building sandcastles next to tropical waters? Eyeing up dinosaur skeletons? Well, you might not, but chances are, your kids do. The US is both easy and safe to travel around and nearly every destination you can think of has child-friendly activities, kid-centred theatres and hands-on science and children's museums. Hotels almost always have family or interconnected rooms and restaurants dole out highchairs and kids' menus. With age-old family attractions like Disneyland, kids' ranger programs at countless national parks, fantastic city parks and that quintessential 'have-a-nice-day' American attitude, it's not surprising that the US is a favourite family destination. Add in a good dose of wildlife and shockingly gorgeous scenery and you've got yourself a dream holiday.

WHAT'S TOPS

- Wobbling on skates across Central Park's pond
- Climbing a spiralling staircase to the top of a Cape Cod lighthouse
- Coming eye-to-eye with snappy crocodiles in the Everglades
- Feeling small next to Arizona's red rocks, as they reach to the sky like giant desert sandcastles
- Snorkelling with candy-coloured parrotfish in Hawaii
- Jumping in the saddle at a Texan dude ranch
- Sliding down the sand dunes on Oregon's coast
- Hugging the world's biggest tree at Sequoia National Park
- Riding a trolley up and down the streets of San Francisco

WHERE

The million-dollar question. If you're after sun and sea but want to avoid the crowds, head for California's northern coast or the Hawaiian Island of Kaua'i. For wilderness,

visit Yellowstone, for quieter woods, Glacier, and for near silence, Alaska. New England offers lovely landscape, small towns and lots of boating, while Texas and the South won't hold your interest forever but do give you the chance to fulfil cowboy dreams and gawk at the Grand Canyon. Cities like New York and Miami are all about living it large.

NEW YORK

Known for its shopping, nightlife and world-class museums, New York isn't commonly seen as a child-friendly destination. But in a city where anything is possible, it's actually quite easy to tailor your visit for a family getaway. Visit the **Statue of Liberty**, soar to the top of the **Empire State Building**, cheer and scoff peanuts at a **Yankees ballgame** and check out the creaking dinosaurs at the **Museum of Natural History**. Visit the progressive **Bronx Zoo** or walk along the boardwalk and sandy beach at **Coney Island**. If your children have a penchant for art, the choices of galleries and museums are endless, and **Broadway** usually has a few shows that are appropriate for children over six. New York is blessed with ample green space, hundreds of delis and cafes, and a public transport system that makes zipping around a breeze. Go on – give your kids a taste of the Big Apple!

SEE

Central Park (+1-212-36-0-3444; www.centralparknyc .org; btwn 57th & 110th St & Fifth Ave & Central Park W) Explore beyond the prominent **zoo** and vintage **carousel** and you'll find lots of hidden gems for kids. Throughout the summer, free afternoon music performances happen at the **Discovery Centre**. Kids (and you) will be bug-eyed at the **Skate Circle** where eclectic roller-skaters from every walk of life perform for the crowd. **A Clearing in the Forest** (Children's Glade & Great Hill; May-Sep) offers free multicultural events for children, from puppets to dance and you'll find **storytelling** throughout the summer at the Hans Christian Andersen statue. At nearby **Conservatory Water**, rent model boats to race over the pond (just like Stuart Little) or strap on skates in the winter.

Children's Museum of the Arts (+1-212-274-0986; www.cmany.org; 782 Lafayette St; $10, 4-6pm Wed pay-as-you-wish; noon-5pm Wed & Fri-Sun, noon-6pm Thu) In addition to temporary exhibits by local and international artists, children's abilities are celebrated through the 2000-strong collection of kids' paintings and drawings from around the world. The Open Art Studio has self-guided stations where kids can get messy with paint, clay, and fabric, or they can participate in Guided Workshops (included in entry fee). Hint: try to encourage small creations that will fit in your luggage!

Hudson River Park Playground (Pier 51, West St at Horatio & Jane) Plonk yourself down on a bench and take in commanding river views or join your kids in the elaborate sprinklers, miniature canal, climbing frames and sand play. There's a separate toddler play area and a resident park ranger. On hot days, the breeze off the river is bliss.

STAY

East Village Bed & Coffee (+1-212-533-4175; www.bedandcoffee.com; 110 Ave C btwn 7th and 8th Sts; $) Run by a creative New Yorker, this artsy place is homey and incredibly reasonable for this neck of the woods. Eleven themed rooms have received lots of TLC. Bathrooms are shared and there's no lift, but the friendly vibe makes it worth it. Rooms on the top two floors are child-proofed, the owner can help find babysitters and there are two parks nearby. Book ahead!

Hotel Beacon (+1-212-787-1100; www.beaconhotel .com; 2130 Broadway; $$) For style united with convenience, this place is tops. Elegantly decorated rooms and one- and two-bedroom suites are all equipped with a mini-kitchenette, plenty of space for playing and tabletops for colouring. Its location on the Upper West Side only adds to its appeal.

NEW ENGLAND

Riddled with tiny harbours, gorgeous coastlines and quaint towns, New England is nothing if not picturesque. Keeping kids interested in the scenery can be challenging but you'll have no problem rousing them if you plan your trip around the beaches, hands-on museums and boat rides. Although one of the country's oldest cities, **Boston** maintains its small-town feel and is easily manageable on foot. **Cape Cod** has more than 640km of shoreline ideal for beachcombing, building sandcastles, biking and exploring dunes. **Rhode Island** is small but jam-packed with festivals and more beaches while the White Mountains of **New Hampshire** are idyllic for skiing and hiking. Drive through countless covered bridges in the rolling countryside of **Vermont** or head out to the rural **Lake Champlain Islands** for a dip in the lakes. In **Maine** teach your kids how to crack open a lobster and head out on whale- and puffin-watching tours.

SEE

Boston Harbor Islands (www.bostonislands.org) are just 16km from downtown Boston. The 34 islands offer 647 hectares of open fields, tidal pools, sandy beaches, woodlands and historic forts. In summer, pack a picnic and enjoy the children's theatre or the walking trails. Several islands have cafes and lifeguard-watched beaches. **Ferries** (adult/child/under 3 years $14/8/free; May-Nov) run from downtown.

Highland Lighthouse (+1-508-487-1121; www.cape codlight.org; Lighthouse Rd, Truro; $4; 10am-5.30pm Jun-Sep) is the Cape's oldest, tallest and brightest lighthouse. Children must be 48in (122cm) tall to scale the 69 steps, followed by a steep ladder into the lantern room. Even if they're not keen on the ladder, just clamouring around inside a genuine lighthouse is exhilarating.

STAY

Falmouth Heights Motor Lodge (+1-508-548-3623; www.falmouthheightsmotel.com; 146 Falmouth Heights Rd; $) may not be flash, but this family-run place is set on 1.8 lush Cape Cod hectares and offers comfy rooms, an outdoor pool, a picnic grove with gas grills, and it's just a short walk from the beach and ferry boats to Martha's Vineyard. A microwave and fridge make life easier, or opt for a full kitchenette and make yourself truly at home. All the rooms are smoke-free and connecting rooms, cots and cribs are all available.

WASHINGTON, DC

Mention monuments and memorials and you'll likely get a glazed over look from your

ABOVE. JUST ADD WATER: PLAN SOME TIME AT THE BEACHES OR LAKES OF MASSACHUSETTS FOR GUARANTEED FUN

kids; thankfully, Washington's got more going on for families. The **National Museum of Natural History** has endless hands-on exhibits while the **National Zoological Park** has everything from beavers to elephants. Few kids won't get a kick out of seeing the rockets, airplanes and moon rocks at the **National Air & Space Museum**, along with regular demonstrations on 'how things fly'. At **Sculpture Park**, wander the lawns to see giant spiders and a bunny-Thinker. And take note: most museums in Washington are free.

Gawk briefly at the **White House** alongside school groups and peace activists and then spend the afternoon at **The Mall**, home to the world's oldest carousel and wide-open spaces that are ideal for picnics and Frisbee-throwing. Also check out the **National Cathedral** where kids can play eye-spy looking for Darth Vader, a pig-tailed girl, a raccoon and an umbrella-toting man on the west tower, commissioned following a children's design competition in the '80s.

FLORIDA

Florida plus kids equals Disney World, right? Not necessarily. At least, Disney doesn't need to swallow your entire holiday. The state's three national parks ensure lots of opportunities to get out and about and, no matter where you go, you're never more than 96km from a beach where you can soak up unending sunshine. Visit the **Keys**, a 200km string of islands with some of the country's best snorkelling opportunities. Here you'll find **Bahia Honda State Park** for warm, shallow water kids can wade in, along with nature trails and water sports. Take wannabe pirates to **Key West**, budding astronauts to the **Kennedy Space Centre**, and marine-biologists to the many **sea life centres**. Consider basing yourself in **Miami** with its

long, sandy downtown beach and kid-friendly museums and eateries. You can always make a side trip to Mickey's.

SEE

Everglades National Park (www.nps.gov/ever) is a subtropical wilderness where you can walk or canoe through brackish water, all the while looking for the beady eyes of crocs and alligators. The Everglades is undoubtedly a holiday highlight and one you can certainly do with small kids in tow. From Miami, head for nearby **Shark Valley** for a shady two-hour tram tour rather than a hike in the heat. A little further south, walk the 0.8km **Anhinga Trail**, a boardwalk over water frequented by bottlenose dolphins and manatees. If you don't get lucky, visit the **Everglades Alligator Farm** (+1-305-247-2628; www.everglades.com; 40351 SW 193 Ave, Homestead; adult/child $19/12; 9am-5.30pm) to hold a baby alligator and take a boat trip into the glades.

Weeki Wachee Springs (+1-352-596-2062; www .weekiwachee.com; 6131 Commercial Way, Weeki Wachee; adult/child $23/16; 10am-4pm) is undeniably kitsch. But if you're going to visit one roadside attraction, little girls will be delighted you chose this one. Opened in 1947, it was once one of the nation's top sights, and glamorous mermaids continue to perform undersea dances in their glass grotto. Afterwards, reminisce about their sequinned tails on a boat ride along the gorgeous Weeki Wachee River or in the waterslide park.

STAY

Loew Miami Beach Hotel (+1-305-604-1601; www.loewshotels.com; 1601 Collins Ave, Miami; $$) has Miami's glamour in its very child-friendly, art deco surrounds. Top views, stylish rooms and a beachside pool are embellished with kid-oriented activities, child-proofing, a games

'SHHHHH!'

~ USA ~

BY KORINA MILLER

Early one summer, I was visiting my sister in New Jersey, just outside New York City. My two-and-a-half-year-old daughter was with me and while my sister was at work, we'd explore on our own. We'd spent one day at a working farm called Fosterfield's, where the staff were dressed like pioneers from the 1800s. Simone loved seeing the pigs roll in mud, she had a go at milking a wooden cow and was truly awed by the opportunity to help one of the 'farmer ladies' find an egg in the hen house. We'd also visited the Crayola Factory in nearby Pennsylvania, where we watched crayons being made and rolled up our sleeves for lots of waxy crafts. So far there had been no shortage of things to do to keep ourselves busy.

On this particular day, we decided to go into the city. I'd travelled with Simone before – she's always very adaptable and loves going to new places and so I imagined that New York would have lots to entertain her. What I hadn't realised was that New York might not be ready for Simone.

We spent the morning living out our somewhat small dreams of the city. Simone was desperate to set eyes on the 'the Big Lady', that giant, green icon in the sea, and so we took a ferry to Staten Island and back. This close encounter was enough to inspire Simone to rename all of her dolls Liberty and to draw nothing but pictures of the statue for the next two months.

I had wanted to wander through Little Italy and past Tiffany's and the Empire State Building and Simone happily came along, marvelling at all of the tall buildings and the 'fancy dressed' people. She pounded those pavements a remarkable amount for a two-year-old, but when the sun beat down its noon-time glare, I was glad to have a stroller for her to ride in. I was also infinitely pleased it was an umbrella stroller that folded up lickety-split and slipped easily into the boot of a yellow cab.

For lunch we took a shuttle to Mars at a space-themed restaurant and were served mammoth portions of slightly stodgy macaroni and cheese by Captain Orion. The look on my daughter's face said, 'Does life get any better?' I suspected it might, because next on the list was the highlight of the day – the Museum of Modern Art.

I should preface by saying that Simone loves modern art galleries. My friends humour me when I tell them this; they seem to think I force Simone in through the doors and then convince myself that she's enjoying it. I mean, what toddler loves Kandinsky? Simone does. In fact, she tends to get more out of some of the more abstract paintings than I do. As I stand gazing on in a bewildered fashion, she'll sigh and say, 'It's a butterfly, Mummy' in a 'what will I do with you?' tone of voice.

So in we went through the revolving doors of MOMA to purchase our rather overpriced tickets. I told myself it was well worth it – Simone was sure to be spellbound by the enormous canvases. I couldn't have been more wrong.

It wasn't that she didn't like them. The problem was that she liked them too much. As we moved from room to room, her excitement escalated. She began to trot ahead of me, standing before a painting and muttering 'Wow – a horse' or 'look Mummy, a flower!' before jogging on to the next image that caught her fancy. Then the jogging turned into a run and the muttering turned into full-scale hollering. I attempted to calm her with low whispers and rules about not running but, not surprisingly, her two-year-old ears didn't hear. 'Shhhhh!', said an obviously unimpressed room attendant in a starched uniform. When Simone continued her enthusiastic tour, he raised an eyebrow and sternly told me that I'd have to get control of her.

We quickly moved to the next room. That's where Simone caught sight of the Lichtenstein. Big, bold cartoon images with 'words, Mummy, words!' She started to dance in front of the canvas, singing a little song about colours in a very loud voice. 'It must have taken a lot of paint to do that one!' she announced to a group of amused onlookers. Nevertheless, a seriously annoyed attendant followed us out of that room and, I suspect, radioed ahead to the next. It was there that we were stopped by a whole squad of starched attendants and

'I mean, what toddler loves Kandinsky? Simone does. In fact, she tends to get more out of some of the more abstract paintings than I do.'

told that we'd be escorted out because we were disturbing the other visitors. 'We're just enjoying the art,' I replied but, not surprisingly, their attendant-ears didn't hear. Twenty minutes after entering, we were back outside on the street.

Any fears that Simone would be scarred for life for having been thrown out of MOMA were quickly banished. We found a fabulous playground in Central Park and our worries were soon forgotten. Now, when she thinks back to that trip, it's the hen house and the Big Lady and Captain Orion that she remembers. And I still take her to galleries. I just head for the free ones instead.

lending library and a family concierge. Bliss. **Bay Harbor Lodge** (+1-305-852-5695; www .bayharborkeylargo.com; 97702 Overseas Hwy; Key Largo; $$) has just 15 bright rooms but this quiet beachside getaway has two-bedroom suites and cottages to fit the whole family. Rooms come equipped with fridges and microwaves and the private patios, paddle boats, kayaks and a BBQ make it hard to leave.

TEXAS

Round 'em up! If you've got kids stompin' for a taste of the Wild West, the vast Lone Star State delivers. Throughout the summer, many small towns and cities host nightly **rodeos** and you can hop in the saddle in countless **dude ranches** around Bandera. Visit **Fort Worth** for the cattle drives at the **Historical Stockyards** and the **National Cowgirls Museum** with interactive exhibits and stars like *Toy Story*'s Jessie. In **Austin**, shriek along with two million Mexican bats taking to the sky each evening and lick your chops at **Salt Lick BBQ** over family portions cooked up on massive pits. Kids can experience launching and life in space at Houston's **NASA Space Centre**. Then head to **Big Bend National Park**, where mountains meet desert, home to mountain lions, bears and reptiles galore. Kids can jump in sand dunes and hot springs and join you on easy trails (but mind the prickly cacti). Y'all have fun, ya hear?

STAY

Dixie Dude Ranch (+1-830-796-7771; www.dixie duderanch.com; Bandera; per day adult/13-16yrs/6-12yrs/ 2-5yrs $135/85/65/45), run by the same family for 100 years, is the real deal: cowboys rounding up cattle and practising for the rodeo. Families love the hayrides, catch-and-release fishing, campfires and fossil hunts. And when the chow bell rings, it's all home-cooked

nosh. Family cabins are rustic and very comfortable. Prices listed include meals, lodging and two rides daily.

ARIZONA

When people think of America's Southwest with its crimson rock formations and big desert sunsets, they're usually thinking of Arizona. Even kids will be wowed by the scenery here. In vibrant **Flagstaff**, check out the **Lowell Observatory** to get up close to that big sky. Take a dip in **Lake Powell's** shimmering waters or rent a houseboat. In Navajo country, ride horseback among **Monument Valley's** flaming rock spires. Kids who are into fossils will love **Petrified Forest National Park**, where logs predate dinosaurs against a **Painted Desert** landscape. Your children will be attempting to recreate its kaleidoscopic skies with crayons for the next month.

And don't forget **Grand Canyon National Park**. If the thought of your child leaning over a mile-high hole in the ground makes you woozy, don't worry – there are lots of ways to visit in a child-friendly way. Hop on the vintage **Grand Canyon Railway** that chugs to the canyon's southern edge, then set out on the **Rim Trail**. Free shuttle buses run between various viewpoints on this trail, the safest section running from Maricopa Point to Pipe Creek Vista. Another option is to visit the western side, where the slightly overpriced but phenomenal glass **Skywalk** is suspended 1220m over the canyon.

PACIFIC COAST

The Pacific Coast, with highways snaking along its sandy coastline, is the ultimate road-trip destination. Drive along **Big Sur** for gob-smacking coastal scenery, forest walks and waterfalls. Stop at **Point Lobos State**

Reserve to look for sea lions and tidal pools of starfish and anemones. At **Yosemite National Park**, an easy, paved trail leads to the stunning **Mirror Lake** and **Yosemite Falls**. Link arms with your kids around the world's largest tree in **Sequoia National Park's** Giant Forest. Further north, the **Oregon Coast** has rugged capes and the largest expanse of coastal dunes in the country, some over 150m (500ft) high, and opportunities for swimming, walking and wildlife watching.

Of course the Pacific Coast is more than the great outdoors – it's also home to some of the country's top cities and child-friendly attractions. While the southern stretch of the coast sees far more sunlight, it also sees more crowds. Surrounding **Los Angeles** are countless amusement parks, including the original **Disneyland** and **Universal Studios**, where you can hang out with friends like *Shrek* and *SpongeBob Square Pants*. Head over to **Santa Monica Pier** to hop on a solar-powered Ferris wheel over a gorgeous stretch of beach. Come face to face with over 3000 animals in the beautifully set **San Diego Zoo**. From **San Francisco**, take a boat over to **Alcatraz** to play cops and robbers. And on a windy day in **Seattle**, listen to the metal tubes singing eerily at **Sound Garden** before checking out the many markets and interactive museums.

It's true – there's just too much to choose from. And with so many of the sights geared for kids, you'll find great family facilities, from hotels to cafes, all along the coast.

SEE

Children's Fairyland (+1-510-452-2259; www .fairyland.org; 699 Bellevue Ave, Oakland; $7 plus $2 for story key; 9am-4pm daily Jun-Sep, Wed-Sun Sep-Nov & mid-Apr–Jun, Fri & Sun Nov–mid-Apr) is ideal for younger children as it's the slow-paced, ecofriendly, story-based 1950s amusement park that inspired Walt to create his Disney. Kids can experience a Wild West town, a pirate ship, Peter Rabbit's garden or Alice's Wonderland, along with gentle rides, farm animals and puppet shows. A short trip from San Francisco, it's a great alternative to bustling, commercial parks and big, scary rides. The lines are short, the crowds are small and children love it.

Zeum (+1-415-820-3320; www.zeum.org; 221 Fourth St, San Francisco; adult/child $10/8; 11am-5pm Tue-Sun mid-June–Sep, 1-5pm Wed-Fri & 11am-5pm Sat & Sun Sep–mid-June) allows you to use clay, cameras and computers to create your own clay-mation DVD; produce and star in your own music video; or design a masterpiece in the digital workshop. Best for kids over five, this place lets their creativity run wild.

Are We There Yet?

Your dream road trip can quickly turn sour with a back seat full of bored kids. Nurture waning attention spans with these tips:

- Play variations of 'I Spy' – something beginning with 'b'; something only Daddy likes; something that rhymes with star…
- Equip kids with a dinner tray, excellent for in-car colouring or doing puzzles
- Bring along favourite music or story CDs
- Have plenty of road snacks and juice boxes on hand
- For more ideas, check out our Games section (p272)

STAY

Farmer's Daughter Hotel (+1-323-937-3930; www.farmersdaughterhotel.com; 115 Fairfax Ave; $$) is a family oasis in the middle of Los Angeles. Wander into the courtyard and you'll find it difficult to remember that you're just down the road from Museum Row and around the corner from Melrose and Beverly. Country-style furnishings (think rocking chairs and rag rugs) matched with urban chic (like high-tech entertainment centres), are rounded off with family-style hospitality. Sunny suites have fully equipped kitchenettes, all bedding is hypoallergenic and all rooms are nonsmoking. And outside your door is Tart, offering home-cooking and fantastic coffees.

ROCKY MOUNTAINS

With big blue skies and snowy mountain peaks, the air seems fresher and the stars seem brighter in America's Rockies. Tumbling through Montana,

Idaho, Wyoming and Colorado, this is a fantastic area to get outside and explore. **Yellowstone**, the country's first national park, offers endless opportunities for hiking, horseback riding, cross-country skiing or even llama-packing. Keep on the lookout for bison, moose, bighorn sheep and bears. Other parks, such as **Glacier** and **Grand Teton**, offer more jagged peaks, trails and wildlife. Bring young moon-walkers to **Craters of the Moon National Monument** to see seas of lava and giant craters. For family-friendly skiing and hiking head for **Sun Valley**, and to **Salmon River** for a rafting adventure. Activities and parks are well equipped for families, with alternative options for younger kids.

ALASKA

Separated from the rest of the country like a long-lost cousin, Alaska has summers that are filled with endless stretches of wildflowers,

CHRISTOPHE TESTI | DREAMSTIME

ABOVE. **EXPERIENCING THE WORLD'S ICONS ANEW: THE GOLDEN GATE BRIDGE, SAN FRANCISCO**

snowy peaks and long empty roads. Its wild beauty is captivating but it's also an expensive destination; getting there is either time-consuming or pricey and accommodation can dig deep into your pocket. Nevertheless, a short trip can be very rewarding and will be easier on your children's attention spans.

The southern tip of Alaska has lots to do and **Juneau** is a great base. Take your kids to **Skagway** where the gold-rush days are continually relived and they can pan for gold or ride the historic narrow-gauge railroad to spectacular **White Pass**. Then hop on a floatplane to **Admiralty Island** to witness brown bears snatching salmon from the sea.

To reach northern Alaska, you need to fly, catch a boat or travel by land through Canada's Yukon Territory. Visit **Kenai Peninsula** to see puffins and sea lions at **Alaska Sealife Center** or to paddle out on family kayaking excursions. For more outdoor wonder, head to **Prince William Sound** for boat tours and marine wildlife, and to **Denali State National Park** for wolves, caribou, dog-mushing and views of **Mt McKinley** (North America's tallest). In **Fairbanks**, kids will be awed by Blue Babe, a 36,000-year-old bison found preserved in permafrost.

At the height of summer, darkness never really falls, making Alaska ideal for camping. Sites are plentiful and well equipped. It's worth considering renting an RV and having your own wheels in Alaska if you really want to explore; public transport is sparse.

HAWAII

Warm, azure water, long sandy beaches, sunshine and all the comforts of home – Hawaii is the perfect destination for tropical family getaways. Drink from coconuts and eat sweet papayas, build sandcastles under a palm tree, take in children's museums and wade in calm waters. While activities like surfing and snorkelling might sound like they're just for big kids, finding options (and even lessons) for younger kids is easy. Hawaiians love *keikis* (children) and show it.

Flung 3220km from the mainland, the Hawaiian Islands are fairly easy to hop between. The most family-friendly options are found on O'ahu, the Big Island, Kaua'i and Maui. On **O'ahu**, visit the **Hanauma Bay Nature Preserve** to see schools of parrotfish in a volcanic ring. For safe swimming, head for **Sans Souci Beach**, which has a lifeguard and outdoor showers, or **Waikiki** for kids' surf and boogie board lessons. The nearby **Ala Moana Park** has a calm lagoon for tots.

On the **Big Island**, don't miss **Onizuka Center for International Astronomy** set high above the clouds. Look through the solar telescopes during the day, or spot star clusters, galaxies and supernovas after 6pm. Wander along the lush, well-marked (and short!) trail at **Akaka Falls State Park** for magnificent waterfall views.

Kids can snorkel in the calm waters of **'Anini Beach** on **Kaua'i**. The can also kayak here along the tranquil **Hanalei River** or swim in the sheltered **Lydgate Beach Park**. On **Maui**, visit **Lahaina** to see the country's largest banyan tree and the **Ocean Centre** for the largest tropical aquarium in the US. Follow the **Wailea Beach Path** for shoreline whale watching or join in at the **Old Lahaina Luau**, with drumming and grass skirts.

Accommodation for every budget is plentiful in Hawaii and it's easy to find somewhere with a kitchenette or guest kitchen. Many restaurants have kids' menus and you can feast on typical American fare, traditional Hawaiian dishes or authentic Asian cuisines. Relax and soak up the *aloha*.

STAY

Ka'anapali Beach Hotel (+1-808-661-0011; www.kbhmaui.com; 2525 Ka'anapali Parkway, Lahaina, Maui; $$) Officially named Hawaii's most Hawaiian hotel, this low-rise complex sits snugly within lush resort grounds. Rooms are dated but comfortable with balconies to enjoy views of the flawless sandy beach. Kids are treated with free hula, lei-making and ukulele lessons and a beach bucket of toys. There's a whale-shaped, shaded pool, nightly music, kids' menus and you can rent a car along with your room.

WHEN

When you go depends primarily on where you go. Summer (June to September) is the most popular time to travel, although cities like New York and Los Angeles can be sweltering and are generally more pleasant in spring or autumn. In winter (November to March), Hawaii and Florida offer tropical holidays while Alaska is frozen and dark and the Rocky Mountains are buried in snow. This is the time to head for ski resorts or the cities, like New York, where you'll find lots of winter diversions.

HOW

Transport

Henry Ford knew what he was doing. America is very much a car culture and, although you can get around by public transport, the distances are long and out of the way places can be difficult to reach. Laws about car/booster seats vary by state, with the most stringent requiring children to be in booster seats until they weigh 36kg (80lb). Rent seats with your vehicle.

Amtrak (www.amtrak.com) runs double-decker trains that connect major cities and are very scenic along the Pacific Coast. It can be good to cover big distances between regions via train then rent a car when you get there.

Shopping & Essentials

Shopping in the US is generally cheap and the choices can be overwhelming. Just making your way down the grocery store's cereal aisle can prove challenging for the indecisive. Rather than pay for extra luggage, buy cheap, reliable umbrella strollers (prams) and all of the nappies (diapers), formula, clothing and toys you could want (and more) once you arrive. Things like organic baby food or allergy-formula may be harder to come by in small-town America; buy it ahead in the city.

Health

Don't leave home without health insurance. Operations and hospital stays can be phenomenally expensive and, with no public health system, the patient foots the bill. Pharmacies are plentiful but you'll often require a prescription for drugs that may be sold over-the-counter at home.

If you've been enjoying the great outdoors in the northeast, check for ticks (which can carry Lyme disease) and protect against mosquitoes which can carry West Nile virus (for updates on affected areas, see diseasemaps.usgs.gov). Avoid wild animals whose bites can cause infection and even rabies, and keep an eye out for large spiders like the black widow and the rare scorpion. These insects aren't deadly but do require immediate medical attention.

Breastfeeding in public is legal in all states, but you'll get more stares (and possibly glares) in mid-American small towns. Be discreet.

Food

At all but the poshest restaurants, you'll find kids' menus and often a bucket of crayons. At roadside diners and chain restaurants, kids' choices are often limited to chicken nuggets and hot dogs and it can feel challenging to get any vegies into your children. Head to markets where you can buy fresh fruit and veg in small quantities. Also opt for family-run restaurants where dishes are often made from scratch and healthier. In cities, you can find cuisine from every corner of the globe. Be forewarned: portions in the US are huge.

CANADA

Rugged Canada captures the imagination with its untamed wilderness, dramatic coastlines and soaring peaks. Canadians are justifiably considered 'outdoorsy' and you'll never be short of ways to indulge in the surroundings. Take your kids on hikes, up gondola lifts or out on a boat. Spot eagles, wolves and black bears, go camping, kayaking or catch a glass-topped train through the Rockies. And when you head back to town, you'll find thriving art scenes, truly multicultural populations, countless kid-geared sights and a laid-back atmosphere that seems to flow across this vast land.

WHAT'S TOPS

- Finding yourself a few feet from an orca on a whale-watching trip
- Slurping Japanese noodles and scoffing Mexican enchiladas in Vancouver or Toronto
- Catching crabs and jumping waves at Long Beach on Vancouver Island
- Feeling the CN Tower sway beneath you from the top observation deck
- Counting mountain peaks and watching for bears and moose in the Rockies
- Scrambling over the colossal rocks at Peggy's Cove
- Being mesmerised by the seaside Celebration of Light, Vancouver's international fireworks competition
- Joining in the winter wonderland – from dog-sledding to snowshoeing to skiing

WHERE

As the world's second-largest country, Canada has a landscape that is as diverse as it is captivating. The east coast has rolling hills, pretty towns and a rocky, lighthouse-dotted coastline. Cities like Halifax and French-speaking Québec have buckets of charm while larger Montréal has a distinctly European feel. Toronto is the country's fastest-paced city with year-round events and festivals, while neighbouring Ottawa is the nation's capital with plenty of red-coated Mounties to prove it. Canada's central plains offer endless miles of fields dotted with tiny communities and Calgary and Edmonton live up to their wild-west reputation. Further west, the Rockies scrape the sky with snowy peaks and adrenaline-packed activities. The west coast has a rugged coastline with long beaches backed by towering forests.

Canada is truly massive. Unless you have a few months to spare, you'll need to focus on one or two areas. A good way to experience the nation's diversity is to head for one of the larger centres – Montréal, Toronto or Vancouver – and take time visiting the surrounding area. From Vancouver you can take in Vancouver Island and Whistler and from Toronto you can head for the lakes or Niagara Falls. Over 75% of Canadians live

DESTINATIONS

It's a Plane...It's a Boat...It's a Seaplane!

Somewhere between a fairground ride and a scene from a James Bond flick, skidding across the water to a halt in a tiny seaplane is undoubtedly thrilling. With phenomenal views over the Gulf Islands, Harbour Air Seaplanes (+1-604-233-3505; www .harbour-air.com; adult/child/under 2yrs $134/67/free) **take off from Vancouver Harbour and land directly in Victoria's Inner Harbour. If you're heading to the island for a day trip, this is the fastest (not to mention most spine-tingling) way to travel. Other options include tours over mountains and glaciers or joining a mail run to tiny coastal and island villages. All flight prices include a carbon offsetting fee.**

within 90km of the US border; venture further north and you'll find a wilderness unlike anything you've experienced before.

VANCOUVER

Vancouver is a wildly popular destination and within five minutes, you'll understand why. Sandwiched between the sea and the mountains, it's possible to build sandcastles, visit the amazing **Science Museum** and go snowboarding within one (albeit long) day. Vancouver has a relaxed vibe; for those used to the crowds and queues in London or New York, it'll seem quiet. With its multiethnic population, you'll find food from every corner of the globe, often with kid-sized portions and wallet-friendly prices. Children are very much a part of this city scene, especially in neighbourhoods like Kitsilano. A short drive away from sights like **Grouse Mountain** (with its breathtaking tram ride, lumberjacks, grizzly bears and snowshoe trails) and **Lighthouse Park** (with picnic areas and endless trails), it's small wonder that Vancouver has a reputation for being 'outdoorsy'.

SEE

Stanley Park (www.vancouver.ca/parks/parks/stanley) To enjoy this park's spectacular scenery and top sights, rent bikes or stroll around the

8.8km seawall; for little legs, hop on the free **shuttle bus** (mid-Jun–mid-Sep) or a horse-drawn **Carriage Ride** (+1-604-681-5115; www.stanleypark .tours.com; adult/child $25/15; Mar-Oct). Kids rule at the popular **Second Beach** with **swimming pool** (+1-604-257-8370; adult/child £6/3; May-Sep). There's also a miniature railway, totem poles, a water park and a farmyard, all paling in comparison to the **Vancouver Aquarium** (+1-604-659-3474; www.vanaqua.org; adult/child $20/12; 9.30am-5pm Sep-Jun, 9.30am-7pm Jul-Aug). Who wouldn't be awed by the whales, caimans and otters?

Capilano Suspension Bridge (+1-604-985-7474; www.capbridge.com; 3735 Capilano Rd; adult/youth/child $28/17/9; 9am-5pm Jan-Mar, extended hrs in summer) Depending on your disposition, skip, crawl or dart across this 137m bridge, dangling 70m above Capilano River. Once on the other side, get a squirrel's eye view of the rainforest in the treetop vantage points joined together by seven more suspension bridges.

STAY

HI Vancouver Downtown (+1-604-684-4565; www.hihostels.ca/vancouverdowntown; 1114 Burnaby St; $) Although it's nothing special to look at, this purpose-built hostel has a five-star location on a quiet residential street, minutes away from Stanley Park, the beach and downtown.

DESTINATIONS

Not surprisingly, it's popular with families. A fully equipped kitchen and laundry make life easier. Rent bikes, join one of many highly recommended tours or quiz the knowledgeable staff for top tips.

Mickey's Kits Beach Chalet (+1-604-739-3342; www.mickeysbandb.com; 2142 W 1st Ave; $) This B&B declares 'we love families' and lives up to its claim. A secluded garden, games, books, cribs and qualified babysitters alongside excellent service, plush bedding and delicious breakfasts leave you entirely content. It's located in funky Kitsilano, just two blocks from a sandy beach a short bus ride to downtown.

VANCOUVER ISLAND

Vancouver Island is like a giant playground. You'll have long days on quiet beaches where you can explore tidal pools and watch for seals and whales offshore. You'll hike through cathedral-like forests with towering trees.

You'll eat ice cream and fish and chips, hang out in warm bakeries that smell of cinnamon and join hundreds of local families at regular festivals and picnics. When it's time to go, you'll be left wondering who had a better time – you or the kids. While the island looks small on the map, it's the size of England; you could easily spend two weeks exploring and still not see it all. Consider making this your sole destination; you don't get more family-friendly than this place.

SEE

Victoria is the capital of British Columbia but it's very slow-paced with a compact downtown that's easy to explore on foot. Exhibits at the **Royal British Columbia Museum** (+1-250-356-7226; www.royalbcmuseum; 675 Belleville St; adult/child $18/12; 9am-6pm Jul–mid-Oct, 9am-5pm mid-Oct–Jun) are often geared for kids – from native masks to life undersea. Hop on a **Harbour Ferry**, tiny tugboats that tour around

ABOVE. **A STUNNING SETTING FOR OUTDOOR ADVENTURE IN THE YOHO NATIONAL PARK, ROCKY MOUNTAINS**

the Inner Harbour, stopping at **Fisherman's Wharf** to wander around (often eccentric) houseboats and to dine on the city's best fish and chips. You'll also find some resident seals here. **Beacon Hill Park** has a petting zoo, a small but fantastic water park, the world's tallest totem pole and endless gardens to explore. Join a whale-watching tour from May to October with **Orca Spirit Adventures** (+1-250-383-8411; www.orcaspirit.com; 146 Kingston St; adult/child $85/59) or **Prince of Whales** (+1-25-383-4884; www.princeofwhales.com; 812 Wharf St; adult/child $95/75) to get up close to these amazing creatures.

If you have a car, head up to **China Beach**. A short walk through old-growth forest brings you to this gorgeous, isolated expanse of beach. A further drive through mountains brings you to **Tofino**. Once a fishing village, then a hippy hangout, it's now an ecotourism destination where you can camp on **Long Beach**, take boat rides to nature reserves and commune with all those big trees.

STAY

Shamrock Suites (+1-250-385-8768; 675 Superior St; $), a renovated family-run motel, is steps away from Beacon Hill Park and the Inner Harbour. Kitchenettes and balconies add to the appeal, as does the excellent service.

Ocean Village Beach Resort (+1-250-725-3755; www.oceanvillageresort.com; 555 Hellesen Dr; $) stands right on the beach's edge. These cedar, arched cabins are equipped with full kitchens and one or two bedrooms. Tranquillity is ensured with no TVs; you can listen to the pounding of the surf instead. Laundry and BBQ facilities and an indoor saltwater pool make it that much more difficult to leave.

THE CANADIAN ROCKIES

Both **Banff** and **Jasper** offer amazing opportunities to get out and stretch your legs – either on skis, in hiking boots or snowshoeing. Lakeside campsites surrounded by forested mountains and gem-coloured glacial lakes would be spell-binding even without the bears, elk and whistling marmots. Both towns are well equipped with hotels, B&Bs, eateries and supplies. And if you're getting much more out of the drive along the staggeringly gorgeous **Icefields Parkway** than your kids are, wake them up for the Athabasca Glacier, a part of the enormous **Columbia Icefield** that reaches down to the road. You can venture out on foot but the thrilling **Snocoach Tours** (+1-877-423-7433; www.brewster.ca; adult/child $26/18; 9am-5pm May-Oct) get you further up the glacier as you rattle and lurch across the ice in huge buses equipped with caterpillar tracks.

TORONTO

At first glance, Toronto might seem all bright lights, big city and you may wonder what you're going to do with tykes in tow. In fact, Toronto is increasingly family-friendly and has the hotels, restaurants and sights to prove it. Ride the glass elevator to the top of the **CN Tower** (553m), the world's highest free-standing structure. Eat peanuts at a **Blue Jays ballgame**, go wild on the rides at **Wonderland** or **Ontario Place** and play at hands-on **Science World**. And don't forget to visit **Niagara Falls** on Toronto's doorstep – a trip on the Maid of the Mist will thrill even the most blasé teenager. Trips to Toronto are planned around the seasons; summer is hot with patio cafes and lakeside fun while winter is bitterly cold but gives you a chance to strap on ice skates.

SEE

Centre Island Chug across the harbour on a ferry boat (+1-416-392-8193; adult/child $7/3;

8am-11pm Apr-Sep) to 240 hectares of laid-back parkland. If your kids aren't yet ready for stomach-churning roller coasters, they'll love **Centreville Amusement Park** (+1-416-203-0405; www.centreisland.ca; day pass adult/child/family $30/21/90, grounds free; 1.30am-8pm daily Jul-Aug, weekends only May & Sep) for its mellow carousel, bumper boats, pony rides and sky gondola. Beyond the grounds, you'll find beaches, cycling paths, a hedge maze and tram tours, along with canoes and paddleboats to explore the island's lagoons. Cafes, restaurants and picnic spots abound.

Royal Ontario Museum (+1-416-586-8000; www .rom.on.ca; 100 Queen's Park; adult/concession/child/under 3yrs $22/19/15/free, half price after 4.30pm Fri; 10am-5.30pm, 10am-9.30pm Fri) Don't tell your child it's a museum and they'll likely think they're in funland. Dinosaur digs, dress-up areas, an active beehive and interactive kiosks will entertain the future palaeontologists and historians in your group. And when they're all out of energy, there's a spacious cafe with organic and locally produced meals.

STAY

Beaconsfield (+1-416-535-3338; www.bbcanada .com/771.html; 38 Beaconsfield Ave; $; Jun-Oct) Located down a quiet street, this eccentric Victorian B&B is filled with murals and creative distractions. Rooms are homely and a full breakfast is served alongside Russian dolls and puzzles to keep small hands and big minds busy. You need to book ahead.

Smiley's B&B (+1-416-203-8599; www.ereld.ca; 4 Dacotah Ave, Ward Island; $$) Treat yourself to a true getaway. With a fully equipped kitchen (including BBQ and basic staples), a DVD player, stereo and miles of bike and foot trails, you'll forget you're only a short ferry hop from downtown. Drop your vehicle and worries in the car park on the mainland, collect some supplies and head to Ward Island. Breakfast is included and dinner is available.

MARITIME PROVINCES

Sprinkled with quaint villages, gingerbread cottages and flashing lighthouses, Canada's far eastern provinces have lots to offer those who enjoy the great outdoors. The enormous moonscape rocks at **Peggy's Cove** are fantastic to scramble over, while hiking or kayaking along the distinctively Scottish **Cape Breton** coast, with views out to passing whale pods, will take your breath away. **Prince Edward Island** has long red-sand beaches where book lovers can re-enact scenes from *Anne of Green Gables* novels. Hopeful captains can climb aboard the *Bluenose* or check out the *Titanic* museum in **Halifax**. And for that end-of-the-earth feeling, ferry over to **Newfoundland** to see icebergs floating off the eastern shore.

WHEN

Canadian weather is notoriously unpredictable, however summer (May to September) generally brings lots of sun and is a great time to visit for outdoor pursuits. The southern west coast rarely gets unpleasantly hot, whereas the rest of the southern regions can be sweltering at the height of summer. In northern Canada, summer comes late – mid-June – and can end as early as September.

Spring (March to May) in Canada's south can be mild and pleasant and autumn (September to October) is generally stunning with spectacular red and orange leaves falling from the trees. Both spring and autumn are quieter with fewer crowds and lower prices.

Winter on the southern west coast is damp while the rest of the country is blanketed in snow and temperatures can drop well below

DESTINATIONS

So You Speak Canadian, Eh?

Canadians sure are friendly. But sometimes you may be baffled as to what they're talking about. Here are a few Canadianisms to help you and your kids converse:

- beavertail – deep-fried pastry made to look like a tail
- Canuck – slang for a Canadian
- chesterfield – sofa or couch
- click – slang for kilometre
- kitty corner – the corner diagonally opposite
- loonie/toonie – slang for the one-/two-dollar coin
- pop – soda pop or soft drinks
- skidoo – snowmobile
- toboggan – narrow sled that is curled upwards at the front
- toque – knitted winter hat

freezing (think -40ºC). At this time of year, ski resorts offer the main outdoor pursuits while many city centres have giant, colourful, winter carnivals.

HOW

Transport
The easiest way to get around Canada is to rent a car. Car seats are mandatory for children under 36kg (approximately eight years old).

Winter driving can be treacherous with ice and snow, and the resulting potholes often mean you'll be held up with road works in summer. Check www.caa.ca for tips on winter driving and www.tc.gc.ca/road for current road conditions and road works. Speed limits are slow in Canada and tickets for speeding are handed out readily.

You can bus around and across Canada but you'll miss many of the excellent side trips and smaller towns and sights. You can also get hop-on, hop-off train tickets for the Canadian railway, a line steeped in history and offering panoramic views. Kids (and parents) may find it a little long, but a short

stretch (particularly through the Rockies) can be breathtaking.

Shopping & Essentials
In city centres and towns you'll find everything you need – from formula to nappies, soy milk to medicine – so pack light. Rain gear is essential all year and in winter you'll need thermal everything; if you don't already own it, pick it up once you arrive. Bug spray is vital from spring to autumn and sunscreen in summer; it's easy to burn on the beaches, even if it's not very hot. In remote towns it may be difficult to find more-unusual food or health products (like allergy formula or holistic medicine). Campgrounds are often located away from towns so bring all supplies.

Nappy-changing facilities are available in most cafes, restaurants, sights and malls.

Health
The majority of health risks you'll encounter will be linked to outdoor activities. Always pay close attention to warnings and age restrictions on activities, hiking routes and ski runs. If you're camping, ensure kids know their boundaries; it is very possible to get lost

in the forest and bear and cougar attacks on small children do happen. Hypothermia is a danger in winter; keep warm.

While Canada has a fantastic public health-care system, it's not available to non-residents. Make sure you have insurance. Check for ticks after exploring outside as they can carry Lyme disease. West Nile virus is passed by mosquitoes and can bring on mild flu-like systems and, rarely, more severe illness. Cover up, wear repellent and check www.westnilevirus.gc.ca for a weekly monitor between May and October.

While breastfeeding is generally accepted in public, locals are usually very discreet. In smaller, remote towns you may get some funny looks.

Food

Canadian cuisine is a rich blend of dishes from around the world and the past decade has seen an increase in innovative cooking that's brought lip-smacking results. On both coasts you'll be spoiled with fresh seafood, while vast expanses of farmland bring thick steaks, plenty of chicken, sausage and fresh vegetables. You can also try hickory-smoked fish, buffalo burgers and quintessential Canadian cheddar and maple syrup. Baking is a highlight across the country, generally with a good dose of cinnamon. British Columbia's warm, dry interior is ideal for fruit – in summer you'll find roadside stalls selling cherries, peaches and nectarines. When you head north and in small, prairie towns you'll find fewer fresh salads and more meat-and-two-veg type meals.

Children are welcomed at all but the fanciest restaurants. If the children's menu looks vegie-less, ask for a half-portion of something from the main menu. Highchairs are normally available and you'll often find crayons and baskets of toys.

ABOVE. **VENTURE OUT ONTO THE COLUMBIA ICEFIELD, ALBERTA**

ON TREVOR'S TRAIL

~ USA ~

BY MARK LIGHTBODY

Our daughter, Ava, was going to camp for a week so we decided it was a good opportunity to do something worthwhile with our son, Trevor. At 14, he was pretty hard to impress and didn't seem overly enthusiastic about the plan Colleen and I had hatched. Or at least it appeared that way. At his age true feelings and outward manifestations are not always in sync.

We wanted to do something alone with him that we couldn't do with his younger sister, something suited to his age and a challenge. We decided on hiking peaks in the White Mountains of New Hampshire. It was an area Colleen and I knew something about from a visit many, pre-child years ago.

After sketching a plan, we showed Trevor the details, looked at maps and listed our mutual equipment and supply needs. We had him select his own clothes and personal supplies, and then divided up the gear. With the packs all loaded Trevor's was heaviest. All he said was 'No sweat'. Colleen and I realised we'd hit a new phase and it held promise. Forget sherpas.

The park warden recommended arriving before 9am so we got up at 4am (Trev loved that!) and drove from Montreal. We breezed through customs and made the camping ground in time to grab one of the few remaining sites.

With chores shared and completed, we tuned up the legs and lungs on a short trail. Later around a quick campfire we joked about tomorrow's adventure. Being alone with one child totally changes the family dynamic and we all enjoyed each other's company and a chance to talk. The absence of the usual bickering and teasing all parents of siblings know, wasn't missed.

With morning came the disheartening patter of rain on taut nylon. I beelined to the lodge for the latest weather service bulletin only to read rain and relentless heavy cloud for the next million days with a chance of something slightly better for the next day only. We all thought briefly (but silently) of quitting but headed for the trail head in the drizzle.

Totally alone we soon discovered this was no manicured path. Aside from the steepness, the muddy trail was endlessly twisted, strewn with rocks of every size and cris-crossed with roots and stumps. Impressively, Trevor dug in. We climbed for hours, stopping regularly to peel off more clothes. We couldn't tell if the clinging wetness was sweat or rain. By mid-afternoon we arrived at the camping area. Stumbling across the slippery rocks to the wooden tent platforms dispersed amongst the trees was like entering a magical world. Trevor picked up on it right away saying, 'It's like the land of the gnomes.' Dripping tree branches hung down, a smiling, straggly-haired munchkin-hiker ambled by and two women swaying in hammocks said, with strong French accents, 'You made it, there are empty platforms further along. Pick one you like.'

As we pitched camp, a lanky, humorous webmaster from Boston strolled up and started chatting, informing us that his stove had died, what that had done to his dinner and what his plans were. Trevor was amazed at the friendliness and camaraderie.

The next morning I stuck my head out of the tent and couldn't see a thing. At first I thought 'My God, the fog's thick,' but then realised that my head was in the clouds. The idea was to hike to the summit and walk along the ridge to some of the other peaks at about 5000 feet. After several hours ending in almost blindly crawling over massive boulders, we reached the tree line and open ridges.

Visibility was nil and the wind so strong it literally nearly blew us over. We found an outcrop to hunch behind out of the wind where we could have lunch. We just got the daypack open when the entire world seemed to brighten. We looked up and a patch of sky opened as though it were a window. The scene took our breath away. There were forests, valleys and mountains as far as the eye could see. In an instant, the window slammed and the clouds folded in on themselves again. Suddenly, the same thing happened again behind us. Loud involuntary oohs and ahhs erupted from our mouths. The same process occurred over and over – our euphoria and jubilation increasing each time. Within

'With the packs all loaded Trevor's was heaviest. All he said was 'No sweat'. Colleen and I realised we'd hit a new phase and it held promise. Forget sherpas.'

10 minutes the entire sky had cleared, the clouds had lifted as if by drawstring and we could see perhaps 50 miles in each direction. We whooped and patted each other on the back, and heard others along the ridge also shrieking with delight. All of us were sharing something we knew was special and well earned. Within minutes various adults joined us tucking into their food bags. Teenagers in North America generally do not get much respect and are not often spoken to, rarely as equals. Here with the incredible scene around us and a collective sense of exhilaration Trevor was greeted, asked questions and treated like a peer.

Days later Trevor led the entire way down. My knees hurt, Colleen's back ached. We stopped for a snack once and that was the last we saw of him until the parking lot. Sprawled out on the grass, he looked tired but happy, healthy and pleased with himself. That look alone was worth the trip for me.

AUSTRALASIA

AUSTRALIA

Koalas, kangaroos, fairy penguins, tropical fish, red deserts, rainforests and golden beaches collude to create an alluring picture for family travellers. The clichéd images of the wide brown land do hold true, but there's a lot going on besides. Bustling, cosmopolitan cities with expansive parks might not seem exotic but they're where most Aussies live and are at the core of the Australian experience.

Travel in Australia is easy, thanks to a well-developed tourism industry. And once you get past the airfares, Australia is an economical destination for those coming from Europe and North America. Transport will be your biggest cost, so it can pay to focus on just one or two areas of the continent. Children can be inexpensively satisfied with beach visits and camping trips.

Travel times in remote areas and for transcontinental trips can be as vast as the landscape, so think carefully about what you want to see and how you're going to get there.

WHAT'S TOPS

- A tour of the Cadbury Chocolate Factory in Hobart, Tasmania
- A ferry ride across Sydney Harbour to Taronga Zoo
- The Crocodile Hunter's Australia Zoo, on Queensland's Sunshine Coast
- A walk to the perfect curve of Tasmania's Wineglass Bay
- The beaches and boulders of Wilsons Promontory National Park in Victoria
- Snorkelling on the Great Barrier Reef
- Queensland's Daintree Rainforest
- A leisurely drive along Victoria's Great Ocean Road, with a platypus-viewing canoe trip at Apollo Bay
- Joining the crowds to watch a game of Aussie Rules footy at Melbourne's MCG

WHERE

Most Australians live on the coast, and you could easily spend a month or more meandering up the east coast to the **Great Barrier Reef**, stopping at gorgeous beaches, lively towns and pulsing cities. **Melbourne**, **Sydney** and **Brisbane** all have plenty to offer, from verdant parks and ferry rides to fabulous museums, aquariums and markets.

Perth is another great city, with some of the country's best beaches (Cottesloe is perfect for children), riveting coastal scenery to the south and boat rides to Rottnest Island to see quokkas – little furry animals found nowhere else. The adventurous may visit the northern city of **Darwin**, jumping-off point for the untouched wildlife zone of **Kakadu**, where you can take fascinating wetland tours that will enthral the whole family.

The **Red Centre** presents a completely different experience, including encounters with indigenous owners, vast expanses of desert, fascinating outcrops such as Uluru and the Olgas, and, most importantly for kids, camel rides.

South Australia's **Kangaroo Island** is the place to really get away from it all. There's not a lot going on (thank goodness) – except pristine beaches, an abundance of wildlife and cute seaside shacks.

Tasmania is a beacon for those interested in hiking, wilderness and food, and getting there can involve an overnight ferry ride that's an adventure in itself.

SYDNEY

There's almost too much to do in Sydney – a world-class zoo, an amazing aquarium (the genuine real-life home of Nemo), stunning beaches and iconic architecture like the Opera House and the Sydney Harbour Bridge to gawp at. Even the public transport has an exciting edge to it – catching a ferry or the monorail is an event in itself. And the city's balmy weather year-round means that sightseeing is a joy even in winter. Exotic eateries and luxe yet kid-friendly hotels round out the picture, making this a top spot for a family holiday.

SEE

Powerhouse Museum (+61 (0)2 9217 0111; www.powerhousemuseum.com; 500 Harris St, Ultimo; 10am-5pm) Covering all aspects of design and technology, this cutting-edge museum has engaging exhibits on everything from costume jewellery to space capsules. There are interactive discovery spaces specially designed for kids as well as a play space called the Pocket, with dress-ups, storytelling, performances, craft activities and more.

Susannah Place (+61 (0)2 9241 1893; www.hht.net .au/museums/susannah_place_museum; 58-64 Gloucester St, The Rocks, 10am-5pm weekends & school holidays, daily in Jan) This row of tiny houses dating from 1844 gives a fascinating insight into the lives of the working-class families who once called them home. Fans of domestic archaeology will love discovering remnants of wallpaper and other 'home improvements'. Make sure you stop at the cute corner shop for some mixed lollies.

STAY

Altamont Hotel (+61 (0)2 9360 6000; www.altamont .com.au; 207 Darlinghurst Rd, Darlinghurst; $$) This sleek boutique hotel has bunks for the kids, roomy bathrooms with big tub, cable TV, a rustic rooftop garden and a friendly dog named Slick. It's a hop, skip and jump from the Cross, and buses run past the front door. Rates are discounted for stays of a week or more.

Price Guide

$** budget **$$** midrange **$$$ top end

Dive Hotel (+61 (0)2 9665 5538; www.divehotel.com. au; 234 Arden St, Coogee; $$) This swanky hotel on Coogee Beach has a relaxed beach-house feel that's perfect for families. Rooms have kitchenette, cable TV, CD player and en suite, and there's a groovy communal eat-in kitchen that extends outside to a bamboo-bordered courtyard. There are three seaside swimming pools in walking distance, including Wylie's Baths with its schools of fish. A stunning cliff-top trail leads to Bronte and Bondi beaches.

BYRON BAY, GOLD COAST & SUNSHINE COAST

The north coast of New South Wales is home to unbroken beaches and resort towns, most famously **Byron Bay**, while the hinterlands mix luxuriant rainforest and alternative lifestyles. Once you hit Queensland's **Gold Coast** it's more about glitz, fun parks and skyscraper condos. Prime attractions are Dreamworld (which includes Wiggles World) and Sea World. Beyond Brisbane, the beaches continue along the **Sunshine Coast** to the upmarket town of **Noosa**, which has its own pint-sized coastal national park where you're guaranteed to see koalas. Other family-friendly spots include **Mooloolaba** and **Caloundra**, with seven lovely beaches, and sights such as the Big Pineapple and the Ginger Farm. Inland and straddling the Queensland and New South Wales border is the lush World Heritage–listed **Lamington National Park**.

STAY

At Byron Bay's Belongil Beach, **Belongil Beachouse** (+61 (0)2 6685 7868; www

.belongilbeachouse.com; Childe St; $) has airy family rooms and self-contained cottages nestled in private gardens as well as a cafe and relaxation spa (perfect for stressed parents).

On the Gold Coast, **Trickett Gardens Holiday Inn** (+61 (0)7 5539 0988; www.trickettgardens.com.au; 24-30 Trickett St, Surfers Paradise; $) is a low-rise block, with a central location and comfy self-contained units.

There are lots of great spots along the Sunshine Coast. In Noosa, **Terrapin** (+61 (0)7 5449 8770; www.terrapin.com.au; 15 The Cockleshell, Noosaville; $) has two-storey self-contained townhouses surrounded by gardens. In Caloundra, **Dicky Beach Family Holiday Park** (+61 (0)7 5491 3342; www.dicky.com.au; 4 Beerburrum St; $) is a well-ordered park right on the beachfront with immaculate cabins, playground, games rooms, plenty of green grass, and tree cover over tent sites.

GREAT BARRIER REEF

This spectacular kaleidoscope of living colour stretches along the Queensland seaboard from just south of the tropic of Capricorn to Torres Strait, south of New Guinea.

Cairns is the most popular jumping-off point for an excursion to the reef, and as such is overtrafficked; it also has no beach, though there is a swimming lagoon that's popular with kids. For beautiful beaches, you're better off heading to **Mission Beach**, **Port Douglas** or nearby **Cape Tribulation**, where the magical Daintree Rainforest meets the reef. Or you can go straight to an island and explore from there. **Heron Island**, **Hamilton Island** and **Great Keppel Island** are just some of the possibilities.

Box jellyfish are a serious problem on the coast north of Rockhampton between October and April, but the Great Barrier Reef itself manages to elude them.

STAY

Hamilton Island (+61 (0)7 4946 9999; www.hamiltonisland.com.au; $$) is extremely popular with families, partly due to direct flights from Melbourne and Sydney. There's a huge range of activities for the whole family (including a kids' club) and good self-catering accommodation. **Great Keppel Island Holiday Village** (+61 (0)7 4939 8655; www.gkiholidayvillage.com.au; $) is a laid-back place with basic cabins and large beach houses.

Back on the mainland at Mission Beach, **Beachcomber Coconut Caravan Village** (+61 (0)7 4068 8129; www.beachcombercoconut.com.au; $) has bargain beachfront cabins that sleep up to five, and loads of amenities.

In Cairns, **Northern Greenhouse** (+61 (0)3 9525 4028; www.deluxeapartments.com.au; 117 Grafton St; $) has centrally located and bright apartments for families. The **Cape Trib Beach House** (+61 (0)7 4098 0030; www.capetribbeach.com.au; $) has rainforest rooms and cabins right on the beach, and organises activities such as snorkelling, horseback riding and kayaking.

TASMANIA

Tassie may be an island off an island at the bottom of the world, but its compact size, friendly locals, intriguing history and diverse, enticing landscapes make it an outstanding family destination. Hire a car (or bring your own on the ferry from Melbourne) and explore natural vistas such as **Wineglass Bay** on the Freycinet Peninsula and majestic **Cradle Mountain**, both of which have short walks suitable for kids. The hilly little city of **Hobart** has a quaint waterfront with Georgian warehouses and floating fish 'n' chip stalls, a hippy market, a chocolate factory and its very own, oft-snowcapped mountain. Tasmania is also one of the best places in the world to sample exquisite food at its source: cheeses, apples, leatherwood honey and oysters can all be tasted on the farms that produce them. Make sure your itinerary features **Bruny Island**, which has beaut beaches, fairy penguins and virtually nil traffic, and **Bicheno**, where there are coastal rock pools and a wildlife park with a walk-through aviary.

STAY

In Hobart, **Edinburgh Gallery** (+61 (0)3 6224 9229; www.artaccom.com.au; 211 Macquarie St; $) is a comfy boutique hotel with a roomy family suite.

Adventure Bay Holiday Village (+61 (0)3 6293 2096; www.adventurebayholidayvillage.com.au; Main Rd, Adventure Bay; $) on Bruny Island has exceedingly quaint cabins and cottages and pretty grounds filled with wildlife. In Bicheno, **Diamond Island** (+61 (0)3 6375 0100; www.diamondisland.com.au; $$) has updated units with ocean views and a penguin colony at the bottom of the garden.

Cradle Mountain Lodge (+61 (0)2 8296 8010; www.cradlemountainlodge.com.au; $$$) has comfy family cabins in the forest, with nearby walking trails and wildlife at your door.

WHEN

In Australia it's high summer from December to February, when the weather and longer daylight hours are ideal for swimming and other outdoor activities across much of the country. Winter is from June to August, with lower temperatures the further south you travel. But this is the best time up north, where the humid wet season has subsided and the temperature is very agreeable (the 'dry' roughly lasts from April to September, and the 'wet' from October to March, with the heaviest rain from January on). Summer in the tropics brings box jellyfish which make

ABOVE. **A VISIT TO THE SPECTACULAR TARONGA ZOO IN SYDNEY WILL GIVE YOU GREAT CITY VIEWS**

the beaches unswimmable. Accommodation can be pricier and harder to come by over the summer months, especially during school holidays (mid-December to late January), though the reverse is true in the tropics, where the winter dry season is high season.

HOW

Transport
Australia is a long way from just about everywhere, and getting there usually means a long-haul flight. That 'over the horizon' feeling doesn't stop once you arrive either – the distances between cities (and opposing coastlines) can be vast, requiring a minimum of an hour in the air or several days of driving.

Travelling with your own car is the easiest way to explore, but flying is essential if you're covering long distances. Car hire is relatively inexpensive, and can be cheaper if you rent with a local firm. Major hire-car companies will supply and fit car seats, usually for a small fee.

Trains are an option for intercity routes, and there are some legendary rail services – notably the *Indian Pacific*, from the east coast to Perth, and the *Ghan*, from Adelaide to Darwin. Trains are certainly much more comfortable than buses, but can be as expensive as flying. See www.trainways.com.au for more information.

A car ferry runs between Melbourne and Devonport, in Tasmania.

You can use your home country's driving licence in Australia, as long as it's in English and carries your photograph.

Shopping & Essentials
Necessities like sunscreen, sunglasses, insect repellent and hats are widely available in Australia, as are baby food, formula and disposable nappies.

Covered markets in the cities are the most exciting places to shop for food and you'll find everything – biodynamic lamb, fresh snapper, organic vegetables and handmade cheeses. But supermarkets are also well stocked and many now have organic sections.

Many motels and the better-equipped caravan parks have playgrounds and pools, and can supply cots and baby baths – and motels may also have children's DVDs and child-minding services. Top-end hotels are well versed in the needs of guests with children, but B&Bs often market themselves as sanctuaries from all things child-related.

Health
Australia has world-class medical services and facilities.

The country's remarkable profusion of dangerous creatures – poisonous snakes and spiders, sharks, crocodiles and the world's deadliest creature, the box jellyfish (or 'stinger') – can be alarming. But you're unlikely to see any of these creatures in the wild, much less be attacked by them, and hospitals have antivenom on hand for all common snake and spider bites.

Surf beaches can be dangerous places to swim because of undertows (or 'rips'). Swim between the flags, if there are any, and talk to locals before taking that dip. The most popular beaches have flags and surf lifesavers watching for anyone in trouble.

Australians have a relaxed attitude about breastfeeding and nappy-changing in public, and shopping centres usually have rooms where parents can feed their baby or change nappies.

Food
Nothing compares to Australia's seafood, hauled from some of the purest waters you'll find anywhere, and usually cooked with care. Fruit and veg, too, are plentiful and delicious and range from mangoes to strawberries and

THROUGH THE OUTBACK & BEYOND

~ AUSTRALIA ~

BY ROSIE WAITT

Baby Harry was only six weeks old when we set off for the second stage of our journey around Australia, from Albany in Western Australia, up the west coast to Darwin.

There were five of us now and suddenly a lot more gear to squeeze into our camper van and trailer; a portable carrycot (although mostly Harry slept between us), a lightweight pram, another car seat, nappies and clothes. After much discussion we included a fold-up rocker which turned out to be a real blessing because he loved it and would rock contentedly outside, surrounded by a mosquito net hung from the van's awning.

It was great to be back in our van and experience once again the joy of leaving, and that wonderful but addictive feeling of freedom that comes with movement. Singing along to nursery rhyme tapes, we made our way slowly up the coast through Kalbarri and Carnarvon, towards the Pilbara region, where the normally harsh landscape was transformed by swathes of wildflowers.

Once again we were surprised at how quickly Nikita, four, and Freda, two, adapted to life on the road. For them it was simple; everywhere was home. With few toys and rare access to television, they had become self-reliant and imaginative, learning to find fun and interest in everything around them. And now baby Harry was thriving too. Having spent most of my pregnancy on the road, the rhythm of the engine was like a lullaby for him so driving was easy. He was totally breastfed too, so we had no worries about sterilising bottles or plates.

But easy baby or not, with the new family dynamics it was difficult at first to rediscover the smooth pattern our previous journey had taken. The broken nights were taking their toll on Tim and me, and now there were three little voices demanding attention. Some days were so heavily punctuated with feed stops, burp stops and (with Freda just out of nappies) toilet stops, that it felt like we would never get anywhere.

Flies were a constant problem. Nikita would regularly become hysterical, start screaming and then swallow a few. We resorted to fly nets and found some relief. Inside the van we put a net over Harry's seat, but outside was a problem. As a deterrent I strung bright beads together into lots of strips and hung them from the top of his pram. Not only did they keep the flies away but the sound, the movement and the colours entranced him.

Then in the mining town of Tom Price, we came under attack from giant kamikaze mosquitoes and tiny midges that flew right through the netting on our windows and stung us all over. It wasn't possible to use insecticides or burn coils because our eldest child had multiple allergies and was sensitive to chemicals. Tea tree antiseptic cream at least temporarily stopped the itching and ensured the bites didn't get infected. But our only defence against the bugs was to shut the windows and cover up. So we were all hot, stroppy and scratchy, and I was starting to wonder if it was all worth it.

Of course it was. My mood quickly passed as we drove into Karijini National Park and set up camp among the wildflowers and the fine red dust, that was like ochre and stained everything it came into contact with. Not surprisingly the children quickly discovered the amazing nature of the soil we were camped on. Just add water! Their clothes would never be the same again.

Coincidentally we arrived in Broome in time for the annual Shinju Matsuri festival, or Festival of the Pearl; a celebration of ethnic diversity. We stayed for a week, watching national dances, fire eaters, jugglers and wandered around markets filled with local crafts and exotic foods. At the festival's spectacular final night concert, Nikita and Freda danced to the music, were half-afraid of the Chinese Dragon, mesmerised by the thousands of candles held by spectators and asleep throughout the fireworks display. Harry slept through the lot.

Twenty kilometres outside of Broome, we heard Freda's little voice in the back, 'Doggy. . . I want my Doggy.' With sinking hearts we stopped and searched the car, to no avail. The worst had happened. We'd lost Doggy – Freda's special (once furry, now plucked), grubby friend that had accompanied her everywhere since she was born. Should we put it down to experience,

'For them it was simple; everywhere was home. With few toys...they had become self-reliant and imaginative'

to the inevitable process of growing up? No way. We were only too aware of the implications (tears, sleepless nights…broken hearts all round), as we drove back to Cable Beach, searched the caravan park and asked hopefully at the office, to no avail.

The air-con in our van was struggling and seated in the back, Freda and Harry weren't reaping its benefits. Both were developing prickly rash and getting pretty whingy. So we bought two small car fans and rigged them above each child. This made a huge difference as we travelled deeper into the tropics, through the dramatic Kimberleys, to the Northern Territory, Katherine and finally Darwin.

Here we did a giant jumping crocodiles cruise, swam in icy cold, crocodile-free waterholes and visited the colourful Mindil Beach market. And when we went to the post office to collect our mail, there was Doggy, patiently waiting for Freda, with a pink ribbon tied around its neck. Freda has never really understood why Doggy got to fly to Darwin and we had to drive.

stone fruit, and from tomatoes to freshly dug spuds, depending on the season.

While Australia lacks a distinctive cuisine of its own, restaurants specialising in Vietnamese, Chinese, Indian, Italian, Lebanese, Turkish, Greek and African food are almost everywhere.

At all but the flashiest places children are generally welcomed. Australia's obsession with cafe culture means that there are plenty of low-key places serving the latest version of a sandwich, such as panini, focaccia or Turkish bread. Pub bistros can usually cater to families dining early. The best news for travelling families is that there are plenty of free or coin-operated BBQs in parks and camping grounds. Beware of weekends and public holidays, when fierce battles can erupt over who is next in line for the barbie.

NEW ZEALAND

Forget about bungee jumping: New Zealand is quite exceptional without all that. Its scenery ranges from stunning to pastoral, the people are always open, warm and friendly and there's an aura of peace and civility that pervades all. Kids will love dramatic spots such as the Southern Alps and Rotorua's mud pools, but they're just as likely to relish a farm stay or a visit to a Maori meeting house.

If you're visiting from Europe or North America, New Zealand is still a fairly economical destination – unless you cling to a jet boat every day of your trip. Meals can be surprisingly pricey, but museums, cinemas and tour and activity organisers usually offer reasonable discounts for children, and there are plenty of open-air attractions available free of charge.

WHAT'S TOPS

- Wellington's Te Papa Museum – crawl through limestone caves, dig for fossils, cross a swing bridge in a rainforest, weave a Maori cloak, and much more
- Rotorua's bubbling mud pools and hot springs
- Sailing or taking a cruise in the Bay of Islands
- The massive walls of ice at Fox and Franz Josef Glaciers, on the South Island's West Coast
- Whale watching or swimming with dolphins at Kaikoura
- A cruise on stunning Milford or Doubtful Sound in pristine Fiordland
- Abel Tasman National Park's beaches and inlets; great for kayaking, bushwalking and sailing
- Aoraki/Mt Cook National Park's stunning alpine landscape, with lovely day walks

WHERE

A third of New Zealand is protected by parks and reserves covering diverse landscapes, from mangrove-fringed inlets in the north to the snow-topped volcanoes of the North Island to the Southern Alps' majestic peaks, glaciers and fiords. Just about anywhere you go there'll be something spectacular to see.

Finding family-friendly accommodation is not always straightforward, as B&Bs often promote themselves as serene grown-up retreats. Hostels concentrating on the young backpacker demographic don't welcome kids either, but there are plenty of other hostels that do. Camper-vanning or staying in a rented house is often the best option for families.

DESTINATIONS

NORTH ISLAND

The top of the North Island is blessed with spectacular scenery, including family-friendly beaches immediately north of Auckland. Centuries-old giant kauri trees can still be seen in the **Waipoua Kauri Forest** on the west coast. **Pakiri**, **Matauri Bay** and **Matai Bay** are the most pristine beaches on the northeast coast. The **Bay of Islands**, punctuated by dozens of coves and filled with clear turquoise waters, is an absolute must-see. The war canoe, meeting house, Maori dances and sound-and-light show at **Waitangi** are also big with kids.

Rotorua boils over with mud pools, thermal springs and geysers. You can take a dip in a spring-fed pool at the Blue Baths or the Polynesian Spa, or visit Waikite Valley Thermal Pools or Kerosene Creek for an open-air experience. Waiotapu and Whakarewarewa geothermal areas have pram-able boardwalks, so bring the stroller for when little legs get tired. Maori culture is strong here, making it a top spot to experience a *hangi* (feast) or concert.

The **Coromandel Peninsula**, near Auckland, has fine beaches, rugged scenery and plenty of alternative lifestylers – it's a great area to tour with your own wheels.

Auckland is a fun place to spend a few days, especially if you take advantage of its fine beaches and make boat trips to islands in the Hauraki Gulf such as volcanic **Rangitoto**, a great spot for a picnic. Kelly Tarlton's Antarctic Encounter and Underwater World (a permanent winter wonderland and superb aquarium housed in old stormwater holding tanks) is the ticket for wildlife fans. And the view from the top of Mt Eden, one of the city's extinct volcanoes, is well worth seeking out.

The Hauraki Gulf is dotted with islands, including arty **Waiheke**, a favourite weekend escape with lovely beaches. Further south,

ABOVE. **ENGAGE WITH LOCAL LIFE ON NEW ZEALAND'S SOUTH ISLAND**

Napier has more pastel-coloured art deco architecture than you can poke a stick at, as well as the National Aquarium and Marineland. The country's windy and hilly capital, Wellington, is a real charmer built on a more human scale than Auckland. It's a lovely place to simply wander around, with cute cafes, pretty wooden houses and interesting shops. Don't miss New Zealand's best museum – the innovative Te Papa – for anything. In addition to kids' discovery areas, it has its own *marae* (meeting house) and loads of truly interactive exhibits. Capital E, a hands-on educational entertainment centre designed especially for children, has circus workshops and TV and recording studios where kids can make their own music and videos.

STAY

Pakiri Beach Holiday Park (+64 (0)9-422 6199; www.pakiriholidaypark.co.nz; 261 Pakiri River Rd; $) has cottages with a magical beachfront setting, plus playground and games room. Whatuwhiwhi Top 10 Holiday Park (+64 (0)9-408 7202; www.whatuwhiwhitop10.co.nz; Whatuwhiwhi Rd; $), on the Karikari Peninsula, has a fine location by the beach; on-site accommodation ranges from single rooms to basic cabins to two-bedroom units and there's a playground. On the Coromandel Peninsula, Opoutere YHA Hostel (+64 (07)865 9072; www.yha.co.nz; 389 Opoutere Rd; $) has family cabins set on a sprawling lawn overlooking the sea; canoes are available for paddling in the estuary and there's a trampoline. On the shores of Lake Rotorua, Cosy Cottage International Holiday Park (+64 (0)7348 3793; www.cosycottage.co.nz; 67 Whittaker Rd; $) has all manner of cabins and a beach where you can dig your own hot spring.

In Wellington, the Carillon (+64 4 3848795; www.carillon.co.nz; 33 Thompson St; $), occupying a mansion just around the corner from

happening Cuba St, has a family room with a kitchenette, cot and toys (on request); downstairs there's a huge communal kitchen and dining room, as well as a lounge with pool table.

SOUTH ISLAND

Crossing Cook Strait by ferry from the North Island to the South Island is very exciting, especially once you reach the intricate inlets of the Marlborough Sounds. The top of the South Island has a magnificent coastline, the Abel Tasman Coastal Track and the sunny artsy town of Nelson, which has a busy market on weekends. Kaiteriteri has a lovely beach.

The West Coast is a wind-blasted stretch of wild beaches and rocky shore rising up through the forest to the summits of the Southern Alps. Rain comes in sideways here and there's an air of hillbilly wildness, so bring your pioneering spirit with you, along with a taste for whitebait patties served with chips, mint sauce and pickled onions. Rain gear and insect repellents are other necessities. The West Coast's glaciers – the Franz Josef and Fox – are mighty to behold and remarkably close to the sea. Punakaiki, with pancake-stacked rocks and indigenous *nikau* palms, feels like a subtropical paradise.

On the eastern coast, Kaikoura is an ecotourism paradise, with dolphin, whale and seal tours galore. The rather staid town of Christchurch needn't divert you for too long, but it does have the absorbing International Antarctic Centre, complete with storm chamber.

The spectacular Aoraki/Mt Cook National Park is a pointy wonderland containing 22 peaks above 3000m. The area is laced with superb walks, some of which are excellent for families.

Touring Middle Earth

Lord of the Rings sites are sprinkled all over New Zealand. Hobbiton is near Matamata, Mt Doom is in fact towering Ngauruhoe, and the Misty Mountains are the South Island's Southern Alps. The visitor information centres in Wellington, Twizel and Queenstown should be able to direct you to local *Rings* sites of interest. If you're serious about finding the exact spots where scenes were filmed, buy a copy of Ian Brodie's nerdtastic *The Lord of the Rings: Location Guidebook,* which includes instructions (including GPS coordinates) for finding all the important scenes. Also check the beautiful online location guide at www.filmnz.com/middleearth. Private companies run *Rings* tours in Tongariro National Park, Wellington, Nelson, Methven, Queenstown and Wanaka.

The rolling **Otago** region has superb lakes and charming historic towns. Top of the kids' list in hilly and increasingly cosmopolitan city **Dunedin** is likely to be a tour of Cadbury World chocolate factory, which features a look at a two-storey, liquid-chocolate waterfall and a taste of the end product. Also check out the world's steepest street (so says the *Guinness Book of Records*): **Baldwin St.** The curvy **Otago Peninsula**, a short drive away, is teeming with albatrosses, seals and penguins. From Dunedin you can catch the famous **Taieri Gorge Railway**, or escape inland to the charming gold-rush towns of **Clyde** and **Arrowtown**. Nearby lies the hyperactive resort of **Queenstown**, where teens will have a ball doing all manner of extreme things. There are also numerous ski fields in the area.

Fiordland National Park, further south, consists of misty mountains and fathomless fiords, with not a township in sight. The park is accessible by the **Milford Track**, which winds through rainforest and past crystal-clear streams, or you can take a boat trip on **Milford Sound** or **Doubtful Sound**. Be prepared for rain, no matter how you tackle the region.

STAY

Sounds Great Holiday Homes (+64 (0)3-574 1221; www.soundsgreat.co.nz) has secluded retreats on Marlborough Sounds. Nelson's **Lynton Lodge** (+64 (0)3-548 7112; www.holidayguide .co.nz/Nelson/LyntonLodge.aspx; 25 Examiner St; $), set high on the hill, has older-style self-contained apartments, including one that opens onto a garden with a play area.

Punakaiki Beach Camp (+64 (0)3-731 1894; 5 Owen St; $), sheltering beside a huge stone escarpment, has clean old-style cabins with ship-shape amenities. At Fox Glacier, **Lake Matheson Motels** (+64 (0)3-751 0830; www .lakematheson.co.nz; Cook Flat Rd; $$) has family rooms with kitchenette, as well as a separate house that sleeps up to seven.

In Kaikoura, **Bay Cottages** (+64 (0)3-319 5506; baycottages@xtra.co.nz; 29 South Bay Pde; $) has tidy tourist flats that sleep four.

Aoraki/Mt Cook Alpine Lodge (+64 (0)3-435 1860; www.aorakialpinelodge.co.nz; Bowen Dr; $) has family rooms with big views and an excellent communal kitchen, lounge and deck on the upper level.

Manor Motel (+64 (0)3-477 6729; www.manormotel .co.nz; 22 Manor Pl; $), in Dunedin, has family units and there's a small park across the road.

DESTINATIONS

WHEN

The warmer months between November and April are best for outdoor exploration. Winter (June to August), obviously, is ski season – but note that if you visit in winter, beachside towns will be in semihibernation. Key sites can become very crowded during school holidays (particularly mid-December to early February) and on public holidays.

On both main islands it gets wetter in the west than the east because the mountains block the moisture-laden winds blowing in from the Tasman Sea. Remember that the weather can change very quickly at any time of year – be fully prepared for this, especially if you're at high altitudes.

HOW

Transport

New Zealand's isolated location in the South Pacific Ocean is one of its drawcards, but it also means that unless you travel from Australia you'll have a long-haul flight. New Zealand has good airline and bus networks, and well-maintained roads, so travelling around the country is very straightforward.

There are several visually stunning rail routes, namely the *Overlander* between Auckland and Wellington, the *TranzCoastal* between Christchurch and Picton, and the *TranzAlpine* which rattles over the Southern Alps between Christchurch and Greymouth. There are boat services between Auckland and various islands in Hauraki Gulf, interisland ferries that chug over Cook Strait between Wellington and Picton, and the passenger ferry that travels between Bluff and the town of Oban on Stewart Island.

Exploring the country by car lets you create your own leisurely, flexible itinerary. For car and camper van hire, local firms are usually

cheapest. International visitors can use their home country's driving licence. Check that hire-car companies can supply a seat, and that the seat will be properly fitted before you pick up the vehicle.

Shopping & Essentials

Insect repellent is indispensable for deterring sandflies; you may want to buy this on arrival after talking to the locals about which kind works best. Also vital is a range of clothing, including winter woollies (yes, even in summer) and raingear, to suit the changeability of the weather. A mobile phone is handy for driving in remote areas and booking accommodation while in transit.

Most shops are open 9am to 5.30pm Monday to Friday, closing at either 12.30pm or 5pm on Saturday. In cities, shops stay open till 9pm on Thursday and/or Friday nights, and Sunday trading is also common. Supermarkets are usually open from 8am until at least 7pm, often until 9pm or later in cities.

Health

There are no deadly snakes or spiders in New Zealand, and no other dangerous creatures either. Medical services and facilities are of a high standard, and formula and disposable nappies are widely available in urban centres.

Breastfeeding in public is common and accepted. All cities and major towns have centrally located public rooms where parents can go to nurse their baby or change nappies; check with the local visitor information centre or city council for details.

Food

Many eateries can provide highchairs and kids' meals. Cafes are often good for families, with a casual vibe and reasonably priced fare. Top-quality fresh produce, from lamb, milk and cheese to fruit and veg, ensures a high standard of food on the whole.

DESTINATIONS

COOK ISLANDS

Scattered over a vast expanse of ocean the size of Western Europe, the Cook Islands are a castaway's dream come true. Rarotonga, the largest island, is a captivating mix of jagged mountains, impenetrable jungle and glorious white-sand beaches. And the other islands – with lagoons, coral reefs and spooky caves – have a lot to offer too.

Everything here is more expensive than it is on Fiji, but Cook Island prices are nowhere near the levels of Tahiti and French Polynesia. Accommodation, in particular, can be hard on the pocket.

WHAT'S TOPS

- Cook Islands Cultural Village on Rarotonga
- The Takitumu Conservation Area on Rarotonga, home to endangered wildlife
- Aitutaki's fabulous glittering-blue lagoon, a perfect swimming spot
- The low-lying islets of Manihiki and its pristine lagoon, with a visit to a black-pearl farm

WHERE

Rarotonga is a great all-rounder of an island, with a lovely lagoon, plenty of activities, classy resorts and fabulous restaurants. Hook-shaped **Aitutaki** sits atop one of the world's largest coral lagoons. The *makatea* (raised coral) islands of **'Atiu**, **Ma'uke**, **Mitiaro** and **Mangaia** are still very traditional, with pretty landscapes, deserted beaches and caves. If you're in search of a really remote experience, you might consider visiting the far-flung islands of the **Northern Group**.

RAROTONGA

Crowned by green mountains, covered with jungle and tall coconut trees, and encircled by a turquoise lagoon, Rarotonga fulfils most people's fantasies about South Pacific islands. The top attraction for children is the fabulous **lagoon**, which is packed with marine life and provides dazzling snorkelling and swimming. **Muri Beach** is the best spot for water babies. Kayaks, sailboards, small sailing boats and snorkelling gear can all be hired, and glass-bottom boats cruise Muri Lagoon.

The **Cook Islands Cultural Village** is great fun, with a cultural show, hands-on activities and slap-up buffet included, and it runs interesting island tours. At the **Takitumu Conservation Area**, kids can learn about the traditional uses of native plants. Children love the traditional drumming and dancing at an **island night**, and you might even get some fire-juggling and acrobatics thrown in for good measure. Island nights are held regularly at all large resorts and at local restaurants.

STAY

The **Rarotongan Beach Resort** (+682-25800; www.rarotongan.co.ck; $$), in a great spot near Aro'a Beach, has a babysitting service and an on-site kids' club. **Kii Kii Motel** (+682-21937; www.kiikiimotel.co.ck; $) has affordable self-contained cottages at Muri Beach.

AITUTAKI

One of the highlights of any visit to the Cook Islands is a **lagoon** cruise on Aitutaki. The lagoon is brilliantly blue and full of colourful fish, giant clams and living corals. Cruises include visits to some of the lagoon's best snorkelling spots and a few of the *motu* (smaller islands) around the lagoon's edge, and you can also explore the lagoon by kayak. On the east coast, there's excellent snorkelling at **O'otu**.

STAY

Gina's Garden Lodges (+682-31058; www .ginasaitutaki.com; $), just out of earshot of the sea, are set around a secluded garden. They're fully self-contained, and there's a small loft sleeping area that's tailor-made for kids.

WHEN

The best months to visit are September and October, when there's a nice balance of warm temperatures and reduced humidity. March and April are also good months, as the cyclone season has passed and the skies are clear and sunny. Rarotonga is often rainy, so bring jackets with you at any time of the year. The wet season runs from December to March, and this is also the most likely time for cyclones. During the wet it can also get quite sticky and uncomfortable. Flights and accommodation can be hard to come by around Christmas, when many islanders return home to spend the festive season with family.

HOW

Transport

The Cook Islands can be visited as a destination in their own right, as a stopover when crossing the Pacific, or as part of a Circle Pacific or round-the-world trip. Many visitors to the Cook Islands come on all-inclusive packages, which can cost about the same price as airfare, or even less. Although there is no visa requirement for short-term visitors to the Cooks, you are supposed to have booked accommodation before you arrive.

Small planes travel between the islands, and an efficient bus service circumnavigates Rarotonga.

To rent a car you need to obtain a local driving licence from the police station in Avarua. Child seats are available from the major car-rental companies on Rarotonga.

Shopping & Essentials

Make sure you bring mosquito repellent, sunscreen, a torch (flashlight), rain gear, old shoes or sneakers for walking, film and books aplenty. If you have your own snorkelling equipment, bring it. Formula is available on most islands and processed baby food is sold on Rarotonga, Aitutaki and Mangaia. Disposable nappies are expensive.

If you plan to attend a church service (definitely fun on the Cooks) make sure you have the right garb – covered shoulders and upper arms, and a knee-length skirt for women; shirt and long trousers for men; and neat attire for children.

Shops are open 9am to 4pm Monday to Friday, and on Saturday morning. Small grocery stores keep longer hours.

Health

Mosquitoes in the Cooks can transmit dengue fever. The disease tends to come in epidemics mainly in the hotter, wetter months so plan holidays accordingly.

Several of the Cook Islands have a problem with ciguatera poisoning, so be wary of eating reef fish; instead, stick to deep-sea fish such as tuna, *mahi mahi* and wahoo (which are generally the only fish served in restaurants anyway). The municipal water supply in Avarua and other large towns on the islands can be trusted, but elsewhere you should boil water before drinking it.

In the sheltered lagoons, it is very safe to go swimming, but you must be very wary of *ava* (passages and breaks in the surrounding reefs), where currents are especially strong. Other risks encountered in the water include 'Man o' War' jellyfish (if you see these in the water or stranded on the beach it is wiser not to go in at all), poisonous cone shells and sea snakes.

Health facilities are reasonable, but you might not find the facilities you would expect in a well-developed country, particularly on outer islands.

Food

One of the culinary highlights in the Cooks is the fantastic seafood, served everywhere.

Locally grown fruits and vegetables are available from local shops, roadside stalls and markets. Imported milk, vegetables and meat available from supermarkets on Rarotonga can be pricey, and costs are higher again on the outer islands. If you're planning on bringing supplies from abroad, you'll have no problem with packaged goods – just remember to declare them on arrival.

Most places to stay offer self-catering or provide meals. If you're self-catering, remember that the choice of supplies is pretty slim – you'll be opening lots of cans (bring a good opener). Turnover can be slow in some outer-island grocery stores, so check use-by dates.

If you're looking for home-grown cooking, head straight for an *umukai* – a traditional feast cooked in an underground oven.

ABOVE: **THE DAZZLING LAGOON IS THE TOP ATTRACTION ON THE COOK ISLANDS' RAROTONGA**

DESTINATIONS

FIJI

Fiji is a major family destination, and the locals love little ones – in fact, your baby or toddler may tire of having her cheeks squeezed! Some resorts cater specifically for children by providing activities, babysitting, cots, highchairs and children's pools. There are even a few resorts that provide free accommodation and/or meals for kids. Most of the islands offer great beaches with activities such as snorkelling, sea kayaking, surfing, coral viewing and horseback riding. Fiji is a very affordable destination, especially if you're travelling from nearby Australia or New Zealand.

WHAT'S TOPS

- Snorkelling on the dreamy, coral fringes of the Mamanuca and Yasawa isles
- Riding the old sugar train on the Coral Coast Scenic Railway on Viti Levu
- Kula Eco Park on Viti Levu, with walking trails through the forest
- The Arts Village on Viti Levu, where you can ride an old-style canoe around an artificial 'traditional' village with local actors dressed the part
- Hindu Holi (Festival of Colours), in February/March, a great chance to squirt each other with coloured water

WHERE

Fiji has over 300 islands, from private resorts to uninhabited coral cays. For swimming beaches, try a smaller coral island such as Mana in the **Mamanucas**, just offshore from Nadi, or those in the **Yasawa** group. Mountainous **Vitu Levu**, the largest island and site of Nadi and Suva, has loads of kid-friendly offerings. **Taveuni**, known as the garden island, has abundant rainforests and wildlife.

VITI LEVU

You won't find many dreamy beaches on Viti Levu (they tend to be tidal, muddy affairs), but the island does have a lush tropical interior with 'authentic', living villages, and you can avoid the claustrophobia that sometimes comes with island resorts. You'll even be able to visit real shops, markets and cafes!

A drive or bus ride along the **Coral Coast** in the south of the island is a highlight. Along the way you can stop at the scenic railway, the Sigatoka sand dunes, pretty Natadola Beach, the fortress at Taveuni Hill and the mock traditional village at the Arts Centre. If you're more interested in visiting real villages, take a tour or bus ride to the **Nausori Highlands** in the interior. **Suva** has a couple of must-sees too. The produce market is a kaleidoscope of tropical fruits and brightly coloured Indian sweets, and the Fiji Museum is worth a visit.

STAY

On Yanuca, linked to Vitu Levu by a causeway, the huge **Shangri-La's Fijian Resort** (+679 652 0155; www.shangri-la.com; $$) has a kids' club and deals on children's stays and meals.

MAMANUCAS

Touted as the isles of smiles, these are your quintessential white-sand eye-popping paradise islands. They are a quick hop by boat, plane or helicopter from Nadi on Vitu Levu.

STAY

There are more than 15 resorts, ranging from backpacker ecoresorts with shared facilities to high-end 'romantic' getaways where kids are more or less banned. **Castaway Island** (+679

666 1233; www.castawayisland.com; $$) is somewhere in the middle, with simple thatched *bures* (cottages; no phone or TV) for families (kids under 16 years stay free). There's a kids' club and activities for teenagers.

WHEN

Fiji has pleasant weather year-round and is a great place to escape winter, whether you live in the northern or southern hemisphere. The Fijian 'winter' (dry season), from May to October, is perhaps the best time to visit. It has the lowest rainfall and humidity, milder temperatures and a reduced risk of hurricanes and dengue fever outbreaks.

HOW

Transport

Most visitors fly into Nadi, sometimes as a stop on a round-the-world ticket, sometimes as part of an accommodation package.

If you want to escape your all-inclusive resort, getting around is fairly easy, by car or bus, and boat or plane. Ferry routes connect most major coastal areas of Viti Levu with the major islands, and smaller boats travel to smaller islands. Unless you take an organised cruise or charter your own boat, however, it can be difficult to hop from island to island. Car rental is relatively expensive but worth a splurge for a day or two on the larger islands. Some rental companies provide baby seats.

A baby carrier is useful for getting around resorts and if you're taking public transport – but it shouldn't be used in villages (nothing should be carried on the shoulders, out of respect for the chief).

Shopping & Essentials

Light cotton casual gear is de rigueur for resorts. Outside resorts men should wear a *sulu*, a sarong-type wrap-around skirt, which can be bought in Fiji. Women should bring below-the-knee skirts. Kids can wear anything. Light raincoats and a small towel are useful for downpours. Otherwise, sunglasses, hats, sunscreen, mosquito repellent and comfy sandals will see you through. It's a good idea to bring your own snorkelling gear.

Nappies and formula are available in supermarkets and pharmacies; if you are travelling to remote areas, take supplies.

Health

Fiji is a safe place, but large reef fish such as snapper, barracuda and grouper can contain ciguatera toxin. Ocean-going fish such as tuna, wahoo and Spanish mackerel are safe, and small reef fish that the locals eat should be OK. Water is generally safe in resorts but in villages drink only bottled water from containers with a safety seal. Fiji is malaria-free but there are occasional outbreaks of dengue fever, a serious mosquito-borne disease, in urban areas.

Breastfeeding is the norm but local women are very modest, so it's a good idea to feed under a muslin wrap or some other covering.

Some resorts have an on-site nurse, which is a real plus as medical help can otherwise be a plane ride away.

Food

Unfortunately food is unlikely to be a real highlight of your trip to Fiji, unless you're eating at the top-end restaurants at the most luxurious resorts, or are lucky enough to sample some genuine home cooking. Locals eat a mix of indigenous Fijian, Polynesian, Indian, Chinese and Western foods. Traditional Fijian foods include starchy taro and cassava roots, and fish served with coconut cream. Indian-influenced dishes are often spicy curries and dhals served with rice or roti bread. Bizarrely, tropical fruits can be hard to find unless you go to markets.

ASIA

INDIA

Sacred India is a land of diversity and contrast, studded with incredible temples and monuments to her fascinating past. But for children, it will be the small wonders that are the most engaging – chai vendors passing clay cups through train windows, monkeys snatching treats from each other on temple roofs, or the colourful flash of a dozen saris as women wash clothes on the ghats.

It's true that India is a challenging destination for families, but the rewards are many and there are ways to make it easier. Stock up on supplies in the major centres and then get away from the crowds and touts and spend time in the more laid-back rural areas. You'll find people welcoming and gently curious, and having the kids along will open doors into homes and hearts.

WHAT'S TOPS

- Joining the rainbow riot of Holi (February/March) when revellers splash each other with coloured dyes
- Sleeping on a boat as you cruise through the gentle backwaters of Kerala
- Scouting for tigers atop an elephant at Corbett Tiger Reserve
- Joining in a casual cricket match at Azad Maidan in Mumbai
- Wandering around a bazaar, such as the one in Mysore, where you'll come home smelling of sandalwood and jasmine
- Wrapping your tongue around the sugary delights of *mithai* (sweets), from fudgelike *barfi* to syrupy *gulab jamun*
- Watching the splendidly decorated elephants, drummers and fireworks of the Thrissur Pooram (April/May)
- Camping out in the desert after a camel trek near Jaisalmer
- Burying your parents in the sand on the sublime beaches of Goa

WHERE

The Golden Triangle tour is a perennial favourite for visitors to India. It takes in **Delhi** and **Jaipur**, two of the country's most impressive capitals, with a stop in **Agra** to see the incomparable Taj Mahal. The kids, however, might prefer a ramble among birds and butterflies on the nearby Taj Nature Walk. You can extend this trip with a tour of the incredible palaces and forts of **Rajasthan**.

Further south you can sample the charms of **Mumbai**, Bombay to its friends, where Bollywood stars mix it in the carnival atmosphere of Chowpatty Beach.

Head south to enjoy the beaches of **Goa**, with its palm-fringed white sands and all the comforts of home – south Goa is more laid-back than the party frenzy to the north.

Next move down to **Kerala** for a tour of its beautiful backwaters. You'll float past villages and fisherfolk in your very own houseboat. You can also see a performance of green-faced *kathakali* dancers here, or stop in to visit the impressive zoo at Thiruvananthapuram (Trivandrum) set among woodland and lakes.

If you plan to visit busy **Kolkata** (Calcutta), stop into Science City, a futuristic theme park with animatronic dinosaurs, and Nicco Park, a colourful amusement park with a rollercoaster and a log flume.

DELHI

Not everyone is a fan of India's crazy capital, but many visitors, passing through on the way to visit the nearby Taj Mahal and Rajasthan, are pleasantly surprised. The cosmopolitan city offers fabulous food, modern facilities and the chance to stock up on essentials such as nappies and formula before you begin your tour of the subcontinent.

SEE

Red Fort Sound-&-Light Show (Red Fort, Old Delhi) The kids' jaws may not drop as low as yours when they see the Mughal majesty of Delhi's Red Fort, but they're sure to enjoy this one-hour extravaganza. Events in India's intriguing Mughal history are recreated each evening with plenty of razzle-dazzle and noise.

Shankar's International Dolls Museum (+91 (0) 11 23316970; www.childrensbooktrust.com; Nehru House, 4 Bahadur Shah Zafar Marg; 10am-6pm Tue-Sun) With almost 6500 dolls from 85 countries, this museum claims to have one of the largest collections of dolls in the world. Apart from its international displays there's an excellent collection of 150 Indian dolls from all over the country, including brides and dancers.

STAY

Home Away from Home (+91 (0) 11 26560289; 1st fl, D-8 Gulmohar Park; $$) Located in a leafy suburb, this place offers stylish home-style accommodation in an apartment with meals available. Hush and Puppy, the resident basset hounds, appreciate a tummy tickle.

Yatri House (+91 (0) 11 23625563; www.yatrihouse.com; 3/4 Panchkuian Marg; $$) A green oasis away from the madness of Main Bazaar, this place has a green lawn, leafy courtyards and a homey atmosphere. The six rooms are scrupulously clean and a good size, all with attached modern bathrooms.

RAJASTHAN

If your kids like fairy tales, they'll love Rajasthan. The desert state is full of stories of kings and queens (or rather maharajas and maharanis), chivalry, poetry and decadence.

Incredible fort cities like **Jodhpur** and **Jaisalmer** will fire up young imaginations with intricate battlements and opulent palaces of carved stone inlaid with jewels.

From the latter you can go on safari through the desert dunes on a camel.

The state capital **Jaipur** has an impressive palace, a weird outdoor astronomical park, and also Chokhi Dhani, a mock-Rajasthani village where you'll be entertained by tribal dancers setting fire to their hats, children balancing on poles and dancers in lion costumes. At nearby **Amber Fort** you can take an elephant ride up to the battlements.

To the south, horse safaris are possible around **Udaipur**, a romantic lake city of island palaces, paddle boats and rooftop gardens.

To the north, visit the creepy **Karni Mata rat temple** at Deshnok, where rats are revered – they're fed sweets and milk and are allowed to run all over your feet!

STAY

A sojourn in a former palace is a great treat for little princes and princesses. The well-heeled can do no better than the **Lake Palace Hotel** (+91 (0) 294 2528800; www.tajhotels.com; $$$) in Udaipur. This romantic white-marble hotel seems to float in the middle of the lake, and features open-air courtyards, lotus ponds and a mango-shaded pool. Babysitting is available.

WHEN

November to mid-February is generally the best time to visit northern India, including Rajasthan, while destinations further south, including Mumbai, Goa and Kerala, are best from October to March.

HOW

Transport
India is a huge country so beware of biting off more than you can chew. Unless you're a fan of long, hot and crowded bus or train

Price Guide

$ budget $$ midrange $$$ top end

journeys, it's a good idea to choose between a tour of the north, through Delhi, Agra and Rajasthan, for example, or a tour of the south, such as one from Mumbai through Goa to Kerala. Delhi and Mumbai are both international hubs with good air connections.

Trains are the best bet for long-haul travel as they're smoother and less hazardous than buses. Overnight services have two- or three-tier bunks to sleep on – not wildly comfortable but kind of fun – or you can opt for a private two- or four-berth sleeper cabin with a washbasin on major lines.

Many families, however, prefer to hire a car and driver for their tour of India. It's surprisingly affordable, comfortable, and allows you to stop where you want and explore out-of-the-way regions. However, don't expect them to come equipped with child seats – consider bringing one along if you're concerned about this. Try to get a driver who speaks some English and knows the regions where you wish to travel – ask at your hotel for a recommendation.

Around town, most families travel by autorickshaw or taxi, which are easier to use than getting to grips with complex local transport routes. Strollers are handy to use as chairs in restaurants, as highchairs are a rarity, but aren't much use outside as India's pavements are uneven or nonexistent. However, if you opt for a backpack you'll get very hot in the tropics or the desert.

Shopping & Essentials
Nappies and formula are available in the big cities but elsewhere are very expensive and very hard to find. Consider bringing supplies from home. Sunscreen, hats, a torch, earplugs

RICHARD I'ANSON | LONELY PLANET IMAGES

ABOVE **ENJOY A DIFFERENT PERSPECTIVE ON THE TAJ MAHAL, INDIA**

DESTINATIONS

THE REAL DARJEELING LIMITED

~ INDIA ~

BY AMELIA THOMAS

Travel in India is something that strikes many parents with a mixture of longing and dread. The longing to share with your children the taste of predawn railway station chai, and the shock of Rajasthani colours after a day in the desert. And the dread: of the chaos, the sunstroke and sickness – the relentless 'Indianness' of it all.

After a successful trip to Goa six months before, our second family jaunt to India took us to dingy, dirty (but endearing) Delhi. I was five months pregnant, and all seemed to be going smoothly. Save for some unwanted attention at Delhi's Red Fort, involving an amateur paparazzi frenzy fit for Brangelina & Co, Cassidy, aged three, Tyger, two, and Cairo, a sprightly one-year-old, were enjoying it too.

'I know', I glanced down at my tea cup, as the children recovered in front of a Disney DVD. 'Now let's go to Darjeeling!'

The *Darjeeling Limited,* or *Rajdhani Express* as it's actually known, departs Delhi daily for the 25-hour journey to New Jalpaiguri, from which it's a further 90km up to the quaint hilltop tea plantation, set amid some of the world's highest peaks. We bought 1st-class tickets, ensuring a cabin to ourselves, and prepared for our trip to the clouds.

'It's quite small', my husband remarked, as he attempted to lever backpacks and children into our minuscule, musty cabin. manoeuvred my cumbersome tummy into a space between the seat and the washbasin. 'Cosy,' I insisted.

Travelling on Indian trains is a lot like childbirth. No matter how many times you do it, you forget the anguish until you experience it again. And just six hours into our Darjeeling Odyssey, it became clear that this time would be no different.

'Good news, Lady and Gent!' came our cheery attendant's call, as he produced piping hot trays of food. 'Dinner! Pure Vegetarian, very tasty!'

We prised open the tin-foil lids. Dhal, rice, and vegetable *sabzi.* Perfectly decent, but strangely similar – make that absolutely identical – to the lunch we'd been served five hours earlier.

'Yummy', I forestalled the children, 'They knew it's your favourite, so you've got it again.'

Their expressions made it clear that I was fooling no one.

'But, Gent and Lady, bad news also', the attendant continued solemnly. 'Train is a little delayed.'

'A little?'

'Ten hours only, madam. Enjoy Pure Veg dinner!' He grinned, and disappeared down the corridor considerably faster than the train itself.

Twenty-five hours with three small children on a train might be a bit of a stretch. Thirty-five goes beyond the bounds of sanity and to another, stranger realm.

Take the regular, identical, five-hourly Pure Veg meals. Throw in toilets beneath which a porthole of railway track sways and shudders, and toddlers who fear they'll fall straight through if they attempt to use it. Take colouring books completed in the first hour. Biscuits crushed to a crunchy powder, and spread liberally throughout your bedding, and games of *I-Spy* with children who don't yet know the alphabet. Add a night on a slim railway bunk-bed whilst your unborn baby tangos in your tummy, and countryside so uninspiring that a pigeon perched on a railway signal begins to look like a Bird of Paradise.

We emerged, ragged and blinking, thirty-five hours after leaving Delhi, to be met by a smart white tea-plantation jeep.

'How long will it take?' I asked our driver.

'Not long', he smiled, 'Seven hours. Maybe eight.' He glanced down at my tummy sceptically. 'But bumpy ride, madam.' He shook his head and sucked his teeth. 'Bumpy, bumpy ride.'

At least the second journey was eventful. After a superfluity of Himalayan hairpin bends, waterfalls, close encounters with oncoming traffic and choruses of *The Wheels on the Bus*, the jeep jolted over the final crevice and up a sweeping driveway. Mossy tea fields, punctuated by pickers, tumbled down steep mountainsides. A planter's bungalow appeared, wicker chairs gracing a bougainvillea-draped veranda. Our host, an elegant Indian lady, stood waiting to greet us. From the drawing room, soothing strains of a children's movie drifted through the clear mountain air.

'Twenty-five hours with three small children on a train might be a bit of a stretch. Thirty-five goes beyond the bounds of sanity and to another, stranger realm.'

There are seven words, magical as a fairy godmother to a tired, pregnant traveller, feeling terrible about dragging her family halfway across India. Our calm and motherly host smiled sweetly, and uttered them.

'Would you like a cup of tea?'

'Tea!' I gasped.

'Teeee!' Cairo galloped on the spot.

'Snow White!' Tyger's attention snapped, keen as a mountain leopard, to familiar music from the drawing room.

As the kids dashed for Disney, their parents took their first sip of real Darjeeling tea and gazed out at Kanchenjunga's snowcapped peak. My husband put his hand to my tummy. The baby turned somersaults. A shriek of laughter erupted from the drawing room. Cairo danced circles on the lawn. Seven simple words and the Seven Dwarves are all it takes to transform the longest journey – and even seven identical Pure Veg meals – into fun for all the family.

for light sleepers and mosquito repellent are also essential items, as well as nonrevealing clothes if you intend to visit sacred sites.

Health

It's important to speak to your doctor about vaccinations and other health issues well in advance of your departure, and make sure you have adequate insurance. Most travellers come down with little more than a case of travellers' diarrhoea, which isn't life-threatening but can spoil the trip for kids and parents alike. Reduce your family's chances by being scrupulous about drinking boiled or bottled water, eating fresh-cooked food from busy eateries and peeling all fruit and vegetables. Also, take along a well-stocked medical kit.

Medical care is hugely variable in India. Major centres have good clinics catering to travellers, but in rural or remote areas medical facilities are basic at best. Warn your kids not to touch animals as rabies is common.

Most upmarket hotels and restaurants have sit-down toilets, but be prepared to use squat toilets too, especially if you intend to stay in budget accommodation. You may even encounter the strange hybrid toilet, which is a sit-down toilet with footpads on the edge of the bowl. Toilet paper isn't always supplied, so carry some with you, and this should be tossed in the bin, not down the loo. It's a good idea to carry soap with you too.

Breastfeeding in public is not condoned in India – you'll need to find a private place at feeding times (ie your hotel room).

Food

India's spectacular food can be roughly divided in two: you'll be served classic vegetarian food in the south and you'll have the chance to sample the meaty traditions of the Mughals in the north. Unfortunately for most little visitors, north and south are united in their love of chilli. Indian kids are expected to toughen up their taste buds from an early age, so don't expect special kids' menus, except in rare Western-style eateries. Happily, however, there are many Indian dishes that don't serve up quite such a spicy kick. Try roti, rice, dhal, curds and soups, or the delicious variety of Indian sweets. Alternatively, there's always fresh fruit available, and most major centres and tourist destinations abound with restaurants offering Western menus of chips, pizzas, burgers, banana pancakes and the like.

SRI LANKA

This beautiful island nation packs palm-fringed beaches, Buddhist mysteries, elephant habitats and verdant green hills into an area the size of Tasmania. It's compact enough to see all the highlights without spending days on the road and the family-centred folk you'll meet will be delighted that you brought the kids along.

Sri Lanka's coast was devastated by the tsunami on Boxing Day 2004. In the intervening years the country has rebuilt – and tourism has been one of the fastest industries to recover – however, the effects of the disaster are still clearly visible, especially at beaches to the south. Be prepared to answer some tough questions from your little ones when they see the temporary camps, razed countryside and reshaped coastlines.

WHAT'S TOPS

- Sitting in on the daily bath for the 60 young residents of Pinnewala Elephant Orphanage
- Kandy Esala Perahera, an unforgettable procession in July/August with drummers, fire-walkers, dancers and decorated elephants
- Eating with your fingers just like the locals – right hand only please!
- Joining the fans in Colombo or Kandy to watch a match of the national obsession – cricket
- Meeting the babies at the turtle hatcheries of Kosgoda
- Getting out the bucket and spade at tranquil Mirissa on Sri Lanka's southern coast
- Touring a spice garden in Kegalle to see plants like cinnamon, clove, nutmeg and vanilla growing
- Boarding a rattling old train for the beautiful ride between Haputale and Ella through green tea plantations

WHERE

You'll probably enter Sri Lanka through the capital, Colombo, and it's worth a stop to visit the small Dehiwala Zoo, with its walk-in aviary and butterfly park, and the sunset carnival atmosphere of ice-cream vendors, kite-flyers and strolling families at Galle Face Green.

Many families head to the **southern beaches** for sandcastling and snorkelling. The town of **Galle**, gateway to the region, features a crumbling 1660s Dutch Fort that you can clamber over.

To the north, the monuments at the **ancient cities** abound in antique mysteries. The flat-topped rock formation of **Sigiriya** was augmented over 1000 years ago with paths and stairways, a carved-lion entranceway, delicate frescoes and a pool carved straight into the rock at the summit. At **Anuradhapura** there's Sri Maha Bodhi, the 2000-year-old sacred bodhi tree at the centre of Sri Lankan Buddhism.

SOUTHERN BEACHES

Offering a truly relaxing beach holiday to suit a tight family budget, Sri Lanka's beaches are laid-back, beautiful and friendly.

Hikkaduwa is probably Sri Lanka's most popular beach town with a wide and pretty beach and plenty of waterfront eateries to choose from. Further south the idyllic resort town of **Unawatuna** offers clean white sands and good swimming.

Many families prefer the quieter resorts further east. The snorkelling is great at sleepy **Mirissa**, there are loads of fish to spot, and sometimes even sea turtles. **Tangalla** is another easygoing town, close to the gorgeous white sands of Medaketiya Beach, while the bay to the south offers shallow, calm swimming for little ones. Further on, head to **Yala National Park** for the chance to spot herds of elephants and leopards.

STAY

Readers recommend **Amarasinghe's** (+94 (0) 041 225 1204; chana7@sltnet.lk; $) in Mirissa for the fantastic food, the huge family bungalows with fridges and the kid-friendly staff who go out of their way to entertain children. In Unawatuna, choose between the **Strand** (+94 (0) 091 222 4358; www.lanka.net/strand; $$) with a garden suite with kids beds, a freezer and atmospheric colonial style-furniture, and **Nooit Gedacht** (+94 (0) 091 222 3449; nooitged@sltnet .lk; $$) with a lovely garden, small pool and a four-bed family apartment.

DESTINATIONS

HILL COUNTRY

When the heat gets too much, head for the hills for a cooler climate and stunning scenery coated in verdant tea plantations. Enjoy the colonial charm of Nuwara Eliya, with its Raj-era resorts and gardens, take a 4km walk to the incredible 880m escarpment known as World's End or try to spot a leopard at Sinharaja Forest Reserve. And don't miss the memorably named town of Kandy, the spiritual home of Sinhalese culture. It features a pretty lake and the temple housing Sri Lanka's most sacred relic – a tooth of the Buddha.

STAY

In Kandy, rest up at the **Golden View Rest** (+94 (0) 081 223 9418; $$) in a large family-owned house with an Ayurveda treatment room and a Finnish sauna. It rents rooms separately or together as an apartment if your family needs more space. Also in town is **Lake Bungalow** (+94 (0) 081 222 2075; $), atop a preschool, which may appeal if you'd like to meet some playmates. The rooms have hot water and kitchenettes and you can rent a floor with three bedrooms as an apartment.

WHEN

If you plan to visit the southern beaches or hill country, the best and driest time is December to March. This is also the peak season, when accommodation is tight and prices are at their highest. For the ancient cities and the east coast, aim for April to September.

HOW

Transport

Sri Lankan buses can be hideously overcrowded and you're far better off taking a train, even if they are infuriatingly slow.

A more convenient, and surprisingly economical option is to hire a car and driver. You can negotiate a trip, even a multiday trip, with almost any taxi driver. Most travellers find this easier than hiring a self-drive car through an agency, although rental agencies can arrange for a child seat, which you won't find in ordinary taxis. Be warned, though, that Sri Lankan roads can be hair-raising and it's often easier to leave the driving to a professional.

If you're tossing up between taking the pram or the backpack, remember that many Sri Lankan streets aren't paved and those that are tend to be uneven, however the tropical heat can make carrying a backpack uncomfortable. It's a tough call.

Shopping & Essentials

Remember to pack plenty of sun-smart gear – hats, sunscreen and shirts with sleeves. The hill country can get surprisingly chilly, so pack some jumpers or parkas for cool nights.

Expensive nappies and baby food are available in a few outlets in major centres – notably Keells and Cargills Food City.

Health & Safety

Visit your doctor well in advance of your trip to discuss vaccinations and health precautions, and make sure you have adequate insurance. Medical care is hugely variable in Sri Lanka – the best, and most expensive, clinics are in Colombo. But don't be scared off by health concerns. The potential dangers may seem ominous, but in reality few travellers experience anything more than an upset stomach. While travelling, be careful of food hygiene – eat fresh-cooked food at busy eateries and drink only bottled or boiled water.

Sri Lankan toilets are a mix of Western-style and squatters – if you need the former, stay in midrange or top-end accommodation. Toilet paper isn't always offered so carry some with you, along with some soap.

Breastfeeding in public is accepted, but try to be discreet.

Sri Lanka has suffered through a violent ethnic conflict since the 1980s. Repeated rounds of negotiations have failed to bring a lasting peace and you should definitely avoid travelling in the north and east of the country. The capital, Colombo, has also been rocked by bomb attacks. However, the tourist areas listed here are generally considered safe and many travellers, including families, rave about the wonderful holidays they've spent in Sri Lanka. Check with your embassy before finalising your plans.

Food

Sri Lankan food is a highlight for many visitors. Rice and curry is the staple meal and comes in myriad delicious forms and flavours, usually featuring a coconut-milk base. The local fondness for lots of chilli can make it difficult for travelling families to order at local places or street vendors, but restaurants will generally go out of their way to cater to delicate young palates.

If in doubt, fruit is available almost everywhere, including bananas, papayas, passionfruit, avocados, mangos, melons, pineapples and guavas. Make sure it's peeled fresh. It's also easy to find buffalo-milk yoghurt, often served with palm treacle as a breakfast treat. You can resort to plain rice or hoppers – bowl-shaped pancakes sometimes served with an egg or banana in the middle – and the kids are bound to love string hoppers, a tangle of steamed rice noodles made into little patties and served with curry.

THAILAND

'The land of smiles' has always been an unmissable stop on the Asian travel trail because of its gorgeous beaches, scrummy cuisine, and fascinating Buddhist traditions. Add in a comfortable and efficient train network, a good health-care system, all the supermarket necessities and plenty of accommodation catering to all budgets and your family is never going to want to leave.

With kids along you'll experience even more of the famously hospitable Thai culture. Expect to be invited into homes and restaurant kitchens, and don't be surprised if temporary nannies appear from nowhere to entertain your little ones while you finish your lunch.

In busy centres like Bangkok it's a good idea to give the kids a copy of your hotel's business card to carry – there's often a map on the flipside with the name and address in Thai. For more Thai travel tips check out the ebook Thailand 4 Kids (www.thailand4kids.com).

WHAT'S TOPS

- Songkran (13 to 15 April), or Thai New Year, the national excuse for a water fight
- Saying hi to a baby elephant at the Maesa Elephant Camp near Chiang Mai
- Khao Sok, a stunning national park of waterfalls, limestone cliffs and jungle trails where you can sleep in a tree house
- Night markets, magical places where fabulous handicrafts are given even more mystery in the light-strung dark
- Watching as small lotus-shaped baskets of flowers, incense and candles are

floated on waterways for Loi Krathong (October/November)
- Swimming in the seven-tiered waterfalls of Erawan National Park, one of Thailand's most beautiful parks
- Taking a pony ride on the beaches of Hua Hin, near the king's summer palace
- Clothes shopping – glitzy malls, street bazaars, or nimble tailors who can whip up something with a perfect fit

WHERE

The long, thin shape of Thailand means that many travellers focus their exploration on either the mountains of the north or the beaches of the south. The capital, Bangkok, has plenty of family-friendly attractions too.

To the north, **Chiang Mai** has a well-developed kids' centre with a playground and animal exhibits. There are also children's art classes in the city, a doll museum, even a skate ramp. Nearby in the **Mae Sa valley**, there are gorgeous waterfalls plunging into swimming holes and exotic animal shows.

To the south, many travellers head straight for the beach, lured by pristine waters and accommodation for every taste. **Ko Samui**, on the east side, is a long-term favourite, and if you like island-hopping, it's convenient to visit the island of **Ko Tao**, famous for wonderful diving and snorkelling. On the mainland nearby you can see shadow puppets being made in **Nakhon Si Thammarat**. On the Andaman coast are the luxurious resorts of **Phuket** – Karon Beach is good for families. Nearby, you can ride an elephant through the monkey-inhabited jungles of **Krabi Province**.

BANGKOK

It's true that Bangkok is congested and polluted, but this gateway city has an exciting energy and there's a lot to offer little ones. If you find yourself here on an international stopover or on the way north or south, it's worth taking a few days to look around.

Most families enjoy a trip to **Dusit Zoo**, where there are rare indigenous animals like banteng and rhinos, as well as paddle boats and a playground. For more exotic animal action, see the cobras milked for antivenin at **Queen Saovabha Memorial Institute**.

If you need to cool down you can head to **Central World Ice Skating**, and for fans of ethnic costume there's the **Bangkok Doll Factory & Museum**.

SEE
Tha Thewet (Thewet Pier; Th Samsen; 7am-7pm) Join the novice monks and Thai kids feeding the fish at this pier. You'll see the muddy waters transformed into a lather of shiny bodies. Fish pellets are sold at the pier.
Children's Discovery Museum (+66 (0) 2272 4575; Chatuchak Park, Th Kamphaeng Phet 4; 9am-5pm Tue-Fri, 10am-6pm Sat & Sun) The hands-on experiences here include climbing aboard a miniature fire truck, or being enclosed in a giant soap bubble. Most displays are geared to 4 to 10 year olds, but for the littlies there's a toddlers' playground at the back of the main building.

STAY
Bangkok Christian Guest House (+66 (0) 2233 6303; www.bcgh.org; 123 Sala Daeng Soi 2, Th Convent; $$) Originally serving Protestant missionaries after WWII, this hotel now takes all comers. It's a good option for families, with a children's activity room, a small garden space, large rooms and connecting rooms available.
Asia Hotel (+66 (0) 2215 0808; www.asiahotel.co.th; 296 Th Phayathai; $$) This enormous hotel has large rooms and good facilities, including a children's pool and babysitting services. It's

connected by a walkway to the Skytrain so you can avoid the *tuk-tuk* onslaught, and cinemas and Western fast-food outlets are nearby if your little ones need a reminder of home.

KO SAMUI

Kids and adults alike are lured by the delights of Thailand's famous holiday isle – white-sand beaches, clear aquamarine seas and swaying coconut palms. Resort hotels generally go out of their way to cater to families and are well equipped with cots, highchairs, kiddy pools and babysitting services.

Older kids might enjoy **Treasure Island Miniature Golf Course** on Hat Chaweng, or a safari with **Namuang Safari Park** which has elephant trekking and croc shows.

STAY

Your best bet is to find a room away from the seedy nightlife and girly bars that can make the more popular beaches less than family friendly. Hat Bang Rak (Big Buddha Beach) is a good option, with a laid-back atmosphere and particularly calm waters for swimming. Plush resorts are well equipped with kids' facilities and activities, but if you can't afford the high rates, try the small **Como Resort** (+66 (0) 7742 5210; www.kohsamuibeachresort.com; $$), which has a wading pool, kids' toys for the beach and bungalows with two bedrooms and two bathrooms available. Another good beach is Hat Choeng Mon, which is clean and quiet. Try **PS Villa** (+66 (0) 7742 5160; $), which has cute wooden bungalows set in a lush and spacious fairy garden of tropical plants, and you can eat at candlelit tables on the sand.

WHEN

The best time to visit Thailand is between November and February, when the rains ease off and Thai people take the

ABOVE: THAILAND'S PRISTINE WATERS AND DRAMATIC LANDSCAPES ARE A STRONG LURE FOR ADVENTUROUS FAMILIES

DESTINATIONS

HOT NIGHT IN CHIANG MAI

~ THAILAND ~

BY FRITZ BURKE

Two am, the Rose Guest House, Chiang Mai, Thailand.

Noah is terribly sick, hot and sticky like the Thai night, and the heat is rising off the street through the attic windows to the bed where he lies shivering with fever. We have to bring his temperature down. Along the hall to the cistern, buckets of water, sponges to the hot skin.

Is it malaria – the deadly cerebral variety extant in these jungles? We researched, and decided against the antimalarial. It would be the dry season, we would stay out of the bush. But there was that elephant ride, a package tour, designed, ironically, as a fun day for the kids. Experience on the road tells me it's intestinal: bad water, street food. But here – where we don't know anyone to call, where we don't even know where to find a phone at this hour – here in this spooky room with its dim bulb, the one bed, the fragile body of my eight-year-old son; in this place I'm profoundly afraid.

Well, it wasn't malaria. Noah is off to college. He's grown up splendidly – self-reliant, outgoing, with a strong moral centre. It's mostly luck or grace I suppose. But it's also the learned confidence, adaptability and tolerance of the independent traveller.

'He's still burning up.' His mother's voice is stretched with anxiety, hollow, in the large unfurnished room. She goes for the night watchman, tries to communicate, ends up leading him to the bed where I'm bathing Noah's forehead. He understands: goes to call a *tuk-tuk*. And we're off, the four of us (Jonas, our five-year-old, is awake now) squeezed on the bench, exposed to the night, wheeling through the sleeping streets – candles in the temples, the night's last prostitutes, the city gate – finally the lighted hospital.

It's not the details of this wild night I've forgotten. It's the sharp, cutting emotional anxiety, the flat-out parental panic, which, mercifully, have been dulled over the last 15 years. I can still feel the air rushing through our ears, the *tuk-tuk*'s throb – which made conversation impossible – leaving me alone with too many questions. What kind of parent knowingly exposes his son to malaria? Would we have to wait all night in some dingy emergency room? Would the doctor – presuming there was one at 3am – know what he was doing?

Our *tuk-tuk* roars up to the front door and we stumble inside. Almost immediately my tension eases. Everything: the light, the colours, even the front desk is perfect. Like many spaces in Thailand – a garden, a noodle shack, a carp pond, now a hospital – it somehow contains a certain lightness of spirit. A team of spotless nurses surround Noah and get to work taking his pulse, measuring and weighing, snapping fresh linens on a bed, and fetching the doctor, who radiates calm authority and speaks excellent English. He asks me a few questions, but his eyes never leave Noah, and he speaks to him kindly, taking his measure. 'Very unlikely this is malaria', he tells us. Probably bacterial; he prescribes an antibiotic. We need to keep the medicine down and Noah will be fine. But I already know this, it could not be otherwise in this place, where even the cafeteria smells like heaven. I'm thinking about checking myself in for a tune-up – perhaps a complete overhaul. Because it occurs to me, now that I've been able to exhale, that I'm badly shaken.

Because of course it could have been malaria. Because in that cheap Thai guesthouse, my wife and I didn't only learn that health is our biggest threat on the road. We witnessed how a parent's fear spans cultural divides. And we got a peek at that dread that lurks somewhere in a parent's heart no matter where she travels. No matter if he travels at all.

Perhaps it is partly because of his exposure to tropical diseases that Noah understands that it is the unknown, often unsettling experience that teaches you the most about yourself and the people you love. It is this lesson my boys have learned on the road. Sure, you try to expose them to the culture – the Royal Palace in Bangkok? They'd rather watch cartoons in the hotel lobby. A history lecture in La Villa de Guadalupe? Boring. In the end, it's the worst times they remember best.

What our family remembers best about our six weeks in Thailand is the Rose Guest House where Noah almost had malaria. After we left the hospital we upgraded to a hotel where we thought Noah would be

'I'm thinking about checking myself in for a tune-up... Because it occurs to me, now that I've been able to exhale, that I'm badly shaken.'

more comfortable. But we continued to take meals at the Rose Guest House. In a small way, the people there had become our family. There was the Korean/Thai couple who were the owners and their baby, as well as the transvestite waiter and the teenage kickboxer who worked the kitchen. They had always been kind to us, but after our trip to the hospital, we understood that it wasn't just because we were customers. The kickboxer spent longer demonstrating his moves for the boys. The transvestite arrived with a plate of American-style pancakes, the owner helped my wife with her Thai lessons. And all of us, Thai and American alike, got a peek at the things that bind us together.

opportunity to kick up their heels – this is festival season. On the beaches to the south the weather is usually good from February to late June. Avoid the rainy season from July to October.

HOW

Transport

Bangkok is a major regional hub, but if you want to avoid the capital you can also connect to airports in Chiang Mai in the north, or Phuket or Samui for the southern beaches.

If you have to travel a long distance, Thailand's efficient train system is definitely a better option than the bus. There's more room to move, a chance to stretch the legs and the scenery outside is far more interesting than you'd see along the highway. Second-class sleepers are fun: at sunset an attendant will come and transform your two seats into two bunk-style sleeping berths with fresh linen, screened off with a curtain for privacy.

Children's car restraints are not required by law in Thailand and it can be hard trying to find a car-hire operator that provides them. If you're concerned about this, consider bringing your own car seat or capsule from home.

Getting around town can be one of the delights of Thai travel. *Tuk-tuks* putter up and down every Thai city and town, allowing an unrestricted view of all the happenings outside – just make sure that everyone's arms and legs stay inside in heavy traffic! On foot, most travelling parents rely on a backpack rather than a stroller, as Thai streets can have uneven surfaces and many are unpaved.

Shopping & Essentials

Nappies, formula, wipes and all the other kid essentials are widely available in Thai cities and resort towns. Bring sun-smart gear for everyone – sunscreen, hats, T-shirts and sunglasses. It's also worth bringing slip-on shoes as you'll be leaving your shoes at the door at most homes and temples.

Health

It's important to consult your doctor before you travel to Thailand for advice on vaccinations and other health precautions. Drink only bottled or boiled water, and avoid drinks containing ice. Also warn the kids not to touch animals as rabies is quite common.

Most accommodation is fitted with Western-style toilets, but be prepared for squat toilets in other places. Also keep some soap on hand to wash up before each meal as bathrooms are not usually equipped with soap.

Large cities in Thailand have good clinics catering especially to travellers. Bangkok is malaria-free, and there's minimal risk in other city and resort areas.

Breastfeeding is common in Thailand, but modesty is expected. Try to breastfeed in privacy or carry a shawl for nursing.

Food

Thai people love their food (they frequently eat five or six meals a day) and most *farang* (Westerners) agree, including kids. Noodles are often the top menu pick for families. Stick to busy places where the food is cooked fresh to reduce your chances of a tummy bug.

However if your kids don't share your enthusiasm for Thai cuisine, plain rice is usually a safe bet and they might be drawn to the range of weird and wonderful fruit available at most restaurants or at markets and street corners. If all else fails, it's not hard to find a Western restaurant or fast-food chain in major centres.

Most restaurants are familiar with the *farang* plea *khâw mâi phèt mâak* (not too spicy please), but *mâi sai phrík* (don't put chilli in) is another handy phrase for parents.

MALAYSIA

With its fascinating mix of Chinese, Malay and Indian communities, its aquamarine waters fringed in white sand, and its unspoilt jungle reserves, Malaysia offers a heady mix of both cultural and natural attractions. A family holiday here can easily combine a little decadent relaxation with some educational cultural experiences.

Attractions and transport generally offer discounts for children and many beach resorts have special family chalets. If the budget is tight, Chinese hotels are a good bargain as they charge by the room rather than the number of people. However, cots are not widely available in cheap accommodation – let the little ones sleep in with you.

WHAT'S TOPS

- Witnessing the feeding frenzy at Sabah's Sepilok Orang-Utan Rehabilitation Centre
- Chinese New Year (January/February) when families open their homes and children receive *ang paw* (lucky money in red packets)
- Visiting the butterflies, rhinoceros beetles and scorpions at the Butterfly Garden in the Cameron Highlands
- Traversing the mountainous interior on the spectacular Jungle Railway
- Spotting leatherback turtles during the egg-laying season (May to August) in Rantau Abang
- Deepavali, the Hindu Festival of Lights (October/November), when tiny oil-lamps are lit outside of homes
- Choosing a souvenir kite at Kuala Lumpur's Central Market

WHERE

The capital, **Kuala Lumpur**, is a modern, cosmopolitan city with plenty to offer young visitors, while in the historic port city of **Melaka** you can learn about Malaysia's fascinating trading history through a sound-and-light show.

If you're hankering for a lazy beach holiday you can head to the stunning island resorts of **Penang**, or **Langkawi**, which features white-sand beaches and jungle-clad hills. The east-coast resorts are another good bet – **Pulau Kapas** and **Cherating** are more geared to family holidays than the other resort towns here. Or try **Pulau Perhentian Besar**, possibly Malaysia's most beautiful island.

For a more adventurous holiday, take the family over to Malaysian Borneo to see the unspoilt wilderness of Gunung Mulu National Park in **Sarawak** and the lovely islands of Tunku Abdul Rahman National Park in **Sabah**.

KUALA LUMPUR

Kuala Lumpur has a great range of kid-friendly attractions, many of them providing calm oases from the busy city. To beat the heat, head to one of the city's excellent water parks: Sunway Lagoon, with its waterslides, giant waterfall and kiddy pool, or Desa Water Park, with three wave pools and a bubble pool.

Wet-weather options include the **National Museum**, featuring displays on kites, shadow play and weaving, or shopping at **Suria KLCC** which houses a couple of great toy stores.

SEE

Lake Gardens This fantastic park is crammed with family attractions. Come here to run around the playground, rent a boat or visit the National Planetarium. Nature lovers will enjoy the enormous walk-in aviary with 160 species of birds, as well as the deer park, butterfly park and the hibiscus and orchid gardens.

Petronas Towers The second-tallest building in the world has a Skybridge linking its two towers on the 41st floor and Petrosains, an interactive science discovery centre for kids. Next to the towers there's a fantastic 0.8 hectare playground with wading pools, a musical fountain and plenty of space to run around.

STAY

MiCasa Hotel Apartments (+60 (0) 3 2081 1188; www.micasahotel.com; $$$) The apartments here, a few hundred metres south of Ampang Park LRT station, are roomy and have fully equipped kitchens so you can prepare your own meals. Rooms with two bedrooms and two bathrooms are available and there are satellite TVs and DVD players. What's more, there's a playroom with scheduled activities and babysitting is available.

PENANG

Penang is a great place to learn a new sport – you can try sailing, windsurfing, waterskiing, parasailing, canoeing or horseback riding.

If the kids need a break from the sun, sand and water, there's also a **butterfly farm** with 4000 fluttering residents and the **Penang Bird Park**, with 400 species from around the world.

Jump on the **funicular railway** up to the top of **Penang Hill** for panoramic views over the city. Or slither down to the **Snake Temple** to see residents curled around the altar among the incense smoke.

During the **Dragon Boat Festival** in June, traditional dragon boats take to the water for a colourful regatta.

STAY

The **Holiday Inn Resort Penang** (+60 (0) 4 881 1601; www.penang.holiday-inn.com; 72 Jl Batu Ferringhi, Batu Ferringhi; $$$) pulls out all the stops in family-friendly accommodation. There's a well-equipped kids' club, a children's pool with a lifeguard, babysitting and water-sports equipment. There are even special 'Kid Suites' which come with TVs, videos, Playstations and bunk beds decorated with themes like 'space' or 'treasure island'. If you're on a tighter budget, try the **Oriental Hotel** (+60 (0) 4 263 4211; www.oriental.com.my; 105 Jl Penang, Georgetown; $$) which has good-value family rooms sleeping four, though the decor's pretty ordinary.

WHEN

The east coast of Peninsular Malaysia receives heavy rain from November to mid-February. Elsewhere in Malaysia rain falls fairly evenly throughout the year and you won't escape it, so plan your trip any time that suits you.

HOW

Transport

Malaysia has a good bus system: it's fast, economical and comfortable, seats can be reserved, and air-con services only cost a little more. The train system is also modern and reliable, but there are only two lines.

Many families, however, prefer to rent a car. By Asian standards the roads are not too hair-raising, petrol is inexpensive and new cars are available for hire. If that's not for you, consider taking long-distance taxis between towns, which are ideal for four passengers. Note however that under Malaysian law car seats are only compulsory for kids sitting in the front seat, although everyone must wear a seat belt.

When you're legging it around town, it's better to take a backpack than a stroller, despite the heat. In many places there are no footpaths and the very high kerbs present too much of an obstacle to pram pushers.

Shopping & Essentials

Nappies, baby food and all the other essentials are widely available in major centres, but stock up if you're planning to head somewhere remote or to an island.

Health

It's important to discuss vaccinations and other medical precautions with your doctor well in advance of your trip, and ensure that you have adequate travel insurance. Most travellers, however, experience nothing more than a stomach bug. You can reduce the risks of this by eating only fresh-cooked food from busy kitchens, peeling all fruit and ensuring you drink boiled or bottled water.

In the major centres, medical facilities are well developed, and there are also special travellers' clinics, but in rural areas services are more basic. In rural areas too, rabies is common, so warn kids not to play with animals.

In Malaysia you'll find both Western-style toilets and squatters, although the former are rapidly replacing the latter and there should be one in your hotel. Toilet paper is not always provided so carry some with you.

Food

Food is a highlight of a Malaysian trip and the kids are sure to love the drama and noise of hawkers as they whip you up something delicious. And it's generally safe to try these delights – great effort has been put into raising the hygiene standards of hawkers in recent years and many have been moved into hawker centres and food courts.

Rice and noodles form the basis of Malaysian cuisine and the rich cultural mix of Malay, Chinese and Indian communities have informed the region's cuisine. Chilli is an important component, but you can usually ask for it to be toned down by saying *kurang pedas* (not too spicy, please!).

But if the local food fails to impress, Malaysian cities are full of the usual Western-style fast-food outlets.

SINGAPORE

Singapore is best known as a cosmopolitan city of skyscrapers, high-end shopping and an efficient public infrastructure that puts the rest of Southeast Asia to shame. Surprisingly, however, the city's family-friendly attractions tend to focus on outdoor activities and nature.

WHERE

Water parks are the city's favourite way to beat the heat and there are loads to choose from – try **Big Splash** or **Wild Wild Wet**. If it's really hot you might need to visit **Snow City**.

If your kids are skaters, they'll want to check out the **National Youth Centre Skate Park**

and Youth Park, or maybe just take the skateboard down to **East Coast Park**, which is also a great place for a stroll with a stroller or a bike ride.

If the city vibe is getting a bit much, there are a surprising number of farms in Singapore that open their doors to the public, often for free. You can visit the **Avifauna Bird Farm**, which specialises in exotic birds, **Jurong Frog Farm**, **Hay Dairies Goat Farm** and two million species of orchid at **Orchidville**, among others.

SEE

Sentosa Island (1800 736 8672; www.sentosa.com.sg; 24hr) Take a cable car to this fantasy land of amusement parks, over-the-top sculptures, imported-sand beaches and laser-light shows. Aquabikes, canoes, kayaks and sailboards are available for hire and there are loads of cool attractions like a Trapeze School and a 3-D cinema. The Butterfly Park & Insect Kingdom is filled with fascinating creepy crawlies, while Underwater World is an excellent aquarium where kids can swim with dolphins.

DUCKtour (+65 6338 6877; www.ducktours.com.sg) While this kitschy amphibious tour is shunned by many tourists as too, well, touristy, it's actually great fun and the kids are bound to love it. The bright yellow buggy will take you on a tour of the city streets before it splashes straight into the water for a cruise around the harbour.

STAY

Allison Hotel (+65 6336 0811; www.allsonhotels.com; 101 Victoria St; $$) Most of Singapore's top-end hotels will welcome you in with facilities like babysitting, swimming pools, family rooms, extra beds and cots, along with steep rates. If you want to keep costs down, you can try this good-value place with rosewood furniture, a small pool and babysitting services.

Sloane Court Hotel (+65 6235 3311; sloane@singnet.com.sg; 17 Balmoral Rd; $) For those on even tighter budgets, this excellent-value mock-Tudor hotel is in a garden setting just 10 minutes' walk from Orchard Rd.

WHEN

Located almost on the equator, Singapore is hot and wet most of the year, so there's little difference between the seasons and any time is a great time to visit. The most spectacular festival is Thaipusam in January/February, followed by Chinese New Year around the same time.

HOW

Transport

With all that heat you'll want to keep walking to a minimum. The efficient public transport system will whisk the family around in air-conditioned comfort – both the bus and MRT systems are good options – or hop aboard one of the 19,000 taxis in Singapore. If you plan to hire a car, child seats should be available – ask when booking.

Shopping & Essentials

Department stores such as Takashimaya (www.takashimaya-sin.com) are your best bet for sourcing nappies, baby formula and other supplies.

Singapore's streets aren't great for strollers, though the heat can make baby slings uncomfortable too. Locals tend to carry their kids around on the hip.

The **YMCA Metropolitan** (+65 6839 8333; www.mymca.org.sg; 60 Stevens Rd) runs a crèche that's open to anyone with kids from 7am to 1pm weekdays. At other times, enquire about babysitting through your hotel.

Health

Singapore has excellent health facilities and in fact runs a lucrative trade in 'medical tourism'. You'll only need vaccinations if you've come from a yellow fever area and it's safe to drink the tap water. Singapore's public toilets are also immaculately clean and widely available.

Food

Singapore offers a huge range of cuisines – from hawker delights to Western-style food courts and high-end restaurants. Singaporean society is very family oriented – eating out with the kids is the norm and restaurants will always make you feel welcome.

CHINA

A country in a state of massive flux, China embodies a huge diversity of people and landscapes. From the sublime karst mountains of the southwest to the fast-changing skyline of Shànghǎi and the historic monuments of Běijīng, this country is varied and vast. A family holiday here is not for the faint-hearted, but if you and your kids are adventurous, a trip through the Middle Kingdom will yield incredible experiences, a deep sense of history and some of the yummiest meals you've ever tasted.

The Chinese love children, and the one-child policy has elevated their status to that of minigods. You'll find that your kids provide an excellent introduction to the locals – people are generally fascinated by *xiao lawai* (little foreigners) and *yang wawa* (foreign babies). But be warned – you may need to prepare your kids to have their personal space invaded by cheerful strangers touching their beautiful fair hair, picking them up or pinching their adorable pink cheeks.

WHAT'S TOPS

- ○ Painting the town red for Chinese New Year (January/February), when children receive red packets containing lucky money
- ○ Sun, sand, surf and the macaques of Monkey Island on tropical Hǎinán
- ○ Balancing your way across the 50 crazy bridges of Shěnyáng's Botanical Garden
- ○ Facing off the army of ancient terracotta warriors in Xī'ān
- ○ Cheering on the colourful boats races and eating *zòngzi* (triangular rice dumplings) at the Dragon Boat Festival (May/June)
- ○ Seeing kung-fu acolytes, many as young as five, demonstrate their skills at Shaolin Temple

WHERE

Travel in China is pretty rough, and one of the more challenging aspects is getting from A to B. Many parents find it easier to visit the larger centres rather than braving long journeys into the wilds – all the cities listed here are accessible by air if you can't face the bus or train. Fortunately you can still experience the diversity of China by basing yourselves in a city and taking short trips out of town.

From **Běijīng** you can visit **Xī'ān** to see the army of terracotta warriors, or head south along the coastal route. **Shànghǎi** has a superfast airport train reaching speeds up to 430km/h, top-notch aquariums and incredible circus acts, while **Guǎngzhōu** offers peaceful parks, world-class museums and cruises on the Pearl River. If you're headed to **Hong Kong** from here, it's worth stopping in **Shēnzhèn** to visit its theme parks. They're cheesy, but offer everything from a miniature Great Wall to an Eiffel Tower and re-creations of ethnic minority villages.

In the southwest, the beautiful city of **Guìlín** is surrounded by gorgeous karst mountains and features underground caves full of stalagmites and stalagtites. Visit the lovely Qixing Park or take the popular six-hour Li River cruise to **Yángshuò**.

To the west, **Kūnmíng** is a modern, safe, laid-back city – Green Lake Park and Grand View Park are family favourites, with boats and playgrounds. **Dàlǐ** and **Lìjiāng**, west again, with stunning scenery, Western eateries and lively festivals, offer respite from the road. You can walk, cycle, swim and relax here.

BEIJING

China's capital is crammed with headlining attractions – the Forbidden City, the Summer Palace, Temple of Heaven Park and Tiananmen Square. Unfortunately children are not generally as awed by the majesty of these sights as their parents. You might need to seek out something more active for little ones.

Young zoologists will enjoy the **Běijīng Aquarium**, or the **Blue Zoo Beijing**, with its shark feeding sessions. Junior scientists can visit the **ExploraScience** museum, with its hands-on displays, and everyone is sure to love **New China's Children's Toy World**, an extravagant emporium of toys.

Events for kids, such as plays or arts-and-crafts events, are listed in the monthly English-language culture magazine That's Beijing (www.thatsbeijing.com).

SEE

Sīmǎtái Great Wall (8am-5pm) If your kids look at the more popular access points for the Great Wall and see an old, yawn-worthy road stretching endlessly into the distance, try this section instead. While the climb is steep and precarious here, there's a cable car to do the hard work for you and you can inspect fascinating 'obstacle-walls' – walls-within-walls for defending against enemies who breached the outer defences. There's also a 3km downhill toboggan ride. Enough said.

China Puppet Theatre (1a Anha Xili, Beisanhuan Lu) Shadow play, puppetry, music and dance are all on the program at this popular theatre, or try the **China Children's Art Theatre** (64 Dong'anmen Dajie, Dongcheng), which specialises in entertaining kids. You can also take in an acrobatic show – this traditional form of street theatre usually features kids performing amazing physical feats.

STAY

Kerry Center Hotel (+86 (0) 10 6561 8833; hbkc@shangri-la.com; 1 Guanghua Lu; $$$) With a large, supervised play area, a pool and a good location close to sporting facilities, this is a great choice for families. Rooms are spacious and there are bathtubs in the bathrooms.

RJ Brown Hotel (19 Xin Nong St, Tian Qiao, Xuanwe District; $$) This comfortable hotel opened in 2005 and features five family suites to combat Běijīng's tendency towards tiny rooms. Cots are available and there's a pizza place next door if you're craving a taste of home.

HONG KONG

With a modern, efficient infrastructure, high standards in food and sanitation and literally hundreds of exciting ways to distract the kids, the bright lights of this big city are sure to thrill the whole family.

Most public transport and museums offer half-price fares and admission for kids under 12, but family tickets are rare. Your hotel can probably recommend a babysitter, or try **Rent-A-Mum** (+852 2523 4868; www.rent-a-mum.com; 12A Amber Lodge, 21-25 Hollywood Rd, Central).

SEE

Ocean Park (+852 3923 2323; www.oceanpark.com.hk; Ocean Park Rd; 9.30am-8pm) Hong Kong Disneyland has given Ocean Park a run for its money, but the attractions here take their cue from Chinese culture, with a terrifying loop-the-loop roller coaster called the Dragon, pandas on display and a Chinese cultural village.

Hong Kong Heritage Museum (+852 2180 8188; www.heritagemuseum.gov.hk; 10am-6pm Mon & Wed-Sat, 10am-7pm Sun) This wonderful museum is crammed with kid-friendly fun from the Hakka fishing village to the computers that let you try on Cantonese opera make-up. The 1st floor houses eight learning and play zones with Chinese cultural themes for kids aged four to 10. For the littler ones there's a hands-on Hong Kong *Toy Story* area. Admission is free on Wednesday.

STAY

Salisbury (+852 2268 7888; www.ymcahk.org.hk; 41 Salisbury Rd; $) Hong Kong's best budget choice is this YMCA-run hostel near the Star Ferry terminal. There are family suites, a children's pool, a climbing wall, even a children's corner in the bookshop. Book well ahead.

BP International Hotel (+852 2376 111; www .bpih.com.hk; 8 Austin Rd; $$) An enormous hotel offering family rooms with bunk beds close to Kowloon Park, with its swimming pools, playgrounds and kung fu corner. Prices are often reduced by 50% so haggle hard.

WHEN

Spring (March to May) and autumn (September to early November) can be the best times to travel as summer and winter often dish up extreme temperatures. Summer is the busiest tourist season when rates go up and it can be hard to find a room. Book well in advance if you plan to travel during the Chinese New Year season (January/February).

HOW

Transport
The simple convenience of family car travel is almost out of the question in China, except in large cities, as hire cars can't be driven out of the city boundaries.

If you plan on getting between cities on the bus or train you'll need to prepare the family for a long ride. Buses average only 25km/h on nonhighway routes and even on the main roads you'll have to contend with the endless noise of the horn and Hong Kong films looped on the overhead TVs. On the plus side, bus services between large cities have reasonably clean and comfortable fleets, and on popular long-haul routes sleeper buses, some with two-tier bunks, are available.

Trains are generally a better option, the safety record is good and you can opt for a sleeper to escape the crowded and uncomfortable sitting carriages. Unfortunately toilet facilities on trains tend to be awful.

Instead, it's worth seriously considering taking flights for long distances. Infants under the age of two fly for 10% of the adult fare, while tickets are generally 25% cheaper than the full fare for children between two and 11.

China's cities are huge and can be tough to navigate – it's best not to try to do it all on foot. Buses are crowded and slow and hiring a bike is only an option if the kids are old enough to brave the crazy traffic, but helmets are hard to find. Taxis are the best way to get around – they're cheap and plentiful.

DESTINATIONS

Shopping & Essentials

Supermarkets are well stocked with baby supplies. Some attractions offer discounts for children, but it's based on height rather than age (generally kids over 130cm or 140cm pay full price). Kids' prices, however, aren't always advertised, so it's worth asking.

Health

China is a reasonably healthy country for travellers, however, it's important to discuss vaccinations and other health precautions with your doctor well in advance of your trip. Also make sure you have adequate insurance.

The standards of medical facilities vary; the best services can be found in major centres where there are often English-speaking clinics catering to travellers. In the case of an accident, it's better to simply get a taxi to the hospital directly; try to avoid dealing with the authorities if possible.

The best way to avoid travellers' diarrhoea is to eat freshly cooked food from busy restaurants. Also make sure you drink boiled or bottled water. Rabies is common, so warn your kids not to touch animals.

Breastfeeding is not a problem, but it's better to find a private place unless you want to be the target of many curious eyes.

Unfortunately, public toilets in China are infamous. Try to get everyone to go before leaving your hotel and if you're caught out on the go, aim for a fast-food outlet, hotel or department store. Toilet paper is rarely provided so keep some with you.

Food

With a huge range of regional cuisines, food is a real highlight of a visit to China. The traditional meal of rice or noodles topped with a vegetable and/or meat dish is usually a winner with kids, and there are loads of more adventurous (and spicy!) foods to try if yours

ABOVE. **CHILDREN GET DOLLED UP FOR A CHINESE NEW YEAR PARADE**

enjoy sampling new tastes. You can pick up quick snacks from delicious dumplings to tea eggs (eggs soaked in soy sauce) and steamed buns, but make sure you stick to clean and busy places. The traditional breakfast of rice porridge is also very kid-friendly.

If your child is a picky eater you can try fresh fruit, which is often served at the end of the meal. Sweetened cereal and the old bland standby – boiled rice – can be found everywhere. It's also not hard to find Western-style fast-food places in major cities.

You'll be hard-pressed to find a highchair or a kids' menu, especially in cheap restaurants, although some upmarket places have started to introduce children's meals, usually consisting of fried chicken or fish. Carry your own cutlery if your little ones haven't caught onto the intricacies of using chopsticks. Many people carry their own chopsticks around too, for cleanliness and to cut down on the forests of disposable wooden sticks that are thrown out after every meal.

JAPAN

With the rise of Japanese influence on Western kid-culture, plane tickets to Japan are sure to excite the whole family. What kid wouldn't want to visit the home of Tamagotchi, anime and Hello Kitty?

Japan is a modern, industrialised country with an excellent transport system and high standards of sanitation. The main barrier for families is the sheer expense of travel, but self-catering and using public transport can keep costs down. For more tips and advice, try *Japan for Kids* by Diane Wiltshire Kanagawa and Jeane Huey Erickson.

WHAT'S TOPS

- Toy shopping in Tokyo
- Stepping into a traditional Japanese town at Hida-No-Sato in Takayama
- Joining kids dressed to the hilt for Shichi-Go-San (Seven-Five-Three Festival, 15 November) celebrating girls aged three and seven and boys aged five
- Diving into the noise and fun of a Japanese gaming arcade
- Catching a glimpse of a kimono-clad geisha down a cobbled lane in Kyoto
- Exploring the world of the samurai among the feudal homesteads of Kakunodate
- Getting cultured with all the ritual of a Japanese tea ceremony
- Sleeping on futons laid over tatami mats at a traditional ryokan (guesthouse)
- Frolicking among the frozen art and ice sculptures at Sapporo's Yuki Matsuri (Snow Festival, early February)

WHERE

The classic quick dip into Japan takes in Tokyo and the Kansai region, speeding between the capital and Kyoto on a breathtaking bullet train.

North of Tokyo, you can sample some Japanese traditions in the northern **Honshū region**. The town of **Aizu-Wakamatsu** preserves the legend of the White Tiger samurais, while nearby **Hiraizumi** features one of Japan's finest temple complexes. Further north, look for impish water spirits in the **Tōno Valley**, a region famous for folk legends.

If the quiet majesty of Japan's most famous peak, **Mt Fuji**, reflected in the pools of **Fuji**

Go-ko (Fuji Five Lakes) doesn't inspire the kids, try the noise and squeals at the nearby **Fujikyu Highland amusement park**.

South of Kyoto you can soak in the public baths at **Matsuyama** or check out the bubbling, spurting 'hells' (geothermal hot pools) of **Beppu**.

Many kids want to pay their respects at the Children's Peace Memorial in **Hiroshima**, where thousands of paper cranes folded by kids around the world are sent annually, inspired by leukaemia victim Sadako. There's also a Hiroshima Children's Museum and planetarium.

To the far south, the islands of **Okinawa** make a great beach destination – bring a snorkel and flippers.

TOKYO

Japan's capital is jammed with enough kid-distracting sights to keep you busy for a week or more.

This is a great place to shop for toys – try **Loft** or **Kiddyland**, which has five floors of the latest in kid-stravagance. Then of course there's **Tokyo Disneyland**, a near-perfect replica of the original in Anaheim, California.

Make a day-trip to Ueno for the **National Science Museum**, with its excellent special exhibits, the **Ueno Zoo**, with its popular pandas and petting area, and the chance to try on Edo-era clothes at the **Shitamachi History Museum**.

Hit www.tokyowithkids.com for more inspiration.

SEE

Sony Building (www.sonybuilding.jp; 5-3-1 Ginza, Chūō-ku; 11am-7pm) If your kids are gizmo fans it's worth braving the long queues at this temple of technology. They can try out new and yet-to-be-released Sony products and there are cool free video and virtual-reality games to play. Big kids usually have just as much fun.

Tokyo Metropolitan Children's Hall (+81 3 3409 6361; www.fukushihoken.metro.tokyo.jp/jidou; 1-18-24 Shibuya Shibuya-ku; 9am-5pm) This place is crammed with cool stuff – there's a rooftop playground with skates and unicycles, a music room, a *manga* (Japanese comics) room, and a human body maze. What's more, it's free.

STAY

National Children's Castle Hotel (+81 3 3797 5666; www.kodomono-shiro.or.jp; 7th fl, 5-53-1 Jingumae, Shibuya-ku; $$) Atop a fabulous children's complex are Tokyo's top family digs. There are indoor and outdoor play areas, art and music rooms, a computer room, wading pool and structured activities like puppet shows and origami lessons. The hotel itself offers comfortable, if bland, rooms although some Japanese-style rooms are on offer for a more cultural experience. Book well in advance.

Suigetsu Hotel Ōgaisō (+81 3 3822 4611; www.ohgai.co.jp; 3-3-21 Ikenohata, Taito-ku) If you want to get down on the tatami and sleep like the locals, try this traditional-style hotel. There's a beautiful Japanese garden, Japanese baths and a tearoom.

KANSAI REGION

The compact Kansai region packs more cultural punch into a small area than any other part of Japan.

In **Kyoto**, you'll find all the contradictions that make Japan so fascinating – neon signs coexisting with ancient temples and tottering geishas sharing the streets with teen punks. If the kids aren't awed by the 2000 **temples and shrines** in the city, step into the **National Costume Museum** to see dozens of models of Japanese clothes down the ages, or go taste-testing in the **Nishiki Market**.

In **Osaka** the over-the-top **Universal Studios Japan** amusement park will scare the pants off the whole family, while the **Osaka Aquarium** has the world's largest aquarium tank and displays on the marine life found at eight different ocean levels.

In the ancient city of **Nara** there are eight Unesco World Heritage sites, but the kids might be more interested in the 1200 resident deer at **Nara-Kōen**, considered to be messengers of the gods in pre-Buddhist times. You can buy biscuits to feed them, but littlies might be intimidated by their pushy table manners.

STAY

Kyoto is a great place to try the traditional ryokan experience – try **Yachiyo Ryokan** (+81 75 771 4148; Fukuchi-chō; $$$) for a ryokan with all the trimmings, or the more humble **Yuhara Ryokan** (+81 75 371 9583; Shōmen agaru-Kiyamachi-dōri; $).

With a spacious quad room for families, bike rentals and free tea and coffee, **Tour Club** (www.kyotojp.com; Highashinakasui, Shōmen agaru; $) is a great budget choice in Kyoto, as is **Budget Inn** (+81 75 344 1510; www.budgetinnjp.com; Aburanokōji-Schichijō; $).

WHEN

The best time to visit Japan is in either spring (March to May) or autumn (September to November). Come in March to catch the spectacular cherry blossoms (sakura).

HOW

Transport

Japanese trains are a pleasure – they're clean, fast, frequent and comfortable. If train travel is an option, it's usually faster than the bus.

The famous *shinkansen*, or bullet train, is one of the highlights of Japan for many young travellers. These superfast services reach speeds of up to 300km/h. It's worth purchasing a Japan Rail Pass (www.japan railpass.net) to save money if you plan to use trains to get around. Children aged six to 11 pay half the adult fare, and up to two children five or under can travel with one adult for free.

Ferries are another fun way to get around this nation of islands. The cheapest fares on longer trips have you rolling out your futon on tatami mats shared by other passengers, but not all passengers are intent on sleep – families may be better off in a private cabin.

Many travellers hire a car, which is a great way to get around and not prohibitively expensive. Child seats, however, are not common, either from car-hire agencies or in taxis. Consider bringing a car seat or capsule from home if you're concerned about this.

Shopping & Essentials

Nappies, formula and all the other essentials are readily available in Japan. There are nappy-changing facilities in many public places, notably department stores and large train stations. Cots are available in most hotels and these can be booked in advance.

Childcare agencies are also available in large cities, though few outside Tokyo have English-speaking staff.

ATMs are common in Japan, but most of them don't accept foreign-issued cards, even if they display the Visa or MasterCard logos. Fortunately, the Japanese postal system has recently linked all of its ATMs to international Cirrus and Plus networks, so head for the post office if you want withdraw cash.

Health

Japan's major centres have excellent, modern health-care facilities but they're expensive, so make sure you have adequate travel insurance. Outside major centres the standards of care can be patchy, and you're unlikely to find an English-speaking doctor – try to take a Japanese-speaker with you.

Food sanitation is generally good, the water is safe to drink and no special vaccinations are required, but ensure everyone is up to date with basic immunisations.

Public toilets are free and there's a mix of Western-style toilets and squat toilets. If you're forced to use the latter, the correct position is facing the hood. Toilet paper isn't always provided, so keep some on hand. You may be given small packets of tissues on the street, which is a popular form of advertising.

Breastfeeding is common, but not generally in public. Try to find a private place.

Food

There's a huge variety of food on offer in Japan, and every area has a regional speciality. The main stumbling block for visitors is usually decoding the menu – choose a restaurant that displays plastic food models in the window so your kids can point out what they want. Noodles and rice are usually safe bets, but if you can't please a fussy eater you'll rarely be far from a fast-food chain like McDonald's or a Japanese equivalent.

During the day you'll find *okosama-ranchi* (children's specials) at most budget restaurants. These consist of Western-style food such as mini-hamburgers or wiener sausages and tend to go down very well with kids.

For dinner you will often find yourself sitting on the floor, which kids enjoy. At Western-style restaurants highchairs are generally available.

When you're out for a meal, you might find the following phrases useful: *kodomo-zure demo ii des[u] ka?* (are children allowed?), *kodomo-yō no menyŭ wa arimas[u] ka?* (is there a children's menu?) *bebii-yō no isu wa arimas[u] ka?* (do you have a highchair for the baby?).

BALI

Bali is a superb choice for a family beach holiday. Quite apart from the stunning tropical scenery and excellent facilities, your children will be doted upon at every turn. The Balinese have a huge affection for *anak-anak* (children). They believe that children came straight from god, and the younger they are the closer they are to god. Children are considered part of the community and everyone, not just the parents, has a responsibility towards them.

WHERE

The best beaches for families are **Sanur**, **Nusa Dua** and **Lovina**, where the surf is placid and the streets quieter than busy Kuta. Check out www.baliforfamilies.com for more travel tips.

SEE

Waterbom Park (+62 (0) 361 755676; www.waterbom .com; Jl Kartika Plaza, Kuta; 9.30am-6pm) If the kids ever get sick of the gorgeous beaches, try this wonderful water park set on 3.5 hectares of tropical gardens. There are waterslides, pools, play areas and a supervised park for under-fives. Let the kids loose under the water cannons or the giant bucket that dumps 1200 litres of water every two minutes. If you can sneak away, there's also a gorgeous spa on site. **Taman Burung Bali Bird Park** (+62 (0) 361 299352; www.bali-bird-park.com; north of Tegaltama; 8am-6pm).

Walk through the aviaries here to see more than 1000 birds of over 250 species, including rare *cendrawasih* (birds of paradise) from Irian Jaya. There's even a couple of non-native Komodo dragons. Next door, Rimba Reptile Park specialises in critters like turtles, crocs, pythons and yet more Komodo dragons.

STAY

Westin Resort (+62 (0) 361 771906; www.westin .com/bali; $$$) Located on the placid waters of Nusa Dua beach, the sumptuous Westin has a kids' club with great facilities and supervised activities like Balinese art and craft. There's also a kids' pool and playground, and two-bedroom family studios come equipped with Playstations, soft toys and board games.

Rambutan Beach Cottages (+62 (0) 362 41388; www.rambutan.org; Jl Ketepang; $$) For those with less cash to splash around, the Rambutan offers very comfortable, Balinese-styled rooms in the mellow north-coast town of Lovina. There's a creative kids' play area, two pools, lovely gardens and even a treehouse!

WHEN

Bali is at its best during the dry season – April to September – but it gets busy and expensive in July and August.

HOW

Transport

There are quick, efficient tourist shuttle buses, like Perama (www.peramatour.com), between major centres but with a family it's usually cheaper and more convenient to hire your own vehicle. It's also fun to take a boat to a nearby island – they pull up on the beach and you clamber over the stern.

Shopping & Essentials

Most essentials can be purchased in Balinese pharmacies, though you may need to ask for assistance with reading the labels. Make sure you stock up on plenty of insect repellent and consider packing some rehydration salts as it's easy for little people to get dehydrated. A folding stroller can be useful as a substitute for a highchair, though as transport they can be awkward because pavements tend to be uneven and have lots of kerbs.

Health

Contact your doctor well in advance of your trip to discuss the necessary vaccinations and precautions, and take out adequate travel insurance. You'll head off the major health concerns however by simply ensuring your family drinks bottled or boiled water and eats fresh-cooked food.

There are still Asian-style squat toilets in Bali but you're unlikely to encounter any in tourist areas. You will, however, need to bring your own toilet paper – carry a supply with you.

The best medical services for foreigners are available at the Australian-run **BIMC** (+62 (0) 361 761263; www.bimcbali.com; Jl Ngurah Rai 100X; 24hr) and **International SOS** (+62 (0) 361 761263; www .bimcbali.com; Jl Ngurah Rai 100X; 24hr), both near the Bali Galeria.

Food

Food in Bali is generally fresh and safe and Western tastes have thoroughly infiltrated the Balinese menu – items including pizza, burgers and fresh fruit are all easy to come by, and the major international fast-food chains all have outlets here. Balinese eateries tend to be casual affairs where children are more than welcome and many even have a grassy area where you can let them run loose while you relax over your meal.

LATIN AMERICA & THE CARIBBEAN

MEXICO

An explosion of colour swiped across a canvas of deserts, rainforests, tropical beaches and cerulean seas, Mexico has something for everyone. In this land of contrasts, those with infants and toddlers can find low-key, easy beaches to relax on or explore, parents with young children will find forests full of animals, birds, fish and insects while teenagers can have a ball learning about the ancient history of the Mayans or how to salsa dance the night away. From hiking to horseback riding to snorkelling and visiting markets, action is the word in this vivacious culture. Mexico has heaps of language schools that families can attend together to learn Spanish, cooking, culture and the arts. While Mexico is one of the most expensive countries in Latin America, it's still a bargain for anyone travelling from the US, Europe or Australia.

WHAT'S TOPS

- Lodging with a local family in the city of Oaxaca while being enrolled in language classes specifically geared towards each age group
- Bosque de Chapultepec in Mexico City has everything from a world-class zoo to an amusement park and Papalote Museo del Niño (a children's museum)
- Taking a pirate cruise aboard the *Sunderland* (www.pirateshipcabo.com .mx) in Cabo San Lucas
- Climbing on ancient ruins, chasing butterflies and lizards and imagining life before European conquest at Cobá in Quintana Roo
- Splashing around in the thermal pools, wave pools and water slides at Ixtapan Balneario, Spa y Parque Acuático in Ixtapan de la Sal southwest of Mexico City
- Boating through the mangroves filled with wild flamingos and crocodiles at Río Lagartos (Yucatán state)
- Watching thousands of turtle hatchlings scurry to the ocean with Grupo Ecológico de la Costa Verde (www.project-tortuga .org) at Playa San Francisco
- Hopping on a happy horse or pony for a leisurely jaunt through the jungle of Mismaloya near Puerto Vallarta
- Snorkelling the shallow, fish-filled reefs and lounge on the white beaches of Cozumel island

WHERE

While **Mexico City** and the hot dry interior hold plenty of interest, they don't compare with the coasts, which offer innumerable oases for families, from the dry cactus beach lands of **Baja** to the surf laden **Oaxaca coast** and the Caribbean calm of the **Yucatán Peninsula**. Resort towns such as **Cancún**, **Acapulco**, **Puerto Vallarta** and **Mazatlan** have plenty of family parks and attractions, but are geared towards party-goers – these are good teen options. While children will enjoy these hot spots, highlights will be the areas out of town that teem with wildlife and adventure. A great beach for kids of all ages is **Sayulita**, about 50km north of Puerto Vallarta, which has a mellow vibe, beginner-level surfable waves and plenty to do.

YUCATÁN PENINSULA

With calm, electric-blue seas, alabaster beaches and enough flora, fauna, history and culture to keep anyone entertained, the Yucatán is an all-round crowd pleaser. Get into Mexican culture in artsy **Mérida** or laid-back **Mahahual**, snorkel and bask in the sun at **Cozumel** or explore Mayan history via jungle

DESTINATIONS

archaeological sites at **Chichén Itzá**, **Cobá** and **Tulum**. Resorts in and around **Cancún** make for an ultimately relaxing vacation while ecolodges along the **Costa Maya** combine creature comforts with a touch of adventure. Small family-run establishments are widely available and offer a warmer embrace into the culture. The calm, blue waters of the Caribbean are great for a first snorkelling experience but will be equally appreciated by experienced divers.

STAY

Children interested in jungle ecology will enjoy **Boca Paila Camps** (+52-984-871-24-99; www.cesiak.org; Main office: Federal Rd (307) Cancun-Tulum, #68 Tulum; $$), near Tulum, run by the ecology group CESiaK. The rustic units are as eco-friendly as you can get – from here guided hikes can be made into Reserva de la Biosfera Sian Ka'an. Right on the beach in Mahahual yet near the jungle, **Margarita del Sol** (+52-55-53-50-8522; www.margaritadelsol.com; Km 7 South; $$) has comfy self-contained studios sleeping four, free snorkel gear, kayaks and wi-fi.

BAJA

This is *Road Runner* land with soaring cacti, vast desert and even a wily coyote or two. The **Sea of Cortez** with its calm waters, whale watching, fishing and clamming is ideal for families. Be sure not to hit this region during the US spring break when hordes of college students descend. **La Paz** is one of the more mellow well-established Baja towns where you'll find an easy, colonial feel and plenty of white beaches. For calm farther north head to **San Filipe**, a sleepy fishing village that can be great fun for beachcombing at low tide. A good travel hub for families, central **San Ignacio** is an oasis of date and coconut palms and a jumping-off point for whale watching.

Price Guide

$** budget   **$$** midrange   **$$$ top end

STAY

Camping and camper vans are the way many families on a budget visit Baja but if you're travelling sans vehicle try **Ignacio Springs Bed & Breakfast** (+52-615-154-0333; www.ignaciosprings.com; $$), a super-deluxe complex of Mongolian yurts in San Ignacio. Family units are available and all have some sort of cooking unit. Kids will love fishing for tilapia and swimming in the spring-fed Río San Ignacia and you can pick dates from palms right outside your door. In La Paz, **Club El Moro** (+52-612-122-4084; www.clubelmoro .com; Carretera a Pichilingue, La Paz; $$) has a pool, parking and peace. It's a bit of a hoof to town with little ones but the tranquillity is worth it. The whole place is gated and most rooms have complete kitchens. Lots of trees and flowers in the lovely gardens make for fun and discoveries.

OAXACA & THE OAXACA COAST

Oaxaca encompasses so much of the beauty of Mexico. The city is small and manageable with plenty of open spaces for children. Don't miss the colourful but not too overwhelming **Mercado 20 de Noviembre** in Oaxaca city where brave children can munch on popcorn-like *chapolines* (crispy grasshoppers). The coasts aren't great for swimming because of the surf, but the beaches are wide and there are often horseback rides and vendors selling little treats. In **Mazunte**, kids will love **Centro Mexicano de la Tortuga** (+52-948-584-33-76; cmt_mazunte@hotmail.com; Mazunte; 10am-4.30pm Tue-Sat, 10am-2.30pm Sun) where all seven of Mexico's marine turtle species can be seen up close in tanks and aquariums. Those wanting a real adventure and unafraid of roughing it should head to the **Lagunas de Chacahua** where bats fish in the mangroves at night and crocodiles bask by day.

STAY

If you are taking language courses in Oaxaca, you will probably have the chance to experience a **Family Homestay** (book through language schools www.iccoax.com, www.mexonline.com/becari.htm, www.vinigulaza.com; Oaxaca City; $). A homestay often means other children to play with, kitchen access and a full-fledged cultural experience. **Beach Hotel Inés** (+52-954-582-07-92; www.hotelines.com; Calle del Morro, Puerto Escondido; $$) in Puerto Escondido is recommended by the author's eight-year-old son because of the plentiful lizards, horseback riding on the beach, and the pool with plenty of other children to play with. Parents like the privacy of separate bedrooms and the kitchenettes.

WHEN

May through September are the hottest, wettest months of the year but if you're on the beach, the weather is rarely a worry except in Baja where it gets very hot. July, August and mid-December to early January are peak tourist months when everything gets booked up and prices soar.

HOW

Transport

Rental cars in Mexico are expensive and roads can harbour hazards like potholes, animals and the occasional car-jacker. Still, if you keep to the main roads and travel during daylight hours it's unlikely you'll have any problems. Rental companies rarely provide car seats – if you bring your own seat, be vigilant about getting a car that actually has seat belts. *Colectivos* or minibuses are a cheaper and

ROBERTO A SANCHEZ | ISTOCKPHOTO

DESTINATIONS

ABOVE. **RELAX AT ONE OF CANCÚN'S PLUSH RESORTS**

CHICLÉ MAN

~ MEXICO ~

BY NOAH BURKE

What sticks in my mind from our family trip to Mexico was not the Diego Rivera murals or the baroque churches. It was Chiclé Man. Every day he made his rounds up and down the beach, his large box of Chiclets gum in one hand, and a jar for his pesos in the other.

It's not like I hadn't seen poor people before. My parents made sure of that. Other 10-year-olds got to go to Disney World; I got the Rose Guest House in Chiang Mai – a $1-a-night dump. In the dirty alleys of Guatemala City my parents held my hand tightly, pulling me away from the beggars' hopeful looks. On the cobblestones of Marrakesh, I was old enough to hold my little brother's hand. Every time we'd walk by a doorway there would be a beggar holding out a cup. My stomach would drop and I'd plead with my parents for money. I couldn't understand why they didn't feel as heartbroken as I did. But in Thailand, I used my parents as a shield to avoid making eye contact with their hopeless faces. I'd learned to do as my parents and pretend not to see the poor, even when they followed you speaking in their foreign tongue. My parents understood something I couldn't at that age: that no matter how much money we gave out we couldn't make a difference in these people's lives.

Nevertheless, when Chiclé Man shuffled up to umbrellas in front of the Vista Hermosa, I'd reach for my peso allowance every day. The other tourists hid behind their books or margaritas, but our eyes met. Canadians would come and Germans

would go but Chiclé Man always managed to find me. 'Chiclé?', he'd ask softly, in a dull monotone, holding out his colourful squares for me to choose. His sun-browned face showed no emotion.

This was our fourth international trip together as a family, the trip where dad and I climbed the volcano. My dad thought hiking would be a good bonding experience despite my protests about hiking two miles to the base of the volcano and then all the way up to the top the volcano. I thought we should just buy a postcard of the view from one of the local souvenir shops. The volcano was a lot further than the guidebook said. We trudged two miles across sandy ash, then another two across rocky lava fields and then up a pebbly slope with no sign of water to refill our empty canteens.

I now remember our trips by stand-out experiences like that. In Guatemala, my brother learnt to walk and my dad shaved his beard (which he's never done before or since) and I rode my first horse. Two years later in Morocco my brother discovered candy and I discovered arcade games. On the walled roof of the Hotel Du Sud in the Anti-Atlas Mountains, I played soccer with Mohamed and his six kids. Mohamed worked from sun-up to sundown, hauling water up three flights of stairs for the tourists' toilets. His children had no shoes, so I took mine off for our soccer games. In Thailand I taught my brother to swim in the Indian Ocean and mum and I fell off a motorcycle. I knew that this trip's memory for me would be Chiclé Man. As I sat on the beach behind the Vista Hermosa hotel, I knew that this would be our last long family trip, since next year I going into high school.

The Vista Hermosa was easily the nicest hotel we stayed in during that 3000-mile bus trek across Mexico. The family rule was my brother and I got to choose one hotel each trip. In Thailand, we had chosen a hotel that had a pool and hamburgers. In Morocco we picked one that looked like a sandcastle. Here at the Vista Hermosa, my brother and I didn't have to share a bed, and more importantly, English-speaking cartoons played on the television in the lobby. There was a balcony with a table and each night we played cards and watched the sun submerge into sea.

At dusk when I was doing my maths worksheets and the palm-tree shadows started to creep up to our balcony, I would watch the vendors trudge home after their long days. Mothers walked by carrying wooden bowls and brightly coloured string hammocks. Following closely behind were preteen daughters with jars of penny candies and baby sisters on their hips. Their little brothers would follow last, with no shoes and wearing *Teenage Mutant Ninja Turtle* shorts and Michael Jordan T-shirts, the cast-off rags of American commercial abundance.

But Chiclé Man walked alone. I don't think he had a family to go to or a little brother to watch out for. Day in and day out he walked, in his brown tattered shirt

'I played soccer with Mohamed and his six kids. His children had no shoes, so I took mine off for our soccer games.'

and ripped jeans, his sunbaked sandals taped to his feet. He never missed a day.

If my family was at home, we probably wouldn't be spending this time together, but here the music and dancing drew us together just like the other families. And although my brother and I always complained about leaving our friends, we both looked forward to playing catch on foreign sands. Even though my Spanish was improving, I was beginning to understand that some words like poverty and family were difficult to translate.

On the plane back to the States, I couldn't get Chiclé Man out of my head. I'm not sure I ever will. But I know that it wasn't fair that this man, born a few hundred miles south of the Rio Grande, had to sell gum for a living while the CEO of Chiclets made Chiclé Man's month's wages in the time it took to blow his nose. I knew that even though I wasn't there to give Chiclé Man my pesos, he was making his rounds – taking his slow steps in the hot sand.

safe alternative outside of cities. In urban areas public transport is often crowded and smelly. Note that on public transport children are expected to sit on a parent's lap. Nearly all towns have roads suitable for strollers. If travelling to and from Mexico as a sole parent, you will probably need a notarised consent form from the other parent or proof of custody or a death certificate – this is mandatory for air travel to and from the US.

Shopping & Essentials

Stores in Mexico are usually open from 9am to 8pm while typical restaurants remain open from 7am to around 10pm or midnight. Most large towns or tourist centres will have everything you need in terms of baby supplies but if you are travelling to small villages it's a good idea to stock up.

Health

To avoid Montezuma's Revenge (diarrhoea) wash hands religiously and never drink any water you aren't certain is clean. Peel fruits and avoid ice. Medical care is relatively good and widely available but nothing you want to explore on holiday. Public toilets are often paid and range from clean to vile – throw used paper into a bin not into the toilet. Hepatitis A (for children over one year; over two years in the US) and typhoid vaccinations (for children over two) are recommended.

Food

Food in Mexico is wonderfully healthy and fresh with plenty of beans, meat and vegetables. *Torterias* (sandwich shops) and *taquerias* (taco shops) have heaps of options so even a picky eater will find something. Hot chocolate for breakfast with fresh bread from the *panaderia* (bread shop) and ripe tropical fruit is something few children will decline. On the streets, there are treats from corn on the cob to biscuits and *paletas* (popsicles). Lots of families eat out and children are welcomed but that doesn't mean you should expect a highchair or special service.

CUBA

Beaches galore, thumping music and some of the friendliest folks on Earth make what might seem like an iffy family destination into a kiddy wonderland. Of course, for parents who want an adventurous edge to their travel, Cuba's got it. It's crumbling, sometimes dirty and you'll have a helluva time finding simple items like decent nappies, but these challenges seem small once you've spotted a manatee or watched a crocodile hatch out of an egg. If you are looking for ease and flashy beaches, Cuba has the biggest resort in the Caribbean with direct flights that let you skip over Havana – of course you'll never see the country's heart this way but it will be easy. Perhaps your biggest worry in taking the family to Cuba is that you might inspire future cigar smoking and revolutionary behaviour in your children.

WHAT'S TOPS

- Parks like Pato de Juegos in Havana are what kids dream of finding in their travels
- Experiencing what pre-resort Varadero would have been like at Playa Santa Maria
- Dolphins, seals and tropical fish get you off the streets of Havana for an hour or two at Acuario Nacional
- Letting your package tour do the talking (and thinking) at the sparkling beach resort area of Varadero

- Searching for manatees, the world's smallest bird, and crocodiles in Ciénaga de Zapata Biosphere Reserve
- Pools, beach and bumper cars await at Club Cienfuegos, Cienfuegos
- Taking a horse carriage from Santa Lucia to the white sands of Playa Los Cocos
- Blowing the minds of the whole family during a 90-minute tour of Gran Caverna de Santo Tomás

WHERE

Everywhere you go in Cuba you'll find friendly people and outrageously gorgeous landscapes. While most families keep to **Havana** and the beach areas of **Varadero** and **Guardalavaca** (both megaresorts), visiting lesser-known destinations is not difficult. Beach areas such as **Cayo Santa Maria**, **Cayo Coco**, and **Playa Santa Lucia** are definitely not off the beaten track but the voyage there will take families through a more authentic Cuba. Inland, **Viñales**, with its picturesque farms and honeycombs of caves, has everything from hiking to swimming. Top towns for children include: **Trinidad**, with its lovely historic centre and nearby beaches, waterfalls and dense forest, **Baracoa**, known for its coconut-based cuisine, jungle boat trips and scientist-led walks and **Holguín**, which oozes with charm, friendly folks and picture-perfect beaches. Great wildlife viewing can be had at **Ciénaga de Zapata** not far off the Autopista National from Havana.

HAVANA

Smiling, spectacularly dilapidated Havana is a vibrant, gritty city that loves children. While it's teeming with animated plazas, it is dirty so be prepared. The **Vedado** municipality is the most kid-friendly area to stay with its pocket parks and less urban vibe. **Habana Vieja** is lovely, heavy on historic sights and a good choice for those wanting to be more central. Ice-cream shops are everywhere and it's a hoot to discover the town by coco-taxi (egg-shaped three-wheeled taxis).

SEE

Patio de Juegos (playground on the Malecón at Tacón) Bounce, ride and swing in Havana's biggest playground. There's an inflatable play room, pony rides, swings galore and kids, kids, kids. For teen or adult shoppers, the nearby Feria de la Artesania with its selection of art, crafts, jewellery and clothing is the city's best.
Acuario Nacional (+53-7-202-5872; www .acuarionacional.cu; Av 3 at Calle 62; $; 10am-6pm Tue-Sun) There's plenty of space for littlies to run from tank to tank at this remodelled aquarium. Dolphin performances are the highlight. Don't miss the sea lions either!

STAY

Casas Particulares (www.cubaparticular.com) Whether you rent your own independent house or apartment or stay with a family, these types of lodgings are the most affordable and can be the most child-friendly in the city. Many come with breakfast so make sure you make your child's needs clear.
Hotel Palacio O'Farrill (+53-7-8605080; Calle Cuba 102-108 entre Chacón y Tejadillo; $$) You can't beat a place that's incredibly central (in Habana Vieja) but also right across from the best park in town. All the charms of Havana are here, with pluses like big bathtubs and a leafy courtyard. Babysitting and baby cots are available.

TRINIDAD & AROUND

Cobblestone streets, restored colonial homes and charming churches have gained Trinidad

DESTINATIONS

World Heritage–site status from Unesco. This town is a fabulous base to explore nearby **Topes de Collantes** for forest hiking past rivers and waterfalls. If you tire of the jungle, the white-sand beaches of **Playa Ancon** are only 10 minutes away and the **Valle de los Ingenios**, a site of historic sugar plantations, can be reached by train for a day trip.

That said, this town is one of the most visited towns in Cuba and can become over-saturated with tourists and aggressive touts. The nearby towns of La Boca and Casilda, only 4km and 6km away respectively, make a quieter alternative to the chaos of the historic centre.

STAY

Trinidad abounds with **casas particulares** (www.cubaparticular.com). Shop around to find the best one for you and don't be led anywhere by touts who get huge cuts when it's just as easy to find a place on your own. Families wanting more peaceful surroundings should head to La Boca which fronts a small beach or the less pleasing Casilda. If you'd rather stay at a hotel, try **Casa del Campesino** (+53-419-6481; $$) 1.5km out of town. There are boat and horseback-riding tours available, cute little rooms overlooking a river and, if there are enough people around, country-style Cuban folk dancing. For something more luxurious, head to Playa Ancón's **Brisas Trinidad del Mar** (+53-419-6500/01/02/03; www.cubanacan.cu; $$$), which has a kiddy pool along with all the regular resort perks and is on an amazing stretch of beach.

VARADERO

Families looking for complete relaxation, package style, should look no further than the Caribbean's largest resort complex, Varadero. Here you can fly in direct and see nothing

of Cuba's gritty side but only beachside beauty. Of course, a visit to this area can also provide a break from the hard travel and intense cultural stimulation of an otherwise adventurous trip. Kids abound so finding playmates is a breeze, there are amazing pools, turquoise ocean, minigolf (Cuban style), a bowling alley, glass-bottomed boat trips, dolphin encounters and even an amusement park. Babysitters and day-care centres are ubiquitous.

STAY

The best deals on lodging in Varadero are through package tours with included airfare – many resorts in this category cater specifically to families. For this kind of holiday consider **Hotel Bella Costa** (+53-45-667210; Av Las Américas, Cubanacán; $$$) which, besides having commendable service and facilities, has individual family-friendly villas, a kids' club and a pool for kids under seven. The base rate is more expensive at the lavish **Meliá** (+53-45-667013; www.solmeliacuba.com; $$$) but kids under 12 stay free with parents so costs are cut considerably. The stretch of beach here is especially nice as is the food and the views. For those arriving in Varadero independently and not wanting to fork out resort-level prices, try friendly **Villa Tortuga** (+53-45-614747; btwn Camino del Mar & Av Kawama, Horizontes; $$) on a fantastic bit of beach.

PINAR DEL RÍO PROVINCE

With its rolling agricultural lands of rice and tobacco, giant caves, wildlife and of course that bright blue ocean always nearby, **Viñales**, with its funky *mogotes* (limestone hills) is a good base for rock climbing, hiking, horseback riding and delving into the **Gran Caverna de Santo Tomás**, Cuba's largest cave system, with a 90-minute tour. For kids who can handle long journeys, the **Península de Guanahacabibes** is a fantastic area for mammals, sea turtles, reptiles and (between March and May) swarms of stinky *cangrejos colorados* (red and yellow crabs). Around the mountainous areas of **Soroa** and **Las Terrazas**, find hiking and horse trails, waterfalls and freshwater swimming spots.

STAY

Just outside Viñales, stay at the working farm of **Ranchón y Finca San Vicente** (+53-8-796110; $$). Trails, orchards, horses, birds and folk tunes at night will keep little ones entertained for days. In town there are oodles of **casas particulares** (www.cubaparticular.com) for that down-home Cuban experience. In Soroa, a good option is **Hotel & Villa Soroa** (+53-9-778218; $$) in a valley of tall trees. Private villas sleep five and have kitchens and TVs.

WHEN

It's probably not a great idea to plan your trip during hurricane season, which is technically June to November – the worst storms generally occur in September and October. Cubans holiday (along with most of the northern hemisphere) in July and August. At this time prices soar, beaches get packed and everything gets rather loud and boisterous. Rainy season is May to October but an afternoon thunderstorm can be a nice relief from the heat.

HOW

Transport

Having your own car can be a boon if you've got lots of gear and rentals are inexpensive, but don't expect rental companies to supply a car seat; they are not known for their customer service. An option is to take the clean and reliable Viazul buses which have received rave reviews from Lonely Planet readers who travelled to Cuba with children. Those with lots of time might consider a train trip – the electric Hershey Train that runs between Havana and Matanzas was built by the famed chocolate company, and other trains run throughout the country. Many cities have horse carriages and bicycle taxis (fun!) and the entire country is set up for biking.

Shopping & Essentials

Cuban nappies have been called 'sweaty' and 'plasticy.' It's best to bring as many of your own brand as you can carry. In fact, finding well-stocked supermarkets and any Western style products, even sunscreen, can be a chore. Many travellers with babies pack extra baby food and formula just in case.

Health

The biggest health risk in Cuba is Hepatitis A. **Servimed** (+53-07-204-48-11) is the for-profit health system created for visitors and payment is expected in cash. You'll want good insurance to get you out of Cuba should any emergencies arise. Pharmacy items are in short supply so bring a good first-aid kit. Public toilets often have no water, paper or even a seat, so look for toilets in hotels, restaurant or gas stations. You'll often have to pay an attendant for paper – note that the paper is thrown into a bin, not the toilet.

Food

Besides beans and rice, which most kids can dig, Cuba is known for its ice cream and pizza – can you say kid friendly? Of course those fresh tropical fruits, shakes and juices are marvellous. Breakfast is rarely served in restaurants so make sure your hotel serves this meal or you have the fixings to prepare your own.

DESTINATIONS

BELIZE

It's a beach destination, it's a jungle destination and it's all wrapped up into one tidy, English-speaking package. If you're considering a first backpacker-type holiday with the kids, Belize is a soft place to start. Of course the midrange to resort-quality options are equally tempting and even the most budget-minded families should seriously consider staying a few nights in a jungle lodge. It boasts the world's second-longest barrier reef, reggae music and a chilled-out beach vibe, and older children and teens will enjoy the beaches as much as tiny tots who can contentedly chase hermit crabs through the white sands. Then hop into the jungle to tube through caves, horseback ride, view an amazing array of wildlife and become enchanted with the ancient Maya.

WHAT'S TOPS

- Cave tubing at Nohoch Che'en Caves Branch Ecological Reserve
- Snorkelling the Hol Chan Marine Reserve at Ambergris Caye
- Fluttering about with the colourful residents of Green Hills Butterfly Ranch
- Kayaking past the wildlife-laden shores around Punta Gorda
- Taking a night tour from the Community Baboon Sanctuary (a black howler monkey sanctuary)
- Belize Zoo, where over 100 native, orphaned, injured or confiscated animals are cared for on 12 beautiful hectares
- Boating deep into the jungle to discover the Mayan mysteries of Lamanai (or just to chase lizards)
- Getting up close to enormous iguanas at the Green Iguana Exhibit and Medicinal Jungle Trail in San Ignacio

WHERE

The entire Caribbean coast from **Ambergris Caye** to **Punta Gorda** is a sparkling beach paradise to snorkellers, divers and beach loungers. Tourism is booming in the **Northern Cayes** while the central and southern coastal areas offer a more authentic Belizean experience. Inland jungles offer a different adventure. **San Ignacio** is a lively centre or ensconce yourselves in the jungle at one of many lodges. Explore Mayan archaeological sites at **Lamanai**, **Caracol** or even **Tikal**, just over the border in Guatemala.

NORTHERN CAYES

Small children can splash around on these beautiful beaches all day while bigger kids can discover a lush underwater world through snorkelling or diving at all skill levels. This is the carefree Caribbean with reggae music, cold fruit juices and plenty of hammocks. From popular but pricey **Ambergris Caye** and its town of **San Pedro** to more budget-oriented **Caye Caulker** or jewel-like **Turneffe Atoll**, a trip to this region means water and relaxation. The more active nightlife makes this a good choice for teens.

STAY
Coconuts Caribbean Hotel (+501-226-3500; www.coconutshotel.com; $$) is a good midrange option in Ambergris Caye where kids under 10 stay free and there's a super-friendly and laid-back atmosphere. Suites have kitchens. In Caye Caulker, **Caye Caulker Rentals** (+501-226-0029; www.cayecaulkerrentals.com; $$) has great deals on a huge variety of houses or apartments.

SOUTHERN BELIZE

Families looking to get away from the tourist hoopla should beeline it to southern Belize for more low-key resorts like **Placencia** and **Punta Gorda** or to the coral gardens of **Glover's Reef**. Inland you'll find a jaguar reserve at **Cockscomb Basin Wildlife Sanctuary** (although jaguars are so shy you shouldn't expect to see any) and lightly visited **Mayflower Bocawina National Park**. A short drive or boat trip from Belize City brings you to the village of **Gales Point Manatee** where you can expect to see at least a head or a back of these likeable sea cows.

STAY

Mama Noots Backabush (+501-670-8019; www .mamanoots.com; $$), right at Mayflower Bocawina National Park, rightly calls itself a 'playground in the jungle'. There are trails, butterfly and hummingbird gardens, waterfalls and just about every other natural treat you could think of. There's a large family cabana or special rates for groups renting a cluster of lodge rooms. Between Placencia and Seine Bight, Canadian-run **Saks at Placencia** (+501-523-3227; www.saksatplacencia.com; $$) has a huge array of accommodation, from beach cabanas to full houses, that is nearly all family friendly.

WESTERN BELIZE

Get deep into the jungle where Mayan ruins, waterfalls, butterfly farms and all-round adventure await. One of Belize's more popular activities is **cave tubing** which is great for kids 10 and up or braver younger children – remember once you're in there's no turning back so think carefully about taking kids that get frightened easily. **San Ignacio** has Belize's most thriving market and is a great base for spectacular day trips. Jungle lodges around this town are a great option if you want to focus on being in the jungle. **Caracoal**, about a two-hour drive from San Ignacio, was once one of the most powerful cities in the Mayan world – while the history is mostly of interest to older children, the jungle setting provides lots of (mostly insect oriented) detours for smaller kids.

STAY

A good base for tubing and horseback riding, **Banana Bank Lodge & Jungle Equestrian Adventure** (+501-820-2020; www.bananabank.com; near Roaring Creek Village; $$-$$$) specialises in family holidays. Well-kept horses graze among jungle critters and there's even a resident jaguar! Near San Ignacio, **duPlooy's Jungle Lodge** (+501-824-3101; www.duplooys.com; near San Ignacio; $$$) is one of the longest-running lodges in the region and features the on-site Belize Botanic Gardens – four different habitats and 18 hectares of planted trees.

WHEN

December through May is the dry season in Belize and the best time to visit. The rainy season from June to November is especially pronounced in the south so if you do plan your trip during these months you might want to keep north. Tourists descend in large numbers in the few weeks around Christmas and around Easter break.

HOW

Transport

Car rental in Belize is expensive but can be the most convenient choice for families. Roads are pretty good and rental companies often have car seats – but it's a good idea to check in advance. If you do decide to take long-distance buses (which are US school buses), taxis and bikes can get you anywhere

DESTINATIONS

once you're in town. To get to the cayes and atolls you'll probably experience an open-air 'water taxi' – bring along rain gear just in case. On Caye Caulker and Ambergris Caye the preferred land vehicle is the golf-cart taxi!

Shopping & Essentials

Boat operators don't carry child-sized life jackets so if you are planning to make any long water journeys, consider bringing your own. Nappies and baby supplies are widely available but there's not much variety. Strollers are great for the waterfront while a baby backpack is much better for jungle visits.

Health

All the regular Central American risks such as hepatitis A, dengue and typhoid are found in Belize. Highest malaria risk areas are the west and the south. Tap water is not safe and be sure to peel all fruits and vegies. When in the jungle be particularly careful of snakes, which are a very real hazard. Medical care is limited and services are expected to be paid in cash but pharmacies are generally well stocked.

Food

Sandwiches, chicken, burgers, fruit and beans and rice are everyday foods in Belize. Other items like spaghetti, pizza and grilled cheese are common in tourist areas. Self-catering is common in the country and avocados, bananas and other wonderfully fresh fruits and vegetables can be mashed or cooked for infant food.

COSTA RICA

If it's wildlife they're after, bring 'em to Costa Rica. Monkeys, crocodiles, giant bugs and lounging sloths are only the beginning of what you're sure to see in forest settings. Besides being touted as the safest country in Latin America, Costa Rica, from its cloud-enshrouded volcanoes to its perfect beaches, is one of the most diversely beautiful regions on the planet. Travel is easy, the people are friendly and love kids and there is so much to do (or not do!) that everyone can find their happiness. Of course this means Costa Rica is a seriously popular destination and you'll probably see more foreigners running around than Ticos. This should not be your first choice if you're looking to give your kids a cultural experience. Prices are very high by Central American standards but will still seem a bargain compared with the US, Europe or Australia.

WHAT'S TOPS

- Pooping porcupines, treetop kinkajous, nesting tarantulas, nocturnal insects and night blooming flowers on a night tour at Monteverde
- Flying through the canopy on Monteverde's zip line – the longest in Costa Rica
- Gazing into the steaming pit of Poas volcano
- Watching groups of olive ridley turtles lay their eggs at night at Refugio Nacional de Fauna Silvestre Ostional
- Watching all the action at the Santa Cruz annual rodeo
- Quietly paddling through jungle rivers of Tortuguero while spotting basking crocodiles and trees full of monkeys
- Learning to surf at Mal País and Santa Teresa

- Hanging out with local families at Ojo de Agua, with its spring-fed swimming pools and a boating lake
- Rafting the gentle Río Corobicí, mellow enough so you can enjoy the wildlife along the way

WHERE

Families could plop themselves just about anywhere in Costa Rica and be perfectly happy. Even **San José**, while not a remarkable city, has sights for children – but it's best to get out of town and into the jungle. The northwest coast, from the dry forest reserve of **Santa Rosa** to the dusty, beach-fringed towns of the **Nicoya Peninsula**, is great for reptile lovers and wannabe surfers. In **Monteverde** the cool mountains dripping with mists and mosses make you feel you're in a land of fairy tales. Adventurous folks with a bigger budget could explore the isolated, scarlet macaw–filled **Osa Peninsula** where you can stay in kid-friendly beachside jungle tents in the national park. A family favourite (and often packed) is **Manuel Antonio** which, although small and resortlike, offers some of the best wildlife viewing. The **Arenal** area offers both a lake with great fishing and sailing opportunities (windsurfing is world class but high winds will present challenges to beginners and children) and a fickle volcano which may or may not be visible when you visit. For something completely different, check out turtles, crocs, white beaches and blue water on the English-speaking Rasta-vibed **Caribbean Coast**.

MONTEVERDE & SANTA ELENA

Natural beauty this intense is rare in the world. This is a cloud forest and it literally feels like you are in the clouds of some mythical perfect world full of wildlife. A great **frog museum**, **night hikes**, a **canopy walk**, **zip lines** and endless trails mean there are activites for everyone. It's a bumpy road to Monte Verde by car but a more fun Jeep/boat combo can make getting here from La Fortuna (Arenal area) much quicker. Horse lovers can also ride (five to six hours) from the Arenal area but make sure you book with a reputable company since unethical practices are not unheard of.

STAY

Milk a cow in the morning and chase monkeys during the day at **Finca Terra Viva** (+506-645 5454; www.terravivacr.com; $$) a 135-hectare farm with pigs, horses, goats and an organic dairy that blends right into the forest. There's kitchen access or the owner can prepare meals for you. More hotel-like is **Swiss Hotel Miramontes** (+506-2645 5152; www.swisshotelmiramontes.com; $$) with expansive grounds to run around and cosy chalets. Those on a budget will like **Pensión Colibrí** (+506-645 5682; Santa Elena; $) which feels like grandma's house and is run by a charming Tico family who will let you use the kitchen.

PENÍNSULA DE NICOYA

Cowboy meets surfer dude on the Nicoya Peninsula where crashing waves hit dusty country and howler monkeys sing into the sunsets. Some of the best swimming beaches can be found around **Sámara**, but the surf, primarily at **Playa Grande**, **Tamarindo** and **Mal País**, is the main draw for big kids. Olive Ridley as well as leatherback and green turtles nest along the coasts and are best seen at Playa Grande and **Ostional**. Tamarindo is a good beach hub that's easy to access and has plenty of amenities (there's a prevalent party-vibe). Most roads on the peninsula are terrible and very dusty so small kids might suffer on long rides. See real cowboys, Tico-style, in the lively town of **Santa Cruz**.

STAY

No trees were cut to build the beautiful **Tico Adventure Lodge** (+506-2656-0628; www.tico adventurelodge.com; 150 N 150 E Plaza Deportes; $$-$$$) a garden oasis right in Sámara and just steps from the beach. The tree-top apartment for four lets you swing on a hammock three stories up, or you can stay in the poolside house for five with a fully equipped kitchen and dining room. In an enviable position on Playa Grande, **Hotel Las Tortugas** (+506-2653-0423; www.lastortugashotel.com; $$) is an ecofriendly base for leatherback turtle watching (October to March), horseback riding and surfing (big kids only). You can get a room or equipped apartment and there's a turtle-shaped pool. The on-site restaurant will keep kids and adults equally happy.

CARIBBEAN COAST

The 'other side' of Costa Rica speaks English and dances to calypso and reggae more than salsa. The city of **Limón** is perhaps too gritty for most families so head to **Tortuguero**, a mini Amazon with lazy crocs and trees filled with slithery snakes and rambunctious monkeys. Down south, the lazy towns of **Cahuita** and **Puerto Viejo** skirt national parks where sloths hang in the steamy jungles and white-sand beaches go on forever. The fringing coral reefs offer the best snorkelling in the country and there are mellow body-boarding and swimming beaches – and also big scary reef-breaking waves for pros. **Finca La Isla Botanical Garden** near Puerto Viejo is a compact, fun way to see trees and wildlife if you are travelling with very young children.

STAY

In Cahuita, **Hotel National Park** (+506-8382-0139; $$) is steps from the beach and the entrance to Parque Nacional Cahuita, and a few more to the grocery store. Beautiful family rooms have kitchens, TVs and separate bedrooms. Beach access and an adjacent iguana farm are only part of the draw to splurge-worthy **Tree House** (+506-2750-0706; www.costaricatreehouse.com; $$$), just east of Puerto Viejo. The architecture is so phenomenal that even the youngest kids will get a kick out of it. All houses have kitchens and the best bathrooms ever.

WHEN

The best time to visit the Caribbean side is from February to June and September and October. In the rest of the country dry season is considered to be December through to April. From around Christmas through to January western and central Costa Rica books solid, so reserve in advance. Prices also soar during this time.

HOW

Transport

Children under the age of 12 get a 25% discount on internal air travel. Cars (4WD are the most reliable) can be rented from most major towns so you can fly and rent. Roads even to popular areas like Monte Verde are very rudimentary so expect to move slowly with lots of bumps along the way. Car seats are becoming more widely available but you can't count on getting one. If you bring your own car seat, leave it with a Costa Rican family when you leave – car seats are expensive and will be very much appreciated as a gift. Kids with a sense of adventure will enjoy the lively local buses – more bland tourist shuttle buses are much less fun but several steps up in comfort. Leave the stroller at home and bring a baby backpack or carrier for jungle jaunts.

Shopping & Essentials

Nappies and baby supplies can be in short supply outside of San José so stock up or be prepared to use cloth nappies and possibly hire a local to wash them.

Health

Costa Rica is one of the cleanest and least risky places in Latin America to travel with children. The medical system, though not first-world standard, is good and should suffice for anything except extreme circumstances. All the common Central American diseases do still exist so be sure to get all the necessary immunisations and don't drink the water. Public toilets are essentially nonexistent but restaurants are very nice about sharing theirs. Carry toilet paper and don't flush it down – throw it in the bin.

Food

The food here is bland and based around beans and rice. Tourist centres have more options. *Batidos* (fresh-blended fruit drinks) either *al agua* (plain) or *con leche* (with milk) are good vitamin injections and come in myriad varieties. Other treats are drinking coconuts, sugar-cane water and *horchata* (cinnamon-spiked rice milk). Fresh dairy products are produced around the country.

BRAZIL

Mention the Amazon River and you won't have to do much arm-twisting to get the kids excited about going to Brazil. Between the nearly fluorescent white-sand beaches along the coast to the jungles dripping with weird bugs and monkeys, there is so much to do and see that it can be hard to decide where to start. Most cities in Brazil are noisy, dirty and crowded, which can make travelling with children stressful. Once you've settled somewhere for a few days, the chaos can start to make more sense. That said, sticking to the jungles and beaches makes for a more peaceful trip. Brazilians love children and many hotels let children stay free although the age limit for this varies.

WHAT'S TOPS

- Knowing exactly how many grams of food it takes to fuel kid-energy at a *por-kilo* restaurant
- Riding the cog train to visit Cristo Redentor, the angel that floats above Rio at night
- Jumping back and forth across the equator in Macapá
- Spotting animals you never knew existed in the Pantanal
- Dances, music and theatre tell the story of the death and resurrection of the bull at the Bumba Meu Boi festival in São Luís
- Shooting down Brazil's highest waterslide (or just watching others do it) at Beach Park water park outside Forteleza
- Chilling out around the Parnaíba Delta
- Staying in the treetop 'Tarzan' Suite at Ariaú Amazon Towers on the Amazon River
- Learning how to order favourite fresh fruit juice combinations in Portuguese

RIO DE JANEIRO

Rio's visitors are sharply divided between those who party all night and sleep it off on the beach all day and the rest of us. But the Cidade Maravilhosa (Marvellous City) has plenty of perks for families beyond the long stretches of white sand and one of the world's most flashy backdrops. There's a zoo, planetarium, amusement park and **Rio Water Planet**, which claims to be the biggest park in Latin America and also encompasses a show and circus area. In 15 minutes you can be in the rainforest at **Parque Nacional da Tijuca**.

SEE

Paddle Boats (Parque do Cantaglo, Lagoa; half-hour US$8) There's plenty of space to run around in all the parks surrounding Lagoa Rodrigo de Freitas then take a pedal in a boat that's a giant plastic swan.

Ilha de Paquetá (ferry +55-21-2533-6661; every 3 hrs 5.30am-11pm; 1hr; hydrofoil +55-21-2533-7524; every 2 hrs 10am-4pm; 25 min) Cavort with the locals on this car-free island where you can rent bikes, take a horse and cart and lounge on unpretentious beaches. It gets crowded on weekends.

STAY

Cama e Café (+55-21-2225-4366; www.camaecafe .com; Rua Paschoal Carlos Magno 5, Santa Teresa; $) This bed and breakfast network links travellers to local residents – you get to pick and choose from over 50 houses by common interest. Although not on the beach, Santa Teresa is a charming, old-time feeling neighbourhood with impromptu street parties and festivals. It's near the *favelas* (shanty towns) which makes the area quite edgy – for the adventurous only.

Ipanema Sweet (+55-21-8201-1458; Rua Visconde de Pirajá 161, Ipanema; $$) With the beach two blocks away and two swimming pools at your disposal, staying here probably means getting in the water – often. Full apartments

ALEX NIKADA | ISTOCKPHOTO

ABOVE. **TAKE IN THE SPECTACULAR VIEW FROM THE CABLE CAR TO SUGARLOAF MOUNTAIN, RIO DE JANEIRO**

have well-stocked kitchens and there's also laundry and a sauna in the building. All the restaurants of Ipanema are a hop, skip and jump away.

MATO GROSSO & MATO GROSSO DO SUL

It's not easy seeing animals in the wild – except in the **Pantanal**. With the greatest concentration of fauna in the New World and considerably less tourism than the Amazon, this is where you might really see all those hard-to-find critters. Further south, **Serra do Bodoquena** around Bonito is lush with waterfalls, crystal rivers, caves and canyons. The whole area is remote and will probably require flying into unless you have lots of time to make the long haul across the continent.

STAY

As best described by a young boy, **Pousada das Araras** (+55-65-3682-2800; www.araraslodge .com.br; Transpantaneira Km 32; $$) is like a zoo and hotel all wrapped up into one, and holds an enviable position in the heart of the Pantanal. It's like a safari camp but the owners are so warm you don't feel like a tourist. If you're on a tighter budget and want a homier experience, **Pousada Ecoverde** (+55-65-3624-1386; www.ecotribal.com /content/64.php; Rua Pedro Celestino 391, Cuiabá; $) is run by well-known guide Joel Souza in his family home in Cuiabá. It's rustic but comfy – families can use kitchen facilities and there's a big garden out back.

CEARÁ, PIAUÍ & MARANHÃO

This mellow area of Brazil has amazing variation in its landscapes from the dry windswept beaches of **Ceará** to the lush vegetation of **Maranhão** and everything in between. One of the loveliest areas and your best bet for wildlife is the **Parnaíba Delta**, with its huge sand dunes, rivers and islands. In Maranhão, **Parque Nacional dos Lençóis Maranhenses** has more amazing sand. Start a lifelong appreciation for reggae in your children by staying in enchanting, cobblestone **São Luís**. Fantastic festivals, nearby beaches and all that good music merit a long stay. When it gets hot, head up to the mountains of **Serra de Baturité** with its coffee and banana plantations and thermal pools. Near **Fortaleza**, you'll find a massive **water park** with waterslides, surf boards and dune buggies – children shorter than 1m get in free.

STAY

Big kids can learn to kitesurf while little ones will love the beach at **Pousada do Toby** (+55-88-421-7094; www.pousada-do-toby.com; Rua Nascer do Sol; $) in Canoa Quebrada. All-day breakfasts at the restaurant and a rooftop pool are bonuses. In the Serra de Baturité, **Estância Vale** (+55-85-325-1233; www.valedasflores.com.br; Sítio São Francisco; $$) has a pool, horse rental and even a minizoo.

THE AMAZON

The dream of many a child is to go the Amazon where crocodiles lurk in murky waters and monkeys swing from the trees. All the animals are there and it's a sure bet you'll see some, but sightings are infrequent enough to test kids' patience. 'White' rivers like the **Lago Mamorí** region have a higher density of animals than 'black' ones like the **Rio Negra** – however, more animals equals more mosquitos. **Manaus**, the gateway to the Amazon for many, is dirty and feels like the anti-ecotour, but it can make a good base.

STAY

Manaus isn't a very kid-friendly town so it's best to splurge on a little comfort here.

At central **Manaus Hotéis Saint Paul** (Rua Ramos Ferreira 1115; $$$) you can have your own apartment including kitchenette – or settle on indulging at **Hotel Tropical** (+55-92-2123-5000; www.tropicalhotel.com.br: Av Coronel Teixeira 1320, Ponte Negra; $$$) which is like an Amazonian Disneyland with its own zoo and spacious gardens. Of course to really experience the jungle, get out of Manaus to a jungle lodge. One of the best is **Ariaú Amazon Towers** (www.ariautowers.com; $$$), where you can rent a 'Tarzan Suite' that is perched in a tree; it's right on that famous river. The whole lodge is at tree level and connected by catwalks so it would be a stressful choice for parents of young children.

WHEN

December to March is the high season in Brazil, when prices soar and lodgings book fast. Besides being the school holidays, the festivities such as Carnaval (which is overwhelming for most children) are what draws the crowds. Brazil's winter, between May and September, is the coolest time to visit as well as being the least crowded and rainy. July is another school-holiday month when tourism takes a quick sprint.

HOW

Transport
Brazil is the world's fifth-largest country and distances are enormous. If you plan on seeing a lot of the country with your children, a Brazil Airpass (www.tam.com.br, www.varig.com.br) can save money and tedious road trips. With all those rivers, boat travel is an exciting way to see the jungle. Driving in Brazil is one of the biggest hazards you'll encounter – fortunately long-distance buses are comfortable and safe although not all have toilets. In cities, it's easy to get around on local buses and by taxi.

Shopping & Essentials
Brazil presents few shopping problems unless you are looking to buy anything beyond the essentials. Nappies are found nearly everywhere but it's a good idea to pack your own creams, medicines or special foods.

Health
It's a jungle out there and all those nasty tropical diseases are part of the territory. Even so, with the proper precautions, Brazil can still be a safe place to travel. Because of the presence of yellow fever, it is not recommended to bring infants to areas outside of Rio de Janeiro, Sào Paulo, the central eastern area to the coast and the coastal areas south of São Luís – the vaccination cannot be given to babies under nine months old. The biggest threat in jungle areas is malaria. Hospitals in major cities have good but expensive health care and everyone will want to be paid in cash. Public toilets are rare beyond airports, bus stations and restaurants and usually charge around US$0.40. The paper goes in that smelly bin next to the toilet.

Food
Burgers, pizza, grilled cheese and, of course, beans and rice are easily found but a good way to encourage your kids to get a little more adventurous is through a *por-kilo* restaurant where food is bought cafeteria style then paid for by the kilo. Fantastic, exotic fruit juices and fresh choices abound and most restaurants have highchairs.

AFRICA

SENEGAL

One of the calmest, friendliest and safest places in West Africa, Senegal is a great destination for independent travellers with children. A francophone nation, it's also a great place to put school French to practice – people love nothing better than a good conversation and will help you to retrieve lost vocabulary. Though it can't compete with the massive wildlife parks of East Africa, there are plenty of places to spot big and small animals. Senegal has some beautiful beaches in easy reach from the capital Dakar, and buzzes with rich traditions of drumming, dancing and music.

WHAT'S TOPS

- Lazing at the beaches of the pea-sized Île de N'gor
- Spotting rhinos at the animal reserve Bandia
- Swinging from the branches of gigantic baobab trees at Accrobaobab
- Adopting a baby tortoise at Village des Tortues
- Twirling and jumping to the drum at the Kaay Fecc Xalé dance festival for children
- Counting pelicans and spotting crocodiles at the Parc National des Oiseaux du Djoudj

WHERE

The **Cap Vert Peninsula** is the starting point of any trip around Senegal, and has several pockets of fun for adventurous families. Dakar, at the tip of this triangular stretch of land, can be hard going with little children, but there are several beaches nearby, some on the fringes of the tiny islands **Île de N'gor** and **Île de Gorée**. At **Lac Rose** with its subtle pink shimmer you can go horseback riding and bathing and relax on its safe shores. Heading southwards from the peninsula, the **Petite Côte** has tiny fishing villages and good tourist infrastructure in close proximity to wide, safe beaches inviting the construction

of sandcastles. In the north, the pretty town of **Saint-Louis** delights parents with its historical architecture and kids with natural parks, such as the **Parc National des Oiseaux du Djoudj** and the **Parque National de la Langue de Barbarie**, inhabited by pelicans, crocodiles, flamingos and many other species. A plane ride to the south, Cap Skiring in the **Casamance** has the best beaches by far, but in recent years a long-standing separatist rebellion has worried tourists. Right now, the greatest risks are probably the region's unpaved roads. Still, check with your embassy before planning a trip to the Casamance.

DAKAR & CAP VERT PENINSULA

Consider Dakar your jump-off base for day excursions around the Cap Vert Peninsula rather than a holiday destination in itself – traffic jams, pollution and street hustlers do nothing to boost the family spirit. If you're kids are into arts, take them to the peaceful **Institut Français**, where children from seven years onwards can take workshops in the beautiful art of reverse-glass painting under the guidance of master Moussa Sakho while parents take in one of their regular exhibitions or relax in the leafy cafe. The fabulously active **Atelier de Danse Keur Jaaraf** frequently runs classes in African dance for children – you need to contact them to arrange the sessions.

In the north of the peninsula, the tiny **Île de N'gor** is reached by a short pirogue ride (life vests provided), and is a perfect spot on which to linger on clean beaches.

STAY

With kids, it's best to stay outside the hassle zones of the inner city. For those on a budget, the tiny **Hôtel Cap Ouest** (+221 820 2469; capouest@arc.sn; Yoff Virage; $) has spacious rooms that can accommodate even large families. The hotel owners are parents, and will gladly give advice on excursions up country.

SAINT-LOUIS & SURROUNDINGS

If your children don't care much for the stunning architecture of this former colonial capital of French West Africa, they'll still enjoy a ride in a horse-drawn cart around the dusty streets of this atmospheric town, and the sight of pirogues rolling in on the surf in the late afternoon. The Senegalese flock here for New Year's Eve, when the majestic **fanal** lantern processions tell ancient stories of the city's beautiful *signare* queens and steep the streets in a wonderfully warm light.

Saint-Louis lies on the edge of the **Parc National de la Langue de Barbarie**, a stunning peninsula where you can spend your days spotting hundreds of colourful tropical birds. Local holiday camps offer kayaking and canoeing adventures, and even short trips with the local fishers.

The famous **Parc National des Oiseaux du Djoudj**, world famous bird sanctuary and foremost winter destination of European migrant birds, sits some 60 km north of Saint-Louis and is best reached by an organised excursion from the city. On a pirogue tour around its wetlands, you'll spot vast colonies of pelicans and flamingos, and plenty of other land and sea creatures.

Price Guide

$** budget **$$** midrange **$$$ top end

STAY

In the city, the classic **Hôtel de la Résidence** (+221 33 961 1260; www.hoteldelaresidence.com; Av Blaise Diagne; $$) has a babysitting service, child-loving staff and the advantage of being run by the owners of the excellent touring agency Sahel Découverte.

PETITE CÔTE

This stretch of coast south of Dakar has brilliant and safe beaches, to be enjoyed either in a resort-style atmosphere or in the surroundings of tiny fishing villages. In **Toubab Dialaw**, you can take your kids horseback riding with **Les Cavaliers de la Savane** or drumming and dancing at the lively hotel and cultural centre **Sobo-Bade**.

A few kilometres further south, **Saly** is a popular seaside resort, with plenty of hotels and distractions. Once sandcastles, seashells and beach ball have lost their edge, you can take your little ones on day trips to **Bandia Reserve**, a brilliantly kept nature park small enough to guarantee sightings of giraffes, rhinos, buffalos, monkeys and crocodiles. Its fabulous restaurant overlooks a busy waterhole. At **Accrobaobab** close by, children from seven years up can climb Africa's mightiest trees, walk on ropes between branches and swing like monkeys. For something calmer, the **Village des Tortues** is the place to learn all about tortoises, touch the biggest ones and even adopt a baby one.

STAY

With its seashell decor, crooked walls, tiny towers and leafy gardens, **Sobo-Bade**

ISHEMA'S NEW WORLD

~ SENEGAL ~

BY KATHARINA LOBECK KANE

My daughter Ishema lolls around on our sofa, keenly following the ski jump on satellite TV. She's put on her tights, scarf and hat for the occasion. I've put on the fan so she won't faint from the heat – it's 30ºC after all, and a hot desert wind blows dust in every corner of our Senegalese home. 'This is what I want to do when I grow up', she announces with that tone of non-negotiation that five-year-olds master. Great. We moved to Senegal three years ago, mainly to give her the chance to grow up in the country and culture that makes up half of her identity. But according to the rule that says that anything a parent does is wrong, she has picked the German half of her being as her current favourite, if only to see whether her mum can really get a snow cannon to work in the Sahel strip.

Taking your daughter to a malaria-infested, one-dollar-a-day country is considered a very odd choice for anyone outside the realms of diplomatic or development services. The image of war-ridden, famine-stricken Africa is so deeply ingrained in the minds of most 'first-world citizens' that a voluntary move there seems nothing short of insane. I'd been to West Africa many times before and knew about the many beautiful, untold stories that make life there so attractive. And yet I was worried about everything – my daughter's health, her schooling, her language-learning, her socialisation – all the way to take-off.

It's hard to imagine a more dramatic shift than the one from our one-room household in London to the bustling, boisterous, constantly interfering and utterly supportive family life in Dakar. While I relaxed, perhaps for the first time since her birth, being able to rely on a hundred helping hands, Ishema was initially overwhelmed. She was an English–German-speaking novelty straight from London, the grandchild that had so far only existed in photographs. She was admired, fussed over and spoken to in languages she didn't understand. She bristled against the sudden love bestowed on her all sides – until she suddenly learnt to command the situation. When even my mother-in-law, who's never spoken a world of English, greeted me one day with a perfect 'Good Morning', I knew Ishema had found her place.

We had only come to Senegal to stay for a few months. It was intended to be a 'taster-mission', a concise introduction to a part of who she is. Yet it turned out to be a lot more. One day, my husband and I arrived at his parents' house to pick Ishema up. The voices of arguing children rose like a cloud of dust from the courtyard. Within the web of inflections, we suddenly detected that of our daughter, who was winning a raging row with an impressive set of Wolof vocabulary and clever turns of phrase. That's when I knew that we wouldn't be able to move back to Europe yet. Language is a key part of one's identity. I'd been rigorous about speaking to my daughter in German, my mother tongue, wherever we lived. She'd benefited from learning English thanks to spending her first two years in the UK. After moving to Senegal she had gradually picked up her first words in French, the language in which her father speaks to her. But none of us had any idea that she was also able to chat away in Wolof, the most widely spoken language in Senegal. Wolof was her language of play, the one she learnt informally through being with other kids, and one she'd never used with us. At only two-and-a-half years, she was a multilingual toddler, able to greet, chat, play, and yes, make perfectly clear demands, in four languages. And as languages contain not only the vocabulary for conversation, but also the keys to a culture, she has also become 'fluent' in the unwritten conventions of four cultures.

Dakar is certainly not a child-friendly city. Not remotely. It's a filthy, frenzied kind of place. Its roads are so potholed and parked-up you can't even push a pram. Daily power cuts paralyse the economy and take the sense of romance out of any dinner by candlelight. I struggle with these realities. My daughter less so. For her, every blackout is an occasion to serve pretend-birthday cakes. And the support of the extended family

"As languages contain not only the vocabulary for conversation, but also the keys to a culture, she has also become 'fluent' in the unwritten conventions of four cultures."

means that she doesn't have to be driven, pushed or carried around at all – she can simply be looked after at home until I return from work. She has beaches to go to, friends that can be visited without having to make complex arrangements of dropping off and picking up. She has streets to rollerblade in, dance classes to attend and donkey carts to ride on during trips up-country. She has learnt the kind of respectful interaction among people that has become impossible to convey in Europe. And she has the cultural and linguistic tools to make her own choices of place and identity later. 'This is a palm tree, mum, not a snowcapped mountain', she says one morning on the way to school, as if teaching me something new. 'They're both big. But really, mum. They're not the same.'

(+221 836 0356; espacesobobade.com; $) in Toubab Dialaw feels like a hobbit habitat and offers dance and drumming courses all year round.

WHEN

The best period to visit Senegal is between November and March. That's when the climate is relatively cool and dry. Malaria is slightly less of a risk, and the national parks brim with animals, including countless migrant birds that escape the European cold. November, December and May are best for festivals and plenty of cultural events.

HOW

Transport
In Dakar, you can get around by hailing taxis. Fares are fiercely negotiated. Travelling outside the city is best done by hire car – if your budget allows for the luxury. If it proves too expensive, negotiate the hire of a bush taxi, but make sure it's in a reasonably good state and the driver reliable. You will need to bring your own car seat.

Shopping & Essentials
The Casino supermarkets in Dakar have the largest choice of imported items, including pricey nappies, formula and baby food. Shops in Saint-Louis and Saly are also well stocked. If travelling to smaller villages, take your own supplies of baby food and nappies.

If you're travelling with children under two, invest in a baby backpack. Sand, parked cars and potholes make it impossible to push a pram anywhere in Senegal.

Most Senegalese are Muslim, and though you won't see many veiled women here, skirts and trousers are worn long. You can save yourself from a lot of stares and unwanted attention by doing the same.

Health & Safety
Malaria is a risk throughout the year, though the dry season (November to May) is much safer than the rainy months. Don't take any risks though: take prophylaxis, sleep under mosquito nets and use repellent. If arriving from other African countries, you need a yellow fever injection – you'll have to show your vaccination certificate at the airport. Typhoid and Hepatitis A jabs are also recommended.

Dakar has several well-equipped private clinics. Your embassy can recommend good doctors, including paediatricians.

Senegal is a fairly safe country, though you need to keep your wits about you in the inner city to ward off pickpockets. The conflicts of the Casamance have largely calmed down, but it's still advisable to check the latest safety recommendations if you are planning a trip to that area.

Food
Senegal's national dish is *ceebu jeun* – a delicious platter of rice boiled in tomato sauce served with generous chunks of vegetables and fish. Rice accompanies most dishes, from the finger-licking *yassa poulet* (rice with onion sauce) to *mafe* (groundnut sauce). Restaurants aren't particularly equipped for children – forget about high chairs and changing rooms – but they'll usually be happy to whip up a children's portion or cut out the chilli if you ask. Thanks to the French influence, crêpes with chocolate sauce are a treat in many restaurants. Steer clear of the ice cream – it's often been defrosted and refrozen several times. Restaurants serve a delicious range of local fruit juices, from the milkshake-thick *bouyi*, made from the fruit of the baobab, to the sugary hibiscus drink *bissap*.

TANZANIA

With its vast plains, abundant wildlife and wide stretches of stunning scenery, Tanzania seems like a picture book drawing of Africa. Just tell your kids you're taking them to the home of the Lion King, and they'll happily embark on this finest of all East Africa adventures with you. Azure waters lick the safe shores of the spice island Zanzibar, where a unique mixture of Middle Eastern, African and European cultures tickles the imagination of young visitors. With good preparation and essential health precautions, you can have the family holiday of a lifetime here.

WHAT'S TOPS

- Viewing herds of elephants from above on a balloon ride across the Serengeti, the original home of the Lion King
- Becoming a mountaineer for a day and hiking up to the first hut of Mt Kilimanjaro
- Riding the waves of the fun-packed Wet'n'Wild water park at Kunduchi, Dar es Salaam
- Building a camp fire and learning how to recognise animal tracks at Sadaani Reserve

WHERE

Most families greet the crowded city of Dar es Salaam only in passing, heading straight to Tanzania's wilderness regions. If you do have a couple of days to spend here, take your kids to the fantastic **Wet'n'Wild** water park, which is more than a splash of fun with 20 water slides, ice cream parlours and a wide range of water sports. From Dar es Salaam, you can jump on the ferry to the tranquil spice island **Zanzibar**, where the ancient Stone Town rests like a legend come alive and turquoise water licks white-sand beaches. On the mainland, the choice is between the northern and southern safari circuits. The north is the most famous, boasting imagination-tingling names such as **Serengeti** plains, **Lake Manyara**, **Tarangire**

National Park and **Mt Kilimanjaro**, Africa's highest peak. But especially with younger children, easily accessible is often better than massively impressive, and the southern national parks **Sadaani** and **Mikumi** as well as the **Selous Game Reserve** cater just for those needs, offering plenty of biodiversity on fairly compact terrain in close proximity to Dar es Salaam. In central Tanzania, the **Usambara Mountains** offer some of the best trekking in the country, with plenty of tours even manageable by under-10s. Start your tours from **Maweni**, a relaxing hotel complete with playground and climbing rocks.

ARUSHA &
THE NORTHERN SAFARI CIRCUIT

The northern safari circuit is arguably Tanzania's most popular tourist adventure. For your children, it will feed Lion King fantasies like no other place. Most safaris start in Arusha. From here, they take you to the elephant-boasting, baobab-specked park of **Tarangire** and the bird paradise of **Lake Manyara**, home to the rare mountain-climbing lion. The tour continues to the ancient volcano crater **Ngorongoro**, where elephants, rhinos, zebras and plenty of other big and small creatures inhabit a stunning diversity of natural habitats. The final stop is the vast expanse of the **Serengeti** desert – famous for the annual wildebeest migration

Climbing Mt Kilimanjaro

Parents of adolescents swear that the hike up Africa's highest peak is the perfect teenager-parent exercise. Differences seem to melt away during a joint battle with altitude dizziness and mountainside camping in the cold. Even younger children can make it to Mandara, the first hut, that sits at 2743m (9000ft). From the base of the mountain in Moshi, Mandara is reached on a leisurely three-to-five-hour hike that leads through magical rainforest brimming with life. Shrieks of tropical birds and the chatter of monkeys accompany your walk along the verdant Marangu Route – the easiest of the ascents. This can be a fun family day out, and your children will glow with pride at having set foot on this African giant.

For any attempts to hike up further, you (and your children) need to come fit and prepared to undertake such an adventure. An experienced guide, good water supply and well-worn hiking boots are essential. The minimum age is 10.

that sees millions of animals gallop from here to Masai Mara (Kenya). You need to be extremely lucky to witness this fabulous event, as the exact time of the migration depends on the annual rainfalls. Even without the thunder of wildebeest hoofs, there's plenty to see in the Serengeti, home to lions and gigantic herds of elephants.

Marangu is a pretty village nestled at the foot of the mighty **Mt Kilimanjaro**. From here, you can take magical walks to thundering waterfalls and tropical gardens. If you're brave, and your children old enough, you can also attempt short hikes up Africa's highest peak (see the boxed text above).

STAY
Gibb's Farm (+255 27 253 4040; reservations@ gibbsfarm.net; Karatu; $$) screams family bliss loudly across Ngorongoro Crater and Lake Manyara. You stay in your own house, complete with romantic fireplace and private verandah. Your kids can try milking cows and see how the vegetables are grown, while tired parents can get pampered at the African Spa. There are forest walks, village trails and mountain-biking tours on offer, too.

ZANZIBAR
Zanzibar – the name alone is like a dose of fairy-tale wonder. A walk around the historic **Stone Town**, where Persian, Omani, Portuguese and Swahili culture have left their mark, is far more than architectural gazing. In the centre of town, **Forodhani Open Market** near the magical **House of Wonders** is a great place to absorb a vibrant trading atmosphere while indulging in grilled seafood or mouth-watering chocolate pancakes and fresh sugar-cane juice.

Surrounded by azure water and lined by white-sand beaches, Zanzibar is the perfect place for beach lounging. On the north-western shore, the fishing village **Kendwa** tempts with privacy, a turtle reserve and a backpackers' vibe, while the tourist centre **Nungwi** is the likely place for families that look for an activity-fuelled beach holiday. The safest waters are however on the east coast, around **Bwejuu** and **Jambiani**. They're great for swimming and shell collecting, and offer plenty of activity. Scuba diving, swimming with dolphins, snorkelling and rides on the dhow boats are all on the menu here.

Halfway between Bwejuu and Stone Town, the magical **Jozani Forest** is a place in which to befriend the cheeky and rare red colobus monkeys. The nature trails leading past gigantic tropical trees are easily managable even for young children.

STAY
A few minutes north of the ancient city, **Mtoni Marine** (+225 24 2250 140; mtoni@zanzibar.cc; $$) has thought of both parents and kids: while the children exhaust themselves at the playground and pool, mum relaxes with an aromatherapy massage.

SAADANI
An easy day trip from Dar es Salaam, **Saadani National Park** packs beach, bush, forests and rivers all into a small, easily negotiated area. On a good day, you can see flamingos, crocodiles and hippos along the Wami River, and observe elephants playing on the beach.

Short travel times make this an ideal minisafari destination for families with young children.

STAY
Saadani Safari Lodge (+255 22 277 3294; info@saadanilodge.com; $$; children under 6 free) welcomes children and offers much for nature-loving youngsters. Friendly guides are happy take your children on a bush adventure, where they can climb trees, learn to build a shelter and light a camp fire, paddle a canoe, go fishing and test their nerve during a night safari.

WHEN

In coastal and low-lying areas temperatures can soar up to 40°C during Tanzania's humid summer months (November to February). During that season, the temperate climate of the north is a much better choice. The peak holiday season is in July and August. It's fairly cool and

ABOVE. **SPOTTING WILDLIFE IS A HIGHLIGHT OF ANY TRIP TO AFRICA**

DESTINATIONS

dry, Tarangire Park brims with wildlife and you may even spot the great wildebeest migration. The rainy months between March and June with their increased malaria risk are best avoided.

HOW

Transport
For independent travel, consider hiring a car in Dar es Salaam, where your flight will arrive. This is fairly expensive, and it's best to hire cars with a driver, as it requires some skill to negotiate the country's potholed, sandy roads.

If you rely on public transport, the Scandinavia Express buses provide good, air-conditioned services to many places. Ferries run from Dar es Salaam to Stone Town – Azam Marine and Sea Express are among the best and biggest companies. Arusha can also be reached by a brief in-country flight.

Shopping & Essentials
For baby basics, try the large supermarkets in Dar es Salaam. The Slipway provides a wide choice in shops, for anything from food to local crafts. Stock up on things like formula or nappies before heading up-country, especially if it's the wilderness of the north you're after. Zanzibar honours its tradition of being an old trading centre, and is a great place to purchase local arts, crafts, fabrics and jewellery.

In the Muslim environment of Zanzibar, women should wear long skirts or trousers, and men should leave their holiday shorts in the suitcase too.

If you're going on a safari, pick a family-friendly provider. Some safari lodges are reluctant to accept children under 10 – if you're travelling with babies or very young children, make sure your chosen hotel welcomes them to avoid disappointment.

Health
Malaria occurs in the entire country, and is particularly prevalent in the rainy season. Be sure to take prophylaxis. Pregnant women shouldn't travel to malaria zones at all, and if you're travelling with very young children it's better to stick to areas where medical help can be found quickly. A yellow fever vaccination is obligatory to enter the country, and it's also recommended to get a Hepatitis A jab.

If your child falls ill, your best choices are the drop-in clinics at the International School of Tanzania and the Premier Clinic.

Food
Tanzania tempts with a great variety of cuisines, ranging from the typically East African millet porridge *ugali* to the finely spiced Arab-African and Indian meals of the Swahili coast. You can the kitchen to go easy on the chilli when travelling with kids; they're usually happy to oblige.

Children are welcome in most restaurants, but rarely catered for. Established hotels and lodges are usually equipped with highchairs and might even have children's menus.

SOUTH AFRICA

There are few places in the world where you find golden beaches backed by majestic mountains, vast natural parks bordering on exciting cities, a vibrant indigenous culture, all wrapped into a pleasant climate and excellent infrastructure. South Africa is about as perfect a holiday destination as you can imagine. Whether your children wish to see elephants and lions in their natural habitat, ride on gigantic roller coasters or build sandcastles from fine white sand, they'll find their happiness in Africa's economic powerhouse. With plenty of family-friendly safaris, accommodation and restaurants to choose from, you won't even need to worry about the organisation of it all.

WHAT'S TOPS

- Being faster than dad at spotting the whale's blow at Hermanus
- Testing mum's nerves on rafting, canoeing, mountain-biking and bungee-jumping trips along the Garden Route
- Spotting the Big Five on a family-friendly safari in the massive Kruger National Park
- Riding on the back of an ostrich at Oudtshoorn
- Becoming a budding scientist at MTN Sciencentre in Cape Town
- Watching dolphins and sharks from below at uShaka Marine World in Durban
- Forgetting about your parents at the excitement-packed Cabanas Children's Park in Sun City

WHERE

South Africa is a vast nation with an amazing variety of landscapes and city scenes and an abundance of wildlife. **Cape Town**, with its mountains, beaches and theme park, and the adjacent **Garden Route**, are the first holiday choices for most families. Its small wildlife reserves, such as **Kwandwe** and **Addo Elephant Park**, are great for watching animals without having to go on long safari drives.

The gigantic **Kruger National Park** in the northeast of the country is the most famous place to spot the Big Five. The magnificent Ngala Camp allows children in. The smaller **Manyeleti Game Reserve** nearby is better for smaller children, who are welcome and especially catered for at the luxurious Khoka

Moya Safari Lodge. **Hluhluwe-Umfolozi National Park** in KwaZulu-Natal is famous for its white rhinos. At the right time of year, you can see turtles lay their eggs on the beach at **Greater St Lucia Wetland Park**. **Durban** is a town dedicated to beach life and holiday spirit, and the slightly artificial **Sun City** is your place, if you feel like being surrounded by endless theme-park fun. Take your kids to Kamp Kwena, if you're happy to loose them all day on excursions, craft activities and the playgrounds of the **Cabanas Children's Park**.

CAPE TOWN

The mother of all holiday cities offers plenty of excitement for parents and children of all ages. Its good infrastructure and pleasant climate make for a worry-free break. **Camps Bay**, one of the city's many white-sand beaches, is popular with the world's beautiful folk, but it's also family friendly, with safe swimming for kids in a tidal pool, and diving, surfing and a picnic area on offer. Teenagers will love **Century City**, Africa's biggest theme park, both for its tummy-tickling roller-coaster rides and the **MTN Sciencentre** where learning becomes fun, as kids can explore the latest in computer technology.

GARDEN ROUTE

Cape Town is the perfect jump-off point for a leisurely four-to-five-day trip along the famous Garden Route, where plenty of wildlife can be spotted in a safe, malaria-free environment. At **Boulders Beach** in Simon's Town, kids can observe thousands of penguins, and even swim with them if they're brave enough. It's also a good area for whale spotting, though the perfect place to observe the sea giants is **Hermanus**, where southern right whales, humpbacks and even orcas come close to the coast or can be watched on government-accredited boat trips.

Following the scenic coastal route at **Oudtshoorn**, adventure-loving kids will adore playing explorer in the **Cango Caves**, and a bumpy ride on the back of an ostrich. **Addo Elephant Park** is the place to spot a variety of animals, and at the nearby **Elephant Game Farm**, you can feed and even ride the thick-skinned giants. Also great with children are the small private animal reserves **Kwandwe** and **Lalibela** that boast family-friendly safaris.

STAY

The Garden Route is blessed with a number of family-friendly camps. The spectacular **Ecca Lodge** ($$) is a favourite with parents, thanks to its packed program of children's entertainment and kids' surprises and a cute bush playroom gives mum and dad a break.

DURBAN & HLUHLUWE GAME PARK

Durban resembles a gigantic resort holiday paradise, raised for the sole purpose of entertaining families. Lined with safe beaches watched over by lifeguards, the **Golden Mile** is great for snorkelling, swimming and water sports. A miniature town, funfair, paddling pools and a saltwater pool are only some of its many attractions. Or just gaze across the pier, counting surfers and observing the fishers.

Even little kids will love a **rickshaw ride** with ice cream around town. Just outside the city, the marine world **uShaka** is so much more than a gigantic pool; it also has dolphin and seal parks, and rock and touching pools.

If this is all a tad too prefabricated, a three-hour trip from Durban takes you to **Hluhluwe-Umfolozi National Park**, one

ABOVE. SOUTH AFRICA CATERS TO ALL TASTES IN OUTDOOR ADVENTURE, INCLUDING SANDBOARDING AT PEPIES FONTEIN

of South Africa's oldest and most stunning wildlife parks. Smaller than the massive Kruger National Park, it allows for plenty of animal sightings even on short drives. It's most famous for the protection of the white rhino, but there are plenty of other animals to be spotted on self-guided or organised walks.

STAY

Durban has great resort-style hotels. Part of a large, family-friendly chain, **Protea Hotel Edward** (149 Marine Pde, Durban; $$) is a good choice, not least because it sits directly opposite an attractive children's entertainment park. In Hhluhluwe-Umfolozi, **Hill Top Camp** (+27 033 845 1000; www.kznwildlife .com; Hluhluwe-Umfolozi National Park; $$) is the most luxurious option and welcomes even children under three years old. Family walking tours and wilderness trails are on offer.

WHEN

There's no such thing as a bad holiday season in South Africa. Cape Town's beautiful summer months last from windy November through to mild April. From June to September, it can be cold and wet, though you'll be guaranteed peace in the tourist centres. With clear blue skies, lots of sun and an average of 20°C, Durban is fabulous in the winter (June to September), while its summers are hot (30°C and up) and humid. And remember that Africa is not only hot – temperatures can drop to freezing in the South African winter.

HOW

Transport

To venture outside the cities, you're best off travelling by hire car. Many providers offer very reasonable rates. Cape Town has safe metered taxis, though sightseeing in Durban

and Cape Town is best done by open-top bus. Your kids will love seeing the city from a bird's perspective. Tickets allow you to hop on and off, perfect for down-to-earth breaks.

Shopping & Essentials

Even the smallest cities provide everything you need for your baby, toddler and youngster. Pick'n'Pay, Checkers and Spar supermarkets have good selections of baby essentials. Toys'R'Us and Baby City have everything else you might have forgotten to pack. In Cape Town, Century City is renowned for its small shops, stylish boutiques and large supermarkets.

Health

There's less risk of illness in South Africa than in most other countries on the continent. Many parts are malaria free – tour operators across the Eastern Cape region tempt worried parents with malaria-free holidays. There's no perfect safety though – the border between South Africa and Mozambique is a risk area, and that includes Kruger National Park. Make sure you take the necessary precautions when going there. Hepatitis B injections are recommended for children; yellow fever is only necessary if you travel from an infected region.

Major cities have good health services, and private clinics around South Africa have excellent facilities.

Food

South Africa offers a fantastic range of food, from African to Indian and finest Italian. Your children might still crave burgers and chips – plenty of fast-food chains can oblige. Spur Group restaurants are great for children, boasting entertainment and supervision by staff. And in all major cities, you'll find cafes and restaurants offering child menus and even colouring books and playpens.

THE
MIDDLE EAST

GULF STATES & THE UAE

With year-round sunshine and a plethora of plush resort-style hotels, the desert-filled Gulf States of Bahrain, Kuwait, Oman and Qatar, along with the United Arab Emirates (a federation of seven emirates, including Abu Dhabi and Dubai) all make easy destinations for travel with children. Oman and Dubai are two particular highlights of the region: Oman a warm, welcoming land packed with traditional Arabic towns and natural delights, and Dubai a playground of dazzling cityscapes, with more child-friendly treats than Disney himself could have dreamed up.

WHAT'S TOPS

- Exploring Old Muscat, filled with forts, palaces, *souks* (markets) and parks
- Oman's Wadi Shab: an oasis of shimmering pools, waterfalls and stunning wildlife
- Riding white-water, white-knuckle rides at Dubai's Aquaventure
- Taking a traditional dhow boat ride along the waters of the Gulf
- Hopping aboard a desert safari out into Oman or Dubai's shimmering dunes

WHERE

OMAN

Clean and surprisingly green, Oman's capital **Muscat** is well worth exploring for its buzzing souks, seaside corniche, and manifold parks. Once you've had your fill of city life, the country hosts a wealth of natural treasures, perfect for families with older children. Hike Oman's numerous **wadis**; take trips out into the **Wahiba Sands** dunes, explore the fjords of the **Musandam Peninsula**, watch turtles on the beaches of **Ras al-Hadd** and **Ras al-Junayz**, and indulge in a host of adventure pursuits, from kayaking to canyoning.

STAY

Muscat's **Shangri-La Al Jissah Resort & Spa** (+968 2477 6666; www.shangri-la.com; $$$), with its plentiful pools and kids' club facilities is great for those with little ones. Older children will enjoy the **Nomadic Desert Camp** (+986 9933

6273; www.nomadicdesertcamp.com; $) in Wahiba Sands, with its simple palm-thatched huts and a Bedouin feast before bedtime.

DUBAI

From roller coasters to top-notch shopping, Dubai has man-made delights aplenty. One of its more adrenalin-filled options is the brand-new **Aquaventure waterpark** (+971 4426 0000; www.atlantisthepalm.com; Atlantis the Palm Hotel, Dubai; adult/child Dh285/220; 10am-sunset), where older children can get a thrill on the heart-stopping Leap of Faith ride, which sends riders flying down an acrylic tunnel and through a real shark-filled lagoon. **Ski Dubai** (+971 4409 4000; www.skidxb.com; Mall of the Emirates, Sheikh Zayid Rd, Dubai; snow-park entry adult/child Dh80/75; 10am-11pm Sun-Wed, 10am-midnight Thu, 9am-midnight Fri, 9am-11pm Sat) encompasses the world's largest snowdome, and offers great respite from the heat for over-threes, who can take a ski or snowboard lesson, build a snowman, or go bobsleighing. Ski slope, lessons and equipment hire cost extra. For fun in the outdoor sun, take an easy desert safari, or board the **Wonder Bus** (+971 4359 5656; www.wonderbusdubai.net; Burjuman Centre, Dubai; over-13s/under-13s Dh125/85; call for tour times), a bus that becomes a boat to take to the water.

STAY

Dubai's Jumeirah Beach Hotel (+971 43480000; www.jumeirahbeachhotel.com; $$$) is considered by many locals the best spot in town for kids, offering an extensive kids' club and unlimited access to the Wild Wadi waterpark next door, which opens early exclusively for hotel guests.

WHEN

The very best time to visit the Gulf is during the cooler months between November and March. Summer temperatures can be searing, and September's month-long Ramadan Islamic holiday makes eating and drinking during daylight hours more tricky.

HOW

Transport

Travel in and between the various emirates of the UAE is easy, with plenty of good buses and decent rates for car hire. In Oman, renting a car might not be all that cheap, but it's definitely easy and the best way to fully explore the country's stunning natural treasures.

Shopping & Essentials

Major brands of baby food, powdered milk, nappies and wet wipes are available right across the Gulf, with major cities like Muscat and Dubai offering the greatest variety.

Health

Aside from the heat of midsummer, there are few health risks in the Gulf, and health care is excellent. If you're bringing medicines into Dubai, double-check lists of banned or restricted substances before travelling, and find out whether you need a doctor's letter of authorisation for prescription drugs.

Since the Gulf is a very conservative place, it's wise not to breastfeed in public. Children shouldn't paddle or swim naked, and – especially outside Dubai – it's best for girls of all ages to avoid skimpy clothes.

Food

You'll have no problems in the Gulf catering to the tastes of any small person. With a wide variety of cuisines, and a generally high standard of cleanliness, you'll find something delicious to please any little palate.

ISRAEL & THE PALESTINIAN TERRITORIES

Despite its reputation as a place of conflict and uncertainty, Israel and the Palestinian Territories' beaches and biblical bonanzas continue to draw many travellers with children. On either side of the contentious border between Israel and the Palestinian Territories, you'll find populations keen to greet, treat, and spoil your little ones rotten, while Israel boasts many facilities tailor-made for families with children. Travel distances are short and there's rarely a drop of rain to disturb long, languid days on Israel's wonderful Mediterranean beaches. Down south, party city Eilat has lots of attractions for children of all ages, from water sports to close encounters with dolphins, while the massive Negev Desert is a stunning centre for desert hikes, camel or horse rides and 4WD expeditions.

WHAT'S TOPS

- Visiting Jerusalem's Biblical Zoo, where the animals come in two by two
- Lazing the days away on Tel Aviv's golden beaches
- Hiking the trails of Israel's many lush, green nature reserves
- Getting up close and personal with dolphins at Eilat's Dolphin Reef
- Sampling the produce at Jerusalem's fragrant Mahane Yehuda market

Price Guide

$ budget $$ midrange $$$ top end

- Strolling Bethlehem's twinkling Manger Square at Christmas
- Riding Jericho's cable car: the world's longest below-sea-level cable-car ride
- Slathering yourself in sulphuric mud, followed by a dip in the Dead Sea
- Observing myriad marine life at Eilat's underwater observatory, without even getting your toes wet
- Trekking into the Negev Desert, on two legs or four, for a night beneath the stars

WHERE

JERUSALEM

SEE

Though undeniably stunning, Jerusalem's fabled **Old City** isn't an easy destination for families with small children or strollers, since its mazes of cobbled steps, alleyways and narrow passageways can fast become something of a trial. Nevertheless, there'll be plenty of willing hands to help hoist your cargo up and down flights of stairs, and even small children love the magical, mystical atmosphere. After all that hard work, there's nothing better than an afternoon at the beautiful **Biblical Zoo** (+972 2 675 0111; Zoo Rd; adult/child 40/32NIS; 9am-6pm Sun-Thu, 9am-4.30pm Fri, 10am-5pm Sun) with imaginative displays and wide, picnic-perfect lawns. Another great distraction from all things ancient is the **Train Theatre** (+972 256 18514; www.traintheater .co.il; Liberty Bell Park; tickets for most shows 40NIS), a children's theatre near the centre of town. For fragrant wanderings, visit the **Mahane Yehuda food market** (8am-sunset Sun-Thu, 9am-2pm Fri) where your young gourmands will be welcome to sample a feast of honeys, halva (a sesame-flour confection), exotic fruits, local cheeses and preserved olives.

STAY

Home Accommodation Association of Jerusalem (www.bnb.co.il; $$) Offers a range of self-catering apartments and studios, perfect for self-catering families, in various price ranges throughout Jerusalem.

American Colony Hotel (+972 2627 9777; www .americancolony.com; Nablus Rd; $$$) This luxurious historic choice in East Jerusalem offers a nice pool, child-friendly staff, and a lovely inner courtyard perfect for afternoon teas and goldfish-spotting in the little fountain.

TEL AVIV

SEE

Without doubt Tel Aviv's principal attraction for children is its safe, sandy **beaches**, close enough to the city to be convenient for whole days on the sand with a break for lunch in a city restaurant. There are few dress codes in town, and restaurateurs are used to kids turning up sandy and in swimming costumes. Great for breakfast or early dinner is the trendy **Old Port** area, with a wide wooden boardwalk perfect for scooters, bikes or rollerblades (all can be hired in the area), and with lots of open space to let off steam. Cute kids' clothes boutiques can be found on family-friendly **Sheinkin Street**, where trendy parents and kids hang out on Friday mornings. Later, take a walk in the **Hayarkon Park**, with its playgrounds, boat hire, trampolines, a skate park and minigolf, then stop for a treat at **Max Brenner** (45 Rothschild Blvd; 8am-1am), a Wonka-style cafe where every dish and drink is based on chocolate.

Oh Little Town of Bethlehem

If you've already had the whole 'Christmas in Lapland' experience and are looking for something new for the festive season, consider taking the kids to Bethlehem, to see where the story began.

Like everywhere else in the West Bank, Bethlehem is incredibly welcoming for children, who can explore its year-round Christmas shops, nativities and mysterious churches and grottos without fear of a 'shhh' or 'hands off'. At Christmas, when the tree springs up in the town square, and the streets fill up with monks, nuns and pilgrims, it's like something straight from a fairy tale, and there's even a possibility you'll see a sprinkling of snow on distant hills.

Bear in mind, however, that if they're not particularly Bible-savvy, the whole thing can be a bit confusing for small children: ours now delight in telling people that they've seen the manger where Father Christmas was born.

STAY

Alexander Suites (+972 354 52222; www.alexander .co.il; Havakuk St; $$) Most of these good-sized suites, accommodate up to four people comfortably. They're close to Tel Aviv's golden beaches and the family-friendly Old Port. If you're travelling with a baby or toddler, call ahead to arrange a baby bed.

Cinema Hotel (+972 3 520 7100; www.cinemahotel.com; 1 Zamenhoff St; $$) A great city-centre choice for those with older children, who'll enjoy the free bike rental and proximity to all that shopping. Some rooms are equipped with kitchenette, and there's free wi-fi throughout.

THE PALESTINIAN TERRITORIES
Though the Palestinian West Bank is cursed with a reputation for violence and lawlessness, the towns of Bethlehem and Jericho, in particular, make great days out for families with children of all ages. **Bethlehem** is particularly atmospheric at Christmas (see the boxed text above) and there are frequent concerts and shows for children at its **International Center of Bethlehem** (+972 227 70047; www.annadwa.org; 109 Paul VI St, Bethlehem;

from 9am), a short walk from central Manger Square. **Jericho**, to the northeast, is a good place for a camel ride and a jaunt on the scenic **cable cars** (cable-car round-trip per person US$12; 8am-5pm) up to the Mount of Temptation where, so they say, the Devil tested Jesus. It's also a quick drive from here to the **Dead Sea** (in Israel) where you and your kids can float the afternoon away, or cover yourself in mineral-infused mud.

STAY

Intercontinental Jacir Palace (+972 2276 6777; www.ichotelsgroup.com; Jerusalem-Hebron Rd, Bethlehem; $$) A palatial property within an easy walk or quick taxi ride to all the major sites, this is a huge and rambling luxury stay, with a decent pool and lots of room in the gardens for little ones to run.

Abu Gubran Guesthouse (+972 2277 0047; www.annadwa.org; 109 Paul VI St, Bethlehem; $) A cosy choice in the middle of town, this place is run by International Centre of Bethlehem, with artwork by local artists adorning rooms. Make sure you call ahead to arrange for a baby cot or foldaway bed.

WHEN

Though summers can be hot and humid, any time of year – outside major Jewish and Muslim holidays – is a great time to visit Israel and the Palestinian Territories. Swimming in the Mediterranean is usually possible from around April to November; winter nights can get chilly in Jerusalem, Bethlehem, the north and the desert, so don't forget to bring the children's hats and gloves.

HOW

Transport

The best way to get around with kids is definitely by car. Rail services, too, are quick and well priced between major cities. All major international car rental companies are represented in Tel Aviv and it pays to shop around for the best rates; almost all will be able to provide baby seats or booster cushions. For car travel into the West Bank, try Green Peace (www.greenpe ace.co.il).

Shopping & Essentials

There's no need to lug nappies, baby food or powdered milk along with you to Israel, as all are readily available in pharmacies and supermarkets. Tel Aviv is filled with designer kids' boutiques and toy shops to cater to every whim, and lots of shops selling beach gear and swimming costumes.

Bear in mind that outside Tel Aviv, many shops, cafes, restaurants and other services are closed for Shabbat (Friday night to Saturday evening), the Jewish day of rest.

Health

Health care in Israel is of international standard, and aside from heat rash brought on by the humidity, there are no specific health concerns. The Palestinian West Bank's health-care system is beleaguered: in the

MICHAEL MAJOR | DREAMSTIME

ABOVE. **DISCOVER TRADITIONAL CULTURE THROUGHOUT THE MIDDLE EAST** event of an accident or emergency, head back if you can to the nearest Israeli town.

In conservative Orthodox Jewish areas and the Palestinian Territories, older girls shouldn't expose their legs or shoulders, and breastfeeding should be done discreetly or in private.

Food

Israeli and Palestinian food is very child-friendly, with lots of easy options such as felafel, hummus, simple salads, kebabs and schnitzels, and is terrific, too, for vegetarian children, who'll rarely feel they're missing out. Don't miss local specialities such as pita with *labneh* (a soft white cheese), *kunafa* (a syrup-drenched pastry) and *sachleb*, a milky winter drink made with rosewater and topped with coconut and dried fruit. In Jerusalem and Tel Aviv, you'll also find almost every cuisine under the sun, and it's extremely rare to find a restaurant without highchairs and a welcoming smile for children.

JORDAN

Hot, hospitable and packed with stunning scenery, Jordan is a great destination for adventure-seeking families whose children are keen to hike and explore ancient ruins, with perhaps a few days at the seaside or a camel trek thrown in for good measure. Aside from the summer heat, there are few hazards to watch out for and, as in the wider Middle East, children will be welcomed with open arms by their local hosts.

WHAT'S TOPS

- Exploring the wonders of Petra, 'rose-red city, half as old as time'
- Hiking or riding into the spectacular Wadi Rum canyon, then overnighting with the Bedouin (nomadic tribes) that live there
- Relaxing in five-star style beside the Dead Sea shores
- Soaking weary limbs in a seaside infinity pool at Aqaba, Jordan's Red Sea playground

WHERE

Undoubtedly Jordan's greatest attraction is the rose-stone city of **Petra** (entry around JD21, children under 15 free; 6am-4.30pm Oct-Apr, 6am-5.30pm May-Sep), built by the Nabateans in the 3rd century BC, and filled with carved rock tombs, temples and palaces. Kids will appreciate Petra's rather free-and-easy approach to conservation – meaning that few structures are roped-off for clambering purposes – and the option of the four-legged visit.

After Petra, don't miss a trip to **Wadi Rum**, with its sublime desert scenery and stunning sunsets. Four-wheel-drive trips are how most choose to see the wadi (only really suitable for the over-fours) though there are also a number of horse and camel trekking options in operation. With older children, there are a number of terrific trekking routes, too, and the added excitement of an overnight stay in a Bedouin desert tent.

If you're looking for something a little more languid, both the **Dead Sea** and the **Red Sea** shores offer repose, with plenty of top-end hotel chains well equipped for children, babies and toddlers. Here, you'll find pools, water sports, and vast buffet breakfasts to cater to every toddler's tastes.

STAY

In Aqaba, a great choice with children is the **Moevenpick Resort & Residence** (+962 3203 4020; www.moevenpick-hotels.com; King Hussein St, Aqaba; \$\$) with its seafront pool, private beach and helpful staff. Adventurous families should head out to **Wadi Rum's Bait Ali Camp** (+962 7955 48133; www.baitali.com) for a night in a Bedouin tent and a trek on camel or horseback through the desert.

WHEN

Since it can get hot and sticky in the summer months – and is prone to snow in winter – April to May and September to October are the very best times to visit Jordan. At other times of year, don't forget to pack your sunscreen and swimming costume, or warm pyjamas and woolly socks, as appropriate.

HOW

Transport

One of the best ways to travel with children in Jordan is by renting private taxis to take you from place to place. The distances are never great, and local drivers know the highways, byways and occasional army checkpoints (where you'll need to show your passport) well, leaving you plenty of time to observe the scenery. They're also in the know about public toilets and snack-food pit stops en route.

Shopping & Essentials

Baby supplies are readily available in Amman, but are less commonly stocked elsewhere, so remember to carry enough with you when you head out on the road. As in all Middle Eastern countries (except Israel), travel during the fasting month of Ramadan, which usually falls in September, will make it trickier to find food for hungry mouths.

Health

The health-care system in Jordan is decent, and except for the dangers of heat exhaustion, heat stroke and dehydration (particularly in summer, and if hiking in Wadi Rum), health risks are minimal.

Food

Outside the five-star hotels of Amman, Aqaba, the Dead Sea and Petra, Jordanian food is tasty, filling and cheap, and is simple enough to satisfy even unadventurous eaters. The usual Middle Eastern spreads consisting of *shwarmas* (kebabs), felafel and hummus apply here, while you'll find seafood galore at Aqaba. If you're spending time with Wadi Rum's Bedouin, jump at the chance to sample some unique Bedouin dishes: *mensaf* (spit-roasted lamb) or *zarb* (barbeque) dishes are seasoned with delicious spices and pine nuts, though not all kids will be thrilled if offered the lamb's eyes, a delicacy reserved for the guests of honour.

LEBANON

Though the precarious political situation has kept many travellers away from Lebanon, the country, in its quieter moments, has an enormous amount to offer intrepid visitors and their accompanying charges. The Lebanese love children, and bringing your little ones along will ensure possibly the warmest welcome you've ever experienced anywhere on your travels. From hiking the lush Qadisha Valley in the north to learning to ski on one of Mt Lebanon's manifold slopes or splashing an afternoon away in the sparkling Mediterranean Sea, there are lots of outdoor pursuits to keep children of all ages occupied. Cities, in general, are less child-friendly, with few pavements worthy of a stroller, and patchy facilities in restaurants. The desire to please, however – from waiters, hoteliers, shop-owners and almost anyone else – will more than make up for what's lacking in practicalities.

WHAT'S TOPS

- Taking the soaring *teleferique* cable car (nicknamed by some the 'terrorifique') from Jounieh to the stunning views at Harissa
- Going underground at the Jeita Grotto, to marvel at some of the world's most magnificent stalactite formations
- Hanging out at the trendy St George Yacht Club in Beirut, with a pool and playground for children
- Taking a gentle hike through the peaceful northern Qadisha Valley
- Blowing four-foot bubbles at Beirut's fun Planet Discovery kids' science museum
- Hitting the slopes at one of Lebanon's many ski resorts

WHERE

Though Beirut's not incredibly well geared up for children in terms of playgrounds and parks, the beach clubs that line the seafront (most, except the most achingly trendy, are child-friendly) and the irresistibly whirring, flashing **Luna Park** (Corniche, Beirut; rides around LL 5000; 10am-midnight) amusement park are both great bets for children. **Planet Discovery** (+961 198 0650; Espace Starco, Rue Omar Ad-Daouk, Beirut; adults & children LL5000; 9am-3pm Mon-Thu, 10am-7.30pm Fri & Sat) has plenty to entertain children from age three to 12, and a great jaunt for animal-loving children is to **Animal Encounter** (www .animalencounter.org; +961 366 7355; Aley; call for opening hours), a nonprofit shelter for injured and abandoned animals.

Further north, plunge into the **Jeita Grotto** (www.jeitagrotto.com) to view its spectacular caves, then allow yourself and your kids to be whisked by **cable car** (www.teleferiquelb.com) in Jounieh to lofty cliff-top heights. There are lots of opportunities for a gentle family hike in nature reserves around the country; check out the itineraries offered by **Esprit Nomade** (www.esprit-nomade.com) to join a group day hike, suitable for older children. Lebanon's half-dozen ski resorts cater well to families (see www.skileb.com for details), and two popular choices – The Cedars and Faraya Mzaar – also have a host of summer activities on offer, with log cabins making a roomy alternative to hotel rooms.

STAY

Beirut's the easiest place to situate yourself with kids. The old-fashioned but still comfy **Riviera** (+961 137 3210; www.rivierahotel.com.lb; Ave de Paris, Beirut; $$) has a big pool accessible from the hotel via an under-road tunnel. Otherwise, consider a homestay with **L'Hote Libanais** (+961 351 3766; www.hotelibanais.com; $$) whose countrywide host families will instantly make your offspring feel one of the family.

WHEN

Lebanon's a great destination for all seasons, so when you should visit depends wholly on what you want to do. For hitting the beach clubs, May to September is best; for skiing, visit from late November to March. Hiking's best in spring (March to May) and autumn (September to November) when the scenery's greenest and the midday sun less severe.

HOW

Transport

Unless you're a very confident driver, you may balk at the state of Lebanon's roads. Traffic is anarchic and unpredictable; roads are poorly maintained and signposted, and the rule of the road is simply to attempt to avoid collisions. However, a lack of decent public transport infrastructure means that travel by car is really the only viable way to reach any destination outside major cities. Consider taking taxis between destinations if you're not keen to drive yourself, or, if your nerves are up to it, take fate into your own hands by renting a vehicle. Advanced Car Rental (www .advancedcarrent.com) is a good local rental agency, with booster and car seats available for children.

Shopping & Essentials

Most pharmacies, even in small Lebanese towns and villages, carry nappies and wipes, but it's best to stock up on baby food and powdered milk before hitting the road.

Health

Beirut's hospitals are world class, and you'll find pharmacies everywhere in the country, usually run by an English- or French-speaker. Except for the sun in summer and the cold in winter, there are few health-related concerns for travellers to Lebanon.

Outside Beirut and the coastal strip, it's wise to be discreet about breastfeeding in public, and women and girls should try to dress modestly.

Food

Children are welcome in all but the chicest Beirut restaurants, and many local families regularly take their children out to dine: it's not unusual to see kids eating out at 10pm on weekend evenings, or even much later. In Beirut itself, you'll have a wide choice of dining styles, with international chains serving Western menus and local concerns dishing up wonderful mezze feasts. Head to the university district (Hamra) for informal cafes, Mexican, sushi, and felafel galore, or to Rue Gouraud in Gemmayzeh for a slightly higher notch of fare, which is still decidedly child-friendly.

Outside the capital, you'll find dining choices more limited and wholly Middle Eastern, but cooks are usually pleased to whip up an omelette or a sandwich for a fussy eater. Indulge, too, in syrupy Lebanese pastries: a great pick-me-up during that four-o'clock lull.

SYRIA

Travellers who journey through Syria comment repeatedly on how friendly the locals are – and if you have children with you, you can expect this to apply tenfold. Though there are few sights specifically aimed at children, most kids will enjoy clambering atop castles and exploring fragrant, tangled souks every bit as much as their parents.

WHAT'S TOPS

- Exploring the evocative castle of Crac des Chevaliers (Qala'at al-Hosn)
- Gasping at the incredible ancient ruins at Palmyra
- Roaming the eerie Dead Cities near Aleppo
- Watching Hama's water wheels, rather like the Wheels on the Bus, go round and round
- Bartering for bargains in the medieval souks of atmospheric Damascus

MOMENTS OF GRACE

~ JORDAN ~

BY VIRGINIA MAXWELL

The Middle East may have many things going for it, but good press isn't one of them. Western media outlets bombard us with images and stories about its wars and terrorist attacks, which must make the work of national tourism offices in Egypt, Israel, Syria, Lebanon and Jordan particularly disheartening.

With this in mind, my partner Peter and I were determined to buck the tourist trends and take our three-year-old son Max to Jordan for a holiday. We're all archaeology buffs (Peter and I indulge this through reading classical histories and watching the Discovery Channel, Max likes to excavate in sandpits and garden beds) and we had long been keen to visit the world-famous sites of Petra and Jerash. The fact that we would be travelling with Max seemed to us to be an added incentive, as our previous interactions with people from that part of the world hinted that travellers with children would be particularly welcomed. Confident that we would be able to steer clear of dysentery, suicide bombers and the wiles of carpet sellers, we managed to escape the concerned clutches of our less-insouciant relatives and set off for a two-week adventure.

And then Max was kidnapped at Petra…

We had allowed three full days to explore the remnants of this extraordinary Nabataean city, and because lots of trekking and some relatively steep climbs would be involved, we heeded the advice of our guidebook and hired a donkey to carry Max for the duration. Negotiations were with an exuberantly entrepreneurial

Bedouin boy called Ali, who was the proud owner of a donkey named Jack. Max was beside himself with excitement, Peter and I were relieved that he was on the donkey's back rather than our shoulders, and Ali was grinning from ear to ear, indicating that we had probably paid considerably over the odds for his services. We set off to visit the Al-Khazneh (The Treasury), made famous in Steven Spielberg's film *Indiana Jones and the Last Crusade*. Carved out of a sandstone cliff, this amazing tomb has a Greek-style facade so visually arresting that we were literally stunned into silence at our first glimpse.

Next, we climbed the steep stairs to Al-Deir (The Monastery), another rock-hewn masterpiece. After an hour or so there, we made the decision to return to the main gate of the site and call it a day. By this stage Max, Ali and Jack were getting on famously, communicating in a bizarre but seemingly effective mixture of toddler English, Arabic and high-pitched grunting and whinnying. Peter and I were enjoying the view so much that we didn't notice that the three had edged ahead of us until we were halfway down the hill. Yelling to the boys to slow down didn't work – in fact, it seemed to encourage them to laugh demonically and go even faster. Soon, the blonde tousled head of our son, the somewhat grubby turban of his Bedouin companion and the rear end of the donkey were out of sight.

Peter and I scrambled down the stone stairs, trying desperately to catch up, but it was to no avail: at the bottom of the hill we looked everywhere but couldn't sight the boys. It was as if they had vanished into thin air.

Trying to contain our growing panic, we ran towards the exit, screeching Max's name as we went. Our demented behaviour got plenty of attention from fellow tourists, but there was no answering cry from Max. We ran along the colonnaded way, past the Great Temple and into the famous Street of Facades. Tourists looked down on us from the hillside tombs and we turned all heads of a Japanese tour group exploring the impressive theatre. However, the boys were nowhere to be seen.

Finally, we turned the corner into the space in front of Al-Khazneh. There, sitting crossed-legged amongst a group of Bedouin men warming themselves by a fire, was our son. Ali, sitting next to him, was showing him how to drink tea Bedouin-style, which involved putting a sugar cube between the teeth and slurping the hot liquid through it. As Peter and I stopped to catch our breaths and calm our racing hearts, Max saw us and flashed the widest and most mischievous smile imaginable.

Most of his tea had clearly been spilt on his clothes rather than drunk, and he was good-naturedly coping with the laughing attention that was being paid to him by his companions, all of whom had weathered

'Pinching his cheek, tousling his hair and urging him to drink, these locals were extending him the very best of Bedouin hospitality.'

faces, rotten teeth and huge smiles. Pinching his cheek, tousling his hair and urging him to drink, these locals were extending him the very best of Bedouin hospitality. Jack was behind him, tethered to a fragment of a Nabataean pillar, and Ali was clearly relishing his duties as host, urging sugar cubes on his new Australian friend.

We too were offered tea, and drank it gratefully. Dusk was approaching, and the rose-pink colour of the surrounding cliffs seemed to take on an almost cinematographic intensity. Sitting around the fire with these gentle and generous people, we felt in turn ridiculous and ashamed that we had allowed ourselves to panic to such a degree. Despite our best intentions, we had fallen victim to the prevailing view that the Middle East is filled with danger for those travelling with children. In reality, it is full of unexpected moments of grace such as this.

WHERE

After you've had your fill of Damascus' ancient, enticing souks, head out to explore the country's numerous historical treasures. There's the imposing **Crac des Chevaliers castle** (adult/student S£150/10; 9am-6pm Apr-Oct, 9am-4pm Nov-Mar), with origins going back a good thousand years, and, around 60km inland, the delightful, languid town of **Hama**, dotted with *norias* (wooden waterwheels). Older children will find their imaginations stirred by the weird Byzantine ruins of Syria's many ghost towns (known as the **Dead Cities**) and there's plenty of room for little legs to play at **Palmyra**, the atmospheric remains of Queen Zenobia's city, which dates back to the 2nd century AD.

STAY

Damascus makes a great base for exploring the country, with several lovely boutique hotels offering child-friendly stays. Try **Beit Zaman** (+963 11543 5380; www.beit-zaman.com; Madhat Basha St, Damascus; $$) with comfortable, antique-laden rooms in the heart of the city, or the swish **Talisman Hotel** (+963 11541 5379; www.hoteltalisman. net; 116 Tal El-Hijara St, Damascus; $$$) whose rooms come with DVD players for a *Toy Story* or two, and deep bathtubs for banishing city grime.

WHEN

Syria is best visited in Spring (March to May) before the summer heat gets into full swing and the countryside is green and flower-filled. Rains in the winter can make sightseeing less fun, and visibility is poor up in the mountains. On the other hand, there's nothing more magical than seeing Damascus under a light blanket of snow.

HOW

Transport

Bus transport in Syria is frequent, cheap and a great way to make friends with the locals. Buses come in all shapes and sizes, from luxury (new and air-conditioned) to Pullman (old and battered) to minibus and microbus (anywhere in between). It's a great way to immerse yourself and your children in Syrian culture, and a highly cost-efficient one too.

Shopping & Essentials

You'll be able to pick up nappies, powdered milk and other baby supplies in most towns and cities in Syria, though the range on offer isn't extensive.

Health

There aren't too many health concerns to consider while travelling Syria with kids, though it pays to keep rehydration salts handy, just in case of any bouts of diarrhoea, and to peel fruit or vegetables, or wash them in bottled water.

It's best for women and girls to dress modestly, and to breastfeed discreetly if doing so in public.

Food

Syria runs on mezze, with spreads of hummus, felafel, savoury pastries and salads that will appeal to many children. A great breakfast dish on a cold morning is *foul m'dames*, a big bowl of brown beans drizzled with olive oil, cumin and lemon and mixed with chickpeas and tomatoes: a sort of Middle Eastern version of baked beans, and a perfect energy-boost for a busy morning ahead.

Part 5

TRAVEL GAMES

TRAVEL GAMES

Most of these games use few props so they're very mobile and require little preparation. This is not a definitive list and we left off classics such as I-spy; rock, paper, scissors; charades and Simon says, in favour of games that will give you ideas for more games. Think of these games as suggestions and change the rules to suit your family.

GAMES FOR ANYWHERE

The best games rely on imagination – a fantastically portable commodity found in most kids.

COPYCAT One player pulls a face or makes a movement (like a robot, a monkey or a ballerina, for example) and the next player must copy it. Play around by giving kids roles they're not used to and working in characters you've met on your travels. More advanced games can use noises.

TWO TRUTHS AND ONE LIE Each player takes it in turns to make three statements, two of which are true and one of which is a lie. The other players try to guess which statement is a lie, holding up one, two or three fingers to indicate the lie. You can keep a score over a couple of rounds or let whoever guessed correctly take the next turn as liar.

CLAPPING CATEGORIES Clapping hands, snapping fingers or slapping thighs, create a rhythm that all the players can keep up (younger players will be better at easier rhythms, such as simple 1-2-3-4 clapping). Now introduce a simple category (such as vegetables, films or colours) each player takes it in turns to say something in the category at a point in the rhythm (try clap-clap-clap-'apple' for starters). Harder than it sounds and it gets harder.

I WENT TO THE SHOP AND I BOUGHT...
Each player chooses something they bought at the shop with the next player having to recite everything the previous players bought at the shop as well as adding something to the list. When a player forgets something they are out of the game and the remaining players battle it out. Longer things might be easier to remember, but try throwing in left-field things like 'a stinky, hairy, man-eating piano' or 'a nice new suit and tie for my pet chimp, Gilbert.'

WORD ASSOCIATION Not just for psychiatrists, this is a quick game to play anywhere with two players. Say a word and the other player responds with the first word that comes into their head. Keep it quick to keep it fun.

SAME NAME One player chooses the full name of a famous person and the next player has to think of a famous person whose name begins with the first letter of the last person's name. For example, Player One might say Winston Churchill and the next player would have to follow with someone whose first name begins with C, say Charlie Brown, and so on.

RHYME TIME Think of a word (children's names can keep it interesting) and go around the group finding words that rhyme with it. Younger players might need hints. The player who thinks of the most rhymes gets to choose the word next round.

TALK TO THE ANIMAL One player chooses an animal character to be for the round and the other players talk to it until they guess what kind of an animal it is. First to correctly guess the animal gets to be the next animal. Throw in family pets, animals you've seen along the way and mythical monsters to keep it tricky.

ODDS AND EVENS A quick easy game for two players. One player chooses to play odds and the other plays evens. Both players shoot by saying '1-2-3-shoot' and sticking out a chosen number of fingers. Add up both hands to see if the total is odd or even, with whoever guessed correctly winning that round. It's such a simple game that it can be played with local children in playgrounds throughout the world.

GAMES FOR CARS

Games that take attention outside the car often prevent car sickness as well as making the trip go faster. Games with activity can stop kids from squirming in the back seat. At night, substitute talking games or use night landmarks like neon signs or tail lights for spotting games.

SINGING IN ECHOES This is a noisy one, so avoid it if you feel a headache coming on or if you've still got a long journey ahead. Take it in turns to make up a line of a song (nonsense words work best) with the rest of the family repeating it as a chorus. Another player sings the previous line and adds one on. Keep adding until your memories fail.

PASSING CARS A nice easy creative game. Get the kids to make up stories about the people in other cars that pass you based on the quick look they get as they pass. Ask questions to get them thinking – What are their names? Where are they going? Is one of them a superhero travelling in disguise?

BUZZ WORDS Gets kids listening to the radio and keeping quiet. Choose a word (start with easy ones like 'song' 'listening' or 'news') and listen out for it on the radio in songs or DJs' announcements. Shout out 'Buzz' when

the word comes up. Readers can look for buzz words on road signs and advertising.

LICENCE PLATE GAMES Make a phrase out of the letters in a licence plate with the first one to make sense winning. Have kids spot their initials in passing plates (first to get all their initials wins). Choose a word and spell it out using license plate letters (use familiar things like pets or school friends to ground kids in unfamiliar territory). Use the numbers to play car 21 – get the kids to add up all the numbers on a number plate in passing cars. GMZ 421, for example, would add up to 7, while 969 would break the bank with 24. Players can ask for another card (the first number of the next car), but if they go over 21 they break the bank. Take it in turns with the closest to 21 (but still under) winning. Or for an easier game, see how many different countries or states you can collect on licence plates.

GAMES FOR PLANES, TRAINS OR BUSES

Getting from A to B doesn't have to be a journey to boredom for kids. The presence of other passengers might restrict the kinds of games you can play, but many of the games from the Games for Cars section can be adapted for other types of journeys.

GEOGRAPHY GAMES Expand your kid's geographical knowledge by taking turns to name a capital city and its country. If this is too easy, try thinking up one for each letter of the alphabet.

WOULD YOU? Read up about the country you're visiting and prepare some questions that will challenge your kids' cultural ideas. Try concepts like 'In Sri Lanka they wash elephants in a river after a long day's work. Would you?' or 'In Chile they eat *chupe de cóngrio* (conger eel soup). Would you?' This a fantastic way to introduce your kids to different customs, languages and foods before arriving in a country to reduce culture shock. Use a Lonely Planet guidebook to research a country.

MAPS Get kids to trace out the journey on world, country or local maps. Some tourist information centres offer free maps, which can be coloured in or cut up.

GAMES FOR WAITING

Kids don't believe everything comes to those who wait. Longer games come in handy in restaurants, queues and stations, because they distract kids from the time it's taking for something to happen.

STORYLINES A good game that is limited only by imagination. Start a story with a sentence ('Once upon a time…' might be a good place to start) with the next family member adding the next sentence. Add one that doesn't make sense or finish your sentence with a cliff-hanger to keep it interesting.

ALPHABET GAMES Alphabet games can run for hours, so they're perfect for long waits. Name a category, then name something from that category for each letter of the alphabet. Animals ('Aardvark, bumble bee, cat') are easier, but harder topics can be famous people or song titles. Double points for double letters, like bumble bee. In other alphabet games, you can choose a category and all the players have to name something beginning with that letter before moving on to the next letter (eg 'Apple', 'Asparagus', 'Artichoke'). For older kids make up a structure, such as 'My name is *blank* from *blank* where they make the best *blank*' filling in each blank with a name, location and object starting with each letter of the alphabet.

GUESSING GAMES Guessing games can be good for shorter waits, as kids can get frustrated or bored. Most guessing games are based on yes or no questions, using general questions ('Is it alive?') to narrow it down to specific guesses ('Is it a rabbit?'). In 'guess the food', one player will nominate a describing word ('crunchy', 'sweet' or 'red') with other players asking questions to guess the food. Use other categories like animals or famous people. You can prepare some cards with categories or names on them. Keep the games based in your travels, using famous people or animals from the country you're visiting.

GAMES FOR QUIET PLACES

Sometimes you might just want your little treasures to keep quiet. Quiet games can teach children that loud behaviour is not always okay, as well as buy a few moments of peace in a hectic day.

GUESS THE LETTER Another one for readers. Draw a letter on the palm of another player with their eyes closed. Try whole words if guessing a letter is too easy.

WHISPERS Pass a whispered message from one player to the next saying the message only once. As players pass it on from one to the next the message will become garbled. In a reasonably sized group (usually more than five people), the message should end up as nonsense when the last player says it out loud.

GAMES FOR OUTDOORS

Exploring the great outdoors is easy (kids love to run and frolic after long journeys). Using simple games can help them to appreciate their surroundings even more or calm them down after too much running around.

TOUCHY FEELY TREE Walk a blindfolded player to a tree and let them explore it using only touch for a while. Then spin them around and lead them away from their tree. Removing the blindfold, ask the player to find their tree.

STATUES A good game to relax with. Move around until the caller says 'freeze', then stay still the longest to win. Another version involves players sneaking up behind the caller to steal a token (anything that's handy will do). Rather than call freeze, the caller turns and sees who is still moving. Anybody caught moving gets sent back to the start.

CLOUDS What do the clouds look like? Can you find a cloud that looks like: a person, your car, your pets, your breakfast?

GAMES FOR MUSEUMS OR GALLERIES

Although many museums are becoming more interactive there are still many old-style museums that will have a 'look, don't touch' ethic that frustrates kids. With a bit of preparation, these games can get children to appreciate looking in a museum as much as you will.

DID YOU SEE? A game that might involve a bit of preparation. Make a list of things to see in a gallery or museum by asking the kids what they think they'll see or prepare a list based on a Lonely Planet guidebook. Kids can check off their list with a prize for the most complete list. Remember to have a range of items, some common (so kids achieve something easily), some rare (to challenge them). You can debrief and talk about items on the list. More complex versions might involve getting more than one of each item (eg seven paintings with a blonde man in them).

HOW MANY... Guess how many of an object you'll see on your visit and get the littlies to count them as they go. Good objects include sculptures, gold frames or security guards.

WHAT WAS IT? A simple game that will get kids looking at exhibits. Give the kids a minute or two to look at an exhibit, then ask them 'What was it?', 'Who used it?', 'When did they use it?' or if it's a portrait ask 'Who was it?', 'What did they do?'. Ask any other questions to stimulate the imagination. Be prepared to answer some tricky questions yourself.

GAMES FOR WALKING

Kids need to focus on something other than how far they're walking, so it's a good idea to have a few games you can play to take their mind off things. These games also highlight differences between their own culture and the culture being visited.

WHAT YOU SAW When passing through scenery ask kids to look around for a minute, then have them close their eyes and tell you what they remember. An observational game that will have kids appreciating their surroundings.

COUNTING GAMES These are easy games to make up in a hurry. Select a frequently occurring local feature – such as windmills in Holland or bikes in China – and two players can count all of these features on one side. First to 100 wins. To keep the game interesting you can count down from 100. Count several things with various points for each sighting and the game can be about addition. If you're near a roadway, counting arrows on signs is always a good one.

STEPPING OUT A quick game, but a good distraction. See who can take the biggest steps, the smallest steps, the silliest steps, the straightest step, a sideways step or the most backward steps (without running into anything).

THE AUTHORS

BRIGITTE BARTA
Coordinating Author

At the age of six months Brigitte travelled with her parents on an ocean liner from New Zealand to Naples, and then lived in a basement flat in Berlin. Her first birthday party was in a French field, with a cake candle that had been nicked from Chartres Cathedral. She has twice travelled with her daughter, Chloe, from their base in Australia to their ramshackle cottage in Greece and, closer to home, they have upended 10,000-piece puzzles in beach houses, been chased by an emu at a farmstay, and managed not to touch the sides of the tent on wet camping trips. Above all else they favour the relaxed beach holiday, where little is achieved each day aside from building sandcastles, swimming and having lunch. Brigitte's travel essentials are a sarong; an up-to-date, detailed map; a mobile phone with local SIM card; and a pocket knife. Her top handy hint is to remember to take your pocket knife out of your hand luggage so that it isn't confiscated.

Brigitte spent eight years working for Lonely Planet in Melbourne and San Francisco and has co-authored guidebooks to San Francisco, Greece and Chile, and contributed to titles such as *Bluelist* and *Going Bush*.

CELESTE BRASH

Celeste Brash was conceived in England, discovered in Mexico and born in the USA. She continues the mobile tradition with her own children, Tevai and Jasmine, who have been raised primarily in French Polynesia. Always on a budget, the family has become avid campers and long-term trekkers and has (among other adventures) discovered the Spanish language in Mexico, rafted the tidal bore in Atlantic Canada, fished for piranhas in the Amazon and kite-surfed in Spain. Their favourite family trip was to the Oaxaca coast where they shared a room with bats, played with an armadillo and got praying mantises in their hair. Luckily, they caught all these moments on film with the handy disposable cameras that they never forget to bring on long trips. Both kids agree that the secret to successful travel with children is to go to lots of zoos and always have good snacks on hand.

FRITZ BURKE

Fritz Burke is a father, writer, humorist, teacher and carpenter. He lives in the house he built on a Maine hilltop with his wife Debbey and sons Noah and Jonas. The family has travelled extensively in Guatemala, Mexico, Morocco, Thailand and the USA. Mexico has been their favourite destination ever since the family walked across the Rio Grande to the Nuevo Laredo Bus Station and began a 5300km journey. They plan to return soon for the warmth of the sun and people, and for the diversity of the landscapes, architecture, festivals, food, cities and coastline. Also for the baseball. The family (except for Debbey – who doesn't understand baseball) always packs gloves.

Fritz has been given awards for his commentary on National Public Radio, for his creative nonfiction chapbook, and for his column about life in Maine. He is also the recipient of The World's Best Dad T-Shirt, although he finds it chafes a bit in the collar. His number one piece of advice for travelling families is to understand that, at its core, the journey is about family.

MONIQUE CHOY

Monique's mum loves to tell people that she had her nappy changed on one of the blocks at Stonehenge. She was nine months old and it was her first overseas trip – she hasn't stopped travelling since.

Monique has authored six guidebooks for Lonely Planet. She researched the Philippines when she was six months pregnant, dragging her poor belly up and down precarious volcanos and out to remote islands. When her daughter Sonnet was born she still didn't stop, taking the baby on a road trip into the Australian desert when she was just four months old.

Sonnet has inherited her mother's itchy feet, along with her own backpack and swag. Their favourite holidays are camping trips in the bush, preferably with lots of mud, dogs and marshmallows.

Monique never leaves home without a stash of ziplock bags in different sizes. They weigh nothing and they're great for carrying around snacks, wipes and soap, and toting home, ahem, wee-soaked undies.

JAYNE D'ARCY

It's the perfect distraction on a long train-ride through the Turkish countryside: a baby yet to wake up, lying on the bottom bunk on his tummy with his bottom sticking skyward. It's one of the zillion photos Jayne has taken since she started travelling with her son, Miles, and yet another where it's not the scenery that's important, it's the tiny travel companion.

Jayne knows that as Miles changes from compliant baby to occasionally defiant toddler and into school-aged boy, the way they travel (and the cost of travel) will change too, but she knows there's nothing quite like that one-on-one, 24/7 contact to bring joy (okay, and sometimes unbelievable frustration) to the journey.

Jayne loves the way that Miles thinks that every foreign language is French, but is less keen that her partner teaches Miles the local swear words before they step off the plane. They rarely go anywhere without their super-dooper Quinny Zapp (a full-size, foldable, lightweight (and tough) stroller), Wet Wipes, and the local words for 'sorry, he doesn't mean it'.

CHARLOTTE HINDLE

When she was 24, Charlotte travelled overland to Australia. In Melbourne, she worked at Lonely Planet's head office for three years. In 1991 she returned to England to set up Lonely Planet's UK office, which she ran for the next 11 years. Her first child, Daisy, was conceived in a rainforest in Costa Rica and her second, Poppy, on a city break to Graz, Austria. Since then, she has travelled with her children to over 30 destinations. Their all-time favourite place to holiday is San Sebastian in northern Spain. Charlotte always travels with the following items in her luggage for the children: Marmite, Calpol, Nurofen, a good thermometer, Kwells Kids travel sickness tablets, no-water antibacterial gel and nail clippers. Her main piece of travel advice for parents is to do a first-aid course.

Charlotte now runs a travel media company called North East South West Ltd (www.northeastsouthwest.eu), and is a freelance travel journalist and photographer. Over the years she has written for several Lonely Planet guides and her photographs appear in many others.

KATHARINA LOBECK KANE
Katharina's daughter, Ishema, claims that she remembers sitting in a baby carrier while Katharina was traipsing around the Faroe Islands in 2004, researching her first Lonely Planet chapter. Later, Ishema accompanied Katharina on further adventurous tours to the Gambia, Germany, France, Belgium, Kenya and Senegal. They now live in Senegal, where Katharina works as a creative consultant, radio presenter and music journalist, making the most of her PhD in Ethnomusicology and background in project management, writing and radio. A large part of each year is still being spent on trips and tours to research travel guides, source new stories and stumble across the next chapter in her biography.

KORINA MILLER
Korina's parents are big believers in family holidays and as a child she travelled across much of North America on road trips. At 16 she started travelling on her own and she hasn't stopped since, taking in more than 36 countries and writing Lonely Planet guidebooks for the past decade. These days, she travels with her daughter, Simone, who has accompanied her on research trips to Copenhagen, Germany and New Zealand, as well as on holidays to Canada, the US, Spain, Italy and France. Thankfully, Simone loves the outdoors as much as her mum and dad, and when they're at home, all three of them are found exploring the Sussex countryside every weekend they can. Korina's top tip for travelling with children? Always teach your kids a few words in the local language – it goes a long way to endearing them (and consequently you!) to waiters, hoteliers and museum staff.

AMELIA THOMAS
Amelia is an author and journalist working throughout the Middle East, India and beyond. She writes for Lonely Planet, *CNN Traveller* and *Wanderlust,* and recently published *The Zoo on the Road to Nablus,* which tells the true story of the last Palestinian zoo. On her frequent jaunts about the globe (and to the zoo), she's usually accompanied by her little troupe of helpers – Cassidy, Tyger, Cairo and Zeyah. So long as their holidays involve sand, sea and plenty of ice cream, they're almost always good, but the family especially loves to head to southern Goa, where the beaches are wide, the curries are delicious, and the holy cows particularly friendly. Her advice for prospective travellers with small children is to book the tickets before you have time to change your mind: it might sometimes be tough on the road with little ones in tow, but you – and your children – will never regret that you just got out there and did it.

PAUL GOODYER
Contributing Author
Paul Goodyer, CEO of Nomad Travel Stores and Travel Clinics (www.nomadtravel.co.uk), started travelling when he was 17. Following a few bouts of ill-health and disasters with dodgy travel equipment, he set up Nomad in 1990. With five outlets combining travel clinics with travel gear shops, Paul and his wife, Cathy, his brother, Professor Larry Goodyer, and his staff, work hard to prepare people for travel. Paul and Cathy travelled independently through pregnancy and then with their children from the age of six months, backpacking through places such as East Africa, South America and the Far East. Paul wrote the health section of the Health & Safety chapter.

AUTHOR THANKS

BRIGITTE'S THANKS

Thanks firstly to my little Chloe for always being hilarious, courageous and adaptable, and my best friend; and to my parents and sister for many happy travel memories. The unflappable commissioning editor Bridget Blair set a new gold standard on this project with her patience, flexibility and talent for listening. Co-authors Charlotte Hindle, Celeste Brash, Fritz Burke, Monique Choy and Jayne D'Arcy all took to the book with enviable enthusiasm and were a fount of great ideas, and Lonely Planet author Duncan Garwood helped me with sourcing child-friendly hotels in Rome. I'm also grateful to Vince Lagioia, from the Parenting Research Centre, for his solid advice on children's (and parents') behaviour, and to Dani Valent for talking Turkey and suggesting we go on a girls' own adventure with our daughters.

CELESTE'S THANKS

Thanks to Josh and kids for putting up with my itchy feet – if you didn't I'd have a lot less to write about. G'ma Diana Hammer has always been an inspiration and offered great advice on kids and dogs while Conner Gory provided essential help on Cuba. Fellow Lonely Planet people, Fritz Burke, Korina Miller, Andrew Bain, Jayne D'Arcy, Michael Benanav, Michael Kohn, David Else, Janet Brunckhorst and Tione Chinula all provided indispensable information on camping and travelling long-term. Thanks to Brigitte Barta for being both a springboard and a rock of support, and to Bridget Blair and Charlotte Hindle for giving us a framework to bring this book into the present and future.

FRITZ' THANKS

Thanks to Deborah Schilder, Noah Burke, Jonas Burke, Genevieve James, Mike Wood.

MONIQUE'S THANKS

Thanks to all the inspiring travellers who wrote in with kid-friendly insights. Kisses to gorgeous Rob and a big squeeze to my beautiful daughter Sonnet for her adventurous spirit, her sunny smile and her patience while I sat at my writing desk instead of playing hide and seek.

JAYNE'S THANKS

A big 'bula' and thanks to Vivien and Bernie Houlgate for dragging me (only occasionally kicking and screaming) around the resort circuit when I was younger. Your idea to sculpt the resort's insignia for sand castle competitions was pure genius.

CHARLOTTE'S THANKS

First and foremost, I'd like to thank Daisy and Poppy for travelling with me and by doing so, giving me the qualifications I needed to help update this book. Thank you sweethearts – I really hope you don't both grow up hating travel because it is something you are doing so much of as you grow up. Next, I'd like to thank all the experts who helped with my chapters: Dr Steve Ray, John Masterson of Trailfinders, Carmel of Direct Line Travel Insurance and freelance travel writer David Orkin. Thank you to all those friends and Lonely Planet parents who shared with me their favourite holiday destinations with children: Dale Rees-Bevan, Geoff Stringer, Celeste Brash, Janet Swainson, Nadine Fogale, Kate Calvert of the Family Travel website, Robin Goldberg, Alicia Pivaro, Eric

Kettunen and Jennifer Garrett. Thank you to my commissioning editor, Bridget Blair, to my coordinating author, Brigitte Barta, for all your ideas and help. Last but not least, thank you to my husband, Simon.

KORINA'S THANKS
Thank you to my parents who first gave me the travel bug and taught me the value of family holidays. Thank you to the many hoteliers, information centres and tour operators who doled out child-friendly information. To the countless people I've met on the road while travelling with my daughter, thank you for carrying the pram, the bucket of crayons, the not-on-the-menu children's meal and for generally making us feel welcome. Thanks to my sister Krista and her family for giving Simone and me an amazing US adventure and for the photo of us hiking in Canada. To Janine Eberle at Lonely Planet, thank you for the gig. And finally, a huge thank you to Paul, my life-long travelling companion, and to Simone who has made travelling a whole new adventure.

INDEX

000 **Photograph pages**

INDEX

000 Photograph pages

INDEX

INDEX